William Nevill

**The manuscripts of the Marquess of Abergavenny**

William Nevill

**The manuscripts of the Marquess of Abergavenny**

ISBN/EAN: 9783337282844

Printed in Europe, USA, Canada, Australia, Japan

Cover: Foto ©Andreas Hilbeck / pixelio.de

More available books at **www.hansebooks.com**

HISTORICAL MANUSCRIPTS COMMISSION.

TENTH REPORT, APPENDIX, PART VI.

THE

# MANUSCRIPTS

OF THE

## MARQUESS OF ABERGAVENNY, LORD BRAYE, G. F. LUTTRELL, ESQ., &c.

Presented to both Houses of Parliament by Command of Her Majesty.

LONDON:
PRINTED FOR HER MAJESTY'S STATIONERY OFFICE,
BY EYRE AND SPOTTISWOODE,
PRINTERS TO THE QUEEN'S MOST EXCELLENT MAJESTY.

And to be purchased, either directly or through any Bookseller, from
EYRE AND SPOTTISWOODE, EAST HARDING STREET, FLEET STREET, E.C.; and
32, ABINGDON STREET, WESTMINSTER, S.W.; or
ADAM AND CHARLES BLACK, 6, NORTH BRIDGE, EDINBURGH; or
HODGES, FIGGIS, & Co., 104, GRAFTON STREET, DUBLIN.

1887.

[C.—5060.—v.]   *Price* 1s. 7d.

# CONTENTS.

U 24962.    Wt. 6696.

# THE MANUSCRIPTS OF THE MARQUIS OF ABERGAVENNY.

The following books and documents are in the library at Eridge Castle :—

A thick volume, small folio, newly bound and lettered—" Officium Beatæ Virginis." It is richly illuminated throughout, and contains sixteen full-page paintings which are said to have been executed by Allan Strayler, illuminator to the Abbey of St. Albans. An inscription on the fly-leaf states that in 1561 the book belonged to Sir Henry Nevill, Lord Burgavenny.

A thick volume, quarto, in old binding, not lettered. It contains the Calendar, the Psalter, the Te Deum, the Athanasian Creed, etc., richly illuminated throughout. At the beginning there are some directions in French concerning masses and prayers to be said in honour of St. Leonard. There are also a few historical notes in a later hand :—Memorandum that on the 2nd of October, 1514, the Lady Mary, sister of King Henry VIII., crossed from Dover to Boulogne, where she was met by the Duke of Brittany, the Dauphin of France, the Duke Langueville, with other nobles, and four thousand armed horsemen (equitibus). Memorandum of the birth of Thomas Nevill of Mereworth, fifth son of Sir George Nevill, Lord Burgavenny, and the Lady Margaret his wife, at Birling co. Kent, March 1, 1482[-3]. Memorandum of the birth of Margaret Nevill, daughter of Thomas Nevill, knight, and the Lady Katharine Fitz-Hugh his wife, at Mereworth, September 26, 1520, and that her godfather was the Abbot of Boxley, and her godmothers, the Abbess of Mallyng and the Lady Wyett, and that her godmother before the Bishop was the Lady Margaret, wife of Sir John Heron of Hakeney, Treasurer of Kings Henry VII. and Henry VIII. Memorandum of the death of Margaret, wife of John Bramswy, of London, May 5, 1556. At the end of the volume are thirteen Latin lines about the Eucharist, beginning :—" Panis mutatur."

A volume of music in a rich binding of the 16th century, lettered " My Lady Nevill's Booke." The title page bears the Nevill arms, etc. and the initials H. N. One of the songs is entitled " My Lady Nevells grounde," another " The Lord Willobies welcome home," and another " Hugh Ashton's grownde." A paragraph at the end of the Table of Contents states that the book was finished on the 11th of September, 1591, by John Baldwine of Windsor. (See Chappell's " Popular Music of the Olden Time," vol. 1.)

A small volume, written on paper, quarto, entitled " The succession of the Baronnes of Bergavenny, briefly sett downe, specially to sett foorth how the digntie of that Barony hath alwayes gon with the possession of the place, and not by proximity of blood," dedicated to Queen Elizabeth by Edward Nevill of Abergavenny. The binding bears the royal arms, and there is a memorandum in the book that Queen Elizabeth gave the book to —— North, who left it to his son, who gave it to —— Haughton, attorney, of Clifford's Inn, who in 1668 gave it to Lady Bergavenny.

A folio volume bound in white, entitled—" A miscellanie of things very observable of that most illustrious and sometime princely family of the Nevills." It contains genealogical notes, copies of charters, drawings of arms, monuments, and seals, and extracts from different historical works, compiled in the seventeenth century.

A small volume written on paper, quarto, bound in rough brown calf, and entitled—" A Treatise of the Nobility of this realme according to the Lawe." It relates to the Barony of Abergavenny, and it was formerly in the library of the late Dr. Wellesley.

A volume written on paper, folio, and bound in green vellum. It contains extracts from court-rolls, escheats, and other documents, concerning the claim of the Lord Abergavenny to the office of Chief Larderer on the occasion of a coronation.

A volume written on paper, folio, and bound in white. It contains copies of the different documents transcribed in the " Registrum Honoris de Richmond," arranged in a somewhat different order. Besides the matter contained in that work as printed, it contains—

Genealogical table of the ancestors and relations of Ralph de Forneux.

Genealogical tables of the families of Manfield and Gartheston.

Memorandum concerning the issue of Simon de Hebden of Craven.

Grant by William Tunstall and four others to Sir William de Nevill, Lord of Fauconberge, of the manors of Busby, Faceby, Carleton, and Hilderwell, in tail male.    March 20, 8 Henry VI.

Grant by the same to Sir Richard de Nevill, son of Sir Ralph de Nevill, late Earl of Westmoreland, of the manors of Dalton, Stotfalde, Newton, and Swayneston, in tail male.    January 20, 4 Henry VI.

Inquisition taken after the death of Ralph, Earl of Westmoreland. November 12, 4 Henry VI.

Petition to James I. concerning the right of succession to Charles, Earl of Westmoreland, lately deceased.

Another petition to the same on the same subject, sent soon after the discovery of the Gunpowder Plot.

At the beginning of the volume there are a few notes on theology and on alchemy, and a copy of a letter from Henry VII. to the Earl of Oxford :—" Thorowe the folly and simpleness of suche as we put in truste to keepe Perkin Warbecke, he is escaped from them, and albeit it is noe great force where he be come, yet to the intent he might be punished after his deserte, we woulde gladlie have him againe.    Wherfore cousyn we will and desyre you to cause good and sure serche to be made for him with all diligence all alonge our portes, creekes, and passages in those partes aboute you, that he in noe wyse passe those waies.    And over this within the same portes and elswhere that shall seeme good ye make open proclamacion that whosoever he be that taketh the said Perkin, he shall have for his rewarde an hundreth poundes with our speciall thankes."    Given under the King's signet at Westminster, June 10 [1498].

A volume written on paper, quarto, and paged (ff. 1-108).    It contains fair copies of the following :—

Order of the Council for revoking the old commission of the Navy and constituting a new one.    July 4, 1660.

Letter from the Duke of York to the Navy Board, Whitehall. January 21, 1661.

A book of the duties of the several officers of the Royal Navy, viz. the principal officers and commissioners, the treasurer, the controller, the surveyor, the clerk of the acts, the storekeeper, the clerk of the cheque, the master attendant, the master shipwrights and their assistants, the clerk of the ropeyards, the porters, the boatswain of the yards, the boatswain of the ship, the gunner, and the purser.

Letters of the Duke of York concerning the purser's duty.  Hampton Court, July 12, 1662, and July 18, 1662.

Letter of William Bridgeman, concerning the victualling of the navy. Admiralty Office, July 26, 1697.

Draft of instructions for the commissioners for victualling the navy. A.D. 1697.

Court-rolls of different manors in the counties of Sussex and Norfolk.

Roll of accounts of Robert Smethcote, chamberlain of Rotherfield Chace.  5–6 Henry VI.

Letter of attorney of John [Kemp], Cardinal of St. Balbina, and Archbishop of York, to William Vyncent and John Ansty, to deliver seisin of the manor of Birling co. Kent, to Edward Nevile, Lord of Bergavenny and Elizabeth his wife.  September 20, 19 Henry VI.

Grant by Cuthbert, Bishop of Durham, Thomas, Earl of Rutland, George Dudley, clerk, Robert Norwych, knight, Chief Justice of the King's Bench, John Spylman, Justice of the King's Bench, John Pakyngton, John Danyster, William Nelson, clerk, and Edmund Turner, to Henry, Earl of Worcester, of the manor of Yaldyng, co. Kent, etc. in tail male.  December 4, 26 Henry VIII.  Signatures affixed and seals attached.

## THE POLITICAL CORRESPONDENCE OF JOHN ROBINSON.

The following documents have been arranged in chronological order, numbered, and placed in a tin box.  Their character, and their bearing upon the history of the reign of George III. are indicated in the general Report of the Commission :—

1.  1770, December 6.—St. James's.  Robert Wood to J. R.  Concerning the stores demanded by the Lieutenant Governor of Minorca. " Secret."

2.  1770, December 14.—Same place.  The same to the same.  Concerning the same.

3.  1771, January 14.—The Earl of Sandwich to John Robinson. Concerning the renewal of a lease.

4.  1771, January 21.—The same to the same.  Tell Lord North that I have promoted Baines, Lutwiche, Wickham, and Holloway.  The Duke of Newcastle some years ago turned out Mr. Harkness from being Receiver-General of Huntingdonshire for no other reason than because he was my friend.

5.  1771, January 21.—Minutes of arrangements, given to Mr. Rice. Lord Suffolk to be Privy Seal.  Mr. Wedderburn at present Solicitor General, Chancellor to the Queen, Privy Councillor, etc.  Mr. Whately to have the Board of Trade, until he can be otherwise provided for. Lords Lyttelton, Hyde, and Thomond, to be first considered whenever any places suitable for them become vacant.  Lord North does not exclude Cabinet places, but does not bind himself to them.  " Private."

6.  1771, February 10.—Hinchingbrook.  The Earl of Sandwich to J. R.  Solicits to be allowed to recommend one of the Aldermen of Huntingdon to be collector of the stamp duties in that county.

7. 1771, February 25.—Admiralty. The same to the same. Introduces Mr. Scott, who is recommended for the living of Worplesden (Waplesden). A bad man may be got out and a good man got in for the borough of Rochester on very reasonable terms.

8. 1771, February 26.—Same place. The same to the same. Recommends Mr. Stephen Arundel to be distributor of stamps at Huntingdon. No resignation from Mr. Thurloe has yet come.

9. 1771, February 28.—Memorandum of the expenses contracted in fitting the " Warwick."

10. 1771, March 23.—Admiralty. The Earl of Sandwich to J. R. Concerning the removal of Mr. Lay. Hopes to obtain the living of Symondsbourne for Mr. Scott from the Governors of Greenwich Hospital. Desires an " ostensible negative letter " for Mr. Gascoigne, that he cannot succeed Mr. Fitzgerald as Receiver of the Quit-rents of the Crown.

11. 1771, July 26.—St. James's. S[tanier] Porten to J. R. Jacques will remain in the country for eight or ten days. Lord Rochford will write to Governor Mostyn. " Private."

12. 1771, July 26.—Same place. The same to the same. A letter to Jacques signed J. Cox is thought by some in the Post Office to have been written by Jacques himself. The postmark of Portsmouth makes me conclude that he is there, and too probably on some bad design. A gentleman went to his house this morning, spoke to his wife, and then went to Cockspur Street, where his servant waited with horses, and they galloped away in a great hurry. " Private."

13. 1771, July 27.—Same place. The Earl of Suffolk to Lord North. The King thinks it is very proper to confer the Lieutenancy of Monmouthshire on the Duke of Beaufort.

14. 1771, August 6.—Same place. The same to the same. Concerning the offers of a discovery made by Jonathan Britain, a prisoner at Reading.

15. 1771, August 7.—Same place. The same to the same. The King has accepted my recommendation of Dr. Alexander Webster as Dean of the Chapel Royal at Edinburgh. Lord Rochford and I have sent Messrs. Sutton and Whateley to Reading about the Portsmouth affair. The utmost caution is necessary in so suspicious a business. It is difficult to bring a person already in custody before the Secretary of State. The King has expressed himself against further delay in the disposal of the Lieutenancies.

16. 1771, August 9.—Same place. The same to the same. Messrs. Sutton and Whateley returned yesterday evening from Reading. On the information which they obtained from Jonathan Britain, Lord Rochford and I judged it necessary to issue our warrant for the apprehension of Rogers and Calene without loss of time.

17. 1771, August 14.—Compiegne. Earl Harcourt to the Earl of Rochford. Report of a conversation between the Duke D'Aiguillon and M. de Merci. Madame du Barri gave a magnificent supper last Sunday to the foreign ministers. The Spaniard was the only one who was not there. He did not expect that the Nuncio would have waited upon the Countess, his predecessor having never visited Madame de Pompadour. Fuentes and the Duke D'Aiguillon are upon very bad terms. Madame du Barri did the honours extremely well. She gave us

music at supper, and afterwards Preville, Brisard, and M^{dle} Vestris acted some comic scenes which they call *jouer des proverbes*. The King came in after supper for more than an hour, and seemed more at his ease than I had yet seen him. (Copy.)

18. 1771, October 12.—The Earl of Sandwich to J. R. Concerning the appointment of a successor to Lay, as Surveyor of the Window Tax in Huntingdonshire. If it should appear that the power of the Government there is in my hands, I shall be able to choose three out of the four members at the next general election.

19. 1771, October 20.—Hinchingbrook. The same to the same. Encloses—
(A.) Letter from William Gordon to [the Earl of Sandwich]. Concerning honorary freedoms of the borough of Rochester. Dated at Rochester, October 16, 1771.

20. 1771, November 14.—The Earl of Sandwich to J. R. Introduces Thomas James, who has been appointed Collector of Window Lights in the place of Lay.

21. 1772, February 8.—St. James's. The Earl of Rochford to J. R. I must draw in the usual official manner for 250*l.*, for a person whom I have employed in France for two years to obtain information. " Private."

22. 1772, March 6.—Dunkirk. Andrew Durnford to ————. Concerning an epidemic on board a Dutch East India ship of sixty guns in the Straits of Calais. " Private."

23. 1772, March 13.—Same place. The same to the same. An abstract of the new ordinance concerning the French navy, with remarks on the same. " Private."

24. 1772, March 22.—Geneva. C. Upton to Lord North. Concerning the extraordinary purchase of corn for the French army.

25. 1772, March 31.—Dunkirk. Andrew Durnford to ————. Details concerning the doggers and fishing-boats sailing from Dunkirk to the cod fishery off the coasts of Iceland and Newfoundland. The traders who sell goods to the English smugglers here were in great consternation a few days ago at a report that the duty on tea was lowered 1*s.* in the pound in England. It is the general computation that the smugglers bring 3,000 guineas into this town weekly in specie, besides what are carried to Calais, Boulogne, Dieppe, and into Holland. Gin is the spirit which is most smuggled into England. A great branch of smuggling is done from here on the coast of Ireland by wherries of about 100 tons burthen, having twenty or thirty men, and eight or ten carriage guns, three and six pounders. Particulars concerning the " Snow," and its captain, Conner, alias the Batchelor, or the Commodore. There are always here about twelve or fifteen of these Irish wherries, and about twenty smuggling vessels of different kinds, mostly from the coast of Sussex and Kent. The wherries load from the quay ; the smaller vessels slip out and in when they please. The destination of the former is generally known.

26. 1772, April 7.—Same place. The same to the same. Chateau Trompette in the centre of Bordeaux is to be demolished. It will produce about 8,000,000 livres, or 349,200*l.* The Pretender, it is said, is going to be married to M^{dle} Stolberg, sister to the Marquise de Jamaique. Complaints of the breach of faith by the French Government concerning the Canada bills.

27. 1772, May 12.—The Earl of Sandwich to J. R. Desires " an ostensible refusal " from Lord North to the application of a clergyman of Huntingdon named Hodgson for a prebend of Worcester.

28. 1772, May 16.—The same to the same. Your refusals are too civil. I wanted " a good set down " about the prebend of Worcester.

29. 1772, October 8.—The Earl of Suffolk to Lord North. Is setting out for Castle Rising.

30. 1782, October 10.—Bushy Park. Lord North to [the Earl of Suffolk]. Reasons for the advancement of Baron Smythe to the office of Lord Chief Baron. (Copy.)

31. 1772, October 12.—Castle Rising. The Earl of Suffolk to Lord North. I beg to be excused from being the channel to convey to the Solicitor General [A. Wedderburn] the news of his disappointment. The Chancellor [Lord Apsley] is at one moment peremptory, at another accommodating, and then again obstinate. His threatened resignation does not strike me as a matter of any mighty consequence.

32. 1772, October 24.—Lord North to A. Wedderburn. Explains the reasons for the advancement of Baron Smythe. (Copy.)

33. 1772, October 24.—Shooters Hill. Alexander Wedderburn to Lord North. Expresses satisfaction at the promotion of so able and so upright a judge as Baron Smythe. He must consider that the vacancy which he expected has not taken place.

34. 1772, November 15.—Hinchingbrook. The Earl of Sandwich to J. R. Concerning the office of Inspector of Window Lights in that district. Hopes to bring in two good members for the borough, and one for the county, at the general election.

35. 1772, November 26.—The same to the same. Desires to see him about the borough of Portsmouth.

36. 1774, June 15.—St. James's. S. Porten to J. R. Concerning the present of 500l. wanted for the Ambassador from Morocco or from Tripoli at his departure.

37. 1774, August 18.—Same place. The same to the same. Lord Rochford desires to see him.

38. 1774, October 5.—Bushy Park. Lord North to ——— Cooper. Inform Sir Ferdinand Poole that Lord Pelham will not be his friend, and that therefore I advise him to retire. I was robbed last night as I expected. Our loss was not great, but, as the postilion did not stop immediately, one of the two highwaymen fired at him and bruised his side. It was at the end of Gunnersbury Lane. Consult with Rigby, Sayer, and Robinson for two good candidates for Westminster. A note should be written to Lord Falmouth in my name, and put into safe hands, informing him that Mr. Pownall can clear himself of the imputation of tampering at Tregony. His Lordship must be told in as polite terms as possible that I hope he will permit me to recommend to three of his six seats in Cornwall. The terms he expects are 2,500l. a seat, to which I am ready to agree. Sir Charles Whitworth must for the present be sent to East Looe, and Mr. Henry Conway to Lostwithiel. (Two sheets.)

39. 1774, October 5.—Islip. The same to J. R. I was detained at Bushy this morning. Let Pownall come in at Lostwithiel, and Conway at Tregony. " My noble friend [Lord Falmouth] is rather shabby in desiring guineas instead of pounds . . . . If he persists I would not have the bargain go off upon so slight a difference." I am afraid that it

MARQUIS OF
ABERGAVENNY'S
MSS.

is too late for Kennett to succeed at Windsor. I have not had a narrow escape, but my postilion had. I lost a very few guineas. I have promised Mr. Graves that he shall come in for East Looe, as soon as we can place Sir Charles Whitworth in any other seat. Lord Boston will pay 2,000*l.* for Mr. Irby. Prospect of success at different places.

40. 1774, October 5.—Queen's House. The King to J. R. Commends his zeal, activity, and prudence. Desires news about the elections.

41. 1774, October 6.—J. R. to the King. Concerning the elections for London, Westminster, and Middlesex. (Draft.)

42. 1774, October 6.—Islip. Lord North to J. R. "Mr. Legge can afford only 400*l.* If he comes in for Lostwithiel he will cost the public 2,000 guineas." Gascoign should have the refusal of Tregony if he will pay 1,000*l.*, but I do not see why we should bring him in cheaper than any other servant of the Crown. If he will not pay, he must give way to Mr. Best or Mr. Peachy. Arrangements for the boroughs of Minehead, Plympton, Lostwithiel, East Looe, and Tregony. As the Duke of Newcastle has come into our proposal, we must strain every nerve for his service. Write in my name to Mr. Luttrell to recommend Mr. Pownall [for Minehead].

43. 1774, October 7.—State of the Court of Aldermen in respect to the scratching for Lord Mayor.

44. 1774 (dated 1772), October 7.—Queen's House. The King to J. R. Desires a list of the elections concluded by Wednesday, with description of the members under the heads of "Pro," "Con," and "Doubtful."

45. 1774, October 7.—Kew. The same to the same. "The very judicious mode adopted for the county [of Middlesex] and Westminster elections cannot fail of success if those employed are thoroughly active; and [I] hope in the City things may turn out well, though the many defeats in that quarter do not give great expectation."

46. 1774, October 12.—Lord North to J. R. Mr. Philips wants money. Demands of this kind will be coming upon us every hour. I ought to know where the fund is upon which we are to draw.

47. 1774, November 19.—Downing Street. The same to the same. Everything in England goes on as well as we could expect. The state of America is neither better nor worse than when you were in London. "I do not find my spirits flag, and am far from despairing of the republick." Let Cooper know whether you promised Masterman 2,500*l.* or 3,000*l.* for each of Lord Edgcumbe's seats. I was going to pay him 12,500*l.*, but he demanded 15,000*l.*

48. 1775, February 1.—Admiralty. The Earl of Sandwich to Lord North. Recommends Mr. Bates, late Fellow of Peterhouse, for the vicarage of Halifax, if it should become vacant.

49. 1775, May 30.—The same to J. R. Concerning the election for Surrey.

50. 1775, May 31.—Admiralty. The same to the same. Concerning the same. Encloses—

[A.] Letter from George Marsh to the Earl of Sandwich. Concerning the same. Dated at the Navy Office, May 31, 1775.

51. 1775, June 4.—Duke Street, Westminster. The Earl of Suffolk to J. R. Encloses a petition.

52.  1775, June 14.—Boston [in America].  General Burgoyne to Lord [North].  " I am in too humble a station to promise myself any hope of contributing essentially to his Majesty's service in the military line in America.  My portion of command, in point of numbers, is inferior to what has often fallen to my lot as Lieut. Colonel, and when I look round me, I am persuaded it is not likely to be mended in point of enterprise."  Desires to return to England for private reasons.  " It would ill become me, and be of little use to your Lordship at present to expatiate upon the untoward state of affairs in this country.  It is but tautology to repeat my assurances of exerting every thought, word, and act that can contribute on my part to retreive (*sic*) them.  My colleagues, Gen^{ls} Howe and Clinton, are equally zealous, and it is with pride and satisfaction I find we do not differ in a single sentiment upon the military conduct now to be pursued.  But it is not within the most sanguine expectation that any stretch of our efforts, nor even the cooperation of his Majesty's councils at home, nor any success attending both, short of the interposition of a miracle, can restore the publick tranquility (*sic*) this year.  My plan therefore to make myself useful towards the proceedings of the next is as follows :—That the commander in chief in America be wrote to in the next dispatches of his Majesty's confidential servants to dismiss me from the army as early as the propriety of any service in which I may be employed will permit—that the Admiral be at the same time instructed to facilitate my passage to New York, Philadelphia, or any other province where in my judgement his Majesty's service may call me, and afterwards to convey me to England.  The friends of Government are suppressed, it is true, but notwithstanding appearances, I am far from beleiving (*sic*) their sentiments changed by the late events. The alarms which are spread and the real evils of the contest which will daily be felt more and more in every part of that continent, must operate to incline many to peace, who, strictly speaking may not come under the denomination of friends to Government.  I therefore am persuaded that, without risk to my person, which I mean at the same time never to spare when the King's service demands it, I could find means to be received in those provinces where the war shall not actively have extended.  In such places as are theatres not of arms but of counsels, it might possibly be expedient openly to profess, that being upon my return to England I wish to inform myself of the general sentiments of the Americans.  Not charged with any direct proposal from Government, nor authorised to treat with them in a publick character, I have not less zeal in my capacity as a member of Parliament, a friend of human nature, and a sincere well wisher to the united interests of the two countries, to forward as far as in me lies the great work of reconciliation upon enlarged, solid, honourable grounds.

"'This sort of language would not commit Government in any thing.  It might nevertheless introduce me to general intercourse with all parties, and it would then be the great purpose to prepare for your Lordship such a delineation of the prevailing dispositions, expectations, proceedings, and powers of men in this country, as might enable you to come to Parliament with a more positive plan than in the uncertainty of these circumstances can be found.  I doubt not your Lordship's consistency in asserting as heretofore the honour and interest of the nation in this great cause, and you shall find in me a steady, zealous, and an active supporter.

" My wish would be to embark upon my undertaking early in October, to arrive in England about Christmas ; always understood that the whole or any part of this proposal is subservent to any military operation that may be thought more material to the King's service, or any wherein my personal or professional honour might suffer by my absence from the   Marquis of army. I likewise mean to disavow any intention of relinquishing the   Abergavenny's service in America, should my presence be found necessary in a second  .   —— campaign." My return may be either put entirely on the footing of private business, or laid before the King as a measure of state. (Two sheets.)

53. 1775, June 16.—St. James's. Sir S. Porten to J. R. Concerning the salary of the English Consul at Corunna.

54. 1775, June 24.—Memorandum in the King's hand as to his manner of receiving petitions from the citizens of London.

55. 1775, June 27.—Plymouth. The Earl of Sandwich to J. R. Concerning the appointment of the Receiver of the county of Huntingdon.

56. 1775, July 15.—Admiralty. The same to the same. Desires to see him.

57. 1775, July.—A. Wedderburn to Lord [North]. Concerning the war in America. "In all undertakings carried on by the arms of this country the beginning has been unpro[s]perous. . . . . This country is never sufficiently prepared. . . . . The misconduct of the General and Admiral is the most obvious cause of the present bad posture of affairs in America." Severe criticism of the former. The conduct of the latter has been spiritless. The removal of commanders is a disagreeable measure, but it has always been a fortunate one. A much greater force is now necessary. "To send troops from Ireland, where they can best be spared, is certainly against law, but it is a breach of law to be hazarded and defended. It is better than a foreign force, because it looks less like a desperate resource." Young men of distinction should be induced to enter the service. A proclamation against the encouragement of treason would be a useful measure. "Addresses from the country in support of Government, which are never worth solicitation, would soon follow unasked." It would be well to give one or two instances of the disfavour of Government to those who have been open and indiscreet patrons of sedition, and have honours dependent upon the pleasure of Government. "The examples should be few, well chosen, and have no air of country politics." The boldest is the safest part. (Two sheets.)

58. 1775, July 31.—Bushy Park. Lord North to General Burgoyne. His Majesty fears that your plan cannot be carried into execution. If taken, you would be a valuable hostage. We cannot send you much above 2,000 men more in the course of this campaign, but in the spring you will have 20,000 regulars or more in the two armies. We are all perfectly sensible of the importance and difficulty of the contest, and mean to exert every nerve to put a safe and honourable end to it. Our wish is not to impose on our fellow subjects in America any terms inconsistent with the most perfect liberty. I cannot help thinking that many of the principal persons in North America will, in the calmness of the winter, be disposed to bring forward a reconciliation. Now they are too angry, too suspicious, and too much under the guidance of factious leaders. Our fleet is daily increasing. Sailors flock in as fast as the ships can be fitted out, and there has been as yet no occasion for pressing. There never was so much business in every branch of manufacture as at present. The interruption of our intercourse with North America must be felt some time or other, but hitherto we are not sensible of it. The desire of establishing our authority in America gains ground daily, notwithstanding the labours of the Lord Mayor and his faction.

Despatch of money and provisions. Measures to be taken if it is decided to abandon Boston. The gallantry and ability of General Howe, and the bravery of the men whom he commanded on the 17th [of June at Bunkers Hill] are the admiration of their countrymen, but the number of wounded and killed makes my heart bleed. I would abandon the contest were I not "most intimately convinced" in my own conscience that our cause is just and important. (Copy. Three sheets.) "Private."

59. 1775, August 4.—Kew. The King to J. R. "Mr. Robinson's accurateness and expedition in executing whatever he is entrusted with can only be equalled by his zeal and integrity. He has judged perfectly right in sending the warrant, which is very properly drawn up, and may be sent to Lord North and two other lords for countersigning. Col. Faucitt cannot set out till next week for Hanover, therefore Mr. Rigby need not issue the money till the warrant has gone through the usual forms. I cannot help saying no Paymaster was ever so accommodating as the present one."

60. 1775, August 8.—Ross. Lord North to J. R. It might have been more prudent to issue the 10,000*l*. to Col. Faucitt out of the civil list in the first instance. No mention of the employment of foreign troops was made in Parliament before the recess. That step is always delicate. If any other person should have the same scruples with myself, the warrant may be withdrawn. Make enquiries about Captain Sauvage. The troublesome Taunton business will probably oblige me both to come up to London and to attend the assizes at Wells. If I find the letter from the Corporation in my private drawers, I shall not choose to put it into the hands of the plaintiff or his attorney, and so shall be obliged to give my personal attendance. This will make me travel about 250 miles extraordinary, and overturn my plans. The news from Sevenoaks about Mr. Evelyn gives me much pleasure. Instructions concerning various applications and proposals made by Mr. Pownall, Mr. Wilson, Dr. Horn, Mr. Prescott, and Mr. Selwyn, etc. (Three sheets.)

61. 1775, August 8.—St. James's. Sir S. Porten to J. R. Sends intelligence. The King has seen it.

62. 1775, August 12.—Syon Hill. J. R. to Lord North. Concerning the warrant to Col. Faucitt. The Solicitor General warmly approved of the proclamation. The Attorney General told me that the expediency of the measure was not determined, and that he foresaw no good to result from it. He promised, however, to see the Solicitor about it. Concerning provisions and clothes for the army in America. Concerning a proposal to establish repositories for British manufactures at Long Island and Rhode Island. Concerning the proposed recall of Gage and Graves. Private intelligence about the turbulent shipwrights at Woolwich. Precautions necessary about the exportation of gunpowder. Concerning various applications. Complaints from the Indian powers should be sent to the Governor General and Council of Bengal, rather than to England. Maclean's reasons for coming over from Bengal. Advice about the trial at Wells. (Eight sheets.)

63. 1775, August 13.—The Attorney General [E. Thurlow] to J. R. He does not know how to speak decisively upon the exigence or expediency of this individual measure, but he agrees with the doctrine contained in the draft of the proposed proclamation.

A.B. [1775, August.]— Drafts of a proclamation for suppressing rebellion and sedition.

C. 1715, July 25.—Copy of a proclamation for suppressing rebellions and rebellious tumults.

64. 1775, August 15.—Lord North to J. R. Concerning Mr. Onslow and Lieut.-Col. Maclean.

65. 1775, August 15.—Sunbury. The Earl of Suffolk to J. R. The Attorney General's note is as sulky as the rest of his behaviour. The Solicitor has not seen the proclamation since it came out of the Attorney's hands. His inspection of it will be necessary.

66. 1775, August 16.—The same to the same. I submitted to the King the expediency of ordering clothing for Maclean's Highlanders, but his Majesty thought it uncertain whether it would be possible to raise them.

67. 1775, August 25.—Freckenham. J. Bates to [the Earl of Sandwich]. Solicits a promise of the living of Halifax, which is likely to be soon vacant.

68. 1775, August 30.—Wakefield Lodge. The Duke of Grafton to Lord North. The inclinations in general of men of property in this country, and the declarations held forth even by the leaders of the Congress in America differ little more than in words. A petition from persons styling themselves the deputies of the United Colonies met in Congress may be inadmissible by his Majesty, but the contents may encourage individuals to state to the whole legislature the wishes and expectations of the different colonies. Your lordship may not know that many persons, hearty friends to Government, have altered their opinions by the events of this year. If Parliament meets early, might not the two Houses address his Majesty that orders should be given to his General to communicate to the rebel army that, from various motives of tenderness, affection, and humanity, no hostile step should be taken if the colonies would depute persons to state their wishes?

69. 1775, September 4.—Hinchingbrook. The Earl of Sandwich to J. R. Concerning the Mayoralty of Portsmouth.

70. 1775, September 6.—Hinchingbrook. The same to the same. My younger son's case is quite desperate. "When a vacancy happens at Huntingdon, I could wish to have a candidate ready to start immediately. I should not like a merchant or a meer (sic) moneyed man, for reasons which I have allready told you, and yet a sum of money will be necessary, tho' upon such terms as no one would refuse. The terms in short that I must have are 2,000l. to be lent to me for five years on my bond, and to pay the expenses of the election, which in all probability would not amount to 300l." The conditions offered to Capt<sup>n</sup> Phipps are "the thinking and acting as I do in all American points, and supporting the present administration in their whole system."

71. 1775, September 10.—Same place. The same to the same. I am sorry to hear that the idea of recalling Admiral Graves is again revived, for I think it is unjust. "I am, however, not so indiscreet as to opiniate this matter after the impression I perceive it has made at the fountain head."

72. 1775, September 22.—50, Margaret Street. Lieut.-Col. John Maunsell to Lord North. Renews his offer to return to America without any expense to the Government.

(A.) Same day. Alternative scheme by the same for recruiting soldiers in the neighbourhood of Limerick.

73. 1775, September 26.—Hinchingbrook. The Earl of Sandwich to J. R. Concerning Mr. Jackson.

74. 1775, October 3.—Cavendish Square.   Lord Barrington to Lord North.   There are no more troops in England than are absolutely necessary for securing the peace and collecting the revenue.  Nothing would please the Irish so much as some indulgence in respect to the exportation of the woollen manufactures of that country.   Encloses—

(A.) A statement of the forces in England on the 2nd of October 1775.   Exclusive of cavalry, guards, and invalids, the whole rank and file from Portsmouth to Newcastle numbers 3,360.   Exclusive of the 42nd Highlanders there are in Scotland 1,120.

75. 1775, October 6.—St. James's.   Sir S. Porten to J. R.   Concerning an address to the King.   Encloses—

(A.) Draft of an address to the King from the Justices of the Peace for the City and Liberty of Westminster.

76. 1775, October 9.—War Office.   A. Chamier to J. R.   Sends an extract from a letter from Lord Barrington adverse to the scheme of Col. Maunsell.

77. 1775, October 13.—St. James's.   The Earl of Suffolk to J. R. The people at Kendal are much divided in opinion upon American affairs.  Dowker wishes to know whether he is to try to obtain an address from thence at all hazards.

78. 1775, October 14.—Sunbury.   The same to the same.   Encloses an application.

79. 1775, November 3.—Hastings.   Edward Milward to J. R. Particulars concerning the election of Charles Jenkinson as Member of Parliament.

80. 1775, November 4.—London.   Charles Jenkinson to J. R. Concerning the election at Hastings.

81. 1775, November 8.  The Earl of Dartmouth to J. R.   "If I take the seals that are offered me, I shall render myself ten times more miserable than I am."   I think it as reasonable that a noble Viscount [Weymouth ?] should be expected to accommodate as myself.  I am divided between my dread of a situation in which I foresee no satisfaction and my love for Lord North.

82. 1775, November 9.—The same to the same.   "The suspence in which I have been since I received your note is a state of no small agony.  Relieve me if you can."

83. 1775, November 10.—Sir S. Porten to J. R.   He has delivered Lord North's message to Lord Rochford.

84. Same day.—The same to the same.   Concerning Lord Rochford's pension.

85. 1775, November 10.—St. James's.   The Earl of Suffolk to the Lords of the Treasury.   Encloses—

(A.) Copy of a letter from the Lords of the Admiralty, dated November 9, 1775.

(B.) Copy of a letter from Captn Pearson, commander of His Majesty's sloop " Speedwell," to Mr. Stephens, dated in Dover Road, November 8, 1775.   He recounts his proceedings with regard to the " Patriote," a snow of Altona, supposed to be laden with arms and saddles for the rebels in America.

86. 1775, November 10.—Sir S. Porten to [J. R.].   Concerning Lord Rochford's pension.

87. 1775, November 19.—Admiralty.   The Earl of Sandwich to J. R. Hopes that Mr. Chamberlain and other members of the University of

Cambridge will go down to support an address to the Crown, which will   MARQUIS OF
be proposed by the Vice-Chancellor, but opposed by the Chancellor's  ABERGAVENNY'S
party and Lord Granby.   MSS.

88. 1775, November 20.—Same place. The same to the same. Concerning the same.

89. 1775, December 4.—The Earl of Suffolk to J. R. The election in Westmoreland is to be on Thursday. There is much dissatisfaction expressed at Sir James [Lowther's] candidate, but no appearance of opposition. I wish that Lord North would dismiss him from his Lieutenancies, which would be a *coup de grace* to his importance in the two counties.

90. 1775, December 4. [Charles] Jenkinson to J. R. Major Whitmore appears disposed to leave opposition. It is surely wise to encourage Mr. Hawke, who is desirous to oppose Lord Rockingham at York.

91. 1775, December 6.—Sir S. Porten to [J.R.]. Concerning Lord Rochford's pension.

92, 93. 1775, December 11, and 13.—St. James's. The Earl of Suffolk to the Lords of the Treasury. Concerning the seizure of the "Anna Catherina" by his Majesty's sloop "Speedwell."

94. Same date and place. The same to the same. Concerning the ship "Patriot."

95. 1775, December 20.—Headington, near Oxford. Charles Jenkinson to J. R. A petition has been presented in his name to the Irish House of Commons without his signature, consent, or knowledge. He desires to know what Lord North wrote in his last despatch to Ireland concerning [the clerkship of] the Pells, and the office of Vice-Treasurer.

96. 1775, December 26. The Earl of Dartmouth to J. R. Concerning the living of Halifax. Encloses—

(A.) Application for the living of Halifax from John Walker of Walterclough.

(B.) Application for employment from James Gardiner.

97. 1775, December 27.—St. James's. The Earl of Suffolk to the Lords of the Treasury. Concerning a vessel in Swansea Bay, supposed to be laden with military stores, saltpetre, or lead.

98. 1776, January 7.—The Earl of Dartmouth to J. R. Recommends the son of Mr. Ferrall of Bristol.

99. 1776, January 12.—St. James's. Sir S. Porten to J. R. Concerning the living of Thurcaston.

100. 1776, January 15. Same place. The same to the same. Concerning the same, and concerning the revocation of the letters patent by which Sir George Macartney was appointed Constable of Toome Castle.

101. 1776, February 10.—Same place. The same to the same. Desires to see the memorandum made about himself in the Treasury Book. "Private."

102. 1776, April 6.—Bushy Park. Lord North to J. R. Concerning the election of Directors of the East India Company.

103. 1776, May 20.—The same to the same. Sir Ralph Payne is eager for the seat [at St. Germans]. If Mr. E[liot] does not approve of him, you had better "liquidate with him," as he proposes. "Mr. P[ownall] having sat but one session out of six, I suppose Mr. E[liot]

will not object to return 2500*l.*, which is the just proportion, of the sum originally paid."

104. 1776, June 14.—St. James's. Sir S. Porten to J. R. Lord Rochford desires that the Custom-house vessel may be permitted to carry him from Calais to St. Osyth on his return from his tour to Holland.

105. 1776, June 17.—Mistley. Richard Rigby to J. R. Desires to find a living for Mr. Pitman, a friend of Lord Weymouth.

106. 1776, July 10.—St. James's. Sir S. Porten to J. R. Encloses a letter from Lord Rochford.

107. 1776, July 24.—Calcutta. Richard Barwell to J.R. " Mr. Hastings and I have been equally disappointed in our views to conciliate our associates, and I fear all our future endeavors will prove as vain and futile as the last. The government and the command of the forces in reversion are objects of too grand a nature to be relinquished voluntarily. . . . If it is judged necessary hereafter that the chair shall be vacated, to promote the General [Clavering] and Colonel [Monson], do me the justice to believe that I will not decline my services while I think I can in any respect render them to the satisfaction of the minister and the Company." " Private."

108. Duplicate of the above.

109. 1776, August 26.—Bushy Park. Lord North to General Carleton. The King has expressed high satisfaction at your conduct in Canada, and his intention of conferring upon you the Order of the Bath. He has also declared his intention of adding some further mark of his approbation. He will give you an annuity for three lives out of any revenue in Canada in the disposal of the Crown. If no such revenue exists, he proposes to order a pension of 1,000*l.* per annum to be made out of the Irish establishment for the lives of yourself, Lady Maria, and any one of your children. You have well deserved this reward from your country. Whether all or any of the colonies do or do not return to their duty, Canada must be the main support of British authority in North America. To establish the Government of Quebec in a manner that shall be agreeable to the people, and at the same time to secure their obedience to this country, is an arduous and important task. Your suggestions will have the greatest weight with us. Particulars about money and provisions. It may not be amiss to put you on your guard against an attack from the French. (Draft, much altered.) " Private."

110. 1776, September 4.—Fort William. Warren Hastings to J. R. Your letters have confirmed me in the line which I had before prescribed to myself for my public conduct. " In spite of every mortification and indignity which I suffer here, and greater from home, I will not abandon the honourable and distinguished trust which was assigned me." Any further steps which may be necessary to create that harmony which you so earnestly recommend, must be made by those who possess the absolute rule of this government, and whose unprovoked attacks I have hitherto suffered without attempting to retaliate them. I have entire confidence in the justice and candor of Lord North. I hope that I shall be honoured with your friendship, of which I know the value.

111. Duplicate of the above.

112. [1776, September.]—Richard Barwell to J.R. Concerning Mr. Wordsworth. Being forbidden to attend public business, I have not lately much frequented the councils. If I do not find myself better, I will take my final leave of India. Now I am totally useless.

113. Duplicate of the above.

114. 1776, September 28.—Sandwell. The Earl of Dartmouth to Lord [North]. Congratulates him on the providential preservation of his life.

115. 1776, October 6.—Kew. The King to J. R. "Mr. Robinson's letter from Paris, and the extract of one to Mr. St. Paul from Dieppe are very unpleasant. I have the strongest reason to believe the French have given ear to the most absurd suspicion that if the troops in America do not meet with success, that they are instantly to proceed to the West India Islands, and wipe out the disgrace of the loss of North America by a conquest on the French. There cannot be the smallest doubt that the friends to the American Rebellion are the fabricators of this lye, and that they will if they can put Ireland also in a combustion. The scene may appear gloomy, but I trust with rectitude and resolution a different aspect will be obtained. It has been a very comfortable gift of Divine Providence to me, that when difficulties arise my spirits also increase, for where the cause is just I can never be dismayed."

116. 1776, October 8.—Same place. The same to the same. The arrangement of the letter of resignation for Mr. Hastings will prevent much irksome business from coming before the House of Commons. "Some delicacy may be necessary in stating the foreign article of the speech, but as to the American, a firm and manly determination of a thorough exertion of every nerf to bring the rebellious collonies to submission, and some spirited expressions to draw forth the resolution of the landed interest to make them chearfully contribute to what so nearly concerns them."

117. 1776, October 8.—Woodsome. The Earl of Dartmouth to J. R. Declines an office (the Lord Lieutenancy of Ireland) offered to him by Lord North, as certain to be productive of disgrace and misery both to himself and to the public.

118. 1776, October 15.—The King to J. R. Concerning the vacant Lieutenancy of Ireland. "There is no one event has given me more real pain than the seeing Lord North so much grieved on this subject, and there is no length I would not go to ease his mind, except the taking a step that would even involve him in the greatest difficulties. Lord Hillsborough has no property but in Ireland; if he is appointed it will set all the Irish peers that live in Ireland to flatter themselves to acquire that office, which must naturally create a constant degree of ill humour in the House of Lords of Ireland. Besides, I am sorry to say, I do not know a man of less judgement than Lord Hillsborough, and consequently less qualified to fill that office with dignity or propriety. Every one of the members of the Cabinet know my sentiments on this subject, and therefore I cannot with any degree of decency accept of a recommendation that I from conviction think an improper one. As to Lord Buckingham[shire], he has been knocking at every door. I am therefore resolved not to accept of him, because he would not appear as recommended by Lord North. Mr. Robinson could not do me a more acceptable service than by suggesting any decent peer to Lord North, whom I ever wish to oblige; but Mr. Robinson would certainly feel the impropriety of my doing it at the expence of what I think no man ought, I mean by doing wrong. Nay, I even told Lord Hillsborough himself that I would never approve of him for that office."

119. 1776, November 25.—Calcutta. Richard Barwell to J. R. The unexpected death of Col. Monson, with the urgent instances of the Governor General have inclined me to forego my design of leaving Bengal. Arrangements concerning Mr. Wordsworth. "Private."

120.—Duplicate of the above.

121.  1776, December 17.—Poland Street.  P. Wentworth to Lord North.  Gives an extract from a letter from Nantes concerning the arrival of Dr. Franklin, and particulars of the mission of M. Carmichel from Paris to Berlin.

122.  1776, December 27.—Hill Park.  Lord Hillsborough to J. R. If Lord North inclines to let me have my plaything no time is to be lost, as Lord Harcourt prepares to come away.  It can be done by King's letter granting me the sum annually, in lieu of my own and ten Warderers' salary.  (Endorsed by J. R. "Fort Hillsborough.")

123.  1776, December 28.—The Earl of Dartmouth to J. R.  Recommends an applicant for an office.

124.  1776, December 29.—The same to the same.  Concerning applicants for offices.

125.  1777, January 3.—Lord Hillsborough to J. R.  My fort is likely to be bombarded by the Attorney General [of Ireland].  Mention of the letters patent of Charles II.

126.  1777, March 2.—Treasury Chambers.  J. R. to the officers of the customs at Dover.  Order for the search of the baggage of a gentleman who is going to France.  (Draft.)

127.  Same day and place.—The same to the Earl of Suffolk.  Encloses copy of the above.  (Draft.)

128.  Same day.—The Earl of Suffolk to J. R.  Approves of the letter.

129.  1777, March 21.—Duke Street, Westminster.  The same to the same.  Acknowledges receipt of letters.

130.  1777, May 17.—Victoria.  Declaration by Count Florida Blanca to Mr. Lee as to the intentions of the King of Spain relative to the United States of America.

131.  1777, May 18.—Victoria.  Reply of Mr. Arthur Lee to the declaration of the King of Spain in favour of the United States.

132.  1777, June 6.—New York.  Sir William Howe to J. R. Major Balfour and I send our warmest thanks for your extreme attention in providing every necessary supply for this army.  We must not expect to see the war terminated this campaign, though I hope we shall strike deep towards concluding it in the next.  "Private."

133.  1777, July 17.—J. R. to P. Stephens.  Concerning the ship " Richard Penn," starting for America.  (Copy.)    " Private."

134.  Same day.—The same to —— Stanley.  Concerning the same. (Draft or copy.)    "Most private."

135.  [1777, July.—Extracts from a letter from a spy (?) at Paris, concerning the relations between England, France, and America.]

136.  1777, August 3.—Bushy Park.  Lord North to [General Carleton].  "General Haldimand is the person intended by his Majesty for your successor in the government of Canada.  That gentleman is now in Switzerland upon a visit to his relations, and it is hardly possible that he should set out for Canada time enough to make his passage this year."  The King has given orders for a warrant for a pension out of the Irish establishment.  "All the letters from Gen¹. Burgoyne and the other officers of the northern army are full of the warmest acknowledgements of the cordial, zealous, and effectual assistance they have received from you."  I have been too busy to give a thorough examination to

your *ordonnances*. Whatever may be the success of our arms, our influence, power, and existence, in North America will henceforward principally depend upon the possession of Canada. " By my other letter to you of this date you will understand that his Majesty leaves you entirely at liberty to continue in the government of the Province of Quebec, if you think fit, and on that account will not permit Mr. Haldimand to set out till after your arrival in England." (Copy.) " Private."

MARQUIS OF ABERGAVENNY'S MSS.

137. 1777, August 7.—Memorial delivered to France and Spain by the three Commissioners of America. (Copy.)

138. 1777, August 15.—Fort William. Warren Hastings to the Court of Directors of the East India Company. Concerning his proposed resignation. (Copy. Three sheets.)

139. 1777, August 24.—Hovingham. Thomas Worsley to [J. R.]. Solicits the appointment of his son to the living of Stonegrave.

140. 1777, August 25.—Greenwich. William Eden to Lord North. Encloses letters from Robinson, Wentworth, and Lupton. There is reason to believe that the Bourbon Court will for the present desist from any measures that might occasion an immediate war. The French, however, persist in sending the additional battalions to the West Indies, and will accompany them with frigates. Lord Mansfield deprecates any measure that tends to war. A resolution that eight additional frigates, from 28 to 32 guns, be employed in the North American service would certainly be a wise measure. " It has for many months been clear to me that if we cannot reduce the colonies by the force now employed under Howe and Burgoyne, we cannot send and support a force capable to reduce them.

141. 1777, August 26.—Hampton Court. The Earl of Sandwich to Lord North. Encloses—

(A.) Statement of the naval forces of England, France, and Spain. Ships of the line in Europe—Spain 21, France 23, England 35; out of Europe—Spain 20, France 1, England 8. " In this situation are we safe at home, and can we on any emergency venture to detach, without more ships being immediately commissioned ?"

142. 1777, August 28.—Kew. The King to J. R. Concerning the living of Stonegrave, and the misfortunes of Captain Brereton.

143. 1777, September 7.—Fort William. Warren Hastings to Lord North. The death of General Clavering has made no change in my intention to continue in the government, although I know not a man into whose hands I should be better pleased to relinquish it, than in those of Mr. Barwell, my immediate successor. I have no cause to suppose that he would be allowed to keep it. " Unless I knew it to be your wish, and his Majesty's pleasure, that I should remain, no consideration upon earth shall prevail with me to solicit it. I wish to approve myself a profitable agent to the Company, a benefactor to my country, a good and loyal subject and servant to my King." (Two sheets.)

144. Duplicate of the above.

145. 1777, September 12.—Kew. The King to J. R. " Friday will be time enough to further prorogue the Parliament to the 20th of November, or to issue the proclamation for its assembling on the 30th of October. If money matters can be so managed as to postpone it to the later day, I should think on all subjects it would be most desirable. I am sorry Lord North seems rather out of spirits, but I am certain when he has seen Mr. Robinson he will be more cheerful. I have

always wished him to be quite open with Mr. Robinson, but much less
so with many others that now and then do more harm than good."

146. 1777, September 19.—Syon Hill. J. R. to the King. " His
Majesty's discernment certainly perceived what oftentimes preys on
Lord North's mind; it is the situation of his private affairs . . .
Lord North's allowance from Lord Guildford on his marriage was not
large, and his estate, including Lady North's, is not at present considerable, or of a nature Mr. Robinson believes very productive . . . He
believes it not to be above 2,500*l*. per annum, and not near so much
nett to him. Lord Guildford, although his estates are 10,000*l*. per
annum, has not made any further allowance to Lord North, except
300*l*. a year to Mr. North while he was at Oxford, and what he may
now be pleased to add for the young gentleman while abroad. Under
these circumstances, without any extravagance, but with so large a
family, when from situation Lord North can't minutely attend to the
œconomy of it, his expenses, he has told Mr. R. repeatedly, have every
year since he was First Lord of the Treasury very largely exceeded his
income. Consequently he has been obliged to borrow money from
time to time, and Mr. R. believes, that what with money borrowed, and
debts outstanding to tradesmen, his Lordship owes near 10,000*l*. At
least Lord North has told Mr. Robinson frequently that that sum will
set him clear, and the thought of this his situation frequently distresses
his mind, and makes him very unhappy." His mind has been agitated
by this, in addition to the perplexities of his public situation, as indeed
it is on every occasion when things press disagreeably. He has said
" that he found his health so much impaired, his abilities fail, and his
mind enervated, and that he was unable to bear the anxieties and
distress brought upon him by these things, which preyed upon his spirits
and shook his constitution." Otherwise he did not feel himself unequal
in any respect to the business of Parliament, and he was ready to meet
faction there in its utmost strength. Mr. Robinson has urged Lord
North to state his situation to your Majesty with great openness and to
depend on your royal munificence, but, from Lord North's delicacy and
natural reservedness, he never could succeed. (Draft. Six pages. See
the King's letter to Lord North, No. 410 in Mr. Donne's edition.)

147. 1777, September 25.—Downing Street. Lord North to — Forth.
The frank declarations of M. de Maurepas, combined with the orders
lately given by the French ministry, and the restitution of the Jamaica
ships, make me more sanguine than I have been for some time past
in my expectations of the continuance of peace. You may assure M. de
Maurepas that it is our fixed intention to maintain peace with our
European neighbours, whatever may be the event of the American war.
(Copy in J. R's hand.)

148. 1777, September 25.—Treasury Chambers. J. R. to the same.
Lord North has ordered 500*l*. to be paid to you, in addition to the 300*l*.
which you will receive in bank notes with this. (Copy.)

Lord North to the same. " At present I am to pay you 400*l*. per
annum salary, and 100*l*. a month, while his Majesty thinks it necessary
for his service that you should live in an expensive manner at Paris.
Whatever else is paid to you must be to answer disbursements." (Copy
in J. R's hand.)

149. 1777, September 26. Lord North to J. R. Concerning
Captain Laurence.

150. 1777, September 27.—Treasury Chambers. J.R. to Sir William Howe. Concerning the same, a most determined enemy to this

country, who constantly sails between Great Britain and New York. (Draft.) " Private."

151. Same date and place. The same to the same. Our anxiety for your success makes us impatient to hear from you. (Draft.) " Private."

152. 1777, October 1.—Tanjore. The Rajah Shree Ram Predaun to the King of Great Britain. Complaints against the Nabob. (Translation. Two sheets.)

153. 1777, October 2.—Fort William. Warren Hastings to Lord North. Until the arrival of Mr. Elliot, 1 neither knew the nature of Mr. Maclean's engagements, nor the degree in which his faith was pledged. Though I cannot recall the past, I can rectify it. It is probable that the death of Sir John Clavering will have removed the object for which my resignation was required. If however any person shall arrive in this settlement who shall have been appointed in form to succeed to the vacancy occasioned by my resignation, and not otherwise, .will immediately yield up the government to the member of the Council who shall be the next in succession to it.

154. [1777, November 14.]—Downing Street. [Lord North to A. Wedderburn.] Desires to remove the suspicion that he is not sensible of his services to Government. Offers public mark of his esteem. (Draft.)

155. 1777, November 14.—Lincoln's Inn Fields. A. Wedderburn to Lord North. Acknowledges his kind letter, and makes an appointment for an interview.

156. 1777, November 16.—St. James's. Sir S. Porten to J. R. Concerning Captain Rush, who is said to be coming to England with letters from the rebels in France.

157. 1777, December 18.—Paris. The three American Commissioners to Samuel Adams. (Copy.)

158. 1777, December 19.—Same place. The same to the same. (Copy.)

159. Same date and same place.—A. Lee to the Secret Committee at Congress. (Copy.)

160. 1778, January 11.—Syon Hill. J. R. to Lord North. Concerning the Board of Revenue in Ireland, the transports for the army, and the policy to be adopted towards America. (Copy or draft. Four sheets.)

161. 1778, January 15.—Paris. The three American Commissioners to Captain Paul Jones of the " Amphitrite." (Copy.)

162. 1778, January 18.—Minutes of a Cabinet Council held at Lord North's in Downing Street. Lord Suffolk communicated a minute of Lord Amherst's opinion concerning the manner of carrying on the war. The Lords were of opinion that 400 men should be sent as soon as the season will permit, to Newfoundland, and a company not short of 50 men to the Bermudas, and that 2,500 men should be sent to Halifax out of the two new corps first raised, and an old battalion if it can be spared.

(A.) Minute of Lord Amherst's opinion that it is not possible to reduce the Colonies by an effective war, without an addition of 30,000 men to the force already in America, and that, under the circumstances, the future operations must be principally naval.

163.  1778, January 19.—Queen's House.  The King to Lord North.  "Nothing can be more detrimental in case of an European war than the idea of sending in our present weak state another old corps out of Great Britain, but I will not object on this occasion, provided it is understood that the 400 men for Newfoundland and the company for Bermudas is of the new levies.  The 70th is the regiment to whom this duty will fall, which is very advantageous to the Admiralty as the 70th Regiment is in Scotland, and Lord Sandwich thinks that he can get transports cheaper at Leith than in the Thames."

164.  1778, February 6.—Calcutta.  Richard Barwell to J. R. Justifies his conduct.  States the arguments for and against the acceptance of overtures made by certain Mahratta ministers at Poona.

165.  1778, February 14.—Paris.  The three American Commissioners to the Secret Committee at Congress.  (Copy.)

166.  An account of the ships that are to sail under the convoy of M. La Motte Piquet on the 17th of February 1778.

167.  Secret intelligence from France.  On the 18th of February 1778, Captain Coulter started from Passy with despatches for America. Lord North's plan of reconciliation is said to be of such a nature that America could not refuse it.  This has alarmed the French Court so much that it would grant any terms sooner than see America reunited with Great Britain.

168.  1778, February 19.—A. Wedderburn to Lord North.  Concerning the naval command to be given to Mr. Johnstone.

169.  1778, February 22.—Calcutta.  R. Barwell to J. R.  Concerning the rupture between the Mahrattas at Poona, and the designs of France.  (Two sheets.)

170.  Duplicate of the above.

171.  1778, February 22.—The Earl of Clarendon to Lord North. Concerning the Ambassador at Paris.  Lady Howe thinks it would be most agreeable to Lord Howe and the General to have leave to come home about the same time.  The King's intended bounties to them would afford a most comfortable relief to their minds.  The General might be scrupulous in accepting anything until he has justified his conduct.  (Two sheets.)  " Private."

172.  1778, February 24.—Minutes of a conversation with Lord Sandwich concerning the naval command [to be given to Mr. Johnstone].

173.  1778, March 1.—Mr. T. to Lord North.

174.  1778, March 2.—Poland Street.  P. Wentworth to [J. R.]. Encloses—
(A.)  Copy of letter from —— Edwards, dated February 19, concerning the supply of intelligence from France.

175.  1778, March 11.—Duke Street, Westminster.  The Earl of Suffolk to J. R.  Nobody can be more ignorant than I am of every part of the business we are to have to-morrow.

176.  1778, March 18.—Parliament Street.  J. R. to Lord North. The Chairman and Deputy of the East India Company are now with me, and, agreeably to your commands, I have opened to them the idea of their giving immediate orders for an attack on Chandenager and Pondicherry. They like the plan, and are ready to proceed therein if his Majesty shall approve.  They can send letters by Leghorn, Alexandria, and Suez, duplicates by Constantinople and Aleppo, and triplicates by

their own pacquet-boat to Alexandria. They have presented a
memorial to Lord Weymouth, desiring that they may have a naval force
for their protection. The subsequent steps must be taken by the
chairs and the Secret Committee, and they cannot commence hostilities
without hearing his Majesty's pleasure. (Draft.)  " Most private."

177. 1778, March 31.—A. Wedderburn to William Eden. Concerning Mr. Johnstone.

178. Memorial presented to the States of Holland by B. Franklin
and A. Lee, Plenipotentiaries for the United States of America.
(Copy.)

179. 1778, April 2.—Chaillot. A. Lee to B. Franklin. Complains
that he was not consulted about the mission of M. Girard and Mr.
Deane to America. (Copy.)

180. 1778, April 14.—Treasury Chambers. J. R. to Mr. Rumbold.
The Nabob has deposited his will in the King's hands. He intends to
lodge a duplicate with you and your Council, and another copy with the
Governor-General and Supreme Council of Bengal. You will see the
absolute necessity of keeping this trust most sacredly. (Draft.)  " Most
private."

181. 1778, April 14.—[France.]  Sir George Rodney to J. R.
" Deprived as I am of the honour of serving my country, by Lord
S[andwic]h's, refusing to employ me yet, 'tis impossible for me
to be an idle spectator, and not from my heart do my best endeavours that the scheems of her enemys may be frustrated, and she
again move triumphant over all her enemys. During my stay here I
shall make it my business to learn the destination of their squadrons,
that his M[ajesty]'s Min[iste]rs may be informed, which I shall send
by every safe conveyance. An officer on the Irish establishment gives
me an opportunity of sending the inclosed, which I must beg you will,
with my sincerest respects, give to Lord N[ort]h. The intelligence
relative to the Americans may be depended upon as fact. Adams, their
ambassador, lately arrived here, is the same as had the conference with
Lord How. He cannot speak a word of French."

182. " Abstract of what passed relative to Lord B[ute] and Lord
C[hatham], with copys of the only two notes Sir James W[right] ever
wrote to Lr. A[ddington] on the subject, and his answers."  (Written
apparently by Sir J. Wright. Endorsed by J. R.  " Suppose to be
genuine and therefore kept." See " Quarterly Review," vol. cxxxi.,
p. 266.)

183. 1778, May 2.—Fort William. Warren Hastings to Lord
North. The Rajah of Birân has expressed his cheerful compliance with
my application that he should allow our troops to march through his
dominions. Concerning the affairs at Poona, and the intentions of the
French. (Two sheets.) Encloses—
    A. Copy of a letter from Modajee Bhoosla to [Warren Hastings],
dated April 20, 1778. (Three sheets.)

184. 1778, May 5.—London. William Pulteney to Lord North.
My friend will stay at Paris if I desire him to stay, but he gives me
notice that he will betray no confidence of his friend there. What I
said to-day in the House of Commons was not meant as any personal
attack. I am agitated to the highest degree at the impending danger of
this country from the criminal delay. If a great fleet was not ready to
sail at an hour's notice, after all the sums allowed by Parliament, and
the knowledge of the preparations of France and Spain, your Lordship

and the First Lord of the Admiralty ought to answer it with your heads. If it was ready and orders for sailing were delayed an hour, the punishment ought not to be less. His Majesty's absence on the Monday is no excuse, much less the intended parade at Portsmouth. I hope to send important information concerning the Court of Denmark.

185. 1778, May 12.—Pall Mall. Lord George Germain to Lord [North]. Lord Holdernesse is dying. To succeed him as Warden of the Cinque Ports has long been the object of my wishes. If your Lordship thinks of asking that office for yourself, I can have no pretensions to it. "I cannot expect to have health and activity much longer to discharge the duty of my present situation, and indeed I have found the attendance of the House of Commons this session too fatiguing and almost intolerable." If any new arrangement is made, I am ready to retire to the private station from which I was called, though it would be more satisfactory to me were I to receive some mark of his Majesty's favour.

186. 1778, June 14.—Treasury Chambers. J. R. to Mr. Rumbold. Sends a letter to the Nabob. Desires a speedy execution of the orders sent. (Draft.) "Private."

187. "Private instructions given to Mr. Smith on his journey to Paris, 16th July 1778." Questions to be answered by Dr. Bancroft. (Two sheets. Draft in Lord North's hand.)

188. 1778, July 19.—New York. William Eden to Lord North. "We are obliged at present to submit to the mortifying spectacle of the French fleet intercepting whatever comes towards us. . . . . If Byron comes before they depart, it seems pretty clear they will never depart. . . . Rhode Island is reinforced with 2,000 troops, and a considerable num ber of the light infantry are aboard the fleet to compleat it. There is great alacrity and good spirits both in the inhabitants and in the forces, but this suspense is trying. . . . . It certainly would be unwise in Lord Howe at present to hazard an action, more especially as we grow stronger every hour. Our supply of fish is interrupted, and provisions are very dear. I tremble for the Cork fleet . . . . By different exertions we might contrive to live till the end of October." If our supplies fail I do not know what will become of us. These islands afford the only means of retaining an effectual hold on this whole country, and America is not lost so long as they are retained. At the same time I believe that they cannot be established with less than 12,000 men. (At the head of the letter is a rough plan showing the positions of the different batteries and of the English and French fleets near Long Island.)

189. 1778, July 20.—Same place. The same to the same. We continue blockaded, but are not dispirited. The manning of the fleet has been completed by the light infantry. A party is to march to-morrow to the east end of Long Island to secure the live stock and the flour. The "Leviathan" has been strongly armed and manned in five days. The General will go to-morrow to Kingsbridge. We believe that the French fleet is in great want of water. (On the third page is a rough plan showing the position of the different batteries, etc.)

190. 1778, August 16.—Fort William. Warren Hastings to Lord North. Describes in detail the events that occurred in India after the 2nd of May. (Seven sheets.)

191. 1778, August.—Maidenhead Bridge. Sir Edward Hughes to J. R. Encloses,—

(A.) Letter from George Stratton to Sir E. Hughes concerning a proposed interview.

192. 1778, September 4.—St. James's. Sir S. Porten to [J. R.]. Private intelligence concerning the movements of Car——l, and concerning the ship "Mary." MARQUIS OF ABERGAVENNY'S MSS.

193. 1771, September 6.—Same place. The same to the same. Concerning the "Mary."

194. 1778, September 17.—Same place. The same to the same. "The noted Beaumarchais is now in London. I could easily find him out, if it were thought expedient to do anything with him." "Private. Read by the King."

195. 1778, September 19.—Same place. The same to the same. Beaumarchais goes by the name of M. Laval. His avowed business is to treat with the noted Morande, and to prevent the publication of some work, but it is said that he has been in the City to deal in the stocks. I have set two men to watch him. His changing his name here seems a matter sufficient to detain him as a spy and impostor. The French Ministers are doing all they can to work up the Dutch, Danes, and Swedes, to maintain the honour of their flags. "Private."

196. 1778, September 22.—Same place. The same to Lord North. Encloses:—
(A.) Copy of a letter in cipher from Lord Grantham to Viscount Weymouth, dated at St. Ildefonso, September 3, 1778. The establishment of packet boats between Falmouth and Santander (St. Andero) might be considered as settled. M. D'Aranda has no power to treat with the Americans, while they are considered by Great Britain as subjects of the Mother country.

197. 1778, October 4.—Head Quarters. General W. Keppel to [J. R.]. Concerning the establishment of packet boats between Chichester and Dover, to obtain intelligence from French fishing craft, and concerning various details of military organisation. Encloses—
(A.) Copy of a letter from Lord Barrington to General Keppel, dated September 27, 1778, concerning the salary of the subalterns.

198. 1778, October 10.—Sandwell. The Earl of Dartmouth to [J. R.]. Concerning the enclosure of common lands in the parish of Stockton co. Warwick, and concerning a prebend of Canterbury.

199. 1778, October 30.—Admiralty. The Earl of Sandwich to J. R. Lord North will lay before the next Cabinet a plan for the better attendance of members of Parliament. I can make good use of the materials with which you mean to furnish him. "Very private."

200. 1778, October 31.—Fort St. George. Thomas Rumbold to Lord North. Solicits some mark of distinction from the Crown, in reward for his services.

201. Same date and place.—The same to J. R. The Nabob could not conceal the joy he experienced from the receipt of your letters. He has been so extremely ill-used, cajoled, and plundered, by promises of assistance. He makes a show of poverty, pawns his jewels, and mortgages his lands at high interest, though his coffers are known to be full. Show him that his country is to be secured to him, at least for his life. The Tanjore country should nominally be given up to him. I am persuaded of his attachment to the English. To dread his power is ridiculous. (Three sheets.)

202. 1778, December 19.—The Earl of Suffolk to J. R. (On the back are various memoranda by J. R.)

203. 1779, January 1.—Downing Street. William Eden to Lord North. Lord Carlisle and I cannot make any claim to a continuance of

the emoluments annexed to the American commission. As to the great object we have been quite unsuccessful. Yet our commission had its uses. We have been the means of transmitting above a million sterling of British property to this country and into mercantile circulation. By accepting that temporary situation, I quitted a profitable office in England.

204. 1779, January 31.—Syon Hill. J. R. to Lord North. Governor Johnstone has just left me. He said that it was impossible for him to hold any office under an administration of which Lord Howe should make one. He blamed Lord Howe's conduct, and said that he did not think him fit to be head of the Admiralty. He believed that Lord Howe would not come in without his brother, and that their appointment to high office would be a declaration that the American independence would be acknowledged. He said he thought that Lord George Germain and Lord Sandwich must go out, and that your Lordship might make a considerable coalition. In that case, he would accept the Admiralty, or the office of Comptroller of the Navy, or even any small office. He said that he did nothing without the consent of Sir James Lowther, who, in that case, would accept some trifling office. He said that he could bring in Charles Fox, and that the Duke of Grafton and all his friends would come in with Lord Camden and the Grenvilles, and perhaps the Shelburnes also. He suggested the Duke of Grafton as head of the Admiralty, and Mr. Grenville as a Lord of the Treasury. He said "I believe you may get Charles Fox even with the Howes, but, holding my opinions it is impossible that I can act with them, for I am convinced that they have ruined their country. If you get Charles Fox it may do for a while, but otherwise you are at your last gasp." He stated clearly that Fox and he and their part of Opposition were separated from Lord Rockingham on the business of Independency. He said that the present calm was owing to him. He spoke rather warmly of Mr. Wedderburn's conduct to him as treacherous. We must have a storm on the promotion of Lord Howe, and it will be impossible to avoid the inquiries in which Lord Howe and Sir William must be parties against the King's Ministers. (Copy. Two sheets.) "Private."

205. 1779, February 1.—Portsmouth. Sir Edward Hughes to J. R. Desires to have the letters for the Nabob.

206. 1779, February 9.—Same place. The same to the same. The Nabob needs comfort. If supported in his own government, he will be a most useful ally to the Company and the English nation. (Two sheets.)

207. 1779, March 6.—Same place. The same to the same. The squadron is unmoored.

208. 1779, March 13. J. R. to the King. Desires to know whether he should hold free and unreserved communication with Mr. Jenkinson on everything relative to the King's affairs. (Draft.)

209. Same day. Queen's House. The King to J. R. "Mr. Robinson may very safely communicate any circumstances he may think necessary for my information, and that requires more explanation than can with ease be conveyed in a letter, or that he may not think worth immediate notice, through the channel of Mr. Jenkinson, who I am convinced will make no bad use of it. I cannot conceive what had depressed Lord North yesterday. This I did not collect from anything in particular that he said, but he was thoughtful and not elated as I expected at having dismissed a business he had taken so much as personal to himself, and certainly considering the strange dislike the country

gentlemen took to throwing out the bill, the majority was very good."
(See the King's letter to Lord North in Mr. Donne's edition, No. 554.)

210. 1779, March 22.—"Superb" off Cape Finisterre. Sir E. Hughes to J. R.

211. 1779, May 10.—"Superb" at Goree. The same to the same. "I arrived here on the 8th inst., with the squadron and convoy, quite prepared for the attack of this island agreeable to the orders I had, but to my great surprise found the French had evacuated it, after possessing themselves of Senegal. Lord Macleod has appointed Lieut. Col. Brooke, the Governor, with 400 men of the 75th." Particulars about the movements of the ships.

212. 1779, May 11.—Parliament Street. J. R. to Lord North. The business of yesterday about the almanacs ought not to rest a moment on your mind. It was one of the most motley divisions I ever saw. The House would, I believe, readily give the two Universities 500*l.* each, or more, towards printing books of literature which would not pay for themselves, but they did not like the business mixed up with the Stationers Company. Our friends said the job was too bad. The Lord Advocate did not wonder at the 60, but at the 40 who were with us. This, therefore, is no test of the sentiments of members towards the administration. Spirit, vigour, and resolution are needed. The Opposition are not liked by the House or the people. The business of Sir William Howe has, it is true, taken a disagreeable turn. Numbers of the best friends of your administration were irritated at the rashness of Lord George Germain, and the imprudence of Mr. Rigby. I must again urge the appointment of the Secretary of State. Lord Weymouth's coldness, inattention to business, and silence in the House, are attributed to a settled design to leave you. Nothing can be better than the appointment of Lord Hillsborough. You have your sovereign's approbation. At times I think that there is some hidden reason against it. (Draft. Three sheets.)

213. Copy of the above. (Two sheets.)

214. 1779, May 12.—J. R. to A. Wedderburn. Lord North acknowledges the engagement to you. If you go to the Common Pleas, or resign your office, he must equally quit his station. He will be glad to see you. (Draft.)

215. Another draft of the above.

216. 1779, May 14.—J. R. to Lord North. Desires to give political advice.

217. 1779, May 25.—Lord North to J. R. Lord Sandwich has such a mean opinion of all my intelligence and all my suggestions, that I would have you send him the enclosed intelligence as from yourself.

218. 1779, July 12.—C. Jenkinson to J. R. Recommends that a small pension be given to the Abbé Jeaurinvilliers, as it is important to engage the writers of foreign gazettes. Encloses—

(A.) Letter from G. Cressener to C. Jenkinson, dated at Spa, July 4, 1779. The Abbé de Jeaurinvilliers, ex-Jesuit, who writes the Cologne Gazette, has had a quarrel with the Chevalier d'Othée, who has the privilege of that Gazette from the Court of Vienna. A pension of 600 livres a year for his life will keep him in our service. Reports concerning the French fleet.

219. 1779, August 15.—Cape of Good Hope. Sir Edward Hughes to J. R. Gives particulars about English and French ships.

220.  1779, August 23.  Paris.  "The embarkation not to take effect at Havre, but at St. Malo and Brest.  In the last mentioned port, besides infantry, 3,000 dragoons on board ships *armés en flutes*; the descent in England to be effected in the latter season.  The operation will begin by attacking Jersey and Guernsey.  La Touche Treville with the flying squadron to cover this.  He is to anchor in Cancalle Bay, as more safe than the road of St. Malo.  Lieut.-Gen. Conway has found notice that the attack will be on the 15th."  (Copy of intelligence, in the King's hand.)

221.  1779, September 13.—Stoneland Lodge.  Lord George Germain to Lord North.  (Printed from a draft among the manuscripts of Mrs. Stopford Sackville, in the 3rd Appendix to the 9th Report of the Historical Manuscripts Commission, p. 97.)

222.  1779, September 26.—Bushy Park.  Lord North to J. R.  I fear that I must have a Chancellor of the Exchequer in my arrangement, for I really cannot do the King's business.  My heart is oppressed with a thousand griefs, and totally disables my head.  "Private."

223.  1779, September 29.—Same place.  The same to Lord George Germain.  (Draft.  Printed from the original in the 3rd Appendix to the 9th Report of the Historical MSS. Commisssion, p. 98.)

224.  Copy of the above in J. R.'s hand.

225.  1779, September 29.—Lord North to J. R.  The Dutch demand must be complied with, so we have nothing to do but to get the money as soon as possible.  I doubt whether we shall persuade Sir G. Pocock to stand.  Mr. Byng will not stand.

226.  1779, October 5.—Windsor Castle.  The King to J. R.  " I am glad to find Col. Tufnell stands for Middlesex.  I hope no pains will be spared to secure the election.  Sir Charles Thompson is every way qualified to represent Beverley, and will be a thorough friend."

227.  1769, October 6.—Kew.  The same to the same.  "The letter Lord North has wrote to the Lord Lieutenant of Ireland seems very proper.  I am pleased to find Mr. Robinson hath effected a ¦meeting between Lord North, the Chancellor, and Mr. Jenkinson, on the Irish affairs.  The more those three can be united, the better for my service.  Now Mr. Robinson knows Lord North's sentiments, I trust he will write to the Attorney General in Ireland, Mr. Beresford, in the same strain."

228.  1779, October 15.—Admiralty.  The Earl of Sandwich to J. R.  "I had a very serious conversation this morning with a great person, and afterwards Lord North came to me, and talked to me more confidentially than he ever did before.  Things are now at the most critical moment, and I think that you should not be an instant from Lord North's side till something decisive is done.  I know not how to go into particulars in a letter which possibly may be dropped between this house and Syon."  I hope to see you to-morrow.  "Very private."

229.  1779, October 16.—Same place.  The same to the same.  " Surely Lord North is not gone out of town without having seen Lord Stormont, and written to Lord Carlisle.  I am convinced that all will go well if you can work him up to decide and to act.  You have therefore more in your hands at this moment than perhaps any one in this country ever had before.  You are the only person who can give good advice to the person upon whom the fate of this kingdom depends."  I enclose a letter which ought to be held sacred in my hands, and which I would show to no other man living.  "Most private."

230. 1779, October 16.—Galloway House. The Earl of Galloway MARQUIS OF
to Lord North. Solicits "an ostensible letter" in favour of the candi- ADERGAVENNY'S
dature of Mr. Johnston in the stewardry of Kircudbright.                          MSS.

231. 1779, October 19.—Lord North to J. R. "I enclose to you
my letters to Lord Stormont, Lord Carlisle, and one to his Majesty, in
which you will see all the proposed arrangements, but what will take
place I cannot tell, till I have seen or heard from the parties concerned.
Lord W[eymouth] will not resign, but, I fear, he will not support. The
King will try no other system, and we must embark and go through it
as well as we can. I have no great expectation of success. The Lord
Lieutenant's letter will show how ill things have gone in Ireland, and how
little support was given to the Castle by those who are the most obliged
to Government." I write a letter to Lord Gower, but I leave you to
send it or no as you shall judge proper. Seal all the letters with my
seal. Order a nomination to the prebend of Ely for the Rev^d G
Downing, and to the living of Wisbeach for the Rev^d J. R. Greenhill.
Send Wentworth's intelligence to the King and Lord Sandwich.

232. 1779, October 31.—Cape of Good Hope. Sir Edward Hughes
to J. R. Introduces Col. Du Prehn.

233. 1779, November 12.—Addiscombe Place. C. Jenkinson to
J. R. "I have just heard all that has passed about negotiations. I am ·
now persuaded there will be none. Lord North has behaved very
handsomely, but is, I see, clearly for going on. I think the Chancellor
is so too, but Lord North is to see him once more." "Most private."

234. 1779, December 12.—Avington. Sir Richard Worsley to Lord
North. Notwithstanding the most favourable returns made by my
agents, I find myself involved in an expense beyond the reach of my
present fortune. Without the assistance of Government I shall not be
able to carry on the poll above two days. My adversaries seem determined to protract it. They have retained five counsel. I have by me
the sum of 6,000l., which I am very ready to exhaust in the cause.
(Enclosed in a memorandum concerning the notes for 2,000l. sent to the
Duke of Chandos on the 14th.)

235. Same day and place.—The Duke of Chandos to the same. Our
adversaries have a subscription purse against which it is impossible for
any individual to fight. This is more than a common contest between
two gentlemen; it is a violent attack upon Government. There can be
no doubt of the event of the poll, if the ammunition does not fail. I
have never used any influence as Lieutenant of the County [of South-
ampton], but shall ever be of opinion that I have a right as a freeborn
Englishman to write to whom I please. "Most private."

236. 1779, December 13.—Queen's House. The King to [J. R.].
"It would be highly improper to neglect the wishes of our friends in
Hampshire. You have my full consent to act as far as you may judge
right."

237. 1779, December 18.—J. Macpherson to J. R. Concerning the
accounts furnished by the Custom-houses, and concerning a seat in Parliament. "Private."

238. 1780, (dated 1779,) January 9.—Dublin.——to Lord [North].
All is safe here pending the bill in England for opening the trade of the
Colonies to Ireland, but when it is once passed, every thing disagreeable,
every thing dangerous may be apprehended here. A majority in Parlia-
ment might be got, but Government here does not know how to get it.
I have seen all kinds of people, and discovered the sentiments of many

His Excellency has talked to me upon public matters. I am to dine
with him again on Tuesday *en famille.* He has not the smallest
suspicion of my real errand to this kingdom. The principal things to
be apprehended here are—(1.) A total or partial repeal of Poynings Law ;
(2.) An attempt to bring an appeal before the House of Lords here ;
(3.) A bill for rendering the tenure of the office of the judges *quamdiu
se bene gesserint,* as in England ; (4.) A money bill for twelve months
only, in order to secure annual meetings of Parliament, as in England,
the Lord Lieutenant being now constantly resident ; (5.) A land tax
upon absentees ; (6.) A separate mutiny bill for the regulation of the
Irish army. " The idea of a union would be sufficient at this time to
excite a rebellion, and yet till a union takes place, how vague, how loose,
a connexion is that of Ireland with Great Britain." (Endorsed by J.R.
" Private and secret letter.")

239. 1780, January 13.— Fort William. Warren Hastings to the
Chairman of the Court of Directors of the East India Company. Recommends Captⁿ. Joseph Price.

240. 1780, January 28.—Syon Hill. J. R. to Lord North. Encloses,
and comments on, letters from General Murray, Lord Hertford, and Col.
Smith.

241. 1780, February 5.—London. James Macpherson to J. R.
Concerning the affairs of the East India Company and Mr. Sulivan.
" Private."

242. 1780, February 8.—Lord Thurlow to J. R. Congratulates him
on his recovery.

243. 1780, February 8.—Madras. Sir Edward Hughes to J. R.
The appearance of the King's squadron and troops has induced Hyder
Ali to recall to his capital the troops he had sent to act offensively. The
treasury at Calcutta has been exhausted in pursuit of wild schemes.
Mr. Hastings has much knowledge, but his politics, since my leaving
India, have been very strange. I have delivered to the Nabob the letters
from the King and the Company. I found Sir Edward Vernon
so debilitated in his nerves as to be totally incapable of service, and I
allowed him to strike his flag. (Two sheets.)

244. 1780, February 11.—Same place. The same to the same. Sir
Thomas Rumbold's health will not permit him to stay longer in this
climate. I must tell you in confidence that the Nabob does not wish him
to be succeeded by General Dick Smith, or General Stuart.

245. 1780, February 28.—Gerard Street. Sir William James to
J. R. Announces the result of the ballot [of the East India Company],
466 for the question, 192 against it, and 4 bad votes.

246. Same day. East India House. Richard Holt to J. R. To the
same effect.

247. 1780, March 18.—The Earl of Hillsborough to J. R. Reflects
upon Lord North's " flimsy way of doing business."

248. 1780, March 28.—Lord Thurlow to J. R. Whoever can advise
about Ireland and find the means to be listened to, might do his country
good service. I enclose a letter from Mr. Baron Eyre. " He is too honest
to be factious, therefore, though a very able man, he has been already
slighted within impunity in the appointment of the last Chief Baron, and
may be so again. But if there be room to take notice of his brother, you
will make him feel that it is not time quite thrown away to do his duty,
and serve his King with loyalty and zeal."

(A.) Letter from James Eyre, Baron of the Exchequer, to the Lord Chancellor, soliciting the Deanery of Salisbury for his brother. Dated at Maiden Early, March 26, 1780.

MARQUIS OF
ABERGAVENNY'S
MSS.

249. 1780, April 5.—Madras. Sir Edward Hughes to J. R. Sir Thomas Rumbold parts with the Nabob in perfect good humour. This is a proof that his Highness is not upon bad terms with every Governor, as his enemies have pretended. His debt has been constantly increasing. His second son, Ameer ul Omrah, seems anxious to promote the interests of the Company. Our arrival has been very fortunate, for the Company's affairs were very precarious. Particulars about the movements of different ships. (Two sheets.)

250. 1780, April 7.—Admiralty. The Earl of Sandwich to J. R. It is absolutely necessary that the matter of the chairs should be settled without any further delay.

251. Same day and place. The same to the same. Concerning a proposed interview with Lord North.

252. 1780, April 10.—Queen's House. The King to J. R. "Whilst at Windsor during the holydays, I may (sic) it my business privately to sound the inhabitants of that Borough, and think it right to state the result of it to Mr. Robinson that he make further enquiry. The Corporation has ever been adverse to Government, and whilst Mr. Fox when Secretary at War represented that Borough, he was chosen by the inhabitants at large. Now the Corporation is desirous of having a candidate recommended by Administration, and the inhabitants will warmly espouse such a person. Lieut. Col. Conway is very ready to state to Mr. Robinson how matters now stand, and says that Admiral Keppel can be thrown without any difficulty, that the assiduity of Lord Beaulieu might make it more difficult to remove Mr. Montagu, through Lord Beaulieu certainly thinks Goverment would beat him. If any one can be authorized to canvas in M. G. Phillips's name, he would certainly be the properest and most acceptable candidate. I wish Mr. Robinson would examine this affair; indeed the subject of elections I know occupies his mind, and is at this hour of the utmost consequence, for it would be madness not to call a new Parliament as soon as we have hobbled through the present session."

253. 1780, April 13.—James Macpherson to J. R. Concerning the election of a "chair" of the East India Company. "Private."

254. 1780, April 20.—Admiralty. The Earl of Sandwich to J. R. Concerning Captain Phipps and Lord Mulgrave. Gives a report of the proceedings at a meeting of the petitioning gentlemen at Huntingdon, when speeches were made by Sir Robert Barnard, Lord Fitz-William, the Duke of Manchester, and Lord Carysfort.

255. 1780, April 21.—Addiscombe Place. C. Jenkinson to J. R. "The unpleasantness of the Chancellor's conversation is owing solely to his want of manners. He had a mind also to show his zeal in the Advocate's cause. I should not conclude from hence that he thought the favour such as should be conferred at present. I think it very likely, for the reasons you mention, that Lord North will enter into some treaty with the Rockinghams, and Fred. Montague will probably be the mediator. If Brummel makes himself an instrument to convey intimidation, he acts a very wicked part." "Most private."

256. 1780, April 23.—Admiralty. The Earl of Sandwich to J. R. Concerning the election at Rochester.

257.  1780, April 28.—James Macpherson to J. R.  Concerning the critical state of affairs at Madras, and concerning certain military promotions.

258.  1780, May 3.—House of Commons.  J. R. to the King.  Concerning the election at Windsor.  Advises that the six houses standing in the name of Mr. Ramus, should be entered in the names of six different members of the royal household.  (Draft.)

259.  Same day.  Queen's House.  The King to J. R.  " This day Lord North acquainted me with his wish of supporting Mr. Powny's inclination of representing the Borough of New Windsor.  I shall in consequence get my tradesmen encouraged to appear for him.  I shall order, in consequence of Mr. Robinson's hint, the houses I rent at Windsor to stand in the parish rate in different names of my servants, so that it will create six votes."

260.  1780, May 29.—Bushy Park.  Lord North to J. R.  Concerning a warrant for the extraordinaries of General Vaughan's army.  Advises that the East India Company should not employ any of their servants who were concerned on either side in the late troubles at Madras.  (Two sheets.)

261.  1780, June 18.—Queen's House.  The King to [Lord North ?].  The Rajah [of Tanjore] should have a civil answer.  " I hoped by this time to have received a copy of the Speech, but as I understand it has undergone some amendments, I suppose I cannot have it till late in the evening, when I hope also to know whether two o'clock is not the best hour for my going to Parliament to-morrow, that will make my arrival at the House about half hour past two.  I must know the hour this night, as it requires some time for sending in the morning the necessary orders for the usual attendants on that occasion."

262.  [Lord North ?] to the Rajah of Tanjore.  Writes by order of the King to acknowledge the receipt of his letter.  The King desires nothing more than that an amicable and equitable termination should be found to all controversies between the different princes in India.  (Copy.)

263.  1780, June 23.—London.  Henry Dundas to J. R.  " I was with Lord Loughborough to-day, who showed me the grant of the survivancy of the Director of the Chancery in Scotland to Sir James Erskine solely, whereas he understood the favour was intended for both his nephews."

264.  Same day and place.—The same to the same.  " I most sincerely rejoice in every mark of honour and friendship which Lord North bestows on Lord Loughborough, because he is my friend, and his splendid talents entitle him to every attention.  But I confess it was with difficulty that I refrained from expressing my astonishment when Lord Loughborough this day showed me the grant.  I however did so, but nevertheless I did feel and do now feel most poignantly the contempt —I will not say disingenuity—with which Lord North has treated me last year and this.  He has uniformly stated to me with apparent regret that the only reason why I did not get my office for life, as my predecessors used to get it, was a rule his Majesty had adopted of not giving offices for life, and to convince me of this he told me a long story about himself and the Cinque Ports.  It seems however that mine is the only Scotch office—or rather I am the only Scotch person—to which this rule is to be applied. . . . . I don't wonder this secret was kept from me with so much care."  (Two sheets.)

265. 1780, June 24.—Lord Thurlow to J. R. In favour of the candidature of Mr. Pott for the office of Resident at Durbar.

266. 1780, July 7.—J. R. to [C. Jenkinson?]. I was with Lord North until past one o'clock this morning. At first he said that he was so entangled by his promises that there was no way left but for him to go out, by which all his promises would fall and his Majesty might make up a stronger government. After a while he agreed to see Mr. Montague, and sat down to form some minutes for the interview, which he agreed to show to the Chancellor and to the King—four questions, and other minutes for conversation. (These minutes, as afterwards amended, are given by Mr. Donne, vol. ii. p. 328.) He is now gone to the Cabinet, and from thence he goes to Court. Mr. Montague is to be in Downing Street at 9 o'clock to-night. I desire nothing so much as his Majesty's approbation. Lord North spoke to me freely about Sir Richard Sutton, Mr. Eden, and Sir Grey Cooper. I told him that for the last three years Sir Grey's place and mine had amounted to above 5,000l. to each. He was so good as to say that I earned it all, and that if I went out he must and would go, for he would not do the business with anyone else.

Postcripts dated 8th and 9th of July. Lord North and Mr. Montague had a very long and open conversation. Mr. M. took with him the paper of questions to lay before the party, but he stated his own thoughts. He did not think that Lord Rockingham would insist on being at the head of the Treasury, but he did not know what the party would do. "The American war, he thought, was now put in such a way as it might be answered, and, he thought, got over. Mr. Keppell's appointment to the head of the Admiralty Board, he thought, was so great a point that it would be insisted upon, and perhaps break off the negotiations. Crew's, the Contractors', and Burke's bill, he seemed to think would not be great difficulties . . . . Upon the whole [he] was rather of opinion that the coalition would not take place, from the points of Keppell, and the Duke of Richmond." Remarks on the noble part acted by the Duke of Northumberland. (Draft. Five sheets.)

267. [1780, July 14?]—Lord Thurlow to J. R.

268. 1780, July 15. Addiscombe Place. C. Jenkinson to J. R. Lord Hardwicke had an audience of the King yesterday, to request that offices in Cambridgeshire should be given agreeably to his wishes, and that the Deanery of Ely, when vacant, should be given to a Cambridge man. "Private."

269. 1780, July 15.—The Earl of Sandwich to [J. R.]. Concerning Mr. Luttrell and Lord Orford.

270. 1780, July 15.—Lord Thurlow to J. R. Desires to see him on the subjects of Gloucestershire and Bombay.

271. 1780, July 16. Syon Hill. J. R. to the Hon. James Luttrell. (Copy.)

272. 1780, July 17.—Edinburgh. Henry Dundas to [J. R.]. Concerning the appointment to offices at the port of Leith.

273. 1780, July 19.—Hanover Square. The Earl of Hillsborough to J. R. Desires to see the box about the East Indies.

274. 1780, July 21.—Parliament Street. C. Jenkinson to J. R. "I was brought to Town to-day, contrary to my intention, by that plaguing fellow, the Duke of Richmond. If there were two Dukes of Richmonds in this country, I would not live in it. I have seen the King, who has

heard nothing more of the negotiation. There is something mysterious in all this, and if Lord North has really heard nothing, I am persuaded that the opposition are disagreeing on the answer they shall return. Poor Chamier is said to be dying. Lord Hillsborough thinks of Sidgwicke as his successor. The King is averse to this, and ordered me to speak to you to promote the cause of Adam."

275. 1780, July 21. Admiralty. The Earl of Sandwich to J. R.

276. 1780, July 24.—Lord Loughborough to Lord North. "You have perhaps been lately told that the office [of Lord Chief Justice] I hold is worth 4,000*l.* per annum . . . . . I state the income only at the certain sum, viz. 2,786*l.*, and consider the rest as patronage, which may be advantageous to a family, though too uncertain to be taken into an account of income . . . . . I cannot assure your Lordship that my gratitude will be increased by an increase of salary, for I feel as much as can be felt for the favours his Majesty has bestowed upon me. I cannot even profess that I shall be more attached to your administration, or more zealous for its support, nor can I pretend that it is impossible to live without an addition, for I confess the income is sufficient for a moderate man."

277. 1780, July 22.—Addiscombe Place. C. Jenkinson to J. R. "If hard words will enable me to get rid of the Duke of Richmond I will lose no proper opportunity of using them . . . . . As Lord North has heard nothing from Mr. Mountague, I am clear there is some dissention among the members of opposition. The King's civil words with respect to some of them, added to distress, have had their proper effect. I wish that Lord North knew how to use this instrument better than he does. One of his great errors is that he thinks that interest alone without any seasoning is the only motive on which men act . . . . . The thing that puzzles me most, is that we hear of no meetings among them. If there has been any, it has probably been at Lord Rockingham's at Wimbledon . . . . Lord North is at heart against the success of the negotiation. He told the King on Wednesday that the expectations of opposition were unreasonably high, and ought not to be complied with. The King answered, he was glad to find that Lord North now agreed with him in opinion on that point . . . . I have been thinking this morning on a subject that would make a very fine pamphlet. The opposition have been for this 15 years stirring up the people against Government, calling the administration violent, when its error in fact was weakness, adopting principles which produced a rebellion in one country, and were near producing one in another, though the evil burst at last on their own heads, when some of them manifested a degree of fear for their own persons and property, and of violence and warmth for the protection of them, beyond what had ever been shewn by administration."

278. 1780, July 29.—J. R. to James Luttrell. Lord Sandwich offers him the post of First Lieutenant on the "Belliqueux." (Draft.)

279. 1780, August 1.—Blackheath. The Earl of Sandwich to J. R. I have had much conversation with Mr. Rigby. "He was very liberal in his disapprobation of many parts of Lord Chancellor's conduct, particularly his absurd jealousy of, and behaviour to, Lord Loughborough, and he ridiculed the weak conduct, and the situation into which Lord Gower and Lord Weymouth had brought themselves. He is most exceedingly eager and anxious about the speedy, or rather immediate, dissolution of Parliament . . . . I think all your reasons for delay are weak . . . . Our opponents are depressed ; the nation is set against

riots and rioters of all kinds; events have been favourable beyond conception.  Will you wait to give our enemies time to rally and reunite, and for some blow in our military operations to turn the tide of popularity against us?"

280.  1780, August 3.—Addiscombe Place.  C. Jenkinson to [J. R.]

281.  1780, August 12.—Same place.  The same to the same.  Concerning the candidates for the county of Kent, and the borough of Wallingford.

282.  1780, August 12.—Bath.  Lord Thurlow to J. R.

283.  1780, August.  The same to Lord North.  Concerning the claims of Mr. Greaves and Mr. Macdonald.

284.  1780, August (or September) 13.—Lord North to J. R.  I cannot tell what to write to Lord Clarendon about the University of Cambridge.  " I do not like to put the King to the expense of 3,000*l.*, to bring in so uncertain a supporter as Lord Hyde, and yet I suppose that you would have me engage to bring him in if he should fail at Cambridge."

285.  1780, August 13.—Bushy Park.  The same to the same.  " I have made it a rule this summer to allow myself no pleasure, nor dissipation, nor vacation whatever. . . . . Provided the Parliament is to be dissolved (which it must now be, although the manner in which it will affect the militia seems to render it much more eligible to dissolve it in winter), it is and always has been indifferent to me when the dissolution shall [take] place.  I only wanted to know from you the state of our affairs and your opinion of the proper moment. . . . . Lord Chancellor, to whom I gave last year constantly all my India papers and propositions, has constantly returned them to me at a great distance of time, without any opinion or assistance at all.  He has never mentioned to me the least anxiety upon that business this year, but has chosen to begin with it in the Closet for obvious reasons.  In short, I see every day more and more the very disgraceful footing on which I am likely to continue while [I] remain in office, which, God knows, I have other causes enough to wish to quit.  I shall never do anything with the Duke of Newcastle by conversation or letter, but I wil ·either write to him or call upon him to-morrow.  He must certainly not see the Duke of Northumberland's letter.  If Mr. Fox stands, we shal have much trouble and more expense, which will all fall upon us Neither Lincoln nor Rodney will contribute."  " Private."

286.  1780, August 14.—Syon Hill.  J. R. to Lord North.  I do not think it at all necessary that you should deprive yourself of all relaxation.  On the contrary, I would recommend that you should have it publicly given out that you were gone into Kent for three weeks or a month.  Parliament should be prorogued until the 31st of October or the 2nd of November.  In the former case the Council should be held on the 31st of August or the 1st of September, and the proclamation and writs issued on the 1st or 2nd of September.  You might stay in Kent until the 28th of August, and return to Bushy on that day, unknown and unexpectedly, for while you and the ministers are still in and about town, a momentary dissolution is expected.  Before your going to Kent I trust to receive all your orders now necessary.  The Duke of Newcastle has written to Lord Lincoln to prevail on him to stand for Westminster, but you are right that it must be all at your expence.  In that case it may be well to fight for both seats.  I will tell Sir Patrick Crauford that if he can secure the second seat at Arundel

undoubtedly, a friend is ready to give 3,000*l.*, but that I doubt that he will find that they must give Lord Surrey one member. (Four sheets.) " Most private."

287. 1780, August 16.—Bath. Lord Thurlow to J. R. I want the lists of those who voted for and against the great questions of last session. " So many people apply to me, whom I have never heard of before, and make no apology for it, but that they are Members of Parliament, that it seems convenient for me to be a little better acquainted with them, and it is impossible to resort to one who can guide me more unerringly. In short if you would send me your list of both Houses, I should certainly know more of the political characters of each House than I have any other chance of doing." Applications for the living of St. Mary le Strand.

288. 1780, August 19.—Same place. The same to the same. Concerning various persons and matters.

289. 1780, August 19.—Addiscombe Place. C. Jenkinson to J. R. " If it is wished to make Lord Edgecombe a Viscount, a certain person will have no objection. Is it not possible to secure a member for each of the counties of Kent and Hants? It is a pity to lose two county members." " Private."

290. 1780, August 21.—Windsor Castle. The King to J. R. " As the dissolution is now fixed for Wednesday, August 30th, I think it right to transmit the money to you which compleats up to this month the 1,000*l.* per month I have laid by. The other payments were made to Lord North himself. I have wrote him word that I have sent it to you. I trust notice will be sent to the Chancellor for his appearance on that day at St. James's, that no delay may issue in issuing the new writs. The amount of the notes is 14,000*l.*" (Endorsed—" His Majesty with *notes* to J. R.")

291. 1780, August 22.—Syon Hill. J. R. to the King. Acknowledges the receipt of 14,000*l.* The account of the distribution of the private fund will be transmitted to the King. He had a conversation of some hours with the Lord Chancellor the day before he left town for Bath, and it was then settled that he would come up to the Council for dissolving the Parliament. (Draft.)

292. 1780, August 24.—Addiscombe Place. C. Jenkinson to J. R. " I have consulted with my brother, and we can think of no man so proper for Bath as General Amherst, and I wish it the more, as it will contribute to strengthen the army interest in the House of Commons, where it is certainly very weak. The General will, I am persuaded, resist this idea himself, but I think it probable that Lord Amherst will be for it. . . . . I continue to think that the King, or Lord North in the King's name, should see the Duke of Newcastle. This, together with an explanation that the Dutchess of Bedford cannot alone command the Bedford interest, and that Palmer is with us, is alone sufficient to influence his Grace, and to induce him to let Lord Lincoln stand." Mr. Mansfield will certainly be chosen for Cambridge.

293. 1780, August 26.—Same place. The same to the same. " Lord Amherst's letter to the general officers commanding at camps will disclose the whole busyness of the dissolution. I submit, therefore, whether it should be sent so soon as Monday . . . . I have a letter from Lady Waldgrave, begging that Mr. Burke may have a copy of the letter given him for the Rajah of Tanjore. If there was no great objection to this I could wish to oblige this Lady."

294. 1780, August 27.—Bath. Lord Thurlow to J. R. "Your MARQUIS OF ABERGAVENNY'S MSS. commands come at a time when I am little able to obey them. But I will do my best, and if I cannot get to London early enough to be at the Council, I will at least be there time enough to seal the Proclamation and writs, which I think, should both be got ready . . . . I grudge the labour of such a journey after the fit of illness I have had since I wrote to you last. . . . . If you have been attentive to Bridgewater and Taunton you can have them both. If not, they are sadly lost."

295. 1780, August 28.—Same place. The same to the same. Desires to see precedents of the forms for dissolving an old Parliament and convening a new one. Prospects of success at Bath, Bridgewater, and Taunton.

296. 1780, September 2.—The same to the same. "Your new Sollicitor General [J. Mansfield] who was sworn in to-night, begins to complain that less sollicitation is used, and less command exercised, than his business requires. I heard him, and have left him to find out and observe the many odd turns which will spring up in the scene he is stepping into ; and, which is worse than all turns, the impracticable restifness ; and, still worse, the stout and all conquering supineness.

. . . . I have heard a bird in the air sing, with the air at least and confidence of truth, that another peerage, and that also a law peerage, is driving fast before the wind ; of which, *causâ quâ supra*, the secret is to be disclosed to me, when the Privy Seal shall announce it. I certainly have little ambition to meddle with the management of such concerns. But I wish that such as affect to express their surprise at my not embarking in more publick business, would reflect a little on the number and nature of my opportunities; when arrangements, which draw to great consequence, and such as principally affect me, are made with such total want of all concert, that if I were ever to talk on publick affairs, my ignorance would be ridiculous, even in those nearest me, under my nose, and wherein, if in any, information might be expected from me ; because it has never, as I believe, happened before that any person in my situation has been left to collect the knowledge of such arrangements from a Privy Seal warrant."

297. 1780, September 2.—Addiscombe Place. C. Jenkinson to J. R. "I sincerely believe that Lord North has a great and real regard for you, but I agree with you that he does not treat you as he ought, that he rewards others who do in no respect serve him, and whom he suffers to enjoy great incomes without doing anything, that he makes you in fact do the whole of his business, and at the same time never thinks of rewarding you." His nature is "more influenced by importunity than by service." I would advise you to have a full explanation, however disagreeable. "You have the comfort to know that you have the favour of your Sovereign. I am sure that you have the good opinion of the rest of mankind, even of those who are the enemies of Administration. You have nothing to remove but the langour of the mind of that person who profits most by your services. . . . The idea of your quitting the King's service can never take place. No one, I am sure, will suffer it. The Government could not go on without you. . . . I have told my office to use all the influence they can in favour of Lord Lincoln, and Sir G. Rodney." (Two sheets.) "Most private."

298. 1780, September 3.—Same place. The same to the same. "The explanation you mean to have will set every thing right. . . . I hope you have found a proper candidate for Bridgewater. If you can get no other candidate for Hants, Sir Richard Worseley would do very

well. Should not Lady Rodney advertise in her husband's name? Has there been any answer yet from Mr. F. Mountague?" "Most private."

299. 1780, September 5.—Hartlebury. The Bishop of Worcester to his brother, Lord North. Concerning the proposed candidature of Mr. Poulter for the City of Worcester.

300. 1780, September 6.—Syon Hill. J. R. to the King. Concerning Mr. Cholwich and Sir John Duntze. (Draft.)

301. 1780, September 7.—Wroxton. Lord North to J. R. "I am sorry for Mr. Brudenell's peerage, which will make him and me ridiculous, and is the cause of Lord Talbot's, and will be the cause of Mr. Thynne's. Particulars concerning the election for the University of Cambridge. Mr. Langlois's dissatisfaction at his appointment is most unreasonable. Instructions concerning the elections for Worcester, Newport, and Lyme. " By Eden's letter I perceive that he is extremely angry, but you see that the King is as angry on the other side. What am I to do?" ·Observations on various elections. (Three sheets.)

302. 1780, September 8.—Harrogate. Lord Loughborough to J. R. Commodore Johnstone is extremely " picqued " at Sir James Lowther's leaving him out in his first arrangement. Before that impression wears off he would no doubt much rather accept a seat from you than from Sir James. "It would be idle to enlarge upon the advantage of bringing in so powerfull and active a friend, who you know does nothing feebly, and would be most warmly attached to Lord North if he felt an obligation to him."

303. 1780, September 9.—Bath. Lord Thurlow to J. R. "I perceive the last letter I wrote you was answered by Lord North (from Sion Hill to prevent mistakes) although, considering what I said in it, I rather wondered it was shown him. We, who are at a distance from that sacred circle, in which the measures of government are formed, must needs see them in another view, and conceive of them more imperfectly than those to whom the whole design is revealed. It is therefore no wonder that we are at a loss to imagine why that which was thought right was not done when it was decided. . . These things however are too much above me to be fit objects of my sollicitude ; and you are engaged in business too much above my small sollicitudes to attend to them."

304. 1780, September 10.—Winchester. C. Jenkinson to J. R. Anyone may be chosen for Hants that Government pleases, without trouble or expense. Encloses—

(A.) Letter from John Cator to the Right Hon. C. Jenkinson, dated September 8, 1780. He has risked his seat in order to get a friend in, and he desires to be assisted to another at a moderate expense.

305. 1780, September 11.—Wroxton. Lord North to J. R. " Our elections seem to go on but ill. Unless you can remedy it, I am afraid Westminster will be lost. Hutton and Calvert both gone, and Bonfield defeated. We are in a bad sort of a way, unless we have some good events to set against these misfortunes."

306. 1780, September 13.—The Earl of Dartmouth to Lord North. Concerning Lord Lewisham. "It is employment I solicit for him, and not mere emolument. I beg he may not be thought of for a place of mere idle attendance at Court. Such a situation will neither suit his inclinations nor my wishes for him."

307. 1780, September 13.—Syon Hill. J. R. to the King. Sends a return of all the members elected, with details about the election for

the counties of Essex and Hants. "Although the poll for Westminster does not look favourable, there is strength enough left to give success to the business if attended to. . . In the City of London it is thought Sawbridge will be thrown out, and the person we push against him is Mr. Alderman Newnham." (Draft.)

308. 1780, September 14.—Addiscombe Place. C. Jenkinson to J. R. Suggests that the Government should assist Newnham, as the less violent of the two candidates.

309. 1780, September [17 ?].—Lord Thurlow to J. R. "Is Lord Powis a friend ?"

310. 1780, September 19.—The Earl of Hillsborough to J. R. "Lord Salisbury died this morning, which vacates Cranborne's seat. . . I enclose to you a character of Foster, drawn by a very able hand, one who is thoroughly acquainted with men and things in Ireland. You may shew it if you please to Lord North."

(A.) A long estimate of the character of Mr. Foster, and of his capacity "as a minister and as a financier." It reckons him wanting in sagacity and political courage, and inadequate to the management of a party. On the other hand it describes him as a great master of business, intimately connected with the aristocracy, and affable.

311. 1780, September 21.—Addiscombe Place. C. Jenkinson to J. R. "Private."

312. 1780, September 23.--Parliament Street. J. R. to the King. Sends a return of all the members elected, and various letters. (Draft.)

313. 1780, September 23.—J. R. to the Earl of Hillsborough. Encloses for the King's approval a list of the proposed new peerages.

314. 1780, September 24. Addiscombe Place.—C. Jenkinson to J. R. "The answer you have returned to Lord Hillsborough is certainly a very proper one. I don't think it of much importance when the Government of Ireland changes. The present is a bad one. I don't think that which is to succeed is likely to be much better. Neither the Principal nor the Secretary are made of stuff to govern that country, and they will be driving perpetual jobs in this."

315. 1780, September 29.—St. James's. The Earl of Hillsborough to J. R. Concerning various appointments in Ireland.

316. 1780, September 30.--London. J. Price (?) to Lord North. Explains his project for the seizure of the Isthmus of Darien.

317. 1780, October 23.--St. James's. Sir S. Porten to J. R. "There will probably be soon an opportunity to risk a letter to Gibraltar by a sloop which the Admiralty will attempt to send thither." Lord Hillsborough desires to be able to send information to General Eliott concerning the provisions necessary for the garrison.

318. 1780, October 24.--Syon Hill. J. R. to the King. Sends a book of the new Parliament, canvassed in the best manner according to their sentiments. (Draft.)

319. 1780, October 28.—St. James's. Sir S. Porten to J. R. Concerning the insurrection in Spanish America.

320. 1780, October 30.—Parliament Street. C. Jenkinson to J. R. Encloses—

(A.) Copy of a letter from the Earl of Bute to C. Jenkinson, dated London, October 28, 1780. Concerning his sons James and Charles [Stuart].

321.  1780, November  3.—Melville.  Henry Dundas to J. R. Your letter is written in so urgent a stile as to make me regret a refusal.  " But the same reasons both of a publick and private nature still remain to keep me to my resolution.  I cannot conceive how my absence could be any disappointment either to you or to Lord North. By a letter from Mr. Brummell more than six weeks ago, it was intimated to me that I was to hear from Lord North immediately upon many points both personal and publick.  Although my curiosity was excited by that intimation, I was not very much disappointed when I did not receive it."  Until the receipt of the circular letter eight days before the meeting of Parliament, I remained in the belief that Parliament was not to meet until the end of November.  " From looking now and then to the newspapers relative to the transactions of Parliament betwixt [this] and Christmas, I may be able perhaps to collect some hints what is the system of government relative to the present very critical state of the interests of Great Britain, foreign and domestick. If there is no system formed, but the friends of Government collected merely to oppose one faction, and to support another, the object is indeed contemptible, and the prospect a most unpleasant one."

Postscript.—" Private."  " Lord North's illness must indeed make the meeting of Parliament a very awkward one.  You regret I have no share.  I feel no such regret. . . .  What brought about the change of resolution of Mr. Montagu being Speaker?  It is a general complaint that the dignity of Parliament has been much let down.  I suppose both sides of the House would concur in that idea."  Mr. Montagu is a man of candour and integrity, and a personal friend of the Minister.  " In his person both sides would concur in maintaining the decency, dignity, and order of the House."  (Two sheets.)

3 22.  1780, November 5.—Pall Mall.  Lord George Germain to [J. R.].  Concerning the order of business in the House of Commons.

323.  1780, November 7th.—The Hon. Col. Charles Stuart to J. R. Solicits a seat in Parliament for his brother James.

324.  1780, November 11.—The Earl of Hillsborough to J. R. Concerning Lord Conyngham's application for an earldom.

325.  1780, November 12.--Henry Dundas to [J. R.].  Concerning the death of Mr. Cardonnel, Commissioner of Customs.

326.  1780, November.—Narrative by C. Jenkinson of the negotiations between the Government and the Earl of Bute concerning the seats to be found for his sons, James and Charles, Stuart.

A few days after the dissolution of Parliament, Lord Bute desired Mr. Jenkinson to carry a message to Lord North that he was so advanced in life that he did not wish to be elected again one of the sixteen peers of Scotland, but that he wished to obtain a seat in the House of Commons for his son Colonel Charles Stuart, through Lord North's favour.  For private reasons he must bring in his son Colonel James Stuart for Bossiney.  Lord North answered that every thing was settled with respect to the elections, but that as several people would be returned for two places, Colonel Charles Stuart should be brought in for one of these vacancies.  He suggested that Colonel Charles Stuart should be brought in for Bossiney by Lord Bute, as James was not in England, and members might be wanted at the opening of the session. Mr. Jenkinson explained that Colonel James's circumstances were such that it was absolutely necessary that he should be in Parliament.  Lord North agreed to the sum which Lord Bute had offered to pay.  Mr. Jenkinson repeated Lord North's answer to the King, who approved of it. He also repeated it to Mr. Robinson. On the 3rd of September MARQUIS OF ABERGAVENNY'S MSS. Lord Bute wrote to Lord North, agreeing to bring in his son Charles for Bossiney, and leaving the elder brother to Lord North's promise. On the 28th of October he wrote to Mr. Jenkinson, asking him to urge Lord North to find the promised seat as Colonel James Stuart could not come home without one, and the trouble of substituting him for his brother at Bossiney would be no trifle.

327. 1780, November 17.—Parliament Street. C. Jenkinson to J. R. Concerning the same.

328. 1780, November 18.—J. R. to Sir S. Porten. Concerning provisions for Gibraltar. (Draft.) "Secret."

329. 1780, November 18.—Parliament Street. C. Jenkinson to [J. R.]. Concerning Col. James Stuart.

330. 1780, November 30.—Henry Dundas to J. R. Concerning Mr. Stodart. "I resolved to be silent, both because he would be warmly recommended by the Duke of Buccleuch, with whom I do not chuse to interfere, and because impartially speaking upon the subject, it is my opinion that it was for the interest of the Government not only to oblige the Duke in the matter, but to do it in this instance in the person of Mr. Stodart, thereby marking in the strongest manner possible your disapprobation of the unprincipled defections which took place in the course of last session of Parliament. . . . . The town of Edinburgh is, I thank God, almost the only place in Scotland where you had an opportunity of marking your disapprobation." (Two sheets.)

331. 1780, December 6.—War Office. C. Jenkinson to J. R. Lord North should write to the Duke of Beaufort, in order to prevent "a flaming patriot" from being elected in Gloucestershire. Hears that the last report of the Commissioners of Accounts is able, but at the same time very hostile to the Treasury.

332. 1780, December 11.—St. James's. Sir S. Porten to J. R. "Private." Encloses—
(A.) Extract from a letter from General Eliott to the Earl of Hillsborough, dated Gibraltar, October 22, 1780.—On the 11th our men of war's boats brought in a Danish dogger laden with lemons, oranges, raisins, and figs. We have numbers ill of the scurvy, and many die. Our bread is "esteemed" to last to June 12, beef to February 7, pork to July 24, pease, etc. to April 8, butter, with oil and raisins, to March 3. We are in the greatest distress for fuel, clothing for the 72nd and 73rd Regiments, strong liquors, and potatoes.

333. 1780, December 14.—Treasury Chambers. J. R. to Sir S. Porten. Concerning "the assistance requested from the Victualling Office for supplying a part of the provisions for the secret and separate service." (Copy.) "Secret."

334. Same day.—Parliament Street. The same to the same. Concerning the same. (Draft.) "Private."

335. Same day.—St. James's. Sir S. Porten to J. R. Concerning the same. "Private."

336. 1780, December 19.—"A letter of importance has been safely delivered with the seals unbroken, but not quite so soon as was, perhaps, expected, from accidents not material enough to mention." (Endorsed by J. R.—"Secret. Lord North's note to Mr. Neckar. Copied in a feigned Italian hand, and sent the same night to Mr. Todd at the Post Office, directed A Monsieur, Monsieur Neckar, a Paris—with a most

secret letter to Mr. Todd, entrusting it to his care, and to be forwarded this night by the mail to Ostend, unperceived and unobserved by any one." See the King's letter to Lord North, No. 655 in Mr. Donne's edition.

337. 1780, December 26.—Henry Dundas to [J. R.]. Encloses—
(A.) Letter from Sir Adam Fergusson to the Lord Advocate, dated Kilkerran, December 24, 1780. He recommends Robert Kennedy, of Pinmore, for the office of Surveyor of Customs at Ayr.

338. 1781, January 3.—Admiralty Office. P. Stephens to J. R. Concerning the provisions for Gibraltar. "Secret."

339. 1781, January 12.—Sir S. Porten to J. R. Desires that Mr. John Snoxell's papers may not be examined at Margate or Dover, on his return from Ostend with papers of great consequence concerning America. "Private."

340. 1781, January 15.—Lord North to J. R. Concerning secret intelligence, and other matters.

341. 1781, January 15.—Bombay. Sir E. Hughes to J. R. Concerning the movements of the English ships, and the general state of affairs in India. (Two sheets.)

342. 1781, January 20.—Addiscombe Place. C. Jenkinson to [J. R.]. "There is something important in agitation. What is it?"

343. 1781, January 23.—Treasury Chambers. J. R. to P. Stephens. Concerning the provisions from Gibraltar. (Draft.) "Private."

344. 1781, January 29.—Edinburgh. Henry Dundas to J. R. Concerning the salt officer at Dysart.

345. 1781, January 15.—Northumberland House. The Duke of Northumberland to [J. R.]. Desires to know whether Lord Macartney has accepted the Chiltern Hundreds.

346. 1781, February 5.—Same place. The same to the same. Concerning the writ for Beeralston.

347. 1781, February 13.—Lord Thurlow to J. R. Concerning East Indian affairs. "To people at a distance things appear to have been going on from bad to worse, and there is no prospect of amendment if the consideration of them is taken up by those who can only speculate upon the matter, instead of those who can act in it."

348. 1781, February 15.—Pay Office. Richard Rigby to J. R. "Have you two hundred and twenty good men ready to take the field to-day? Or are we (which will be the wisest course to take, if you cannot answer my question in the affirmative) to give way as far as to let the Bill [for the reduction of the Civil List] to be brought in?"

349. 1781, February 17.—Addiscombe Place. C. Jenkinson to [J. R.]. Concerning the state of the House of Commons.

350. 1781, March 6.—Queen's House. The King to J. R. "Mr. Robinson shewed his usual propriety in transmitting to me last night the list of the speakers in the debate, as well as the division. I take this opportunity of sending 6,000l. to him, to be placed to the same account as that sent on the 21st of August. I have given notice of it to Lord North."

351. 1781, March 6.—Parliament Street. J. R. to the King. Acknowledges the receipt of 6,000l. (Copy.)

. 352.  1781, March 19.—St. James's.  Sir S. Porten to J. R.  The  MARQUIS OF
warrants for the appointment of the nine gentlemen as Baronets of Great  ABERGAVENNY'S
Britain have been sent to the King for signature.                        MSS.

353.  1781, March 19.—Queen Square.  Lawrence Sulivan to J. R.
Concerning the appointment of writers in India.

354.  1781, March 23.—Saville Row.  Henry Dundas to [J. R.].
Concerning appointments at the port of Leith.

355.  1781, March 23.—The Earl of Hillsborough to J. R.  Concerning Jebb's pamphlet, and Heron's pension.

356.  1781, March 24.—Addiscombe Place.  C. Jenkinson to J. R.
" I am glad to hear that Lord Hillsborough disapproves of the raising
the six new regiments as I do.  I apprized Lord Amherst of my dissent
a month ago at least, and Lord North a fortnight.  Besides other objections, I knew they were jobbs as you now state."  I will quit my
office rather than have anything to do with them.

357.  1781, March 29.—London.  The same to the same.  I had a
long conversation with the King yesterday, when he was as usual very
gracious.  Lord Hillsborough was very accommodating, and, after a long
conference this morning, we settled all that should be done in order to
bring this affair to an amicable conclusion.  He sent to Lord North to
obtain his concurrence, but no answer has come.  I conclude that Lord
North is determined that I shall go out, which I now imagine will be
the issue of this business.  " Private."  (See the King's letter to Lord
North, No. 673, in Mr. Donne's edition.)

358.  1781, April 9.—Parliament Street.  The same to the same.
" Lord North opened the E[ast] I[ndia] busyness to day in the House of
Commons very well.  Mr. Burke was absurd, and made a long speech
that was not much to the purpose, but very mischievous.  Sir G.
Cooper was taking every advantage that he could to find fault with the
measure, and to create every possible obstruction."

359.  1781, April 13.—Bushy Park.  Lord North to J. R.  " I
understand Mr. John Craigie is very fit for his office, and that the
resignation of Mr. John Drummond is complete . . . . I suppose we
must comply with the requests of Lord S[heffield] and Mr. D[aubeny].
The expenses of both were incurred without my privity, or any promise
on my part . . . I suppose the following sums will do.  L[d] S[heffield]
2,000l., Mr. D[aubeny] 1,500l., being 500l. more than he asked for at
first . . but perhaps Mr. D. will not be satisfied, and it will be necessary
to give him more.  Try to do this business as cheaply as possible.  You
will find it difficult enough to raise even the lowest sum.  Mr. Powney
[at Windsor] stipulated at first only for 1,000l.  He has, I believe,
had 1,500l. or 2,000l.  What does he want now ? . . . The demands
on this occasion are exorbitant beyond the example of any former time."

360.  1781, April 14.—Bushy Park.  The same to the same.  I have
sent Mr. Craigie's commission to the King.  Mr. Hamilton is so sensible
and so agreeable a man that I should be much pleased with his friendship.  In Parliament he is a vote, and he might be much more if he
would.

361.  1781, April 14.—Addiscombe Place.  C. Jenkinson to J. R.
Concerning the debt of the East India Company.

362.  1781, April 22.—Bushy Park.  Lord North to J. R.  " Mr.
Johnes wants to have his seat vacated on Tuesday, in order to be elected
at the first County Court . . . . The Bishop of Winchester is dying."

MARQUIS OF
ABERGAVENNY'S
MSS.
— I shall solicit for the Bishop of Worcester, who, I believe, will be succeeded by the Bishop of Lichfield and Coventry. Does Dr. Graham expect to be the next Bishop? Will he be satisfied with a less Bishoprick than Lichfield? In the latter case, we may be able to oblige one person more than we should otherwise, though, under my present circumstances, it is inconvenient to me to recommend any Bishop who has nothing to quit.

363. 1781, April 27.—Henry Dundas to [J. R.]. Encloses—
(A.) Letter from Lord Maitland to the Lord Advocate [Dundas], soliciting appointment as one of the secret committee to enquire into the cause of the losses in the Carnatic.

364. 1781, June 24.—Addiscombe Place. C. Jenkinson to J. R. Concerning the affairs of the East India Company. "The whole is a game of interest. The proprietors will bid above the Directors, and the Directors above the proprietors, and will not support Government in any one point, and between the two the publick interest will be abandoned and neglected."

365. 1781, July 5.—Lord Thurlow to J. R. Concerning an error in the East India bill.

366. 1781, July 8.—Henry Dundas to J. R. Hopes that Lord North will not give himself a moment's difficulty in order to make a vacancy for him at the Treasury.

367. 1781, July 10.—The same to the same. Wishes that Lord North will think no more of any arrangement for placing him at the Board of Treasury. It would neither augment his fortune nor gratify his ambition. The public would think that he meant to make a sinecure either of the office of King's Advocate, or of that of Commissioner of the Treasury. While he remains in Parliament, he will give a steady and cordial support to Lord North and his administration.

368. 1781, July 6.—The same to the same. Baron Maule is dead. Lord Stormont is as eager for the success of Steuart Moncrieffe as Lord North can be, but care must be taken that no injury be done to Andrew Steuart.

369. 1781, July 15.—Headington. C. Jenkinson to J. R. Lord Amherst has assured me that the idea of raising Swiss troops for the East Indies has been given up.

370. 1781, July 17.—London. The same to the same. Concerning Mr. Ricketts.

371. 1781, July 29.—Addiscombe Place. The same to the same. "The Chancellour has been here and passed a morning with me. His conversation was, as usual, very kind to me, and more civil than it commonly is with respect to other people." Complaints of Lord North's personal unkindness in the matter of Mr. Ricketts.

372. 1781, August 7.—Smallberry Green. The Earl of Sandwich to J. R. Concerning the Receiver-General for the county of Huntingdon.

373. 1781, August 8.—Admiralty. The same to the same. Concerning the same.

374. 1781. August 19.—Bushy Park. P. Wentworth to Lord North. Gives a long account of his interview at Amsterdam with Mr. Rendorp, the President Burgomaster, Mr. Vander Hoop, and Mr. Deutz, with regard to a treaty between Great Britain and the Seven Provinces. (Three sheets.)

375. 1781, April 25.—Perthshire. Henry Dundas to [J. R.]. Encloses and recommends—

(A.) Application from Lord Elphinstone to the Lord Advocate, for the pension of 400l. a year, vacant by the death of Lord Crawford.

(B.) Application from Lord Mountstuart to the same, on behalf of Lord Elphinstone.

376. 1781, August 29.—Kew. The King to Lord North. " I have carefully perused the hints Lord North transmitted this day, and which I now return, for a seperate peace with the United Provinces, which arrived a few days since from Holland. The proposition from Russia certainly makes it impossible to settle finally with Holland without passing through the channel of Russia, but I doubt very much whether the French party has not got so decided a majority that no seperate peace with that Republic will be effected, yet it is advisable to be informed what terms the friends to negotiation think attainable. Lord North having read the dispatches from Petersburgh must see that no kind of reliance can be placed on the solidity of that Court, that therefore it is absolutely necessary to know how far the Court of Vienna will consent to the seperate peace under the sole mediation of Russia, before any answer is given to the joint offers of the Northern Courts. Therefore Lord North has my consent to go to Wroxton and to stay the next week, unless the letters from Vienna shall enable Lord Stormont to lay (*sic*) the Dutch business on Thursday sevennight, of which Lord North shall have notice."

377. 1781, August 30.—Admiralty. The Earl of Sandwich to J. R. " Our Cabinet is just broke up. Everything went on very quietly and well, though Lord Stormont showed a disposition against Mr. Stables, and Lord Amherst was clear against him, and wished for General Monckton. Lord Chancellor was clear for Mr. Stables. I said what I thought necessary in his behalf, and mentioned Lord North's approbation of him. Lord George said nothing, but was quite for Mr. Stables. . . The conclusion of course has been that Mr. Stables is to be recommended to the King as a proper person to fill the office destined to him by the India Company." " Very private."

378. 1781, August 30.—Syon Hill. J. R. to L. Sulivan. Concerning Mr. William Burke at Bussora, a relation of Mr. [Edmund] Burke. (Copy.)

379. 1781, August 30.—Christ's Hospital. Thomas Burfoot to J. R. 'This morning I was informed of the death of Alderman Hayley. We are told that there will be three candidates, the Lord Mayor, Alderman Townsend, and Crichton. I think we shall benefit by the three standing, and they will " cut " one another. (Copy.)

380. 1781, August 31.—Syon Hill. J. R. to the King. Concerning the election of a member for the City of London. (Draft.)

381. 1781, August 31.—Kew. The King to J. R. " We have so frequently failed in attempts in the City that I am not sanguine in my expectations of success on this occasion, but must think it advisable to encourage Mr. Clarke on this opening, should the three opponent candidates stand. He may have some chance of success, but he certainly has not an hour to lose, and the writ ought to be in the Gazette as soon as the necessary forms will admit of which I am certain Mr. Robinson will not lose sight."

382. 1781, September 1.—Wroxton. Lord North to J. R. " If Mr. Clark does not succeed, I should, from the respect I bear to the chief magistrate, wish that he may be preferred to the other two. I am

not inclined to spare any trouble in this business, or, indeed, any legal
method of supporting Mr. Burfoot and his friends.    .   .   .   If we are
obliged to engage in any expense, the sum should be fixed.    .   .   .   .
Lord Amherst wishes that Genl. Monkton may go out as Counsellor [to
India], and so does Mr. Jenkinson, who I believe to be at the bottom
of this difficulty, and to have suggested it to Lord S[tormont].  I know
the disposition of his Lordship not to be favourable to me.   .   .   .   .
If it is thought of importance that Genl. Monkton should be upon the
spot to receive the command when Sir Eyre Coote quits it, I suppose it
would not be impossible to persuade the Directors to give a salary to
Genl. Monkton as a retaining fee."    Remarks concerning Mr. William
Burke, Lord Dunmore, a candidate for the East Indian Direction, and a
prisoner for debt.  (Two sheets.)

383.    1781, September 2.—St. James's.  Viscount Stormont to Lord
North.  Concerning the negotiation with Russia, to be discussed by the
Cabinet on the 6th.  It seems better to make a stand upon the terms of
peace than upon general reasoning against a separate negotiation with
Holland.  "Most private."  Encloses—

(A.) Note to be read to the Cabinet.  There are many strong objections to a separate peace with Holland in the present temper of the
Republic, and little reliance can be placed on the impartiality of the
Empress of Russia.  These considerations decided the first answer given
to her offer of mediation between Great Britain and Holland.  Now that
the prospect of a general negotiation appears distant, she has resumed
the idea of a separate mediation with great warmth.  If this is refused,
she will be highly exasperated, and as she is so much governed by
passion and pride there is reason to fear that she will endeavour to draw
upon us the whole weight of the Northern League.  Sweden, which is
in the hands of France, would gladly join in her plan, Denmark re-
luctantly, but wherever Russia leads Denmark will follow.  The most
dignified part for this country would be to abide by the first answer, and
stand by the consequences.  "If we are equal to such a contest but for
one campaign, perhaps the wisest as well as the most spirited conduct
would be to risk the fate of it, and throw a die for the whole."  The
Northern powers, however, can wound us in a vital part by cutting off
our supplies of naval stores, while they themselves are scarce vulnerable.
An extension of the war would raise the hopes of France, Spain, and
the Rebels.  "It is to be feared that one of the first steps these new
enemies would take would be to acknowledge the Rebels as an independent state, and in this they would be joined by Holland, and probably by
the King of Prussia.  An acceptance of the sole mediation of Russia
would retard these evils, if it did not prevent them."  The Empress
"will never venture a rupture without the assistance of the other two
Northern powers, and in the event of the failure of this negotiation, she
would have no pretence for calling upon them.   .   .   .   The mediation
would engage her attention and feed her vanity, at least for a time.
.   .   .   The failure of the negotiation would not be liable to the same
inconveniences as the refusal of her mediation."  This mediation might
make her less solicitous about the negotiation for a general peace, from
which, after the unfriendly proposals fabricated at Vienna, we can expect
no good.  If your Lordships should advise his Majesty to decline the
mediation offered by Russia, great resentment is to be expected, haughty
and insolent language, and perhaps an open rupture.  If you should
advise his Majesty to accept it, the acceptation should be accompanied
by a statement of the terms we shall accept, which may be stated to be
our *ultimatum*.  (Three sheets.)

(B.) Seven heads for a separate treaty with Holland. (French. Two sheets.)

384. 1781, September 3.—Wroxton. Lord North to J. R. Concerning messengers, and the day of the meeting of Parliament.

385. 1781, September 7.—Admiralty. The Earl of Sandwich to J. R. Concerning the representation of the borough of Portsmouth, advocating an agreement between the two parties. " Private."

386. 1781, September 12.—Seamore Place, Mayfair. The Earl of Ailesbury to J. R. Solicits the appointment of Mr. Robert Anstey, son of a gentleman well known in the literary world, as a cadet in the East Indies.

387. 1781, September 25. –St. James's. Sir S. Porten to J. R. Concerning the case of Mr. Daubenny. " Private."

388. 1781, September 26.—St. Cross. C. W. Cornwall (Speaker of the House of Commons) to J. R. Concerning Mr. Dunn. " I am happy to find that Parliament will not meet till the end of November. I have long thought it not good policy to suffer the longer sitting of Parliament than was necessary for the public business, and that public business took up more or less time, in proportion to the provision which had been made, not to the substance only of the business, but to the paper and packthread which enveloped it."

389. 1781, September 27.—Windsor. The King to J. R. " By the appearance of yesterday I had flattered myself that Alderman Clark would have been at the head of the poll this night. I now suspect the. Lord Mayor will be successfull. The measures taking at Colchester seem to promise success. Rebow was so bad an attender and so doubtful in his conduct that the change seems advantageous."

390. 1781, September 30.—Bushy Park. Lord North to J. R. Concerning the contracts for victualling, the letters of Lieut. Col. Debbieg, the application of Lord Dunmore, and the Lord Lieutenancy of Essex.

391. 1781, October 1.—Waldershare. The same to the same. I have quite done with elections in London. " We have now been led three or four times into idle and foolish expenses there, at a time when the principal persons in the City, after having embarked Government, have seemed not very earnest themselves, as Mr. Harley showed himself in the last instance, by going out of Town in the midst of the poll. In this case of Colchester I am inclined to give way . . . . The sum however must be limited, and should not exceed 1,500l. or 2,000l. at the most." Potter, being a contractor with the Treasury and Victualling Office, should be deterred . from the ruinous plan of disobliging us and hurting himself, by opposing Affleck. My near relation, Mrs. Boydell .wants the place of Painter to the Navy for her husband. I do not know that such a place exists.

392. 1781, October 31.—Melville. Henry Dundas to [J. R.]. Concerning a cadetship promised to Mr. Cruikshanks.

393. 1781, November 1.—Same place. The same to the same. Concerning Mr. Hay's appointment as Secretary to the Supreme Council in Bengal.

394. 1781, November 11.—St. James's. Sir S. Porten to J. R. Sends despatches from Commodore Johnstone and Major-General Medows.

395. 1781, November 19.—Bushy Park. Lord North to J. R. Concerning the mover of the address, and Mr. Joliffe. " My body and mind are feeble and unfit for exertions, and I shall not be able to go through the next Session. I wish that his Majesty would prepare himself in case of accidents."

396. 1781, November 21.—Admiralty. The Earl of Sandwich to J. R. Concerning different members of Parliament summoned to London, and concerning the representation of the borough of Portsmouth.

397. 1781, November 25.—Same place. The same to the same. Concerning the representation of the borough of Portsmouth. Letters from France bring a certain account that Lord Cornwallis surrendered on the 19th past. " Private."

398. 1781, November 27.—Same place. The same to the same. Encloses, and asks for advice about—

(A.) Letter from J. Rawlinson, to the Earl of Sandwich, dated at Lincoln's Inn Fields, November 27, 1781. Being now convinced that the prosecution of the American war must end in ruin to the mother country, he can no longer vote with the Ministry on this question. As he is unwilling to vote against them, he is ready to absent himself, or to vacate his seat.

399. 1781, November. Lord Thurlow to J. R. Concerning the Commission of Sewers.

400. 1781, December 1.—Samuel Wilks to J. R. Concerning letters received from India.

401. 1781, December 9.—Admiralty. The Earl of Sandwich to J. R. Concerning Mr. Cecil. " The King mentioned to me the other day his not having lately seen any lists how people voted in the House of Commons, which used formerly to be frequently communicated to him."

402. 1781, December 10.—Queen's House. The King to J. R. " Mr. Robinson has done very right in returning the state of the House of Commons, as he did not want it longer. It is certainly very useful to me, as it shows who can be most depended upon. A copy of the division on the address and of that on the supply would be very agreable to me, if they can be easily made out. I should also wish to see the minutes on the receiving of the petition from the Common Hall of the City of London, and the proceedings at Westminster Hall this day, and at the previous meeting for that of the county of Surry, Lord North having but very slightly mentioned the one of Westminster, and not one word on the other two."

403. 1781, December 13.—Admiralty. The Earl of Sandwich to J. R. I am clear in my opinion that it is my duty to court an enquiry into naval affairs, unless there is a party among Lord North's supposed friends who have formed connections adverse to me. " Private."

404. 1781, December 14.—Same place. The same to the same.

405. 1781, December 26.—Lord North to J. R. Concerning the proposed candidature of Mr. North [at Taunton]. " I send you a most important and extraordinary letter, which I received to-day, and which I must desire you to bring or send to me to-morrow. I must then return some answer. You see that there is no great objection to changing men, but a very great one to changing measures, and that it will be expected from me to take upon myself *alone* to carry on that plan which appears to me in our present circumstances ruinous and impracticable." (En-

dorsed by J. R. "His Majesty's letter." See the King's letter to Lord MARQUIS OF<br/>ABERGAVENNY'S<br/>MSS.
North, No. 702 in Mr. Donne's edition.)

406. 1781, December 27.—Salt Hill. Lord Thurlow to J. R.
Concerning the Post Office.

407. 1781, December 27.—Thomas Exon to J. R. Concerning the
representation of the borough of Taunton.

408. 1782, January 13.—Blackheath. The Earl of Sandwich to
J. R. Concerning the proposed naval enquiry. A meeting with Lord
North and some of the principal members of the House of Commons
before the opening of the session seems to me absolutely necessary.
"Should that not be obtained with chearfullness on the part of the
friends of Government, I should not augur very well of the event of the
enquiry; with that kind of support I fear nothing, but am inclined to
flatter myself that Government, as well as myself, will gain credit from
the enquiry." I look upon you as my chief and confidential friend.
I believe that Ellis is a decided friend, and that Jenkinson is very
favourably disposed. "The Advocate [Dundas] I consider as an enemy,
and as being led by the Lord Chancellor to be adverse personally to me.
Nothing but Lord North's interposition will draw him from pursuing
that line of conduct. . . . If Administration gets well through the
naval enquiry, Mr. Orde must gain credit by taking a leading part and
shewing his abilities on such an occasion. . . . I fear no enquiry
unless there should be a party among those who profess themselves
friends of Government who think that a change in the Admiralty would
strengthen the Administration. On this point I differ from them in
opinion, but decency makes it improper for me to give the reasons upon
which my difference of opinion is founded." (Two sheets.)

409. 1782, January 20.—Admiralty. The same to the same. Encloses letters to which he desires to have "ostensible answers."

410. 1782, January 24.—Same place. The same to the same. Concerning Mr. Smith, an alderman of Huntingdon, and Mr. Hampshire
his deputy, "the cleverest fellow in England."

411. 1782, January 24.—The same to the same. "My wish is that
by all means it should be a Committee of the whole House, that the
enquiry may be as publick as possible."

412. 1782, January 25.—Admiralty. The same to the same. "I
hope yesterday was a good day for Administration as well as for the
Admiralty. . . . We are preparing and digesting at this office a
narrative of everything that seems necessary as materials to answer the
several heads of enquiry, as far as we collect them from Mr. Fox's
speech, and the orders of the House of Commons."

413. 1782, January 27.—The Earl of Hillsborough to J. R. "The
conversation [with the King] you mention passed, but it was of my seeking not his. It was not explicit as you wish, but very confidential. I
agree with him upon the necessity of a S[ecretary] in the H[ouse] of
C[ommons]. I recommended pressing J[enkinson] again, and telling him
that he was resolved to have one there. Probably this may make him
accept, for he will be afraid of the A[dvocate] getting before him. The
A[dvocate] however cannot do at present. At all events then take
E[llis] for the present, and give the T[reasurership] of the N[avy] to the
A[dvocate]. This will put him in a situation not too agreeable to
J[enkinson], and if at the end of the Session it should be thought
desireable E[llis] and A[dvocate] may change, or alors comme alors
At least it will enable N[orth] to make use of J[enkinson]'s jealousy,

and the A[dvocate]'s ambition. These were the poor politicks I suggested. He left me undetermined as usual. I am ready to stir my old bones as well as I can, but convinced it will answer ill to put it in my hands."

414. 1782, January 31.—Pall Mall. Lord George Germain to Lord North. "When I had the honor of seeing your Lordship yesterday sevennight in Downing Street you were so good as to assure me that you would on the next day send me a note acquainting me with the King's pleasure whether I was to continue in office or resign the seals. A decision upon that subject is absolutely necessary, as my remaining in this precarious state prevents all business being done in my department, and till the measures of Administration are finally determined, no preparations can be made for carrying on the war, for maintaining our present possessions, or for taking any step towards propositions of peace." Instructions should be sent to the Commander in Chief, and some answer should be given to the Duke of Newcastle, who presses for the recall of Sir Henry Clinton. "The uneasiness which is universally expressed at the inactivity of Government, the conjectures which are occasioned from those high in office, and supposed to be high in your confidence, absenting themselves from the House of Commons, call aloud for some declared plan of Government, and for exertion in every department of business, and I should think myself inexcusable if I did not in the strongest terms once more beseech your Lordship to dispose of me in that manner which may best answer your Lordship's views for his Majesty's service and the publick good."

415. 1782, February 1.—Admiralty. The Earl of Sandwich to J. R. Concerning the arrangements to be made for the management of the debate on naval affairs. "My whole mornings are taken up from ten till five in digesting the papers that are to be laid before the House."

416. Same day and place. The same to the same. "I am glad to hear that you have made some impression on the Advocate." The "Thetis" is unengaged. I do not know when the court martial will be held.

417. 1782, February 3.—Same place. The same to the same. I desire to meet Mr. Orde and Mr. Percival. Wednesday evening is fixed for the large meeting at Lord North's. Lord Mulgrave suggests that I should invite Mr. Ellis and the Solicitor General to meet him at dinner. "It is absolutely necessary that you should see the Advocate without delay, as it is very material to know whether he is adverse or not."

418. 1782, February 8.—W[elbore] Ellis to J. R. Lord Hillsborough entirely approves of the stopping of the packet if it is not gone, but says that he cannot take upon himself to give the King's orders for stopping it.

419. 1782, February 9.—The same to the same. Todd imagined that the object of your note was to stop the Jamaica, West India, and North American packets. I told him there was no such intention, but merely to stop the New York packet, or, if it had sailed, to have another ready to carry the letters of Tuesday.

420. 1782, February 9.—Whitehall. Lord George Germain to Lord North. As I am now at my office for the last time, I desire to support the request of Mr Knox who has rendered me constant assistance, and also to recommend Mr. Pollock, the first clerk in the Secretary's office. From the expressions in your last letter I was apprehensive that my

conduct had not been agreeable to you, but the King has assured me that I have every reason to be satisfied with your sentiments in regard to me. I wish you all possible success and happiness both in your public and private capacity. Encloses—

(A.) Application from Mr. Knox concerning a pension.

421. 1782, February 10.—W. Ellis to J. R. " I called this morning on Mr. [Gabriel] Steward to inform him of what, I suppose, is to happen to-morrow, for I have not yet had any direct signification of the King's pleasure to come to receive the seals. . . . . I found Steward a little out of humour, and thinking himself slighted because he had not had any signification from Lord North or from you." He was Mayor [of Weymouth] at the time of the dissolution, and therefore obliged to prevail on Captain Lisle (Lyel) to be returned in his place. He accordingly bore a fourth part of the expense of that election, but he complains that when his Mayoralty expired, the whole expense of the election after Captain Lisle's retirement fell on him alone. Is it worth while to put him out of humour for the value of 500l. ?

422. 1781, February 13.—Admiralty. The Earl of Sandwich to J. R. Concerning Mr. Fox's motion for Wednesday (the 20th).

423. 1782, February 14.—The same to the same. " I think something ought to be thrown out in the House upon the strange language held by Mr. Viner, but by whom or how I cannot at present decide."

424, 425, 426, 427, 428. 1782, February 15.—The same to the same. Concerning the attendance of Members of Parliament on the 20th.

429. 1782, February 15.—Lord North to J. R. Concerning Newcastle and concerning General Tryon. " I inclose a summoning letter sent to me by Sir Francis Bassett to give him the decisive answer I promised. I cannot give it him, but I have no right to expect him to remain undetermined, so that, I fear, I must let him take his course, the consequence of which will be the defection of himself and his three friends to the enemy. We can but ill spare them."

430, 431, 432, 433. 1782, February 15.—Admiralty. The Earl of Sandwich to J. R. Concerning the attendance of Members of Parliament.

434. 1782, February 16.—C. Jenkinson to J. R. The case of those bankers who are not admitted to the subscription seems hard, as it gives the rest of the trade a great advantage over them. Encloses—

(A.) Letter from Messrs. Brown, Collinson, and Tritton to C. Jenkinson, dated Lombard Street, February 16, 1782.—Having no connexion with any of the gentlemen to whom the loan is to be allotted, they fear that they will be excluded. The list of applications for themselves and their friends amounted to 500,068l.

435. 1782, February 20.—Admiralty. The Earl of Sandwich to J. R. " The story about the five ships detained from Rodney is as follows :—Rodney was first to sail with ten ships. Five more were then ordered by Cabinet to be added, and five additional ones to be prepared to be sent after him. However, upon his having got the start of the French fleet the second five were by order of Cabinet stopped, upon an idea that they are more wanted at home. However, two of the second line are notwithstanding sent out to strengthen Sir Richard Bickerton, and to leave him in a certain latitude and proceed then to join Sir George Rodney. This is also done by Cabinet. As to stopping the French fleet, after the detachments of seventeen to

the West and six to the East Indies, it is utterly impracticable, as we have no force in any readiness to attempt it."

436. 1782, February 25.—Same place. The same to the same. Concerning the attendance of Members of Parliament.

437. Same day and place. The same to the same. "A certain very considerable person desired me to endeavour to see you, in order to press you to use every possible exertion to secure attendance on Wednesday, as he is fearfull that Lord North cannot give his attention to this very important part of our present business."

438. 1782, February 26.—Same place. The same to the same.

439. 1782, March 3.—Same place. The same to the same. Encloses a letter (from Sir John B. Warren) explaining that he makes a distinction between voting for Lord North and voting for Lord Sandwich.

440. 1782, March 3.—Sackville Street. Henry Dundas to J. R. "Our last conversation, joined to the idea that Lord North should not in the present situation of affairs act any part inconsistent with honour and the dignity of his publick character, suggested to me the idea of putting something in writing in the shape of arrangement of an administration. I do it for Lord North only, as I have consulted with nobody. . . . . I have put the matters in two views, and have only to add upon them, that one or other of them appears to me absolutely necessary. Lord North's remaining in his situation would certainly be attributed to motives very dishonourable to him, and even after having so disgraced himself, still his duration in office would be very short. . . . . After having fought so long by his side upon personal considerations, I would not be part of an administration formed upon the coalition I have suggested exclusive of him. . . . . I feel it as a point of private honour in my own breast, which I value more than any situation, to stop my political career with the fall of the minister whose friend I have been. . . . . When I talk of removing Lords Hillsborough and Dartmouth, you will naturally understand that I mean their retreats to be perfectly comfortable. Lord Talbot's office naturally suggests itself for one of them. Allow me further to add that when I suggest myself for a Cabinet situation in place of the Treasurer of the Navy, it is truly giving up what is both more lucrative and more comfortable in every respect, and no motive whatever would make me think of such a thing, except a notion that my being in the Cabinet at the same time other people were introduced, would give weight and comfort to him." (Two sheets.) "Most private." Encloses,—

(A.) "1st View. If Lord North is to remain at the head of Government, the following seems a very strong arrangement without anything expensive in the execution of it,—

| | |
|---|---|
| Treasury - - - | - Lord North. |
| Chancellor - - - | - Lord Thurlow. |
| President of Council - - | - Lord Gower. |
| Privy Seal - - - | - Lord Weymouth. |
| Secretary at War, in Cabinet - | - Mr. Jenkinson. |
| Secretary of Foreign Affairs - | - Lord Stormont. |
| „       „ Domestic Affairs - | - Mr. Ellis. |
| India and Plantation - - | - Lord Advocate [Dundas]. |
| Admiralty - - - | - Lord Howe. |

Mr. Pitt, Treasurer of the Navy, with a seat at the Treasury, Admiralty and Trade, to some of his young friends.

A peerage to Sir James Lowther, and a Blue Ribbon to the Duke of Rutland.

The general principles of the above administration must be, an end to the American war, the best peace to be got, universal economy, and a high-handed executive authority.

2nd View.--If Lord North is not to remain, it appears to me that the safest thing for the King is not immediatly to throw open his Government, but to appoint Lord Gower to the Head of the Treasury, Mr. Jenkinson Chancellor of the Exchequer, Lord Weymouth President of the Council, Lord Howe First Lord of the Admiralty, Lord Thurlow remaining Chancellor, with power to him to give such intimation as he thinks proper to the Rockinghame and Shelburn parties separatly that the King is ready, upon the foundation of the Government as above stated, to dispose of the other places both in and out of the Cabinet for the purpose of a coalition with either of the above two parties, for it appears impossible to coalete with both, and at the same time preserve any part of the former system of Government."

441. 1782, March 6.—The Earl of Sandwich to J. R. "I think we have had a good day in the House of Lords—the numbers 37 and 72. Lord Beaulieu and Lord Bessborough went away without voting, and several others that I cannot yet recollect.

442. 1782, March 7.—Parliament Street. C. Jenkinson to J. R. Desires to see him, particularly after his interview with Lord North.

443. 1782, March 7.—Apsley House. Earl Bathurst to J. R. My nephew [John] Buller has desired me to ask his Majesty to give him the Chiltern Hundreds, as you have told him that Lord North will do nothing for him. I shall be under the necessity of telling a long story of repeated ill usage. I shall be obliged to mention your name as one from whom, as from Lord North, I have received the most solemn promises. I am not sure that I shall have interest enough with my nephew to prevail with him to bring in a friend to Government in his place. " But if you will recommend a gentleman who is willing to pay handsomely, I will endeavour to get him chosen [at West Looe]."

444. 1782, March 8.—Admiralty. The Earl of Sandwich to J. R.

445. 1782, March 9.--Henry Dundas to J. R. "I will fight your battle while a rag of you remains, but it is a wild idea to suppose that with a majority of only ten votes the Government of this country in time of war can be carried on. A few changes two months ago would [have] left us all upon our legs. But Lord Sandwich was a favourite with too many of you, and by that partiality we are reduced to what we now are. As to what you say about myself, you know I have long felt *seriously* hurt that I am the only person in Scotland whose office is not for life. The conclusion naturally arising out of that circumstance galls me perhaps more than you think. . . . Without any other feeling but personal love to Lord North himself, I am determined to stand and fall with him. I think both the President's warrant and my own should be in my possession before Wednesday. . . . I ought to be left dependent upon the goodwill of nobody but the Minister by whose side I have fought, and whom in no moment of difficulty I have ever forsook in thought, word, or deed. Postscript.—Never omit one moment to remind Lord North of the absurdity of not giving a good reversion to his son, but above all enforce upon him that he will not gain any credit by not doing it, and does not take the chance of benefiting one of the best young men I ever knew." (Two sheets.) "Private."

446. 1782, March 9.—Parliament Street. C. Jenkinson to J. R. Desires to see him before going to the King.

447. 1782, March 9.—Copy of circular letter proposed to be sent to Members of Parliament to request their attendance on the following Monday and Wednesday.

448. 1782, March 13.—Admiralty. The Earl of Sandwich to J. R. Concerning the attendance of Members of Parliament on Friday (the 15th). Encloses answers received—
   (A.) From Lord Wentworth.
   (B.) From Lord Sheffield.
   (C.) From J. Burling (M.P.)
   (D.) From Sir Charles Frederick (M.P.)
   (E.) From Lord Hinchingbrook.
   (F.) From Lancelot Brown, junr. (M.P.)

449. Same day and place.—The same to the same.

450, 451. 1782, March 14.—Same place. The same to the same. Concerning an Indiaman, the " Princes Royal," believed to be intended for foreigners. " If an Act of Parliament is not instantly passed to prevent these illicit practices, it will be a great disgrace indeed to Government which has allready suffered disgraces enough."

452. 1782, March 15.—Same place. The same to the same. Concerning the attendance of Members of Parliament.

453. Same day and place.—The same to the same. " If we go out of office I should hope that I shall not be forgotten. Unless I retire with a pension, my finances will be in the utmost disorder. I wish to consult you in the course of to-morrow as to the measures to be taken upon this subject."

454. Same day and place.—The same to the same. " From what I have heard to-day I am persuaded that if Lord North did not despond and talk of giving the thing up, matters would not be yet irretrievable."

455. 1782, March 17.—Same place. The same to the same. " I am very much obliged to you for the detail you have sent me of the division of Friday last. It gives me a very bad opinion of the present state of affairs, as I percieve (sic) the rats increase, and I do not know that we can make any further exertions."

456. Same day and place.—The same to the same.

457. 1782, March 19.—Same place. The same to the same. " I saw a certain considerable person yesterday, who is much to be lamented. He is very firm and seems to be inclined to do every thing that is dignified and judicious. I afterwards saw Rigby who desponds totally, and thinks that further resistance is in vain."

458. 1782, March 19.—Sackville Street. Henry Dundas to J. R. Concerning the office of surveyor of the duty on houses and windows in the counties of Berwick and East Lothian. Encloses—
   (A.) Letter from Lud. Grant to the Lord Advocate concerning the same.

459. 1782, March 25.—Sir S. Porten to J. R.

460. 1782, March 25.—Treasury Chambers. J. R. to Mr. Eliot. (Draft.)

461. 1782, March 22.—Admiralty. The Earl of Sandwich to J. R. Hopes that Lord North will dine with him the following evening at " the *last* cabinet dinner."

462. 1782, March 26.—Sir S. Porten to J. R. Encloses—
   (A.) Copy of a letter from the King to Sir S. Porten concerning various warrants.

463. 1782, March 26.—Admiralty. The Earl of Sandwich to Lord North. "I saw the King yesterday and urged my suit to him upon the ground of the letter I had written to him, and upon your interposition in my favour. His Majesty expressed much feeling, and I think a strong wish to give me assistance, but he made made no promise, and went no further than to say that he allowed the propriety of my behaviour during the whole time I had been in his service, that he felt exceedingly for me, and that he would consider of my application. If my judgement is right, I think his inclination is with me, but he may doubt of his power, and that he may possibly have other applications of the same nature. . . . At present my Parliamentary interest is very considerable. Your Lordship knows that it is so without my naming names, but if I am reduced by my circumstances to live in absolute retirement, that interest will soon sink to nothing, and my means of doing any service to this distressed country be utterly annihilated." MARQUIS OF ABERGAVENNY'S MSS.

464. 1782, March 26.—W. Ellis to J. R. Concerning the proposal to give a pension to Mrs. Arnold, which has been approved by the King. Suggests that the amount should be 600*l.* a year, as there are five boys.

465. 1782, March 27.—Sir S. Porten to J. R. Concerning various warrants.

466. 1782, July 6.—Lord North to J. R. "I do not think it impossible that Mr. Fox may be persuaded to resume his office. Lord Shelburne must certainly wish to have been some time in possession of the Treasury Board before he separates from the other party in the Ministry, and Mr. Fox, finding that the Duke of Richmond and Mr. Conway are not inclined to resign, may fear that his resignation will not have the effect he expected. If therefore some point should be conceded to him which may enable him to return to office with some decency, I do not think it improbable that some peace may be patched up for a time, but the grounds of the disunion are too deep to admit of a sincere reconciliation. Mr. Fox's silence yesterday renders it possible that they may reunite for a time. If he had made any personal attack, the breach would have been irreparable. Many of his friends will, to be sure, wish to see him continue in office."

467. 1782, July 6.—Addiscombe Place. C. Jenkinson to J. R. "I am told that Lord Shelburn[e] is determined to go on, and does not think the seceders are so numerous as he expected. Lord Keppel does not resign at present."

468. 1782. July 23.—Same place. The same to the same. "I cannot help thinking that Lord S[helburne] is sure of the Advocate [Dundas] . . . I am of opinion that you should tell Lord North that Lord Sh[elburne] has desired to see you, that you should go to Lord Sh[elburne] at the time appointed, and converse with his Lordship on any subject he may mention to you, as a man of honour ought to do . . . You may be assured that the Chancellour is at the bottom of all this busyness, and that he gives his full support to Lord Shelburn[e], and I am confident that the Advocate will not give his answer without consulting him. Nor would he have come from Scotland, if he had meant at once to refuse. I should be glad to meet you for the purpose of receiving such information as you could give me, but I dare not come to Town as I should be observed, and a meeting on Battersea Bridge or Battersea Rise is too uncertain."

469. 1782, August 7.—Windsor. The King to J. R. "Mr. Robinson is desired to send the enclosed to Lord North. I cannot at the same time avoid expressing my approbation at his having undertaken to

furnish Lord Shelburne with an accurate state of the House of Commons and the connections of each of them as far as can be ascertained. This will be very material to counteract the activity of Mr. Fox, who, every honest man and those in the least interested in the support of this constitution must wish to do the utmost to keep him (*sic*) out of power."

470. 1782, August 7.—Syon Hill. J. R. to the King. He will render every service which he can in favour of his Majesty's Government and the constitution. (Draft.)

471. 1782, August 14.—Wirksworth, near Matlock. Lord North to J. R. "Your letter with its enclosure has overtaken me. It was very important and remarkable." I send an answer which you will take care to have carefully and speedily delivered.

472. 1782, August 17.—J. R. to the King. Transmits letter just received from Wirksworth, near Matlock, using the same channel through which he received the King's commands. (Draft.)

473. 1782, August 19.—Windsor. The King to J. R. "Mr. Robinson has acted with his usual punctuality in using the same channel to convey the answer by which he had the letter to which it relates. G. R."

474. 1782, August 21.—Upper Harley Street. Thomas Orde to J. R. "Lord Shelburne desires to have the pleasure of seeing you at Wycombe on Saturday next to dinner at five o'clock, and hopes that you will stay Sunday."

475. 1782, September 3.—Wroxton. Lord North to J. R. "I return you inclosed the letter you sent to me at Lord Bagot's, which you will be so good as to take care of, and to put it (*sic*) with the others which you have of the same hand (*i.e.* from the King). Be so good as to keep it very private, and shew it to no person breathing. Read it however over carefully yourself, for I shall want to converse with you upon the subject of it. . . . . In the meanwhile I wish you would prepare for me an exact copy of the note of hand which I gave some time ago to Mr. D[rummond]. You will perceive by the inclosed letter that no notice is taken of it, nor a word said to relieve my mind on that subject."

476. 1782, September 7.—Same place. The same to the same. Expresses anxiety about the safety of his last letter.

477. 1782, September 8.—Same place. The same to the same. Concerning the [King's] letter enclosed on the 3rd. "There is not the most distant hint of any intention to do me justice, and I very much fear that if the matter is not now settled it never will be settled as it ought. I want therefore some pretence for renewing the business, which, if I am furnished with the paper I want, I shall be able to do with a tolerable grace, as Lord Brudenell has called upon me once or twice for a line of explanation on the subject."

478. 1782, September 16.—Orton. C. Jenkinson to J. R. I conclude from your visit to Wycombe and other circumstances that Lord S[helburne] is pleased with your conduct, and I have no doubt that the King will be pleased with it also. "I am sorry to hear that Lord N[orth]'s answer was cold and reserved. . . . . I dread the advice which Eden will give him, for I am perswaded that his Lordship wants to drive a bargain, and to this Eden will direct him till he has profitted himself by it. This is however a very shabby and undignified conduct for a man who has held such great situations, and who has received

such favours from the Crown. Think what he, his father, his brother and son now receive from the Crown, and that his debts have been paid, which is a personal favour never before conferred but once on any subject. I hope however he will think better and act otherwise. He at least should not be cold and reserved to such a master. He had better give a flat negative, and *assign his reasons.*" " Private."

479. 1782, September 22.—Same place. The same to the same. " I agree with you perfectly in opinion on all you have said concerning Lord North's conduct. I know through a private channel that a certain person is displeased at the answer that was returned, and says that Lord N's present language is very different from the strong and repeated declarations he used to make him. I am perswaded however he will act right in the end, though he will lose all the merit and grace of it." I approve your idea of having a pamphlet written. Would Macpherson undertake it ?

480. 1782, October 1.—Walmer Castle. Lord North to J. R. Concerning his movements, etc.

481. 1782, October 1.—Orton. C. Jenkinson to J. R.

482. 1782, October 12.—Addiscombe Place. The same to the same.

483. 1782, October 27.—Dillington. Lord North to J. R. " Your express has distressed and perplexed me beyond expression. Since the rising of Parliament, I have heard nothing respecting India affairs, and I imagined that all attempts to recall the Supreme Council had subsided, at least that since the last advices the idea of removing Mr. Hastings would be dropt for a time. But now I find myself called upon suddenly and without the least notice to take an active part in order to preserve a gentleman in the government of Bengal of whose conduct on several occasions I have often expressed my disapprobation, and whom I myself have endeavoured in vain to remove. If I desisted from that pursuit, it was partly from despair of success, and partly because since the death of Sir John Clavering and General Monson, I know no person whom I wished to see in his place.    .   .   .   As to the recall of Mr. Hastings I am certainly of opinion that it is a rash and ill advised measure, especially at this time, when the circumstances of India require in a Governor-General the most tried abilities, the greatest experience, and the most perfect knowledge of the country, and when the last advices from thence have given the Company every reason to be satisfied with the late conduct of Mr. Hastings. To send a perfect stranger there at this moment, appears to me so impolitic, and so little likely to give satisfaction, that I wonder the Ministers have attempted it." I shall therefore be very glad to act with Governor Johnstone, unless you should think it improper for me to interfere for following reasons :—

1. I have frequently expressed my wish that Mr. Hastings might be recalled, and do now think that many parts of his conduct have been very exceptionable, and that his constant disobedience to the orders of his superiors may, if not discouraged, prove of very pernicious example to the public."

2. " I proposed, promoted, and encouraged the Secret Committee who first advised Mr. Hastings's removal."

3. Most of my friends are out of Town, and others may not admit that circumstances have altered.

I leave it to you to decide whether to ask my friends to vote against the recall of Mr. Hastings, or to stand neuter. " It is impossible for me to wish that my friends would join the Directors in a measure which appears big with danger to the public." (Two sheets.)

484. Same day and place. The same to the same. I have referred Commodore Johnstone to you for my reasons *pro* and *con* about interfering in the ballot. "Unless the objections are weighty, I had rather consult the public good than my own reputation of consistency. This, however, is not to be risked lightly, and if you are perfectly certain I can be of little service." "Private and separate."

485. Same day and place.—The same to the same. Upon maturer reflection I have thought it better to enclose my letter to Governor Johnstone to you, leaving you free to send it or not as you think best. "Private and separate."

486. 1782, November 4.—Bushy Park. Lord North to the King. (Copy by J. R. Printed in Mr. Donne's edition, No. 729.)

487. 1782, November 24.—Rochester. Lord North to J. R. "I do not expect to see the Address, but wish to know enough of it to be able to judge whether we shall be driven to oppose any part of it."

488. 1782, December 3.—Bushy Park. The same to the same. "I do not understand the nature of the treaty with America. . . . One thing, however, is very apparent, that peace will not be concluded when we meet, that the most we are to expect will be some provisional articles with one of our enemies, which will be binding or not at the will of another. The Ministry will be open to every sort of attack upon all matters in dispute between us, France, and Holland, and it appears as if they would do better, not having made the peace, to apply to Parliament for assistance to carry on the war. But it is nonsence to talk about this subject till we know the articles."

489. 1782, December 10.—Same place. The same to the same. Concerning the impending debate on naval affairs. Desires that his friends in London should go to the House of Commons on the following day, so that there may be a competent number of "*Hear hims.*"

490. 1782, December 13.—Same place. The same to the same. "I hope that your good news will prove true, but as an Englishman I am most anxious for a tolerable peace. I am afraid that the French had no sincere intention of concluding anything before the meeting of Parliament, and that they deceived the Ministers, while they and their friends and their agents were trying to make money in the funds. But still I will not despair. These fortunate events, if true, will hasten it, and so will a manly language well supported in Parliament, which will express a reasonable [desire] of peace, without betraying too much apprehension of the continuance of war."

491. 1782, December 15.—Calcutta. Francis Pierard to J. R. Concerning his arrival in Bengal, etc.

492. 1783, January 6.—Addiscombe Place. C. Jenkinson to J. R. Advises him to keep up his spirits, and not to mind what the rumours of party may say or write against him. It may be well to prepare a few words by way of answer to anything that may be said in the House of Commons.

493. 1783, February 1.—Syon Hill. J. R. to Lord North. Your discourse a few days ago appeared to me to have a great tendency towards a change of the conduct which you have so honourably held in parliament. "The question to be decided is what line you are to take on consideration of the Articles of Peace in the House of Commons."

To discuss those articles is not necessary for deciding your line of conduct. " A most extensive dominion and valuable part of the Empire was dismembered and irretrievably lost, in your opinion, before you quitted his Majesty's service, and your uniform language has been that peace (although not an ignominious one) was necessary to this country. . . . Your Lordship has hitherto in this session of Parliament on public grounds supported the measures of Government, with great credit and reputation, and that conduct has put you in high estimation with your country. . . . Does your Lordship think that the objections to the Articles of Peace are such as would justify you to say that we should go on with the war ? Will the country in general, although many exclaim against several Articles of the Peace, support this idea ? . . . Are you sure of your following ? May it not happen that Mr. Fox may approve of those very Articles of the Peace to which you would object ? " If you and Mr. Fox should overturn the present administration and form one, your heart will tell you that it could not be permanent or pleasant. " Speak your sentiments upon the various Articles of the Peace as they strike your mind, but do not join in any motion for an amendment of the address which may be proposed, or in anything which may tend to a disapprobation of the Peace, or towards overturning the Government. . . . When I am told, as I mentioned to you in the coach three days ago, that the Advocate had declared expressly to you by authority from Lord Shelburne, that his Lordship meant coalition with *the old Government*, that he was extremely desirous of shewing to you every possible attention in his power, as well as to your son, and that his Lordship would leave the Advocate, *your friend*, to be the judge whether his Lordship did not deal fairly and honourably by you ; What am I to say ? What can one think ? Can one credit that there is an intention to dupe you ? . . . The two questions over, which, I am sorry to say, I think may shake the Government and the constitution of this country to its foundation, arrangements may be made to form a strong and a stable government perhaps of the most efficient men in this country to bring it out of its almost overwhelming difficulties, but to entertain an idea of making terms now, or to have any bargain made, in my opinion (not to use harsher terms which suggest themselves to me) would surely not do you honour." (Draft. Seven sheets.)

494. 1783, February 6. Fenchurch Street. R. Atkinson to J. R. " The general fact of a letter having been written is undoubtedly known, and the general purport will infallibly be related. I have not an idea that the Advocate feels the least want of confidence in what has passed."

495. 1783, February 7. Hertford Street. C. Jenkinson to J. R. " I am by no means in the secret of all the intrigues which are now going forward, and which are indeed without number. I see that Lord North and the Lord Advocate have in effect quarrelled. I have taken some pains to procure an explanation between them, but without success, and I am not sure whether it is possible at present to reconcile them."

496. 1783, February 19.—The same to the same. " None of the present Ministers saw the King till to-day after the Levee, and, as I understand from Mr. Orde, Lord Shelburne had come to no resolution as to what he would do."

497. 1783, February 28.—Fenchurch Street. R. Atkinson to J. R. " The present Administration, in whose hands the King has been brought into the present dilemma, are called upon to give an advice concerning their successors. This step appears to me a wise one, inasmuch as it

tends to bind them down to support what they recommend.  The
Gowers, etc., seem determined not to hazard an Administration upon
their own strength, and not to trust to probabilities concerning the
strength of others.   At the same time it appears clear to me that a little
encouragement would lead them to make the attempt . . supposing the
present Ministers to recommend an attempt in the Gower quarter.  This
I think the present Ministers *must* do, unless Mr. Pitt again plucks up
his courage, of which Mr. Townsend was not without hopes, or unless
he has secret communication with Mr. Fox, about which I confess I am
not without fears . . . . Your being out of reach may in half an
hour's time lead to consequences never to be repaired . . . The times
are beyond all example critical; the characters of the Dramatis Personæ
not remarkable for their inflexibility (excepting always one whose
obstinacy seems to have petrified the powers of all the rest), and if a
leading card can be managed, I think you will agree with me in thinking
it may govern the whole game."

498.  1783, March 7.—Hertford Street.  C. Jenkinson to J. R.
"I have passed many anxious hours since you left me, and have been
kept up the greatest part of the two last nights at the place where I
was then going.  Nothing could exceed the anxiety and almost despair
which I have seen.  Lord Gower has engaged to try to form something,
and is now about it, but God knows whether it will succeed."  "Most
private."

499.  [1783, March 8.]—London.  The same to the same.  "I am
this instant come home . . . . Nothing is yet settled.  Lord Gower
endeavoured yesterday to form something, but has failed . . . .
Everything in short is at sea, and the King in the utmost distress."

500.  1783, March 10.—Same place.  The same to the same.
"Everything still remains unsettled.  Lord Gower has done all that he
could do in order to form an administration, and that project seems to
be at an end.  Lord Mansfield has had an audience on the recommendation of the Duke of Newcastle, but he had nothing to propose.  He
condemns the conduct of Lord North and the Coalition, and I do not
think that Lord Stormount will take any share in an administration
formed by it.  Lord Ashburton has also had an audience.  He advises
the King on no account to give way.  He has suggested some projects,
but they appear to be chymerical . . . . Much the majority of
mankind pity the King, detest the Coalition, and abuse Lord North
beyond anything you can conceive."  "Most private."

501.  1783, March 12.—Same place.  The same to the same.  My
Friend [the King] after having done everything that man could do to
resist the combination that was formed against him, has found it necessary at last to give way.  He sent for Lord North this morning, and
told him that the Duke of Portland might be First Lord of the Treasury,
and desired that an administration might be formed on as comprehensive
a plan as possible, and Lord North and his new associates are now met
for that purpose."  "Most private."

502.  1783, March 14.—Fenchurch Street.  R. Atkinson to J. R.
"Nothing transpires of the arrangements between Lord North and Mr.
Fox, from which I am led to believe the detail is not found very easy
to settle."

503.  1783, March 22.—London.  C. Jenkinson to J. R.  "Another
hitch has happened, and one that is not, I think, likely to be got over.
The D[uke] of P[ortland] has behaved to the K[ing] in a manner that
has offended him highly.  If this continues we shall have a strange **day**

in the House of Commons on Monday. Your absence from Town is at present very detrimental." " Private."

504. 1783, March 24. The same to the same. " Before I went to-day to the House of Commons I understood that Mr. Pitt accepted, and I have reason to suppose that the K[ing] thought so, and had acted accordingly. When I came to the House, it was clear that he had not accepted, and the whole of Mr. Pitt's conduct was inexplicable. If it is not cleared up, I shall begin to entertain a bad opinion of him. He was of opinion that the address should not be opposed. He told me he should not oppose it, and therefore I would not."

505. [1783.] Sunday [March 16 or 23]. R. Atkinson to J. R. " Yesterday Lord North went to the King with the list of the Cabinet, and a proposition to remove the Chancellor, to which the King gave for answer that he would not. As far as I can learn there was in the proposed cabinet.

| | | | |
|---|---|---|---|
| The Duke of Portland | - | - | Treasury. |
| Lord Carlisle } <br> Mr. Fox } | - | - | Secretaries. |
| Lord Keppell | - | - | Admiralty. |
| Lord Stormont | - | - | President. |
| Lord North | - | - | Lord Warden. |

I know not the rest. Whether Lord North was merely the carrier of the proposal to turn out the Chancellor, or accompanied it by his advice so to do, is not known. The general report is that *all's abroad.* What the King means to do next is not yet known, but it appears to me that nothing short of a message to Parliament, and a vote of a great majority grounded thereon, will be likely to move Pitt's mind. The Advocate might I think be moved, but I understand Lord Gower would not venture with the Advocate without Pitt . . . . I have burnt your letter, which was opened by the Advocate, and recommend your doing the same by this."

506. 1783, March 25.—Conduit Street. The same to the same. " The blossoms of yesterday are finally blasted. . . . . Mr. Pitt informed the King last night that nothing had passed in the House to remove those obstacles which had before operated upon his mind, to which the King replies that he hopes he will still accept. The King does not come to Town till to-morrow. The King's situation appears to me more deplorable than ever. The notes he wrote on Sunday night both to Lord North and the Duke of Portland were peremptory, that he should give them no further trouble. There now remains, I apprehend, nothing but to send them carte blanche.

I have had a conversation this morning with Lord Surrey, who told me the purport of the King's notes, and from whom I gather a confirmation quite decisive to my own mind that Mr. Fox did not fully inform his own party of the true conditions entered into with Lord North, and that the divided Cabinet was treated by them as an incroachment, and not as part of the bargain.

Upon a very recent conversation between Mr. Pitt and the Advocate, the latter gives the business up as wholly at an end, and that not another word can be said to him about it. All that can remain will be to give such support as one can to the Government, for by Heaven I am convinced there are not materials in the country to form another. This young man's mind is not large enough to embrace so great an object, and his notions of the purity and steadiness of political principle absolutely incompatible with the morals, manners, and grounds of attachment of those by whose means alone the Government of this country can be carried on."

507.  1783, March 28.—The same to the same.  "I believe that no message has yet been sent, and that all is dark and desperate.  The A[dvocate] and I intend to spend an hour with you on Sunday forenoon, not on politicks, but to enquire how fast your health is returning."

508.  1783, April 2.—The same to the same.  "The writs are moved for Lord North, Lord John Cavendish, and Mr. Fox."

509.  1783, April 12.—The same to the same.  Concerning the loan.

510.  1783, April 15.—Lord North to J. R.   Encloses—
(A.) Application for 10,000l. of the loan for Thomas Farrer, and for the like sum for John Ruse.

511.  1783, April 21.—Hinchingbrook.  The Earl of Sandwich to J. R.  "I cannot say that I was much edified with what passed when Lord Hinchingbrook and I had an interview with the Duke of Portland, Lord North, and Mr. Fox.  The whole was a trial whether I would be satisfied with loose assurances of what should be done for me hereafter.  As to a specifick office to be given me at a fixed time no such thing could be done."  Lord North afterwards called on me, and I saw the Duke the same evening, and I am very well satisfied with what passed.  "I am here in hourly expectation of his final answer, which if not favourable will leave me to take my political line according as my own judgement will direct me, which certainly will not lead me to a connection with the new coalition."

512.  1783, June 21.—Lord North to J. R.   Concerning Mr. Fothergill, and concerning the allowance of the Prince of Wales.

513.  1783, September 4.—Fenchurch Street.  R. Atkinson to J. R.

514.  1783, September 17.—Addiscombe Place.  C. Jenkinson to J. R.  "I shall be anxious to know the substance of your conference with Lord North.  I am not surprized to hear that they are not in love with their situation.  No man of honour would act as some of them have done. . . . .  I am mistaken if the present possessor of Bushy can reflect on his conduct with any satisfaction, and this is proved by the pains they are forced to take to keep up his spirits."

515.  1783, September 24.—Same place.  The same to the same.  " By all I hear a certain person has not in the least altered in his disposition to the present Ministers.  He complies with their advice in all publick matters, but they generally find him out of humour.  He grants them whatever he can take from them again, but nothing permanent. . . . .  I was always sure that he would refuse Ellis's peerage, and I am now curious to see what he will say to the Duke of Portland's request with respect to the offices vacated by Sir John Shelly's death. . . . .  I suspect that North and the Duke of Portland oftener agree than either of them do with Fox, and of this Fox is jealous.  They are now sensible that the King is personally stronger and themselves weaker by the operation of Mr. Burke's bill . . .  Fox has said that his principal hopes are built on the present disunited state of opposition."

516.  1783, October 18.—Dublin.  [John Beresford] to J. R.  Review of the political situation in Ireland.  (Two sheets.)  "Private."

517.  1783, October 31.—Addiscombe Place.  C. Jenkinson to J. R.  Concerning the political situation in Ireland.  "I was today at the

Levee. His Majesty was kind to me. I thought particularly so. I met there Lord Mount Stuart. I observed from his conversation that he was attached to Fox. . . . He told me that Fox had made a great many friends during the summer, that Lord North had lost many, and that if *he* was now to go into opposition he would carry only his own family. . . . His Lordship added that the King had of late been very civil and kind to the Duke of Portland, but the very reverse to Fox. . . . Besides all this information I in short perceived that the present Ministers were jealous of each other and not well together. . . . Your idea of a Constitutional Club is a good one, but I do not think that things are sufficiently ripe for it."

518. 1783, November 4.—Same place. The same to the same. There is hardly a circumstance which you have learnt from Rigby that I did not also hear from Lord Mount-Stuart. You may be sure that his Lordship was right when he said that Rigby was gained. I am not at all surprised. You know what has always been my opinion of him. " I do not think however that all Rigby's efforts will influence Lord Thurlow, or induce him to abandon the King. This I say after having had a long and confidential conversation with his Lordship. . . . . I conclude Lord Weymouth will act a doubtfull part, at least till Lord Thurlow is satisfied. . . . Fox wants to put himself at the head of the whole, and to get rid of the Duke of Portland and Lord North."

519. 1783, November 19.—Lord North to J. R. Desires the attendance of his friends in the House of Commons at the second reading of the East India Bill.

520. 1783, December 3.—Fenchurch Street. R. Atkinson to J. R. " Every thing stands prepared for the blow if a certain person has courage to strike it. . . . The matter will probably be submitted very soon, perhaps indeed ere this. . . . Our India Directors will, I fear, make a bungled business of the account. However in one shape or another I hope to get it through the General Court tomorrow."

521. Same day. The same to the same. " Inclosed is the result of this day's Court. It was thrown out by Potter (the Welsh judge) and eagerly caught by the Court that it would be better to surrender our violated rights to the Crown in a solemn way, if the bill passes the House of Peers, than let these new potentates have the power of mismanaging our property without controul. . . . The bill has undergone no alterations worth mentioning, and is to be read the third time on Monday."

522. 1783, December 4.—Fenchurch Street. The same to the same. " The aspect of things is hopeful. . . . Nothing decisive however has come to my knowledge."

523. 1783, December 5.—H[ertford] S[treet]. C. Jenkinson to J. R. " I approve very much of your paper of minutes. I only think that the instructions to the Council are not sufficiently ample. . . . I have talked with Lord Thurlow on all this, and have settled with him what should be done. . . . You cannot do too much to obtain the votes of Lord Abergavenny, the Duke of Beaufort, and Lord Montague. You may be assured that the King sees the bill in all the horrors that you and I do. . . . Lord Gower comes to Town on Sunday, and things will then get more in train. I shall be curious to see what Lord Sackville's members will do on Monday. I hope tomorrow to receive your list of peers."

524. [1783, December.] Canvass of the House of Lords for the East India Bill.

525. 1783, December 8.—Fenchurch Street. R. Atkinson to J. R. Concerning the canvass, and the petition of the East India Company.

526. 1783, December 12.—Same place. The same to the same. "A *direct* communication has been had, and all goes right. As far as I understand, the case is, that on Wednesday a letter was written declaring the readiness of certain persons to receive the burthen, to which a reply was made full of assurance that he would go every length they desired him. He afterwards wrote, commanding Lord Temple to go to the Levee or to Court yesterday, and to have an audience. He also (I think) saw Lord Gower. He has written to Lord Gower to come to Town, and has given authority to say (when it shall be necessary) that whoever votes in the House of Lords for the India Bill is not *his* friend. This however is, as I understand, to be kept secret some days." ".Secret."

527. 1783, December 12.—St. James's Place. Richard Rigby to J. R. "Peers and their proxies are hunted after all the world over, and the House of Lords will be numerous next Monday. The Duke of Bridgewater, who is always eager and sanguine, thinks they shall throw out the Bill, but it will be carried by a majority of 25 at least."

528. 1783, December 13.—C. Jenkinson to J. R. "I had learnt of Lord G[owe]r all that past, but as I understand that letters are now frequently opened at the Post Office I dare not write particulars. This is a bold measure, but things are in the hands of men of resolution."

529. 1783, December 14.—Leicester Fields. R. Atkinson to J. R. "I understand generally that all goes right."

530. 1783, December 15.—The same to the same. The Lord Advocate wishes "to get an appointment made for you and he and Mr. Pitt and myself to meet as soon as possible, and in the most secret way, not from any improper desire of secrecy but lest the measure in agitation should be guessed at if an interview was known. It has ended in appointing this evening at seven o'clock at the Advocate's house in Leicester Fields, when he will have some dinner for us . . . I understand in general that all goes right." (Endorsed—"Answered immediately, and went accordingly.")

531. 1783, December 16.—Burlington Street. G[eorge] A[ugustus] North to J. R. Urgently requests his attendance at the House of Commons by three o'clock to support Lord North. Desires to know how matters stand at Harwich, with regard to the probable dissolution of Parliament.

532. 1783, December 17.—Syon Hill. J. R. to G. A. North. He cannot be at the House at the time named, by reason of the gout. He has honestly spoken his sentiments to Lord North on the 13th of November, and also repeatedly to Mr. Rigby. To show personal attachment to Lord North has ever been the leading principle of his heart, and he will do all that he can do with honour and propriety concerning Harwich. (Two sheets. Draft.)

533. Extract from the above.

534. 1783, December 17.—St. James's Place. Richard Rigby to J. R. A dissolution of Parliament is in everybody's mouth as likely to take place in a few days. "Being to be set adrift for a seat in Parliament, I am determined to try the good-will of my neighbours at Harwich to represent them, I therefore sollicit you as a voter, as well as to be a joint candidate with me. I know no pretensions that George North has there better than myself. Nor can the Treasury, whoever they may be, claim any influence over the present voters. And why good neigh-

bourhood and good fellowship is not to prevail in my person as well as in another's I cannot tell." MARQUIS OF ABERGAVENNY'S MSS.

535. 1783, December 17.—R. ¦Atkinson to J. R. " I am dragged into the India direction," on the recommendation of Lord Thurlow quite unexpectedly. " Lord Thurlow wanted explanations of the account. He is ill, which I am confident is the ground of his apparent low spirits. He expects to throw out the bill tonight. T'is expected Fox will stop the third reading of the Land Tax, and vote an address against dissolution, and censure upon interference, that the Ministry will in that case be changed. You stand high with Mr. Pitt."

536. 1783, December 18.—St. James's Place. Richard Rigby to J. R. " My old friends must be grown bolder than they used to be if they advise the King to dissolve, when a majority of two to one have voted him an enemy to his country who gives such advice. Not being present I can only tell you from report that there appeared in the House of Commons last night such a spirit in support of Fox, and after the news came from the Lords of the considerable majority by which the India Bill was rejected by their Lordships, that nothing can overcome in this Parliament, and who is the bold man will advise its dissolution ? "

537. Same day.—Syon Hill. J. R. to R. Rigby. Concerning Harwich. Regrets that he is to be set adrift for a seat. Hopes to see him. (Copy.)

538. Same day.—St. James's Place. R. Rigby to J. R. I perfectly understand the delicacy of your situation respecting Lord North's son and Harwich. I am determined to stand, and I have sent to my friends to canvass the borough tomorrow.

539. Same day and place.—The same to the same. Concerning the same. " I dined with the late Advocate today, who left us early to go and settle the new Ministry. Fox and the Duke of Portland were with the King, who said nothing to either of them of an intention to change his Ministers. But Lord Temple and Mr. Pitt were also in the closet at different times, which is a sufficient indication of what is intended. The dissolution is expected tomorrow." " Private."

540. Same day and place.—Half-past twelve at night. The same to the same. " I was just going to bed when Mr. Fox sent and desired to come and speak to me. He told me all was over, that Lord North and he had late tonight received their dismissions, and the King had said that as altercations were disagreable they might send their seals by their Commissioners. Mr. Fox wished to mention a few circumstances concerning various elections, and amongst others about the Duke of Bedford's boroughs." I told him that I was determined to stand for Harwich. He thought that North had a right to your interest. He will not oppose the Land Tax, " but he will keep the House sitting as long as he possibly can without essential detriment to the publick in stopping the Land Tax." He stands for Westminster, but he concludes that the Duke of Northumberland will oppose him.

541. Same day, noon.—R. Atkinson to J. R. " The Lords negatived the committment of the Bill by a majority of 18 present and of 16 including proxies. Fox carried the kind of questions I described by a great majority." I expect Mr. Dundas at Johnstone's after he shall have seen Mr. Pitt. " I am clearly of opinion that after the debate of last night disguise will no longer disguise anything, and is therefore absurd. I have suggested the sending you an ostensible signification of commands to give information, and hope you will agree in opinion that the kind of communication which will now become hourly necessary

cannot be carried on at ten miles distance, and that you will come to
Town tonight or tomorrow. We are to have a committee and a general
court tomorrow where we must lay our groundwork . . . I should
suppose the Duke of Portland and Lord J. Cavendish would to day receive
dismission, and perhaps the whole gang, and the rest kiss hands tomorrow,
and be in the Gazette on Saturday. Lord North was again great in
debate last night. I prophesy that that man's powers will revive in opposition. What a constitution of character this is!"

542.  1783, December 19.—Treasury Chambers.  Draft of circular
letter [from J. R. to certain persons at Harwich].

543.  1783, December 23.—Draft of an agreement between Mr.
H[enry] D[rummond] and Lord M[ountague] concerning the representation of the borough of M[idhurst].

544.  1783, December 24.—Addiscombe Place.  C. Jenkinson to
J. R.  I rejoice to hear that some administration is at last formed. It
shall have my hearty support. "I am ready to accept office, or to
support without office, as is most agreeable to the wishes and opinions of
those who are at the head of the Government . . . and if it be
thought necessary you may move for a new writt; but I do not think it
creditable to come to Town, and wait there in expectation of an office,
when I have not heard as yet a word from any one on that subject.
. . . I have as much zeal and enthusiasm in this business as you
can have.  I wish to hear and hope I shall hear that some proper provision is made for you."

545.  1783, December 24.—Tidwell.  John Rolle to J. Sinclair.
List of the boroughs in Devonshire, with remarks on the political
influence dominant in each.

546.  1783, December 25.—Cowdray.  Lord Montague to J. R.
Confirms the memorandum of Sunday last.

547.  1783, December 26.—Syon Hill.  J. R. to Lord North.  "In
consequence of the declarations I have repeatedly made, and the conduct
I have uniformly pursued since your Lordship left the Treasury, and,
with your approbation, to Lord Shelburne when he was the head of
Administration, I have been called upon for such information as is in
my power to give from the official situation I held. . . . I ought
now to follow the same line." (Copy.)

548.  Same day and place.—The same to R. Rigby.

549.  1783, December 29.—Fenchurch Street.  R. Atkinson to
J. R.

550.  1783, December 30.—The same to the same.

551.  1783, December 31.—Fenchurch Street.  The same to the
same.  Mr. Dundas will hardly be able to attend the Cabinet tonight,
and therefore, I presume, nothing will be decided.  The bill is good as
far as it goes, but it leaves a vast deal to be done by a subsequent
bill for the regulation of affairs in India. This is the whole of the
difficulty.

552.  1783, December 31.—Addiscombe Place.  C. Jenkinson to
J. R.  The Lord Chancellor was here on Sunday, and Lord Gower has
written me a very kind letter, but I have not heard a word from Mr.
Pitt, as Mr. Dundas said I should. "He has not even paid me this
small mark of attention." I want to see an abstract of the present state
of the House of Commons.

553.  1784, January 1.—Fenchurch Street.  R. Atkinson to J. R. MARQUIS OF "I am under no apprehension about Fox's attack, because a plain tale ABERGAVENNY'S MSS. will easily put him down."

554.  1784, January 3.—The same to the same.

555.  1784, January 5.—Isleworth.  J. R. to Lord North.  The examinations you have desired me to make cannot be speedily done, and it is not possible to send the papers by your servant as you desire.  The notes you mention were all regularly sorted for several years, as they came to my hands.  (Copy.)

556.  1784, January 5.—J. R. to Lord Montague.  (Copy.)

557.  1784, January 5.—Fenchurch Street.  R. Atkinson to J. R. Concerning the government of India.  Fears that the bill "will be whittled down to a state of inefficiency."

558.  1784, January 6.—Syon Hill.  J. R. to Lord North.  I send herewith a copy of the note you gave to Mr. Drummond, and also his Majesty's notes for the years 1779, 1780, 1781, and 1782, sorted regularly and put into books.  I have several old ones from 1768 to 1778, which I will tie up in parcels and send hereafter.  I intended to have made an index of the whole.  I send also four packets sealed up by your order, viz. (1) relative to Close and Buck's affair, January 1779; (2) to the Chandos negotiations, December 1779; (3) to the negotiations with Lord Montague, July to September 1780; (4) to the transactions with Jones, American army, and Clinton, 5 October 1781.  (Draft.)

559.  Same day.  The same to the same.  Sends seven parcels of the King's letters from 1768 to 1778, and a small parcel marked "Duke of Gloucester and Cumberland."  (Copy.)

560.  1784, January 7.  R. Barwell to J. R.

561.  1784, January 10.—Addiscombe Place.  C. Jenkinson to J. R.  I begin to be confident that we shall be victorious on Monday, although I thought it hardly possible before.  Your own conduct is very noble.  You do right in despising all the foolish talk respecting yourself.  It would be wise, however, to prepare some "topics" on what may be said in the House about yourself.  I much like what has been done this week at the India House.

562.  1784, January 20.  Ed. Boehm to J. R.  Declines to stand for Parliament.

563.  1784, January 22.  R. Rigby to J. R.  Desires to see him.

564.  1784, January 23.  Lothian's Hotel, Albemarle Street.  J. R. to Lord North.  Concerning——Fothergill.  (Draft.)

565.  1784, January 25.  The same to the same.  Concerning the same.  Regrets that Lord North would not see him.  Desires to justify his conduct to him and other private friends, but declines to notice the abuse of the newspapers.  (Draft.)

566.  1784, January 25.  J. R. to R. Rigby.  Concerning his own relations with Lord North and Rigby.  (Draft.)

567.  1784, January 25.— 31 Suffolk Street.  Major Joseph McVeagh to J. R.  Concerning a seat in Parliament.

568.  1784, January 27.—Lower Grosvenor Street.  Lord North to J. R.  Concerning——Fothergill.  "I trust that you have too good opinion of my spirit and understanding to suppose that I can accept any civility from the present Treasury or from you upon this occasion . ."

.   . I do not desire any explanation of your conduct.   You say that you had to choose between being my friend and my enemy, and you have chosen the latter course.   Your option has necessarily determined mine "   (This letter begins " Sir," instead of " Dear Robinson.")

569.  1784, January 28.—St. James's Place.  R.  Rigby to J. R. Complains of his treacherous conduct with regard to the representation of Harwich.  J. R.  had urged in excuse that he was trustee for the borough for every Treasury.  He bids him remember this expression after the fall of the Ministry in the week to come.  (Three sheets.)

570.  1784, January 30.—Hertford Street.  C. Jenkinson to J. R. No pains should be spared to procure a full attendance in the House of Commons on Monday, when the opposition expect a majority of 16 on their motion for an address for the dismissal of the Ministry.

571.  1784, January 31.—Syon Hill.  J. R. to R. Rigby.  Justifies his own conduct.  (Draft.)

572.  Same day and place.—The same to Lord North.  I must draw to your recollection the line which you laid down for me to follow when you went out of office, which was to inform, to assist, and to support his Majesty's Government, in whose hands soever it was, as far as it could be done with propriety and consistency.  I have repeatedly explained the reasons why I could not follow the line you had taken in the East India Bill, although I did not vote against it.  Read the letters which I wrote to you in February last.  (Draft.  Two sheets.)

573.  Same day and place.—The same to Mrs. Broomfield.  Concerning——Fothergill.  (Draft.)

574.  1784, February 6.—London.  C. Jenkinson to J. R.  It is of the greatest importance to secure the largest possible attendance of members on Monday next.  The Ministers continue very firm.  The attendance of the Lords who went up yesterday with the address was greater than was ever known.  Lord Mansfield was very temperate in his conversation yesterday evening.

575.  1784, February 6.—Hertford Street.  The Earl of Sandwich to J. R.  Concerning Mr. Poyntz.

576.  1784, February 12.—Memorandum by J. R. of Lord Oxford's application to Mr. Pitt on behalf of Mr. Wolfe.

577-584.  1784, February 17, 18, 20, 21, and 23.—Hertford Street.  The Earl of Sandwich to J. R.  Concerning Mr. Poyntz.

585.  1784, February 14.—Hertford Street.  C. Jenkinson to J. R. " You may be assured that a certain person is firm, so that nothing will shake his resolution.  I know also that his Ministers are firm and resolute at present, and I trust that they will continue so."  They have in this respect exceeded my expectations.  Lord Sandwich's conduct does not entitle him to a favour.  We have his son.  " I am assured that Mr. Fox was defeated to-day in Westminster Hall by 5 to 1.  Others make the parties more even.  It is clear however that Mr. Fox was forced to leave the Hall and to leave the other party in possession of it, and that he afterwards harangued the mob from one of the windows of the Kings Arms Tavern.  He was then drawn in his chariot by a low mob of about 100 to Devonshire House, but what will astonish you is that Col. Stanhope, Mr. Hanger, and Mr. O'Byrne (?) were on the coachbox, and that Mr. George North, Mr. Adam, and a third person, stood as footmen behind.  How disgraceful!  I am glad that, with the assistance of Mr. Beresford, you have made for Mr. Pitt

a state of the Irish House of Commons. I am sure he is much indebted to you for all your labours."

586. 1784, February 24.—Fenchurch Street. R. Atkinson to J. R.
Concerning the affairs of the East India Company.

587. 1784, February 26.—Same place. The same to the same.
Appointment for a private meeting at Mr. Dundas's.

588. 1784, February 26.—Duke Street, Westminster. George
Rose to J. R. Concerning affairs at Liverpool.

589, 590. 1784, March 8 and 9. The Earl of Sandwich to J. R.
Concerning Mr. Poyntz.

591. 1784, March 10.—Fenchurch Street. R. Atkinson to J. R.
Concerning Mr. Boehm, and various matters.

592. 1784, March 16.—Petersfield House. William Jolliffe to J.R.

593. 1784, March 20.—No. 13 Piccadilly (opposite to Lord William
Gordon's Lodge in the Park). J. R. to Mr. Harbinge. Concerning
the representation of Seaford. "Most private." (Copy.)

594. 1784, March 20.—Anthony Bacon to J. R.

595. 1784, March 23.—No. 31 Suffolk Street. Major Joseph
McVeagh to J.R. Concerning his candidature for Parliament.

596. 1784, March 24.—Fenchurch Street. R. Atkinson to J. R.
Concerning his candidature for Parliament.

597. 1784, March 24.—Copt Hall Court. Anthony Bacon to J. R.

598. 1784, March 26.—Colchester. Sir Edmund Affleck to J. R.
Solicits assistance in his canvass.

599. 1784, March 29.—London. R. Atkinson to J. R. Concerning
his candidature for Parliament. Encloses—

(A.) Copy of certificate by John Purrier, Fr. Baring, and William
Greenwood, arbitrators between the Lords of the Treasury and Mr.
Atkinson, that they are satisfied with the uprightness of his conduct
relative to contracts for rum during the late war. March 29, 1784.

600. 1784, March 31.—The same to the same. "Nevill is returned
for Seaford. In spite of newspapers and reports, depend upon it, I am
safe for the City."

601. 1784, April 2.—Colchester. Sir E. Affleck to J. R. Thanks
him for his assistance.

602. 1784, April 15.—London. R. Atkinson to J. R. Concerning
the affairs of the East India Company. If we very much press Mr.
Sulivan to take the chair, he will consent, though greatly against his
own feelings. "'The alternative he holds out is the leaving the present
chairs in office, in order the better to explain the necessity of parliamentary regulation, and to look to Parliament for that purpose. Now
you know that Sulivan cannot be requested to take the chair, nor supported in it if he had it; and therefore after all that we have done to
support the honour and efficient character of the India Constitution, and
after overturning a Ministry for invading it, Mr. Pitt is to be driven
to the necessity of bringing forward a coercive regulation very similar
in its principle to that of Mr. Fox, or else remaining a silent spectator
of a scene of stupidity and inefficiency perhaps unparalleled in the
history of any government, or else facing the topicks of declamation in
the House of Commons." There will be difficulty in carrying the
chairs for Baring and me, even with Sulivan's best assistance. " A

E 2

single vote upon the present occasion may decide upon all the future
system and fate of the Company. . . . . Nothing new in my
scrutiny." (Two sheets.)

603. 1784, April 17.—Same place. The same to the same. •

604. 1784, April 18.—Addiscombe. C. Jenkinson to J. R. Expresses great pleasure at the results of the elections. Desires to see
a state of the House of Commons. Declares himself curious to know
the sentiments of North and Rigby, if they can be learned.

605. 1784, April 19.—London. R. Atkinson to J. R. We are all
in confusion. The old gentleman [Sulivan] is immovable.

606. 1784, April 20.—Same place. The same to the same. "Sulivan stands in spite of all advice and opposition. . . . . Eleven
will be an equality. Supposing we were clear of Sulivan, Baring would
have at least seventeen out of the twenty-two."

607. 1784, April 21.—Same place. The same to the same. We
should have lost it by one. Having determined that Sulivan should
never be trusted in the chair, we brought back the old chairs. "The
advices from Bengal are distressing. Hastings on one side—Wheler,
Macpherson, and Stables on the other other. Hastings *must* be
recalled."

608. 1784, June 2.—London. Robert Drummond to J. R. Concerning a proposed reconciliation with R. Rigby.

609. 1784, June 5.—St. James's Place. R. Rigby to J. R. Invitation to dinner.

610. 1784, June 21.—House of Commons. R. Atkinson to J. R.
Concerning the candidature of Mr. Thornton at Ipswich.

611. 1784, June 22.—R. Atkinson to J. R. Concerning the same.
Postscript by William Pitt, dated at Downing Street on the same day,
requesting J. R. to exert himself on behalf of Mr. Thornton.

612. 1784, June 24.—R. Atkinson to J. R. Concerning the affairs
of the East India Company in Parliament.

613, 614. 1784, July 1 and 5.—The same to the same. Concerning
the same.

615. 1784, July 30.—Fenchurch Street. The same to the same.
Concerning the same. "We have fixed the dividend in the Committee
to, night at 8 per cent., without either Fox or Eden making their
appearance. They have unchained Burke, who raved like a Bedlamite
for two hours."

616, 617. 1784, August 16 and 17.—The same to the same. Concerning the opposition of the Lord Chancellor to the bill for restoring
forfeited estates.

618. 1784, August 19.—Kew. The King to J. R. Concerning
his pecuniary relations with Lord North and Mr. Drummond in 1782.
Expresses his thorough approbation of the honorable part acted by Mr.
Robinson in the late critical times which, by the assistance of Providence, have wonderfully changed since the assembling of the new
Parliament. Although he has "both public and private reasons to be
displeased with Lord North," he does not wish conduct so shameful to
be known further than to prevent Mr. Drummond's being a loser.

619———622. 1784, September 4, 22, 25, and 29.—R. Atkinson to J. R. Concerning the affairs of the East India Company, the
state of funds, etc.

623. 1784, October 3.—Addiscombe Place. C. Jenkinson to J. R. Observations on Mr. Dundas and Mr. Eden.

624. 1784, October 24.—Windsor. The King to J. R. Concerning his pecuniary relations with Mr. Drummond.

625. 1784, October 26.—Syon Hill. J. R. to the King. Concerning the same. (Draft.)

626. 1784, December 2.—Fenchurch Street. R. Atkinson to J. R.

627. 1784, December 7.—Addiscombe Place. C. Jenkinson to J. R. I incidentally saw Shelburne in Town, who told me his own tale. The notice taken of him was brought about by the Duke of Rutland. "I think I see that his Lordship is not pleased with Pitt, is very angry with Dundas, and that he will not himself be satisfied till he is once more got into office." I also saw Lord Gower, who said that there were to be no more changes. The Chancellor came here on Wednesday. He appeared dissatisfied, and knew less of what had lately happened than even I did. He was to see Mr. Pitt confidentially on Friday. "I have some confidence in the friendship of the Chancellor, but not in that of any of the rest. I do not choose to give up the game as yet entirely."

628. 1785, March 22.—Downing Street. W. Pitt to J. R. Acknowledges the receipt of papers about Parliamentary reform.

629. 1785, April 8.—Hertford Street. C. Jenkinson to J. R.

630. 1785, April 9.—Syon Hill. J. R. to William Pitt. During the recess I have revised the short minutes on the rise and progress of boroughs, basing them on Prynne's returns. When I was with you, you seemed desirous to give as clear and concise an account as could be, lest by detail you might tire the House. Precise statements given with your perspicuity will have the contrary tendency. This is a business that calls for minute detail to show the history of Parliamentary representation. I have talked with some of the gentlemen on the subject of reform, whose opinions you asked me to learn. I find them in general very much against meddling with it in any shape, fearing to open a door to confusion. Although they would vote against you with great reluctance, to induce them to accede even to bringing in a bill it must be stated that the bill proposes to be declaratory as well as remedial. The idea of voting a large sum of money to accumulate for the purpose of purchasing boroughs, as talked of, appears to be much disliked, and it will be greatly contested. It would be better that decayed boroughs should relinquish their rights, and receive from others that have increased in population and wealth such a sum of money as Parliament may assess. I did not venture to state any knowledge of your plan. Some gentlemen wish to propose an essential reform in the constitution of the House of Commons, by bringing in again the qualification bill which was offered a few sessions ago. (Copy. Four large pages.)

631. 1785, July 8.—Stangate Street. Francis Pierard to J. R. Encloses—
(A.) Long extracts from letters from Francis Pierard at Calcutta, dated in 1784.

632. 1785, December 6.—The Earl of Dartmouth to J. R. Concerning the voyage of Captain Pointing.

633. 1786, April 24.—Sion Hill. J. R. to F. Pierard. (Copy.)

634. 1786, December 28.—Calcutta. F. Pierard to J. R. Concerning appointments in India. (Two sheets.)

635. 1787, January 24.—London. Lord Hawkesbury (C. Jenkinson) to J. R.

636. 1787, May 2.—Syon Hill. J. R. to Lord Hawkesbury. Concerning the votes likely to be given by different peers on the expected motion relative to the Prince of Wales. "Most private." (Draft.)

637. 1788, November 11.—A[ddiscombe] P[lace]. Lord Hawkesbury to J. R. "I think that the physicians assume too melancholy a tone. They suppose that a King must even in illness be as wise as Solomon, and that he must not be subject to delirium like other men."

638. 1789, January 9.—James Macpherson to J. R. "The Committee are at daggers-drawing, and have not, as yet, finished their report. . . . They speak of an application to the House for further powers." "Private."

639. 1789, January 9.—Brompton. Sir J. Macpherson to J. R. Concerning the King's illness, etc. "My own business of the I[ndia] House is put off to Wednesday. Friends are cold and opponents obstinate. This is hard after saving to my country a million and two hundred thousand a year of expence." "Private."

640. 1789, January 10.—J. R. to Sir J. Macpherson. The reports of the surgeons and persons who sit up with his Majesty ought to be given in evidence. Advice about the Regency. "Most private." (Draft.)

641. 1789, January 18.—Brompton. Sir John Macpherson to J. R.

642. 1789, January 18.—James Macpherson to Sir John Macpherson. Encloses—
(A.) Summons to James Macpherson to attend in the House of Commons at 4 o'clock on the following day, an important division being expected.

643. 1789, January 19.—Brompton. Sir John Macpherson to J. R. "Private."

644. 1789, January 24.—James Macpherson to J. R. Tuesday will probably be "the great day."

645. 1789, January 26.—Brompton. Sir John Macpherson to J. R. "It is now said that the Ministers will agree to an address, and drop the Great Seal creation."

646. 1789, January 26.—James Macpherson to J. R. Parliamentary intelligence.

647. 1789, January 29.—The same to the same. "The Prince is to give his answer tomorrow at three. There are apprehensions of Burke's being in the Board of Controul. He insists upon it for the services and adherence of thirty years. If they will agree, all the fat will be in the fire. A hint to the P[rince] would prevent it, for I plainly see his object is to carry on business as smoothly as he can. But how to give the hint is the question. They have carried the question against Mr. Pitt in the Common Council. . . I am told the [Prince's] answer is guarded but decisive—his *own* ideas. He has written a very proper letter—an ostensible one should the King recover—to the Queen. That also his own."

648. 1789, February 6.—The same to the same. "Private."

649. 1789, April 5.—Sir John Macpherson to J. R.

650. 1789, December 12.—Harwich. The same to the same.

651. 1790, January 28.—Colchester. Robert Thornton to J. R. Solicits his assistance in his canvass at Colchester. MARQUIS OF ABERGAVENNY'S MSS.

652. 1791, May 7.—Addiscombe Place. Lord Hawkesbury to J. R. Concerning the appointment of Mr. Dundas as Secretary of State. Copy of J. R.'s answer dated Syon Hill, May 8.

653. 1791, May 25.—A[ddiscombe] P[lace]. Lord Hawkesbury to J. R. Mr. P[itt] saw the D[uke] of G[rafton ?] in private on Saturday, and I strongly suspect that the person whom his Grace is to succeed sold his vote in Hastings's business for the promise of a pension."

654. 1791, June 10.—Same place. The same to the same. "I have heard nothing yet from Mr. P[itt], extraordinary as it may appear. He cannot, I think, go from his engagement to call me to the Cabinet, as he has by letter announced it to Lord Chancellor."

655. 1794, August 25.—Putney Common. James Macpherson to J. R. Concerning Indian affairs.

656. 1794, September 6.—Same place. The same to the same. "Private."

657. 1794, October 24.—Belleville, N.B. The same to the same. Desires to know whether Parliament is to be dissolved. "Private."

658. 1795, March 23.—Putney Common. The same to the same. Concerning the Nabob, and Indian affairs. "Private."

659. 1795, April 5.—Same place. The same to the same. Concerning the same.

660, 661. 1795, April 27 and 28.—Same place. The same to the same.

662. 1795, June 15.—Same place. The same to the same.

663. 1796, March 30.—Wyke House, Isleworth. J. R. to Henry Dundas. Mentions the schism in the borough of Harwich. "Most private." (Draft.)

664. 1796 (endorsed 1797), April 16.—Dublin. J. Beresford to J. R. "Our session ended yesterday, much to the honor and credit of Lord Camden and Mr. Pelham. The publick business has been effectually done, without noise or parade, and the opposition so kept down that 16 was their highest numbers during the whole session. The wickedness of the late Administration, and the weakness of their principal, gave me much trouble as to my own particular situation and character. . . . I have completely triumphed over my enemies, who were obliged to acknowledge on their legs that there was not the smallest foundation for the scandalous reports which were industriously raised against me. . . . I should hope that the very numerous sacrifices which the laws have made, both in Dublin and on the circuits, would cool the zeal and madness of Presbyterian and Popish Republicans, at least for a time, but you may be assured that although the spirit may lie dormant, it still exists in the breasts of those sects."

665. 1796, December 12.—Brompton. Sir John Macpherson to J. R. Condolences on the death of Lady Abergavenny.

666. 1797, May.—Hertford Street. The Earl of Liverpool to J. R. Concerning the coinage.

667. 1799, June 26.—London. The same to the same.

MARQUIS OF
ABERGAVENNY'S
MSS.
668--671.  1799, January 1, 25, 26, and February 13.—Sir John
Macpherson to J. R.

672.  1799, March 9.—Hertford Street.  The Earl of Liverpool to
J. R.  Concerning the appointment of his eldest son, Lord Hawkesbury,
as Master of the Mint, and the studies of his second son.

673--675.  1799, April 1, May 1, and September 12.—Sir John Macpherson to J. R.

In another box are several bundles of papers and tabular statements
showing the state of political parties in Parliament, and the probable
results of general elections.  A.D. 1772–1782.

Besides the above there are at Eridge Castle a number of official
papers of John Robinson, relating chiefly to the affairs of the East India
Company and those of the Borough of Harwich.

H. C. MAXWELL LYTE.

---

# THE MANUSCRIPTS OF G. F. LUTTRELL, ESQ., OF DUNSTER CASTLE.

## (SECOND REPORT.)

MR. LUTTRELL'S
MSS.
Soon after the appointment of this Commission, the late Mr. Horwood
drew up a short account of the manuscripts at Dunster Castle, which
was printed in the Appendix to the First Report.  Since that time I have
had occasion to examine them more carefully, and I have given many
notes and extracts from them in a series of papers on "Dunster and its
Lords," which have appeared in the "Archæological Journal." Inde-
pendently, however, of those documents which illustrate the history of
the families of Mohun and Luttrell, there are in the muniment-room at
Dunster Castle some ancient deeds relating to other knightly families
in the west of England, and a few manuscripts of more general interest.
Of these I now subjoin a list.

Grant by Reginald Fitz-Urse (filius Ursi) to his brother Robert
Fitz-Urse (Ursi filio) of a moiety of Williton (Gilletone), and of the
house in which he was wont to dwell, with the whole enclosure (purprisio),
before the Knights of the Temple to whom he has granted the other
moiety of the vill in alms for the benefit of his soul.  Witnesses :—
Hugh de Moreville, Richard Brito, Gilbert Engaine, Walter de Penedhoc,
Richard de Mustiers, William de Chocheleberge, Ralph par sa fei,
Robert de Nottune, Ralph Passemer, Girard son of Reginald.  (12th
century.  The first two witnesses were associated with the grantor in
the murder of Archbishop Beket.)

Confirmation of the same by Henry II.  Witnesses :—Saher de
Quenci, Robert de Stutevill, Reginald de Pavilli.  Fragment of Great
Seal attached.

Charter of Savaric, Bishop of Bath and Glastonbury, granting to
Robert Fitz-Urse and his heirs that every canon of the prebend of St.
Decuman's shall cause a chaplain to reside in the vill of Williton (Wile-
tone) and celebrate daily in the chapel, provided that the parishioners
who are the men of the said Robert and of the brethren of the Temple

of Jerusalem shall do no prejudice to the mother church of St. Decuman's, and shall resort thereto on the greater festivals of the year. Witnesses:—Alexander, Dean of Wells, Master W. de Sancta Fide, Precentor of Wells, Thomas de Monteacuto, Treasurer of Wells, Herman de Wivelescombe, Master Nicholas de Lovariis, Sir Ralph Fitz-William Simon Buzun, and two others named. Fragments of episcopal and capitular seals attached. [A.D. 1192–1205.]

Charter of Robert de Curt', addressed to all his friends and men, French and English, clerks and laymen, future and present, confirming to Robert Fitz-Urse and his heirs the land of Sunleweclive which Reginald Fitz-Urse his brother gave to him, and the land of Williton which the said Reginald apportioned (divisit) to him, according to the charters of the said Reginald and of the King. He also ratifies an agreement made by himself on behalf of his wife Matilda, with the said Robert, concerning an exchange of land at Lokinges, etc. Witnesses:—Reginald de Curt', William de Curt', Geoffrey de Corneville, Thomas ——, Richard Cotele, Geoffrey de Turberville, Ralph the clerk, William son of Geoffrey, Luke, Roger de Mai ——, Robert de Brianne, Clement, Robert Chanterel, Hugh, Geoffrey de Wireville, Osbert ——, William de Cornevill, Hugh de Luffewic, Robert de Wittone, William de Holt, Geoffrey ——, who made the charter. (It is almost certain that the surname Curt', which occurs several times in this deed, should be extended Curtenay. The grantor was clearly a person of high position, having property on both sides of the English Channel, and it was at Swallowcliff that William de Courtenay afterwards founded the Priory of Worspring. This deed then appears to be one of the earliest memorials of the English branch of the illustrious family of Courtenay.)

Agreement between Reginald de Mohun and John Bretasch and Eugoretta de Roingny his wife, for an exchange of lands at Carhampton (Karempton). 39 Henry III.

Grant by John de Mohun, lord of Dunster, to Simon le Baker and Joan his wife, of the land, garden, etc. in Carhampton, which he had of the grant of William de Mohun, son of Sir William de Mohun. 10 Edw. I.

Grant by William de Mohun of Carhampton, son of Sir William de Mohun, to Walter Trenchard, of a messuage at Carhampton, between the tenement of Sir Roger Perceval on the north, and the king's highway which leads to the church of St. Karentoc on the south. 5 Edw. II.

Grant by William Fitz-Urse and Lucy his wife to Thomas in Theburne and Agatha his wife, of a tenement, etc. at Theburne near Watchet. 2 Edw. I.

Assignment by Ralph Fitz-Urse to Elizabeth his daughter, of land at Withycombe (Wydecumbe) and Gildencote. 3 Edw. I.

Grant by John Fitz-Urse son of Ralph Fitz-Urse to Annora daughter of Alexander Luterell, of land, etc. in his manor of Williton.

Grant by Philip son and heir of Henry Pyck by Isabel his wife, to Ralph Fitz-Urse and Annora his wife, of the moiety of a burgage, etc. at Watchet. A.D. 1293. (Ralph Fitz-Urse and Annora his wife are parties to two other deeds of the 22nd and 34th years of Edward I.)

Grant by Simon de Meriet, lord of Withycombe, to John de Mohun lord of Dunster, of Andrew, son of Ralph de la Cumbe, his villein (nativum meum), with all his following. Witnesses:—Sirs Warin de

Raleye, John de Brutache, Philip de Cantilupe, knights, and four others named.

Grant by Robert Martin, knight, by consent of Amy his mother-in-law (socre), to Geoffrey Dobel, of a messuage at Withycombe (Wydecumbe) in free marriage with Isabel de Bonevile. 15 Edw. I. Heraldic seal attached.

Letter of attorney of Robert Martin, son of Sir Nicholas Martin, knight, to Hugh de Wollavington, chaplain, to give seisin to Edmund Martin his son, of lands at Withycombe, Cutcomb (Codecomb), and Watchet. 32 Edw. I.

Grant by John de Fitzurs, parson of the church of Brompton Ralph, to Edmund Martyn and Isabel his wife, of his third part of the manor of Withycombe (Wydecombe). 3 Edw. III.

Grant by Ralph de Fizurs, knight, lord of Williton, to William Poyer, tucker, and Dionisia his wife and Cecilia their daughter, for the life of the survivor of them, of all the lands in Beredone which Richard de Beredone formerly held of him in villenage. 2 Edw. III. Fragment of seal attached.

Grant by Edmund son of Sir Robert Martyn to John de Fitzurs, parson of the church of Brompton Ralph, and William le Cras, parson of the church of Hawkridge (Hauckeregge), of lands, etc. at Withycombe, Cutcombe (Codecombe), and Watchet. Palm Sunday, 3 Edw. III.

Grant by John Alford of Williton, clerk, to Sir Ralph le Fizours, knight, lord of Williton, Sir Robert le Fizours, brother of the said Sir Ralph, Annora daughter of Sir John de Memburi, knight, Sir John de Pouldoune, chaplain, Ralph Darderne, John Ylebrouwere, and Hawis daughter of the said Sir Ralph [le Fizours], of a tenement, etc. at Williton. 9 Edw. III.

Grant by Ralph le Fizours and Matilda his wife to Hugh de Durburgh and Hawis le Fizours their eldest daughter and to the heirs of their bodies, of land, etc. at Withycombe and Carhampton. 18 Edw. III.

Release of the same by Matilda, relict of Ralph le Fizourz, knight.

Grant by Ralph le Fizours, knight, lord of Williton, to Sir John de Durburgh, knight, Hugh son of the said John, and Hawis wife of the said Hugh, James, son of the said Hugh, and William Dygon, of land, etc. in his borough of Watchet. 23 Edw. III.

Grant by Geoffrey Loni, vicar of St. Decuman's, and John Ilond, to John Fizours and Joan his wife in tail, of land between the two roads that lead from Watchet to Williton, with remainder to the commonalty of the borough of Watchet, for the sustenance of a chaplain celebrating in the chapel of the Holy Cross at Watchet, who in all his masses shall pray for the souls of William Fizours and Lucy his wife, John Fizours and Joan his wife and Annora and Joan their daughters, John de Trebourghe, Adam de Trebourghe and Cristina his wife, Ralph Fizours and William his son, Richard Fygere and Joan his wife, and all faithful departed. 43 Edw. III.

Confirmation by Hugh de Durburgh, son and heir of John de Durburgh, knight deceased, of a demise by his said father to Thomas atte Pole and Sabina his wife, and Elizabeth their daughter, of a tenement, etc. at Stogumber (Stokegomere). 33 Edw. III.

Grant by Geoffrey Loni, vicar of St. Decumans, to John Basynges and Joan his wife in tail, of lands, etc. at Kentsford (Camisford) in the parish of St. Decuman's, and in the parish of West Meon (Westmunc) co. Hampton. 41 Edw. III.

Grant by **William Powton** and Richard Orchard to Gilbert Basynges Mn. Luttrell's and Agnes his wife, of lands, etc. at Kentsford and Watchet, and in the MSS. fee of Brompton Ralph. March 2, 2 Henry IV.

Deed of Gilbert Basynges making provision for his wife Agnes, and for the payment of his debts in the event of his dying in foreign parts. He mentions his lands, etc. in Cancsford, Watchet, and Sampford Bret. 4 Henry V.

Grant by Richard atte Brygge of Wachet to Walter de Durreburgh and Margery his wife and John their son, of land, etc. at Watchet. 6 Edw. II.

Release by John de Mohuu, lord of Dunster, to Sir John de Durburgh, Joan his wife, and Hugh their son, of all his right in certain lands at Carhampton. 23 Edw. III.

Grant by John de Ralegh of Netelcombe, knight, to Sir Hugh de Durburgh, knight, and Hawis his wife, of a tenement, etc. in Watchet, on the west side of the street called Swynstret. 38 Edw. III. Fragment of heraldic seal attached.

Grant by John Rogus to James Durburgh, son and heir of Hugh Durburgh, knight, of the manors of Heathfield, Stogumber, Preston, Almsworthy, and Withycombe. 2 Richard II. Heraldic seal attached.

Agreement between Hugh Durburgh, knight, and Robert Cheddre of Bristol, that James, son and heir of the said Hugh, shall take to wife Alice daughter of John Bathe, late burgess of Bristol, before Michaelmas next. Hugh undertakes to settle rents to the yearly value of 40l. out of his manors of Magor, near Chepstow, and Withycombe. Robert Cheddre undertakes to pay 350 marks to Hugh Durburgh, and 50 marks to James Durburgh for the chamber and apparel of his wife. Sept. 2, 3 Richard II.

Grant by James Durburgh and Alice his wife to Robert Pyppyng, Cristina his wife, and John their son, of a cottage at Withycombe. 11 Ric. II.

Release by James Durburgh to Ralph Durburgh his brother, of all his right in all the lands, etc. at Carhampton (Karampton) which Hugh Durburgh ever held. 10 Ric. II. Heraldic seal attached.

Agreement between Ralph Durburgh, esquire, and Alexander Anne and Alice his wife, relict of John Durburgh, concerning parts of the manors of Withycombe, Wilhton, Batheneston, Watchet, and Almsworthy, co. Somerset, and Magor, co. Gloucester, after an award by William Kynwoldesmersshe, Treasurer of England, and William Wenard, apprentice of the law. Feb. 13, 9 Henry V.

Grant by Ralph Durburgh to John Courtenay of Godenlegh, and Joan his wife and to her heirs for ever, of lands, etc. at Durburghes Cantock, co. Somerset. 8 Henry VI. Heraldic seal attached.

Agreement between John Courtenay, esquire, and Joan his wife, and Edward Grevyle, for a marriage between the said Edward and Isabel daughter and heir of the said John and Joan. July 8, 10 Henry VI.

Demise by Thomas St. Leger (Seynt leger), knight, Richard Pomeray, James St. Leger, Bartholomew St. Leger, and John Brokeman, esquires, to James Courtenay and Alice his wife, and Joan their daughter, of lands at Medecomb in the parish of Merwode. 20 Edw. IV. Seals attached.

Grant by Alexander Hadley and Alice his wife, one of the daughters and heirs of Ralph Durburgh, to John Stokes, John Stopyndon, Nicholas Wymbussh, clerks, and Thomas Morstede, of rents issuing from their manors of Williton and Watchet. 10 Henry VI.

Grant by Alexander Hadley to John Hadley his son, of all his lands, etc. at Stogursey (Stoke Cursey) and Bourton in the hundred of Cannington, which formerly belonged to Ralph Durburgh. August 23 35 Henry VI. Seal attached.

Letter of attorney of Thomas Kyngeston, for delivery of seisin of lands, etc. at Williton and Watchet, to Alexander Hadley and Alice his wife, with remainder to John Hadley their son and heir apparent. 2 Edw. IV.

Release by Elizabeth Hadley, gentlewoman, daughter of John Hadley, esquire deceased, to Richard Hadley her brother, of all her right in the manor of Withycombe. 7 Henry VIII. Seal attached.

Agreement between Christopher Mathew of the county of Glamorgan and of Morgannock in South Wales, esquire, and Richard Hadley of Withycombe, esquire, for a marriage between James Hadley son and heir apparent of the said Richard, and Frideswide, daughter of the said Christopher. Feb. 26. 8 Henry VIII.

Release by John Hadley, son of John Hadley, esquire deceased, to James Hadley, of all his right to land, etc. at Withycombe, under the will of his father. 17 Henry VIII.

Indented will of James Hadley of Withycombe, esquire, dated December 13, 19 Henry VIII. He makes mention of his mother Phelippa, his uncle John, his wife Elena, his eldest son James, and his other children Christopher, Richard, John, Alice, and Catharine, some of whom were the children of the said Elena, and some of a former wife.

Inquisition taken on the death of James Hadley, esquire, Oct. 6, 31 Henry VIII. Christopher his eldest son is twenty-two years of age and more.

Grant by Thomas de Hallesweye, son of Thomas de Hallesweye, to Walter Lucy son of John Lucy of Watchet, of a burgage at Watchet, etc. (13th century.)

Release by Robert de Lucy son and heir of Walter de Lucy to John de Brattone, of all his right in a burgage, etc. at Dunster. 8 Edw. III. Heraldic seal of Robert de Lucy attached.

Grant by Hamo de Basinges to his son William de Basinges, of all his land of Kentsford (Kanesford), rendering the service of a quarter of a knight's fee. Witnesses:—Sirs Ralph Fitz-Urse, and William le Britt, knights, Adam de Treberge, Nicholas de Sancto Decumano, John de Basinges, rector of the church of Chauberge, John de Tottesford, clerk, son of Philip de Totteford. (13th century.)

Grant by Hubert de Frechenevill, son of Sir Ralph de Frechenevill, knight, to Alexander Loterell, son of Sir Andrew Loterell, knight, of all his land, etc. in the vill of Cullesworphe. (13th century.)

Grant by Simon Everard to William Everard his younger brother, of all his rents, services, etc. at Williton, in tail, with remainder to the grantor in tail, and to his brother Robert Everard in tail. 49 Edw. III.

Probate copy of the will of John Everard dated August 6, 1494. He desires to be buried in the parochial church of Carhampton, and he bequeaths a cow towards the fabric of the new seats in the said church.

He appoints his wife Isabel to be his executing and residuary legatee, and John Hadley gentleman to be the overseer of his will.

Letter of Friar John, Minister of the House of Hounslow of the Order of the Holy Trinity, etc. reciting divers privileges conferred on his order by several popes, and admitting Thomas Cooker and Joan his wife to the benefits thereof. A.D. 1506. On the back is a form of absolution.

A small roll of one membrane, giving a list of the Scottish knights who were taken or slain at the battle of Homildon Hill, A.D. 1402 :— " Les nouns des Contes, Seignurs, Barons, Bancrettz, et Chivalers qui feurent prises et tuez a le Bataille de Homelden le iour de lexaltacion de la seinte Croix, lan du regne nostre tresredoute sire le Roy Henri, tierz, sauz les nouns des Esquiers et autres gentz qui feurent aussi prises occys et noiez a le Bataille suisdit.

### Contes.

Le Mordyk de Fyff leisne filz au Duc Dalbaine.
Le Conte de Douglas.
Le Conte de Murree,
Le Conte Dorkeney.
Le Conte de Angos.
Le Conte de Strathern.

### Barons et Bancrettz.

Le Sire de Gordon.
Le Sire de Mongomery.
Mons<sup>r</sup> Johan Levyngston, Sire de Kalendr.
Mons<sup>r</sup> Johan Swynton.
Mons<sup>r</sup> David Flemyng.
Mons<sup>r</sup> Johan Styward de Endermeth.
Mons<sup>r</sup>  „  de Erskyn.
Mons<sup>r</sup> James Douglas de Dalketh le filz.
Mons<sup>r</sup> Johan le Seton le filz.
Mons<sup>r</sup> George de Lessele.
Mons<sup>r</sup> William Arth.
Mons<sup>r</sup> Johan Lyon.
Mous<sup>r</sup> Johan de Edmundeston.
Le Sire de Heillys, Franceys.

### Chivalers.

Mons<sup>r</sup> Robert Logan.
Mons<sup>r</sup> William Douglas de Niddesdale.
Mons<sup>r</sup> William Douglas de Strabrok.
Mons<sup>r</sup> James Douglas de Aberdour.
Mons<sup>r</sup> Alisandre Ramesey.
Mons<sup>r</sup> William Preston.
Mons<sup>r</sup> Archibald Edmundeston.
Mons<sup>r</sup> William Hay.
Mons<sup>r</sup> William Styward de Forest.
Mons<sup>r</sup> Robert de Levyngston.
Mons<sup>r</sup> Johan de Hamelton de Fyngalton.
Mons<sup>r</sup> Johan de Hamelton leng[ne].
Mons<sup>r</sup> Johan Moubray, Sire de Bernbogell.
Mons<sup>r</sup> Fergos Donaldson.
Mons<sup>r</sup> Thomas Malkolagh.

Mons' Thomas Makkelagh.
Mons' Johan Styward le filz de Sire William Stiwar.! de
Foreste.
Mons' Johan Glendenwyn.
Mons' Thomas Conyll.
Mons' William Morhede.
Mons' William Englys.
Mons' William Conyngham.
Mons' Hugh Walleys.
Mons' Thomas Somerville.
Mons' Johan de Cambele.
Mons' Thomas Kyrkepatryk.
Mons' William Synclare.
Mons' Johan Syward.
Mons' Roger Wygemore.
Mons' William Monypeny le filz et heir.
Mons' William Arth.
Mons' Johan Sybaldby.
Mons' Wautier Scot.
Mons' William Crouforth.
Mons' Robert Erskyn, filz et heir.
Mons' Thomas Erskyn.
Mons' William Erskyn.
Mons' William Dalyell.
Mons'      „      Dalyell le filz.
Mons' Robert Styward de Endermeth.
Mons' Patryk de Levyngton.
Mons' William de Akenhed.
Mons' William de Abernetthe.
Mons' William Gledestanes.
Mons' Car de Semelston.
Mons' Wautier de Boghanan.
Mons' William Hamelton.
Mons' Johan Dromonde.
Mons' Robert Lyle.
Mons' Thomas Carr.
Mons' William Menteth.
Mons' Adam Forester.
Mons' Johan Forester le filz.
Mons' Wautier Bykerton.
Mons' Jaket de Haplee ⎱ Franceys.
Mons' Piers de Haresy ⎰
Mons' Johan Danyel leisne.
Mons' Johan Chattaw.
Mons' Archibald Stiward de Endirmeth.
Mons' Johan Howden.
Mons' Laurence Ramensay.
Mons' Johan Lyndesay de Walghopp.
Mons' Aleyn de Carthcarte. ·
Mons' Johan Senclare.
Mons' Johan le Blare."

Documents relating to the election of successive Priors of Bruton.
Six of them have impressions of the conventual seal attached. They
give a continuous list of the Priors for nearly three hundred years :—

Stephen de Kari.
1255. William de Sancto Edwardo.

1255. William called le Sheftysbery (probably identical Mr. Luttrell's MSS. with the foregoing).
1267. William de Deverell.
1270. Stephen de Carevyle.
1274. John de Gryndenham.
1298. Richard de la Grave.
1308. Walter de Legh.
1334. Robert de Coker.
1361. Richard Cokkynge.
1396. John Cosham.
1418. John Schoyle.
1429. Richard Glastenbury.
1448. John Henton.
1495. William Gilbert, Bachelor of Theology.
1532. John Elye.

Petition of the inhabitants of Minehead to Queen Elizabeth. They state that from time out of mind a pier, or quay, has been maintained by them "agaynst the grett see," to their yearly charge of 50*l.* or more, always levied upon such shipping and "traffyke" as belonged to their town; that by reason of sundry wars their ships are now few, and the pier is now so decayed that, if speedy redress be not had, no ship or boat will be able to take succour there, to the great annoyance of that west part of Somerset, and of Devonshire, and Cornwall, and the decay of an ancient and daily passage from the parts of Glamorgan, by means of which the fairs and markets of the said counties are furnished with cattle, sheep, wool, yarns, cloth, butter, stones, coal, oysters, salmon, and other kinds of fish and flesh. They anticipate the destruction of such ships as shall happen to be in that part of the Severn in stormy weather, and the displacement of a hundred seafaring men from their houses, and the utter undoing of the petitioners. They therefore pray for the grant of a [charter for a] borough, port-reeve, and burgesses. They desire that they may choose a new port-reeve yearly, and that no persons, save such as shall be burgesses and shall bear their portion towards the charges of the said pier, shall sell any kind of merchandise, except victuals, coming from any outward parts until twenty-one days after their arrival within the said pier, or road, of Minehead. They furthermore desire that the port-reeve and the burgesses shall have authority to make such orders as be beneficial for the said pier. (Copy.)

Depositions in support of the foregoing petition. It is stated that if the pier at Minehead be not made new before Michaelmas next, "the same is not to be recoveryd and made wythowt the charges of a prynce."

February 4, 1564. Resolution by eleven burgesses of Minehead that Mr. Thomas Luttrell shall be the principal burgess of that town.

July 1570. Circular letter from Thomas Luttrell of Dunster Castle, asking for the assistance of his good friends and "welwillers" in making a new quay, or pier, at Minehead. He desires to make such a harbour as there is not the like of in the west part of England. The bearers of his letters have also testimony under the seal of the town of Minehead that they are appointed collectors for the same. (Copy.)

" An old rate of the weare dewties at Mynhead 37° Eliz. renovat ' as hath byn paied tyme out of mynde for and towardes the mayn-

MR. LUTTRELL'S MSS.

tenaunce of the port or weare of Mynhead, called by the name of wearieg to be paied for comming and going to and from the sayd port or to any other creeke belonging of right unto the lorde of the mannors of Mynhead and Dunster." Among the items are the following:—

For every barrell of herrings, 1d. For every " meaze " of red herrings, ½d. For every hundred of hake, 2d. For every "burder" of white fish, 1d. For every hogshead of salmon, 2d. For every tun of wine coming from France, 4d. For every tun of wine coming from Andalusia, 6d. For every tun of sweet wine, 6d.

" Reasons why the Towne of Mynhed should not be incorporated by Her Majesty." It is stated that the town of Minehead was better governed before the granting of the corporation which is now forfeited in law than it is now; that the magistrates and burgesses, of whom the corporation consists, are but simple and rude handicraftsmen who are fitter to be governed than to govern others, and that by their mis-government there have been many affrays in that town, and some murders in Dunster; that there are twenty-three persons (besides a tavern there) licensed by the port-reeve to be "tiplers," of whom two only are fit or able to give entertainments; that the town is much "depopulated" since the granting of incorporation; that the weekly market is altogether decayed since the granting of incorporation; that whereas there was a very ancient and good harbour having thirty or forty barks and bonts, there are now only five; that the whole manor and town of Minehead, with the liberties and franchises thereof, is the inheritance of George Luttrell, Esq., Justice of the Peace, who has, within the last two years, at his own expense begun to make a new harbour there on a far fitter plan than the former, and about 300 paces from the former, wherein he has bestowed 600l., besides 200l. or thereabouts collected by his means from his friends and tenants, the finishing of which will cost him very near 1000l. more; that the said harbour when finished will be able to receive her Majesty's ships, and will be the fittest in all the west for transporting seldiers, munitions, and victuals into Ireland, and is the common passage of all commodities from Wales to the counties of Somerset, Devon, and Cornwall, and from them to Wales, and that it will be a great succour to the ports of Bristol and Bridgewater ; that her Majesty's customs will be greatly increased by the maintenance of the said harbour; that divers Justices of the Peace of the County of Somerset, and the principal burgesses of Minehead have, by petition to the Privy Council, desired the suppression of the corporation; that certain burgesses have, by virtue of the incorporation, engrossed some commodities brought by sea to the said town, in order to sell them at excessive prices; that the town of Minehead has no lands or other profits belonging to it, in right of its incorporation, whereby it may be main-tained, and that it is unable to maintain the harbour without the aid of Mr. Luttrell; that the port reeve and burgesses have, by permission of Mr. Luttrell, taken the duties of the harbour for fourteen years towards the repair thereof, but that they have suffered it to decay, converting the profits to their own private use.

Petition of the gentlemen, merchants, traders, and principal inhabitants of Minehead. They state that Queen Elizabeth, by letters patent dated the 10th of October in the first year of her reign, incorporated the borough by the name of the Port-reeve and Burgesses of the Borough of Minehead, upon proviso that the grant should be void if they should at any time fail to keep in repair the port and harbour of Mine-

head; that the inhabitants were so impoverished by the long wars MR. LUTTRELL'S
between England and Spain in the reign of Elizabeth that they MSS.
were not able to keep the port in repair, and that thereupon the letters
patent became forfeited; that by the aid of several Acts of Parliament
the port has since been kept in good repair; that trade has of late years
flourished in the said borough which has become very populous; that
the borough suffers extremely for want of a reasonable power within
themselves to compel strangers resorting thither to pay their debts
before their departure. They therefore pray that the charter granted
by Elizabeth may be restored to them, so far as it relates to the good
government of the borough. (Copy.)

December 16, 1716. Order made at the Court of St. James's that the
foregoing petition be referred to the Attorney-General for examination.
(Copy.)

" Heads humbly offered by the gentlemen, merchants, traders, and
principall inhabitants of the borough and antient port of Minehead in
the county of Somersett, for a new charter." They suggest the appointment of a Port-reeve and Coroner, a Recorder and Senior Capital
Burgess, twelve Capital Burgesses, a Steward, and a Serjeant-at-Mace,
bailiff, and keeper of the gaol. (A.D. 1716 or 1717.)

" An account of the expences of Edward Cleeve, Keeper of the Prison
at Ivelchester in the yeare of Sir John Trevelyan, Bar$^t$, late Sheriffe
of the county aforesaid. Anno Domini 1704 and 1705." The following are among the charges :—" Carryeing 13 prisoners from Ivelchester
to Taunton assizes, being great rogues, and gardsmen's charges
2l. 19s. 3d. Burning in the cheek John Taylor and Edward Follett,
13s. 4d. Richard Wiccary hanged, 1l. 6s. 8d. John Bridgment
whipt, 6s. 8d. Mary Webber put in pillory, 13s. 4d."

A true copy of the circular letter of John Speke, Esq$^r$, to the freeholders of the county of Somerset, on behalf of his son.

Sir. This is to desier you to know that my son, George Speke,
Esq$^r$, does stand for Parliament man for this county at the request
of severall freeholders of Bristoll, Milborne Port, and other places, and
severall Dukes, Erles, and Lords of the King's Majesty's Court
above have sent down to the stewards in the countrey to make interest
for my son George Speke, Esq$^r$. Now this is to desier you to know
that there is one S$^r$ William Wyndham that they say does design to
sett up likewise, but this S$^r$ William was lately turned out of a very
profitable place at Court, for he was very intimate with one Lord
Bollenbrook, who had a hand in making the base and scandalouse
peace, and was turned out of his place even before the King's Majesty came over. Had they not made that peace, we had had but
some towns before we had gotten to the gates of Parris. Sir, your
interest and vote is desierd for my son George Speke, Esq$^r$." [A.D.
1714.]

Letters from Charles Blake to John Fownes Luttrell, Esq$^r$, dated
respectively, Quebec, Nov. 17, 1776; La Chine, nine miles above Montreal, June 22, 1777; and Montreal, Sept. 19, 1777. They describe in
detail the military operations in Canada.

H. C. MAXWELL LYTE.

REPORT ON THE MANUSCRIPTS OF PHILIP PLEYDELL
BOUVERIE, ESQ.

MR. BOUVERIE'S
MSS.

Some papers formerly belonging to John Pym, the great Parliamentary
leader, were presented to the British Museum in 1840, by his descendant
the late Hon. P. P. Bouverie. Others, however, still remain at his seat,
Brymore, near Bridgewater. I append abstracts of the most important
of these, and of other documents in the same collection. ·

1514, December 26. Greenwich.—The Lords of the Council to the
Archbishop of Canterbury. The King has been credibly advertised
that the French King is preparing sundry great armies, wherewith
to molest his Majesty and his subjects in sundry places. His Highness is
therefore enforced to prepare like force by land and by sea, the charges
whereof are so "importable" that it is more than requisite that he
should be speedily "aunswered of suche sommes of money as be due. to
hym." Although the tenth and subsidy of the clergy now due to him
at Christmas is not yet so soon payable, he doubts not that the clergy
will be content to "prevent" the day of their payment. He therefore
desires that the money should be paid to the Archbishop's ministers
before the 15th of January, and by them to the Court of the Tenths
and First Fruits before the end of the month. (Copy.)

[1544.] December 27. Lambeth.—T. [Cranmer] Archbishop of
Canterbury to Peter Hayman and Thomas Hales. Encloses copy of
letter received from the Council this day concerning the tenth and subsidy
money due by the clergy of his diocese, and desires them to proceed
speedily in the matter. Signature and heraldic seal.

[1545 ?] St. John's Day. London.—Peter Hayman to Thomas Hales
at Canyngton. I was imprisoned on Saturday last for 40l., and to day
I had been sent to the Fleet but only that my Lord Chancellor, at great
suit, has given me some days' "respect." I owed not 20l. Since my
coming up, I have paid above 280l.

N.D. The same to the same, concerning money due.

A small note-book, unbound, entitled "Memorable Accidents." It
contains brief biographical and historical notes by John Pym, written
continuously down to the year 1618, and a few of later date. Some of them
relate to well-known public events, and others to the births and deaths of
the writer's nearest relations, but there are others again that seem to
deserve mention in this report.

" A.D. 1591. My father died at Oxford."

" A.D. 1596. My mother died at Morton in Marsh."

" A.D. 1602. The Kinge was proclaimed upon our Lady-day at
Oxford by my Lorde Norris."

" A.D. 1604. There was a great plague at London, wherof there died
2,000 a weeke, so that the Kinge kept his courte at Wilton by Salisburye, the Queene and Prince Henry and Duke Charles. The terme
was kept at Winchester because of the plague at London, where my
Lord Cobham, Sir Walter Raleigh and others were arraigned for
treason. I lived then at Salisbury because the plague was at Oxforde."

" A.D. 1605. I returned to Oxforde and there lived about the space
of a yeare in studyes. The King and Queene came to Oxforde, and lay

at Christchurch, where there were playes, Latin and English, the Prince MR. BOUVERIE'S<br>
Henry at Magdalen Colledge, where there were likewise playes and MSS.<br>
orations. There was an Acte kepte in St. Maryes."

" A.D. 1606. I went into Somersetshire where, having a dangerous fall, I lived about halfe a yeare."

" A.D. 1607. I went to London and was admitted into the Innes of Courte, the Middle Temple, where I remember the tresurer, a grave man, for my uncle William Ayshcombe's sake abated me 20*l.* in my admittance, saying—We must nourishe the line of good studentes."

" A.D. 1608. I fell upon a dangerous rocke, a false frende, and through his perswasions ranne into many inconveniences and expencefull courses. My brother dyed upon Fridaye morning about foure of the clocke at the end of Michaelns terme. I lived in Milforde Lane amongst the wilde beastes, etc. I proved a warde and was betrayed by my frend whome I will forget to name. I was drawne by him into a project of water workes. I lent to the projector about 400*l.*, and spent in and about the busines I know not what, but I knowe that it was all lost. I was much importuned to marry my Lady Garrardes daughter of Dorney by Windser, Mrs. Martha Garrard, a fine gentlewomen truly. I sawe her and no more."

" A.D. 1609. I was drawen by my frend into a busines of one Mr. Lees of weaving silke stockinges, wherupon I layd downe 140*l.* besides what I spent about it. I received of the Venetian Ambassador forty poundes for it ; all the rest I lost. I was importuned to see a brave spirited gentlewomen named Mrs. Kate Howarde, beinge one of the two daughters and heyres of the Viscount Bindon's brother. I saw her not far from Bath, was earnestly sollicited to proceede ; being halfe afraid of the greatnes of her spirit, I did not. Shee was since more worthily bestowed, and she was most worthy so to be. I did hazarde myselfe twise or thrise for the defense of my frend aforesaid.

" A.D. 1610. I did redeeme my wardships by the assistance of my cozen R. J. and my cozen J. Bl., and then I did shake of my sharkinge comrades. I was wished unto a fine gentlewomen. I saw her, upon further acquaintance I disliked, and did not proceed. I sued my uncle Oliver Ayshcombe and my cozen his eldest sonne for my house and land at Ashampsted in Berkes in the Courte of Wardes. Upon my information they came in and compounded, and I did enjoy the land. My Lorde Wharton's eldest sonne and Sir [James] Stewarte killed each other by Islington by London. Mr. George Carewe a freind and an old acquaintance of mine was killed by one Mr. Deane at Thistleworth" (Isleworth).

"A.D. 1611. . . . Sir John Spencer the Alderman died. My Lord Compton havinge maryed his only daughter oppressed with the greatnes of his sudaine fortunes fell madde. The Erle of Suffolke havinge begd the keeping of him would have seized upon his money and jewelles at Islington ; my Lord Compton's mother the Countesse of Dorset playinge the valiant virago, withstood him, and he was therby defeated ; my Lorde Compton, being kept in the towre a little while, recovered. The Erle of Suffolk marryed in one day three daughters, the elder to the Lord Knowles, another to the Erle of Essex, the third to the yonge Erle of Salisburye. These t[w]o last to be referred to the year 1609." (The date of the marriage of the Earl of Salisbury, is given in Collins's "*Peerage*" as December 1, 1608. Mr. Gardiner has given his reasons for believing that the Earl of Essex claimed his young bride " shortly after Christmas, 1609." " History of England," vol. ii. p. 167.)

"I was credibly informed by his stewarde Mr. P. that my Lorde Compton at the first comminge to his great estate after the death of Sir John Spencer did within lesse then 8 weekes spende 72,000*l.*, most in great horses, rich saddles, and playe."

A.D. 1612. Sir Thomas Overbury was "mortally maliced" by the Countess of Essex.

"A.D. 1613. I seeing so much wickednes in the world and so much casualty among men, thought good to chuse out a companion for me in an honest course and tooke a wife."

A.D. 1614. "Sir Edwarde Sackvill brother to the Erle of Dorset killed the Lorde Bruse beyond the seas in single fight. The Erle of Montgomery was lasht with a riding rod by one Mr. Ramsey a Scotchman, but I think twas taken up by the King, and the Erle well rewarded by the King for his patience. The Ladye Honoria daughter and heyre of the Lord Denny and wife to the Lord Hayes (*sic*), cominge in her coach out of the towne somwhat late either from a masque or from supper about Ludgate Hill had a very rich jewell pulled violently from hir forehead by a fellowe, who was presently taken, and although shee was an earnest suiter to the Kinge for him, was hanged for it in Fleet Streete; shee beinge great with childe and by reason of the sodaine fright miscarying dyed about a weeke after. Sir Roger Owen, a fine gentleman, good scholler, a great speaker in the parliament house, fell madde at London, and shortly after dyed. . . . Sir Edward Phillipes, Master of the Rolles, the Kinge having killed a very fat bucke at Wansteed (the report went) sayd to the King—I hope your Majesty and I shall live to kill many more here as fat as this, the Kinge answeringe him in contempt—Yes, you and I, the good old man tooke it so the heart that he died shortly after. Sir William Wade, Lieutenant of the Towre, put out of his place."

"A.D. 1614. Mr. Richard Martin, beinge made Recorder of London, and havinge bine suspected heretofore of the murder of one Mr. Ferrers (the fame went) that one of Mr. Ferrers' sisters, whether the Lady Somerfeeld or other, should saye—God forbid that ever he should sit upon bloud before he hath paid the price of bloud himselfe; but it seemes the Recorder goinge to the recett [of the] Venetian Ambassador dranke somwhat deepe with him in theyr strange kinde of drinke, and therof surfettinge presently after dyed, never keeping any sessions, which are every three weeke . . . Sir Henry Nevill standinge for the place of Secretary to the Councell and missing of it, tooke it so to the harte that he shortly after died."

"The Lord Clyfton having maryed his daughter to the Viscount D'Aubigny, since Earl of Marche, who was at lawe with him for his landes, and being put into [the] Fleete, did or would have cut his own throate. Yong Sir Thomas Sherley being in the Fleete for debte attempted to poyson himselfe."

[A.D. 1616.] "The Lorde Boyle made a Baron, who (they say) not above sixteene years afore, being a poore fellowe and in prison at Monster in Ireland, borrowed sixpence, and now hath a great estate 12,000*l.* yeerly of Irish land."

"Mr. Palmer sent a challenge to the Erle of Sussex by Mr. Manwaringe and L. Huntley and others being with him upon St. George's daye as he was going to the tilte yearde; he received it; the busines was hearde before the Councell and there argued by the haroldes, and agreed upon that a gentleman of three descents might challenge an Erle and he was bound upon point of honour to answere him, but because this was done upon St. George's daye when the Erle was as it were a companion to the Kinge, therfor Mr. Palmer was put into the towre, and I think fined 300*l.*"

A.D. 1618. Sir Walter Raleigh "had the favour to be beheaded at Westminster, where he dyed with great applause of the beholders, most constantly, most christianly, most religiously."

Later in the book are notes of various commercial projects.

1630. A sheet of accounts in the hand of John Pym, relating to the Isle of Providence. The receipts amount to 1,355*l.* 6*s.*, among which are payments by the Earl of Warwick, Mr. St. John, Lord Brooke, Sir Benjamin Rudyerd, and others, for their "adventures." The charges are mostly for arms, ammunition, and provisions. A copy of Purchas's "*Pilgrimages*" cost 2*l.* 14*s.* 6*d.*, and "6 dozen Catechismes bought for the plantation" cost 12*s.*

N.D. John Pym to John Akehurst. Instructions as to the management of Estates in Somers Island with particulars as to leases already granted. (Draft.)

1633, October 23. Island of Providence.—William Rudyerd, William Rous, Roger Floyde and John Brigham, to [John Pym?]. We do not find here the largeness that was reported. At the arrival of the Sea-flower, the country was furnished with an overplus of provisions for the number of persons here. In October following, the new-comers had a crop of corn._ In that month eighty more came from Bermuda, who had been dissuaded by the seamen from bringing provisions. Although they had felled a great quantity of ground by the end of November, and planted it with corn, the dry season came on so fast that little of it came to good. These Bermudans (Baremoodians) had little help of the provision of store which was spent in the fruitless work of Warwick Fort. Thus many have endured great hardness. The island is full of hills and not so fertile as was reported. At New Westminster, and where Captn. Axe lives, the ground has this year twice failed in corn. This allotment of two acres a head will no more than find food. Even if tobacco were as vendible as ever, the quantities from here would never cloy the market. The tobacco that can be made between January and August may be as good as that of any country out of the Indies, if we observe the Spaniards' course of keeping it a year before sending it home. The worms eat our rafters, and the dust falling on our tobacco hinders the burning, and makes the taste bitter. Most men will have plantains and papawes in their season. Pines, orange trees, and lime trees grow, but do not bear. Potatoes are the most thriving and certain food we have. Fortification goes on slowly, and we are environed with enemies. From Fort Henry on the South West to Fort Warwick on the North East, a distance of seven miles, the land is inhabited. The 29 pieces of ordnance here, if fitly placed, would free the West side. The North side is not inhabited, and it is partly defended by breakers. 20 pieces of ordnance are requisite for its defence. In the harbour there is good riding for twenty ships. Whatever others may relate, this is the truth.

1640, December 21. Speech of John, Lord Finch, Lord Keeper of the Great Seal, made in the House of Commons. (Printed in the "*Parliamentary History.*")

1641, April 29. [London.]—Sir Thomas Peyton [M.P. for Sandwich] to Robert Hales. The London petition for expedition of justice has been transmitted by us to the Lords, "with a special enforcement of our own," upon which they have read the Bill of Attainder twice.

MR. BOUVERIE'S
MSS.

They have appointed Thursday to hear our counsel. The Court of the President and Council at York is voted illegal. We have spent three days in debating how to raise money that all armies may be disbanded this month. By the 16th of May we shall owe 200,000*l.* above the stock of our six subsidies. If this sum can be had for the present any where, it will be charged upon the rich men, at the rate of 5*s.* for every 100*l.* of land, and none under 100*l.* per annum to be charged. This will come to a mighty sum. But this is not yet the final resolution of the House. If used, it must not be repeated, for a second or third tax like this would drink up all the treasure of the Kingdom. The King has told us that the Papists will be disarmed according to law. Because all things are in an ill condition and nothing has yet succeeded according to the hope and expectation of men, we are about to have a second fast.

1641, October 5. Marshalsea of the Four Courts in Dublin. Gabriel Jenninges to John Pym. Complains at great length of his arbitrary imprisonment at Westminster and at Dublin.

1641, December 6. Sir William Balfour to John Pym. "Give me leave to arrest your noble promise of endeavour on my behalfe that I may receive these severall moneyes due unto me viz.

For sex monethes pay due to my selfe as Commissary and Capten of a troup in Irland, 470*l.* 8*s.*

For two monethes for my troup there by way of advance, other wyse it will bee impossible for that troup to subsist, I not being present in person to relieve them, as other Captains are, 501*l.* 12*s.*

There is also due unto me since I was Lieutenant of the Towre (as appeareth by the quarter books signed by sex of the Lords and Sir Robert Pye) the summe of 1,173*l.* for my owne ordinary fees, the dyett of prisoners, and other necessary disbursements for one yeare and 3 quarters ended at Christmas 1641, whereof 823*l.* appeareth by the said bookes to be moneyes disbursed by mee, I say due in all, 1,173*l.*

More due to me 56*l.* which I did disburse by direction of the house of the Lords, dureing the tyme of the Erle Straffords committall, for interteynement of a company of souldiers at 8*d.* per diem, who were appoynted to watch in the Towre some weekes before his death. I say 56*l.*"

1642, September 21. Shrewsbury.—Sir Edward Nicholas to Sir William Boswell, Resident at the Hague. His Majesty arrived here yesternight, the High Sheriff, Sir John Weild attending him from Wellington with a train of thirty-four liveries. He was received near this town by three fair foot companies of the trained bands and a hundred horse, afterwards by the Mayor, Aldermen, and liveries, all ranked in a very comely manner, they and all the people shouting with great joy throughout the whole town to the Court-gates. After his Majesty there entered the Banner Royal at the head of the Lord General's regiment, then the cannon, munition, and six foot regiments more, which are quartered about the town.

Sir John Byron with 300 foot and 150 horse defends the city of Worcester against divers forces under Mr. Nathaniel Fiennes and others, whom he has put to flight and loss, without any at all of ours. We now hear that they have retired far away in great haste upon news of the approach of some of our horse and dragoons. The arms and munitions that came last to Newcastle are now at Chester, and will be employed as soon as they arrive here. Plenty of men come in daily to serve, insomuch that his Majesty's army increases beyond imagination. Yet Lord Strange and divers Welsh regiments are not yet come up to join us, making about 5,000.

The Lord Lieutenant of Ireland had his instructions and full despatch from his Majesty at Stafford on Sunday last, where he took leave. He is gone to London about some particular affairs of his own, and from thence he is to go "in diligence" to his charge. Our army there is much disheartened at getting no supply of necessaries from London. We are in hourly expectation of the Queen's arrival at Newcastle. The Duke of Richmond and the Earl of Newport are gone thither. I hear that my letters written to you from Derby on Wednesday last have been intercepted, and that they are to be printed. Mr. Glyn is to make a comment on them. " I know not how my actions may be misinterpreted or my words misconstrued, but I sure there is no man to my power hath more seriously endeavoured and more hartily prayed for peace and a happy accomodation than I have done. But this I must say, that I had rather perish in the King's cause, if God for our sinnes shall bring us to the worst of extreames, then prosper by taking arms against God's anoynted." Heraldic seal.

[1642 ?] October 6. Derby House.—The Earl of Northumberland and the Earl of Loudoun to ————. The King having marched towards Newark with all his forces, it is necessary that he should be followed, to prevent the plunder of the country and to hinder his recruits. The taking of Chester is also a matter "of very great concernement." We have appointed Col. General Poyntz to follow the King, and we desire you to march to Chester to endeavour to reduce that place, and to receive orders for that purpose from Col. Jones.

[1642 ?] ———— to the Earl of Northumberland and the Earl of Loudoun. According to your command of the 6th inst., I have appointed the officers of the few scattered and broken troops who have marched with me to receive their orders from Lieut. Col. Jones. By the many wounds I have lately received I am at present altogether impotent, and unfit to judge whether I shall ever be able to serve you. I hope the committee will not permit me to endure overmuch the vexation of other men's commands, and to be undervalued in my own. (Copies on one sheet.)

[1642.] October 7. Worcester.—Viscount Mandeville to John Pym. I fully agree with your way, in having some of us to quit our commands to Scotch commanders who will be more useful. If you were here with us, you would find it of absolute necessity. I have not yet consulted with our General about it, but I sent him your letter and the note of the commanders, and I intend to speak with him about it to-morrow. We are still at Worcester, watching what the King will do. It is rumoured that he will march towards London on Monday next. Others think that he will advance towards us, which may be probable, because he has sent 2,000 foot into Bridgnorth. I pray haste down the Scotch commanders. There is some suspicion that our artillerymen are not as they should be. If this prove a truth, we are but in ill condition for action.

1642, October 18. (N.S.)—Memorial presented to the States General of the United Netherlands by Walter Strickland, Envoy from the English Parliament. He mentions the friendship subsisting between the two countries, and complains that soldiers and arms are being sent over to England without permission. (French.)

Declaration by the States General that they wish to adhere to their intention to remain neutral, and that they will again write to the different boards (*colleges*) of the Admiralty to forbid the issue of arms and ammunition. (Dutch.)

MR. BOUVERIE'S
MSS.
——

1642, October 15.   Cork.—William Jephson to his cousin John Pym. We are now brought to the last pinch of being able to subsist, and if you be not active for us in Parliament, the business must necessarily perish.   Nothing in the world is to me so sad a spectacle as to see those soldiers now in rags, languishing for want of natural food, whom I lately saw behave so gallantly in the field that all the officers wished them in scarlet.   A good part of the harvest is saved round about us, but it will not suffice to relieve the very poor, stripped by the rebels, and sent in for the protection of our charity.   We should have perished long ago if we had not been very active.   Our success in the field has been beyond imagination.   We have now desired, in our letter to the Speaker, that a regiment of dragoons may be levied for this service. You cannot do Lord Inchiquin justice for his activity and engagement of himself so freely against his countrymen for the maintenance of the cause of religion.   He is desirous that Capt$^n$ Min and Capt$^n$ Chudleigh should be his field-officers, which we all wish.   Ever since I came over, I have been authorised first by the Lord President, and since by the Vice-President, to execute the place of Major of the horse.   I hope my friends will not let me suffer an affront by Lord Leicester's " aversenesse to me," which I never deserved.   Capt. Chudleigh is well able to inform you of the state of this province.   Heraldic seal.

1642, October 18.   Worcester.—The Earl of Bedford, Viscount Mandeville, Lord Wharton, Lord Brooke, Denzell Holles, and three others, to the Committee for the Safety of the Kingdom.   In obedience to the commands of the Houses, the Lord General despatched Mr. Copley, Commissary General of the Musters, to desire a safe convoy for such as his Excellency should send with the petition of both Houses to his Majesty.   Yesterday morning, Mr. Copley returned with the enclosed answer, by which you may perceive that his Majesty absolutely refuses to receive any petition by any address of the Lord General, as one who is there expressed to be the principal of those whom the King has proclaimed traitors.   This we humbly conceive to be " a most high indignity " and scorn cast upon the authority of the Parliament in the person of his Excellency, and a final and utter rejection of the " submissive," dutiful, and earnest desires of peace so often laid at his feet, " with the cryes and groanes of his loving and loyall subjectes."   We beseech you to take care that when any ammunition " or other carriages " are sent, we may be acquainted beforehand of the road they take and the places where they lodge every night.   Heraldic seal of the Earl of Essex.

Same day and place.—The Earl of Essex to the same.   In obedience to your commands, I sent Mr. Copley with a letter and three votes of both Houses, with a desire of a safe conduct.   I have sent you the letter and the answer.   This answer did not take me unprovided, for since the first answer I sent up to the Parliament I expected no better. " And for my head that is soe much louckt after (and pleas God), I intend to sell it at such a rate, the buiers shall bee noe great purchasers."   My secretary has put up Lord Dorset's letter.   Smaller heraldic seal.

1642, November 1.   N. S.   The Hague.—Walter Strickland to John Pym.   This gentleman, Mr. Knight, is well known to Mr. Lawrence and Serjeant-Major Skipham.   He is a gentleman of merit and a true lover of religion.   All that I can commend to your care is the Queen's coming over, which I fear will produce some disadvantages.   Officers and commanders will pass with her, not in that name but as followers and servants.   I hope you will cause her ships to be visited.   Mr.

Percy has gone to England, to Newcastle I think.  So is Davenant, Sir Mr. Bouverie's MSS. Thomas Dorrill, and Philpot, and one Mr. Smith.  They say that Lord Newcastle, with the help of Sir William Widdrington, and Lord Dunbar, will raise 8,000 or 10,000 men.  I hear that officers, both English, Scotch, and High Dutch, will go with the Queen as followers and servants.  I will do all I can, but I wish that the seas may be kept. They say that she will be going within ten days.

[1642.]  $\frac{\text{October 31.}}{\text{November 10.}}$  [The Hague.]—Walter Strickland to John Pym.  The Queen has demanded ships and appointed the 17th of this month for her departure, but it is thought that she will not go until she hears from England by Davenant, Percy, Philpot, or Sir Thomas Dorrill.  Captⁿ. Stradling came here some four days ago.  He reports that Lord Essex's men will not fight, and that they go from him.  I hope you will have regard to what passes with the Queen.  Orders here are not punctually executed; officers will not do their duties.  The Council of State and the Admiralty have order to execute the answer to the declaration.  I desire to hear how you like it.  I hear that the Queen intends to take over horses and ammunition.  Great endeavours are made to raise money by borrowing and pawning jewels.  The Prince, I hear, forwards this business.  Col. Goring will go over.  All that I could obtain by my complaint was that the Council of State and the Admiralty should stay all officers and soldiers, but for all that he will pass by ship from some private place.  I learn that your letters and mine are opened on the way.  Heraldic seal.

[1642.]  November $\frac{3.}{13.}$  The Hague. — Walter Strickland to John Pym.  I am glad that your armies are in so good a condition.  Lady Stanhope's husband, Mr. Hanifleet was sent by the States to enquire when the ships should be ready, and the Queen returned answer on the 20th.  Most people, however, think that she will await the return of those sent over, of whom the last was Sir Frederick Cornwallis, who went to England two days ago.  Lord Goring has lately come from Amsterdam, where, I hear, he has bespoken five or six thousand muskets, which are to be paid for out of jewels sold or pawned.  These are to come with the Queen, or before.  The levy of men in Hamburgh continues, and they say that four or three thousand will soon be shipped to England.  I send the order of the States General upon my complaint of Col. Goring's coming over.  It is not so particular as I could have wished.  Some say that Prince Talmont, brother of Lady Strange, will go over with the Queen, but in what condition I know not.  General King has been here three or four days.  It is doubtful whether he will accept the employment of England, though he will be much pressed to it.  Colonel Cockram is to be here in a day or two.  Some say that he sent word that the soldiers levied by him were ready to be sent to Newcastle.  Lord Arundel came here yesterday from Flanders.  He is going away to-day.  Some say that the Catholicks contribute money to this war.  I hear that Lord Craven will shortly go to France.  Colonel Goring, Sir Henry Mackworth, and Captain Wyndham (Windam) are likely to go over.  The soldiers of most esteem here seem to be very good friends to the Parliament, as Sir Henry Herbert, Lieut.-Col. Cromwell, and Sir Ferdinando Knightly.  It is said that the magistrates of Rotterdam furnish 15,000l. sterling upon pawn of ten great pendant pearls and other jewels, and that divers other jewels of the value of 100,000l. have been offered to be pawned at Amsterdam, but that they will not raise half the money.  Mr. Henifleet, Lady Stanhope's husband, Mr. Jermyn, and Lord Goring, are used in these matters.  Heraldic seal.

[1642.] November 13. (N.S.) The Hague.—Walter Strickland to
John Pym. Since I wrote my "packet," I hear that Sir Frederick
Cornwallis has taken over some twenty commanders with him. The
wind is now contrary, but I am told that he went to sea yesterday for
Newcastle. It is said that Mr. Percy is not gone to England, but to
Germany, to the Emperor or some other princes. The Queen leaves
about the $\frac{13\text{th}}{23\text{rd}}$ Money has been raised here by means of the Prince.
Mr. Jermyn has had great sums here—some say 15,000*l.*, some say
more. It is said that Mr. Percy is to borrow 100,000*l.* I hope the
seas will be well kept. They have two troops of horse, and if they
cannot embark here, they will embark at some port in Germany.
Heraldic seal.

[1642.] November 3. Stamford Bridge.—Sir Hugh Cholmeley to
John Pym. I have this day come to Stamford Bridge, where I purpose
to quarter the few forces that I have, being scarcely 500 foot, Capt[n]
Mildmay and Alured's troops, and about 20 more horse sent to me from
the gentlemen in the country, and by me armed. I expect as many
horses "suddenly" as will make up a troop, if I had arms for them.
Mr. Sykes has brought into Hull arms which he desires to furnish for
the service of the King and Parliament, upon public faith. I desire the
Committee for the Safety of the Kingdom to give me leave to take 40
pair of pistols and as many carbines upon public faith, and that I may
complete a troop. If we had six troops of horse here, there would be
employment for them. The enemy is very strong in horse, and
especially in dragooners. They drove into the city many horses in
droves, before we came hither. Our horse are much employed in the
day in bringing provisions from the city, which is the more difficult
because we are upon the forest, six miles from the city. There is no
good quarter nearer York, and our forces, being not equal to the enemy,
lie safe here upon a river which " carryes " most of the mills that supply
the city with corn. I will make most of them unfit to grind, except
these at Stamford Bridge. I expect 200 men more within two days,
and as our forces increase I shall endeavour to draw nearer to York.
We are informed that there are 2,000 in the town, but I do not believe
the number to be so great. They use all art that may be to unite the
city to them, making bonfires for the great overthrow of the Parliament
forces, and the taking of the Lord General as a prisoner. I cannot much
confide in Capt[n] Alured. Both at Hull and since his coming to me,
he has much magnified the King's party in London, till this defeat [at
Edgehill]. I have furnished Capt[n] Alured with 100*l.* and he has not
a penny. My money slips fast away, and yet I am as careful as if it
went out of my own purse, and I am both Paymaster and Commissary
myself. I have disbursed 200*l.* in repair of the castle, mounting
ordnance, etc., but before the platforms are finished, the breaches repaired, and the castle made habitable, it will cost 200*l.* or 300*l.* more.
We found three pieces of ordnance there. If victualled, my captains
think that it may be made tenable with 300 or 400 men against any
number. I have left 100 men in the castle under Capt[n] Cowleby. We
hear of great preparations in the north. They are brisk in fortifying
at York. One Mr. Francis Thomson " owes " the castle. He had
within these two years contracted to sell it to Sir Francis Wortley
for 600*l.*, and truly I thought he would not have required more
of the Parliament, but he holds it now not a penny under 800*l.* He is
a malignant man, and, I am informed, sent a horse to the King against
the Parliament. His son, Christopher Thomson, helped to send the
ship with arms from Scarborough to Newcastle a little before my

coming, else Sir John Hotham's ketch would have met with her. It were not amiss to send for them, but I would not have it done on my information, for reasons which I cannot now express. Heraldic seal.

1642, November 4. Southampton. — John Button and Edward Hooper to John Pym. In obedience to your letters of the 1st inst., we went to-day to Southampton privately, and there conferred with the Mayor, the two Burgesses who serve for the town, and some other well affected persons. They told us that all was quiet yet, but that there are some ill affected. Yesterday a servant of Sir John Millin, who with his master came on Monday last from the King's army, gave ill language of the Lord General, for which he was committed, and since let out on bail. On Monday there was a meeting about exercising arms, at which there was some difference of opinion, but it was pacified by the care of the Mayor and Burgesses. We think it fitting, if you so please, to add to the Committee of Hampshire, Mr. Peter Seale, Mayor of Southampton, and Mr. George Gallop and Mr. Edward Exton, Burgesses for the Parliament, whom we find very vigilant and faithful. There are three companies in Southampton, whereof one is without a captain; the other two they can scarce confide in. It is therefore desired that any six of the Committee may have power to supply the place wanting, and to displace the others if there be occasion.

[1642.] November 19. N. S. The Hague.—Walter Strickland to John Pym. I am more and more confirmed that there are designs upon Harwich, Yarmouth, Hull, and Portsmouth, and that it is intended to have considerable forces at sea to beat the Parliament's ships if it be possible. A ship called the *Ralph* has come here from Newcastle; the master's name is Hudson. She belongs to one Coole of Newcastle, who has offered her to serve the Queen. It is said that she is to take in ten pieces of cannon. I have made complaint to the States General, but there is so much form in their resolutions as to make the work fruitless. Whatever is concluded one day must be read the next in the council, and then be perfected, which gives time enough for the ship to be gone. When I sought to hasten it, the Secretary, or *Greffier*, who is to despatch the order, told me that he cared not whether she were gone or not. I find him harsh in all that concerns the Parliament. I beseech you therefore be careful that a good fleet be at sea when the Queen goes over, which they say will be this day sevennight if Knowles and Skipwith come over. I hear that Sir Frederick Cornwallis is gone to London disguised. He has been a great taker-up of men. Colonel Goring, Sir Francis Mackworth, Captain Wyndham, and Captain Byron, are principal agents in the design for taking up men. I hear that General King has deserted the service, and that he will not be employed. You will hear that Hudson's ship is gone, whilst I am put off with delays. The Queen has packed up, but it is said that she will not go till this day sevennight. She has eight ships by the States, and is angry that she has no more. When the States of Holland meet in two or three days, I shall haver better expedition. I shall endeavour that their ships may not have orders to conduct men or to fight with ours. Heraldic seal.

1642, November 19. N. S. The Hague.—Walter Strickland to [John Pym ?]. I have received you letter of the 28th of October. It seems to me that the great number that fell off from the Lord General was a real demonstration that the victory was not by men but by God. I have made known to the Prince-elect what you wrote concerning him, in your own language. It satisfied him much, as he knows the worth of your person. He told me of a letter whereby he was earnestly pressed to put himself into the Queen's affairs, to go over with her, and so to go to the King. I told him that in doing so he would forfeit the opinion which he now has in the hearts of the best men, and that it might engage him in designs he knew not of, which at best must tend to ruin his interest among all Protestants in the world. He told me plainly that he was dependent on the King, but he asked whether the Parliament would preserve him in case he should not follow that way. I told him that it was not for me to judge what the Parliament had not declared, but that it was not likely that the Parliament would suffer a Prince they loved so well to be prejudiced for loving them. Let me know how far he may expect satisfaction in this particular. You may loosen him from them and fasten him to you. One way or the other, the kingdom must pay the money. He is sweet and noble, and you have an opportunity of gaining him, by making him assured of his subsistence.

The Queen is not satisfied with the small number of ships. Some think that others will meet her on the way, and make her able to do something against our fleet, or to get some place in England, Harwich, Yarmouth, Hull, or Portsmouth. Serjeant-Major Dolman was offered employment, but he would not accept it. He has been very fair since he came from England. If what we hear of the Scots' march be true, Newcastle will be no place for the Queen. I have a new order to the Admiralty concerning the *Ralph*, but I fear that she will be gone before she can be stayed. They intend " to steal into her by night " ten pieces of cannon and some powder, for they cannot have leave. No man here was more busy than Sir Frederick Cornwallis, nor more active against whatever I did for the Parliament. You will receive from me a letter which I was entreated by the States General to write on behalf of Lady Derby. They entreated me to do this office to the Parliament because their Ambassador was coming away. I could not refuse to do it, but I told them that I heard that she had deserved ill of the Parliament. You will give them a fair answer, and for doing or not doing the thing it is all one to me.

1642 [November], 19 (N. S.). The Hague.—Walter Strickland to John Pym. Concerning the *Ralph* of Newcastle, and the projects of the Queen. Heraldic seal.

1642, November $\frac{10.}{20.}$ The Hague.—Walter Strickland to John Pym. The States General have lately received a letter from England from the Countess of Derby, of which they communicated the effect to me by my Lord Vosbargen, a person of great esteem who has much obliged me. She desires the States General to mediate for her with the Parliament that her person, her children, and her house, may be secured from the dangers to which she may be exposed by her Lord's following the King's party. She gives as reasons that they should interest themselves for her that " her marrying into England was a thing communicated to them," that her grandfather lost his life in their service, and that she is nearly allied to the Prince of Orange. I told my Lord Vosbargen that some of her letters were said to show but little good affection to the Parliament, and that I knew not how far the Parliament had power to exempt any from these common dangers, but I promised to make known their desire. I beseech you to acquaint both Houses with it, and be pleased to use your power to favour it. Heraldic seal.

Same day and place.—The same to the same, " for yourselfe." I am informed that there is one Mr. Clarke, a gentleman living near Charing Cross, and having some relation to the Court, who pretends to be a friend to the Parliament only in order to be trusted. He discovers all

that he can to those here. Many here speak "desperately" against
Parliament men. An Englishman was heard to say in a passage boat
that he would kill the Lord General, the Earl of Essex. Before I
could have the order, Hudson's ship was gone, with ten pieces of ordnance and about a hundred soldiers. The Queen has packed up. Some
think that she will go to Newcastle; others to Ireland. I hear that Sir
Richard Cave, Captain Gerard, and Captain Blake are in service against
you, and that Captain Wyndham is gone over in Coole's ship [the
*Ralph*] with the ordnance and men. The States give the best
orders, but they are badly performed. I will complain. Do what you
please about Lady Derby's business; a civil answer will serve, though
it be not to expectation. I desire not to speak for malignants, but I
could not do less. Signet.

1642, November 11. Plymouth.—Alexander Carew, Francis Butler,
J. Eliot, John St. Aubyn, John Trefusis, Francis Godolphin, John
Carter, Richard Erisey, and T. Arundell, to John Pym and the rest of
the Committee for the Safety of the Kingdom. We wonder much that
our county of Cornwall should be so much neglected by you. Since
our last, Col. Ryven with some of ours were invited by the insolency
of our Cornish adversaries and their invasion of Devon to try their
mettle by falling out upon them as they lay in Milbrooke, whence on
our appearing they immediately fled, leaving to our mercy five of their
company, of whom one was a Lieutenant, with their horse and furniture.
The Sheriff of Cornwall not only continues his malignancy but gives it
new " accression." The posse comitatus is now raising a second time.
This town is doubted. Their strength is great—five or six thousand
well armed, and plentifully furnished with money by their taking up
the subsidy contribution for Ireland and the county stock. Ours is
small, which again provokes our old petition for a speedy supply,
especially of money and arms—pistols, carbines, and saddles in the
first place. Devon pretends but little, and will act less. Each pro-
crastination is dangerous to us. We dare not give our reasons. Papers
are not safe. We again implore your speedy succour.

1642, $\frac{\text{November 28.}}{\text{December 8.}}$ The Hague.—Walter Strickland to [John Pym].
I have complained to the States General, and likewise to the States
of Holland, concerning the Captains who were to come over, but
I can get no relief from either. They are to be shipped to-morrow for
Newcastle with divers soldiers. All these Captains are intended to be
Colonels. There is Colonel Goring, and Captain Byron, Sir Francis
Mackworth, Captain Flood, Captain Brett, and Wyndham who went
before in Coale's ship. I cannot hear the number of soldiers, but I
think that it is two or three hundred. I was likewise informed from
Amsterdam that twenty pieces of ordnance, with powder and other
ammunition, were shipped at Midenblick, a port in North Holland. I
gave a memorial to the States of Holland desiring that the ships might
be stayed, and I went likewise to the States that came from Amsterdam. The next morning I went to the President of the States General,
who fell out to be then Van Reade, or Rinswowd (for he is called by
both these names), one of those who was intended to be one of the
Ambassadors to England. He has always expressed himself against
the Parliament, but never so much as at this time. I offered him a
note of the ships, desiring that they might be stayed, but before he saw
it, he said that I could not prove it, and that I must tell who informed
me. Such a demand was never yet heard of, for there is no English or
Dutch merchant who dare be known to give any information for fear of
the displeasure of " great ones." I refused to tell him. I had the

MR. BOUVERIE'S information from an honest, able man from Amsterdam, where Lord
MSS Goring was making these provisions. If the Parliament will not let
them know by letter that I am not to be so used or slighted, I shall be
able to do the House no service. They should be told that you will not
pass by without resentment so many breaches of their promise. Otherwise I would have leave to come home. No discouragements ever stuck
with me whilst I was able to serve you. If I come home, it will be but
to tender myself to your commands. If I can do nothing else, I can
add one sword more to those that wait on the Lord General [Essex].
Some here think that the King of Denmark might be " sweetened." I
know not how you treat of peace at home, but all things here seem to
be carried to conclusions of war. Mr. Knowls came here from Scotland
not long since. The Queen's alteration in not going into England was
very sudden, after her ships were ready. They hope to make Newcastle able to command Yorkshire, and " be a seed-plott for greater
hopes." Some say here that two thousand soldiers are to be sent from
Hamburgh to Newcastle. If the Ambassador from Holland be not
gone away, it were fit to make him understand your sense of these
things. The President Van Reed told me that I had sent arms to the
Parliament, which I never did.

1642, December 2. (N.S.)—Protest of Walter Strickland concerning the breaches of the order of the States General against the transport
of soldiers and arms to England. (Copy. French.)

N.D. The Earl of Warwick to John Pym. I have received
your letter of the 6th inst. and have accordingly despatched Captn.
Harris with Mr. Strickland's man to Helvoetsluis, to look after Dunning
and Achelees. I will send Captn. Wheeler into the Maas. I will also
send another ship to bring away Mr. Estwick's arms from Rotterdam.
All our merchant-men are near the end of their victuals; some have
sprung leaks in this stormy weather. I have sent in several of them.
Some of our ships of his Majesty's have victuals for only twenty days.
They must go in at fourteen days, the winds being so constantly west
at this season that they may lie ten days at anchor in the Gore, before
getting a wind to carry them over the flats. A bark of Blakeney in
Norfolk has told me that divers Irish pirates are abroad, well manned,
and that they have taken a Yarmouth man and hanged all the English,
and their dogs also. None escaped but a French pilot of St. Malo.
They lie about Ushant, Conquet Road, Belle Isle, Croisic, and Nantes.
If they be not prevented, they will take many of our merchant men who
have no defence. It grieves me much that I cannot help them, or send
any of our ships to take those rogues. All our ships are out of victuals,
and none go well enough to catch them, except the *Providence* and the
*Expedition*, which might be fitted out for this service. I expect the
commands of the Houses for my stay here or my return home, for about
the 20th inst. my ship's victuals will do no more than carry her to
Chatham. If you do not make sure of Ketelby, he will give you the
slip. If his company be examined, you will find foul matter against
him. I send you enclosed the accusation of Captn Ketelby for this last
misdemeanour, as sent to me to day by my Vice-Admiral from the Gore
near Margate.

N.D. Verses " upon Sir John Suckling's hundred horse." Forty-
two lines. They begin :—
" I tell thee Jack, thou'st given the king."
They end :—
" By carding and by dice."

Sir John Suckling's Answer. Forty-two lines. They begin :—
"I tell thee fellow, what ere thou bee."
They end :—
"To venter for a crowne."

[1643.] March 14. Coventry.—John Berker, H. Mackworth, William Purefoy, and George Abbott, to the Earl of Essex, at Windsor or elsewhere. We enclose letters which we have intercepted. Our danger is the more by reason of our weakness occasioned by late disbandings of many men for want of money and supplies sent to Killingworth and Maxstoke Castles and two companies to Lichfield, which are withheld from us by the forces that lie between. We have written, according to your advice, to Lord Grey, to join with Sir John Gell, and also to Sir John to entreat the like of Sir William Brereton, " which joint power is likely the only way to amuse their designe together with your Lordship's diversion." We are assured that there are mortar pieces as well as battering ordnance intended against us. Besides this warrant for 100 horse to be raised in Warwickshire, there was another of the same to the Earl of Northampton for that shire. If we should be besieged, we should be in great defect of a commander of experience. We hear extraordinarily well of Lord Forbes, who would, we doubt not, readily undertake this employment, being now out of action. Heraldic seal—a fesse chequy between six roundles.

1646, May 9. [Somers Island, Bermuda.] — William Rener to Alexander Pym at Derby House in Westminster. Concerning his estates in Padgett Tribe and Pembroke Tribe, and the estates of Lord Say and Sir Benjamin Rudyerd. The Government is changed. Within twenty days after his arrival, the Governor called an assembly, pretending thereby to reform certain things amiss. All the ministers in the island, Mr. White, Mr. Goldinge, and Mr. Copeland, were Independents, and they had set up a Congregational church, of which most gentlemen of Council were members or favourers. The burgesses of this assembly were picked out of those who were known to be enemies to that way, and they did not suffer a Roundhead (as they term them) to be chosen. Particulars of tobacco send to England in chests of cedar.

1646. November 14. Woolavington.—James Hayward to Alexander Pym at Wilmot House near Whitehall. The payments for beds and pioneers' wages for the garrison at Bridgwater were raised by a general rate over all our parish. When such a burden is laid on our parish, you will not expect that your poor tenants should bear it all and your farms go free. Colonel Jepson quartered 50 men and 50 horses in our parish for ten days, and of them I had, for my own tenement and your farms, Major Gifford, his wife, child, and five servants and nine horses. For your farms I have craved allowance for only three men and three horses. Of a foot company I have had the ensign, his horse, his boy, and one soldier, yet I craved of you only for the ensign's diet at 5s. a week. I have thus borne a greater burden myself for my own tenement which at best was worth only 30l. a year than I craved for your farms which in good times were let for 150l. a year. A foot company of Taunton garrison is at present quartered in our parish. This will be chargeable to you. The Commissioners of water-sewers have also ordered a great sum of money to be raised in our parish for repairing a sea-wall in Huntspill. Your rate thereof is above 20s. for your farms.

1648, August 11. Mungeham.—John Sackett to Robert Hales, Captain of the troop of horse for the Lath of St. Augustine [co. Kent]. Last night I was warned to send a light horse to appear before you this morning at Bridge Hill. I am glad that you are entrusted with the command of this troop, and I hope that it will be more carefully managed than heretofore. I am not fitted to send so speedily, my house and arms being swallowed up in that general deluge which was upon us in the late unhappy tumultuous insurrection of the county. I hope that I shall not be charged with the whole furniture of a horse, man, and arms, especially at this time when the burden of quartering soldiers lies so heavy upon us, which will continue as long as the "leaguer" last, my parish being assigned for wounded men. However, I shall be content to bear proportionately with the rest of my brethren of the ministry who are free from the charge and trouble that I daily suffer. I am content to find a horse, or the man and arms. We have great difficulty in obtaining our maintenances, yet we have no abatement of our taxes. I do not envy the calling of a soldier, yet they, whose wages are double and treble to ours, are wholly free from taxes which are imposed on us.

1662, August 15. Surinam.—John Treffry to Charles Pym. We have been long in expectation of my Lord [Willoughby] who by his last told me that he would soon be ready to sail, having fully agreed with his Majesty concerning Barbados and this place. I hope that we shall see this colony wonderfully prosper by reason of the decline of Barbados, whence we daily expect sixty passengers and planters by the *Guiana*. All things are excessively dear, and the sugar so bad that it will hardly be received. Money is as fluent there as in England, and taverns take nothing else—no goods, which must occasion a decay of their old trade. The Spaniards, we understand, have bought 500 negroes from the island for ready money at high rates. Our colony is daily improving. Seven ships have already gone hence laden with sugar, specklewood, and other commodities.

Major Noel has a windmill up, and ours will be the next to be made. Every one is striving for the good of the public. Our sugar is far better, and of greater price than that of Barbados. Our noble Governor may justly bear the honour, having won every one not only to himself but also to industry. Some debauched persons have lately tried to make the world believe that he intended to poison Lieut.-Col. [Robert] Sanford. It was a plot of Sanford's. Particulars given.

1667, December 15. Barbados.—Lord Willoughby to Sir Charles Pym. "I am going to Leeward to settle things there, and I may chance try my skill in Indian-hunting. Their late barbarities have been such that they deserve no law." Heraldic seal.

1668, November 8. Antigua. William Byam to Sir Charles Pym at Hatton House, London. I have deserted our unfortunate colony of Surinam, war and pestilence having almost consumed it. As it is to revert to the Dutch, I have with great loss removed to Antigua, where I am hewing a new fortune out of the wild woods. Resettling is hard, the island being ruined by the French and the Indians. The titles of our lands are established to the satisfaction of all, and the inhabitants are more now than ever before. Heraldic seal.

1685, September 15. [London.]—William Longueville to Thomas Hales. The new Lord Lieutenant is to be over [in Ireland] next month. The Lord Keeper, North, died on Saturday at his house in Oxfordshire. Who shall succeed is not yet fixed, but Lord Jeffreys is most likely, and the Bishop of Ely [Francis Turner] has some thoughts among us. Judge Walcott of the King's Bench is dead, and the Master of the Rolls very dangerously ill. Heraldic seal.

1685, December 17. [London.]—William Longueville to Thomas Hales. Yesterday the Lord Lieutenant went on his way for St. Alban's, attended by the Lord Chancellor, the Lord Treasurer, the Dukes of Mr. Bouverie's MSS. Ormonde and Beaufort, and others. Heraldic seal.

1685[–6], January 9. [London.]—William Longueville to Thomas Hales. The Earl of Northampton is at the Countess of Conway's, and like to be married to that very rich, hunting lady. The Earl of Nottingham has been above a week married to Lord Hatton's only daughter.

1685–6, February 4. [London.]—William Longueville to Thomas Hales. There has been too much bloodshed here. You will hear of duels—the Duke of Grafton and Mr. Talbot, Vario's (Verrio's) son and another, Mr. Henry Wharton and a Lieutenant. The Earl of Northampton has at last given over Lady Conway, and come to town. Heraldic seal.

1685–6, February 23. [London.]—William Longueville to Thomas Hales. One of the first obligations I had to your Lord [Clarendon's] family was by reason of your grandfather's patent of baronetcy which was stopped. My father and I applied to Lord Clarendon, then Lord Chancellor, and I had five hundred broad pieces to present to him on the occasion, but the good old Lord told us that he would oblige us, and never had a penny. It is expected that all the baronets of the late King's time will be brought by Exchequer process to pay and plead the discharge of 1,000l. recited to be paid in the usual patents of baronet. Some quietuses or discharges will not be allowed. Sir Thomas Osborne and Sir William Temple have applied to the Lord Treasurer, and have gained stop of this process against themselves. The King will ease those who have family merit or personal merit. I have sent for your father that we may resolve what to do "under this rod." You must show all diligence for the Lord Lieutenant, "his talent being in his over-measure diligence." There has been duelling about Lord Northampton's match or no-match. If either of the wounded who are in danger—Mr. Conyers or Mr. Seymour—happen to die, the King will let the law run with severity against all the six concerned. Heraldic seal.

1686, May 8. [London.]—William Longueville to Thomas Hales. Books instruct and "gentilize a man." The Earl of Northampton is to marry Sir Stephen Fox's daughter to-morrow. The King goes to Windsor on the 14th of this month. The case of Mr. Williams as to his formerly licensing Dangerfield's Narrative comes on in the King's Bench on Tuesday. "It lookes cloudely on Mr. Williams." Sir Edward Hales is prosecuted at the suit of one Godwyn of Kent for 500l. for not taking the test as Colonel, but whether it be "a prosecution adversary," or on purpose to draw on the question of the dispensing power is doubtful. Cousin Lydcot, secretary to Lord Castlemaine, is come from Rome in fourteen or fifteen days. Our common people say that His Holiness objects to our King's titles of supremacy. Heraldic seal.

Besides the above, there is a bundle of letters to Sir Charles Pym from several persons living at Bermuda in the time of Charles II.

The following documents are on parchment:—Certificate by Thomas Gudibour, Prior of the cathedral church of Carlisle, Christopher Moresby of Highened, knight, Master John Whelpdale, Official of the Bishop of Carlisle, Master William Rea, Official of the Archdeacon of Carlisle, John Radclyff of Derwentwater, and Henry Denton of Cardue, esquires,

that Robert Lowther son of Robert Lowther, knight, died without issue
and was buried at Sebergham, that Geoffrey Lowther, brother of the
said Robert the son, also died without issue, and was buried at the same
place, that William Lowther, brother of the said Geoffrey, had issue
John, and was buried at Dalston, that the said John died and was
buried at Dalston, leaving issue Christopher who is alive and "enherit-
able," and to whom ought to belong the manors of Well and Garyngton
co. Kent, according to a fine levied in the 26th year of Henry VI.
Attestation of Richard, Bishop of Exeter.   Shap, January 8, 1498-9.
Fragments of five seals attached.

Rental of property co. Kent belonging to the Prior of Christ Church,
Canterbury, made by John Hales, Baron of the Exchequer.  35-36
Henry VIII.

Taxation of all benefices in the diocese of Canterbury.  35 Henry VIII.

Rental of Christ Church, Canterbury.  26-27 Elizabeth.

Subsidy roll of the Lath of St. Augustine, co. Kent.  33 Elizabeth.

Illuminated genealogies of the families of Engeham of co. Kent,
A.D. 1572 and 1651 ; Hales of Hales Place, A.D. 1621, with continua-
tion by Sir Isaac Heard ; and Pym of Brymore, A.D. 1583 by Dethick,
and 1643 by Ryley.

There are also at Brymore many bundles of small mediæval deeds
relating to property at Cannington and other places in the county of
Somerset.

Mr. Bouverie has kindly given me every facility for the examination
of his manuscripts.

H. C. MAXWELL LYTE.

---

## SUPPLEMENTARY REPORT ON THE MANUSCRIPTS OF
## THE LATE W. BROMLEY DAVENPORT, ESQ., M.P.

SHORTLY before his sudden death, the late Mr. Bromley Davenport
submitted for examination a number of ancient deeds from Baginton
Hall.  By his desire some of them were selected for exhibition in a
cabinet or glass case, and the remainder arranged in bundles, as
follows :—

Selected deeds :—

Confirmation by W. Giffard to William son of Hunger of his land at
Sunger (Suhanger), granting it to the use of the church of St. Mary of
Bordesley in free alms.  Witnesses :—Henry, brother of the Earl [of
Warwick], Henry the sewer, Edwin de Piru, Walter the chaplain,
Ralph the scribe, Walter son of Girard.  Fragment of equestrian seal
attached.   (12th century.)

Confirmation by William Giffard to the church of St. Mary of
Bordesley of the land of Sunger (Suhanger), for the benefit of the soul
of his lord, Roger the Earl [of Warwick], who gave it to him, and of the
souls of their respective ancestors, and for the good estate of his lord,
William the Earl [of Warwick], and Gundreda the Countess [of War-
wick] his mother, and of himself and his heirs, on condition that Richard
de Dercet and Gilbert his son, and William son of Hunger, who claim
it by hereditary right, shall release it to the said church for ever.  He
confirms also to the said church the grant of Suan Eaveth of a hide of

land at Oxhill (Occeshull). Witnesses :—Ralph, Prior of the Holy Sepulchre [at Warwick], Henry brother of the Earl [of Warwick], Robert the butler, Henry the sewer, Ralph the scribe, Walter son of Girard, Gundreda the Countess [of Warwick], Geoffrey the chamberlain, Hugh de Arden, Robert Murdac and Thomas his brother, Robert son of Odo, John de Kinton, William de Cirecester. Fragment of equestrian seal attached. (A.D. 1153–1184.)

MR B. DAVENPORT's MSS.

Confirmation by G[eoffrey] the chamberlain of Clinton of the charter of William Giffard, granting the land of William son of Hunger of Sunger (Sudhangra) to the church of St. Mary of Bordesley. Witnesses :—Robert de Crest, Roger son of William, Simon his brother, William son of Ralph de Tamworth (Tamewarda), William de Moi, William Estreche of Felcheham, Roger Bastard of Tamworth (Tamewarda), Ralph monk of Winchester, Haste the villein, the man of Robert de Crest (Haste villano homine Roberti de Crest), Engelram. (12th century.)

Confirmation by R[oger], Earl of Warwick, of the grant of William Giffard to the church of St. Mary of Bordesley, of the land of William, son of Hunger, at Sunger (Suhanger). Witnesses :—Henry his brother. Henry the sewer, Walter the chaplain, Geoffrey the chamberlain, Walter son of Girard, Edwin de Piru. Dated at Warwick (before A.D. 1154).

Grant by Walter Cumin to the church of St. Mary of Bordesley, and the monks thereof, of his land adjoining the road which leads from Sturcheneston (?) to Edston (Edricheston), for the benefit of the soul of his uncle William Cumin. Witnesses :—Jordan the chaplain of Wire, William Cumin, and twelve others named. Seal attached. Endorsed in a later hand " Confirmatio Walteri Cumin de quadam terra Suangre."

Grant by Reginald, son of Roger de Claverdon, to the church of St. Mary of Bordesley, of an acre of land at Sunger (Suhanger). Witnesses :—Robert son of William de Wolverton (Wlfardintur), William de Burle, Robert de Walefort, Alan de Bleiz, Helias the bishop. Fine seal attached.

Grant by Alan, son of Alan de Blez, to the church of St. Mary of Bordesley and the monks thereof, of fifteen ridges (seiliones) of land at Langley. Witnesses :—Peter de Wolverton (Wolwardington), and six others named. Large seal attached—device three ears of corn.

Letter in French from John de Cantelou to the Bishop of Worcester, concerning the right of John de Wolverton (Wolwardynton) to present to the church of Wolverton. A.D. 1307. Heraldic seal attached.

Grant by Gerard de Allispath of a yearly rent of 30d. in free alms, for the sustenance of two wax torches before the altar of St. Mary in the church of Allispath, and of a lamp before the altar of St. Laurence in the same. (13th century.)

Grant by John Odingsels (Oddyngsels), knight, to Robert Wolfes of Sowe, and Richard Wolfes, clerk, of the custody and marriage of Guy Breton, son and heir of John Breton, and, if he die under age, of the custody and marriage of Agnes his sister. 41 Edward III. Heraldic seal attached.

Grant by Joan, relict of William Bretoun, knight, to William de Folkeshall, chaplain, and William the clerk of Offchurch, of all the lands, etc. which she had, jointly with her late husband, of the feoffment of Nicholas de Somerton and Nicholas Salomon, chaplain, in the hamlets of Hay and Gorcote, in the parish of Studley. 6 Richard II. Heraldic seal attached.

Indenture tripartite whereby William, Abbot of Westminster, and the Convent of that place, in consideration of the sum of 300 marks paid to them by Master Walter Cook, Canon of Lincoln, and of the patronage of the chantry of the chapel of SS. John Baptist, Laurence, and Anne, lately established and built by him in the hamlet of Knowle (Knoll), co. Warwick, assign a yearly stipend of 10 marks to the chaplain for ever. August 11, 1404. Conventual seals attached.

Grant by John Shakespere of Wraxale, son and heir of Richard Shakespere, to Humphrey Blyke of Aspeley co. Salop, of a croft called Newland, in the domain of Shrewley. January 18, 7 Henry VII. Fragment of seal attached.

Certificate of Edmund, Prior of Henton, and the Convent of that place, of the admission of William Gellet, M.A., as a partaker of the prayers of that house, in life and in death. A.D. 1533. Fragment of conventual seal attached.

A bundle of twenty-nine deeds of the 12th and 13th centuries relating to property at Claverdon and Kington, in the hundred of Barlichway, co. Warwick. Among them are the following :—

Grant by Walcran, Earl of Warwick, to William de Arden, in fee, of certain lands at Claverdon, for a yearly payment of one bezant. Witnesses :—Thomas, Prior of Warwick, Nigel de Mundevill, and eleven others named. (A.D. 1184–1205.)

Grant by William de Ardern to the church of St. Mary of Bordesley, and the monks thereof, of twenty-five acres of land at Claverdon, for a yearly payment of 4s. 2d. Witnesses :—William Cumin, and four others named. Fragment of equestrian seal attached.

Release by Michael, son of William de Ardern, to the church of St. Mary of Bordesley, and the monks thereof, of the said yearly payment of 4s. 2d. Witnesses :—Nicholas the chamberlain, and seven others named. Seal attached.

Confirmation by Walter, son of Hugh de Burley, to Christiana his sister, of a messuage in the vill of Kington, in the fee of Claverdon. (13th century.)

Grant by Hugh de Burley to the Abbot and Convent of Conches, and the Prior of Wotton [Wawen], of seven ridges (sellones) of land at Claverdon. Witnesses :—Sir Simon Bagot, Sir Robert de Clopton, knights, and five others named.

Grant by Hugh de Burley to the church of St. Peter of Conches, and the monks thereof, of part of his clearing (assarti) at Claverdon. Witnesses :—Sir Peter de Wolverton (Wolvardinton), knight, Sir Robert de Clopton, knight, and four others named. Seal attached.

Grant by Hugh de Burley, son of William de Burley, to the church of St. Mary of Bordesley, and the monks thereof, of the homage and service of Julinna, niece of his wife, and a yearly rent of 1d. Seal attached.

Grant by Nicholas Curli and Juliana his wife to Henry Smith (fabro), son of John Smith, with Alice their daughter in free marriage, of a tenement called le Hoo, to be held of the Abbot of Bordesley. Witnesses :—William de Waleford, Henry de Nort, Nicholas de Curdeshale, and six others named.

Release by Nicholas, son of William de Burley, to the Abbot and monks of Bordesley, of the land which he held of them at Claverdon, adjoining the land of Hugh, son of William de Burley. Witnesses :—

Sir Peter do Wolverton (Wolwardinton), Sir Simon Bagot of Preston, knights, and four others named.

Release by William, son of John de Burley, to the church of St. Peter of Wotton [Wawen], and the monks thereof, of all his right in the land at Claverdon which they had of the gift of his uncle, Hugh de Burley, and his grandfather, William de Burley. Witnesses :—Walter de Wolverton (Wlvardinton), and eight others named. Fragment of heraldic seal attached

Confirmation by Walter, son of Hugh de Burley, of the grants of his father to the Abbot and Convent of Conches and the Prior of Wotton [Wawen].

Grant by Thomas de Colehull, son of William de Colehull of Claverdon to the Prior and canons of the Holy Sepulchre at Warwick or half an acre of land at Claverdon. Witnesses :—Nicholas de Cardeshale, and six others named.

A bundle of twenty-seven deeds of the 13th and 14th centuries relating to property at Edston (Edricheston), co. Warwick.

A bundle of four ancient deeds relating to property at Sunger, in the parish of Claverdon, co. Warwick. Among them are the following :—

Confirmation by Andrew Gyffard of the charter of his uncle William Gyffard, granting the land of Sunger (Suhanger) to the church of St. Mary of Bordesley and the monks thereof. This he confirms for the benefit of the souls of his said uncle, his own brother William, and others. Witnesses :—William Cumin, William de Curle, Peter son of Robert de Wulward, Philip the parson of Haleford, Alan de Blez, John de Burle, and others.

Agreement between W. Abbot of Bordesley and the Convent of that place, and the rector of Claverdon, concerning the tithes of Sunger (Suthanger), as made by the papal delegates. Witnesses :—Richard the chaplain of Wolverton (Wolwardington), Peter de Morbi, William de Colehull, Nicholas de Cruddeshal, Simon de Bles, Robert de Lamore. A.D. 1297.

A bundle of forty ancient deeds relating to property at Hatton co. Warwick. Among them are the following:—

Grant by William Reynfrey of Hatton to William le Porter and Giliana his wife, of half an acre of arable land with two "chikenes" adjoining, in the field of Hatton on Wodefurlong, situate between the land of the Lady Scolastica de Mewes and that of Robert le Mason 2 Edw. III. Seal attached.

Grant by John Hastanges, knight, lord of Budbrook, and Eva his wife, to William le Porter, son of Roger de Grendon, and to Juliana his wife, of three and a half acres of land with headlands (chereciis) and all other appurtenances, which William Franceys de Walda bondman (nativus) of the grantors, bought in the territory of Hatton by Haseley, of which half an acre "que est forera" lies on Asschefurlonges, half an acre on Whetefurlonges, half an acre on Wodefurlonges "cum uno chevecto," half an acre on Middelfurlonges, two half acres on Whetefurlonges, and half an acre "cum chevecto" on Benehull. 3 Edward II. Two seals.

A large bundle of ancient deeds relating to property at Shrewley, in the parish of Hatton, co. Warwick. Among them are the following :—

Demise by John de Dufford, knight, to Matilda relict of Walter de Culy, of lands, etc. which Helisencia relict of John de Shrewley (Schreveleye) formerly held in dower. 2 Edw. I.

Demise by John de Dufford, knight, to Matilda daughter and heiress of John de Shrewley (Schreveleye), of all the lands, etc. which Helisencia, relict of John de Shrewley, held in dower. 35 Edw. I.

Grant by John atte Cros of Hatton in the Woodland to John de Brokshawe and Emma his wife, daughter of the grantor, in free marriage, of a messuage in Shrewley " cum octo chevectis et duabus selionibus terre cum foreris, haiis, et fossatis ad so spectantibus cum suis pertinentibus," which he had of the gift of the said John. 7 Edw. III.

Grant by John de Meaux, knight, to William de Filylod and Nicholas his brother, of lands in Shrewley, Hatton, and Haseley. 30 Edw III.

Release by Matilda de Culi, widow, to William de Fililed, son of Roger de Fililod, and Nicholas his brother and heir, of a rent in Shrewley, Hatton, and Rowington. 30 Edw. III.

Release by Agnes Warde of Shrewley, daughter and heiress of John Warde and Magota his wife, to John her son, of all her right in lands, etc., which came to her after the death of her said parents. 12 Hen. IV.

Among other persons named in deeds in this bundle are the following:—Sir John de Thacham, called also Sir John Draper, vicar of Rowington (27 Edw. III.), Sir Gilbert de Lokkesleye, chaplain of the parish of Hatton (7 and 20 Edw. III.), Richard Shakespere of the parish of Wraxale (5 Hen. VII.), and John Shakespere of Wraxale, son and heir of Richard Shakespere. (7 Hen. VII.)

A large bundle of ancient deeds relating to property at Haseley.

A bundle of twelve deeds of the 13th and 14th centuries, relating to property at Wolverton, co. Warwick. Among them is the following:—

Grant by Michael son of Robert de Wolverton (Wolwardington) to William son of Richard Geri of Bearley (Burleg), in free marriage with Florence his daughter, of the service and homage of Simon de la Hulle of Wolverton (Wolwardington). Witnesses:—Sir Elias Giffard, Gilbert his brother, Sir Robert de Clopton, Sir Peter [de Wolwardington], knights, and three others named.

Among other persons named in deeds in this bundle are the following:—Sir Peter de Wolverton (Wolwardington) and Alina his wife, Peter son of Walter de Wolverton (Wolwardington), William de Brome, lord of Wolverton (31 Edw. III.), and William Bruton, knight, lord of Wolverton (45 Edw. III.).

A bundle of fourteen deeds of the 13th, 14th, and 15th centuries, relating to property at Langdon and Knowle, in the parish of Solihull, co. Warwick.

A bundle of three ancient deeds relating to property at Harborough Magna, co. Warwick.

A bundle of three ancient deeds relating to property at Long Itchington, co. Warwick. In each of them mention is made of Guy le Bretoun of Wolrichestone and Joan his wife (11, 12, and 16 Edw. II.).

A bundle of ancient deeds relating to property at Coventry. Among them are the following:—

Grant by John Smythier of Coventry and Robert Litelman of the same, to John Wyseman of Hurst, co. Warwick, of a yearly rent at

MR. B.
DAVENPORT'S
MSS.

Christmas of a tunic of the value of 3*s.*, a pair of hose of the value of 8*d.*, a pair of shoes of the value of 6*d.*, and linen of the value of 7*d.*, during his life. Witnesses :—Sir William Bagot, knight, John Wychard, esq., John Wizteladdo, and others. Dated at Baginton (Bakyndon) 5 Kalends July, 8 Ric. II.

Demise by Master Nicholas Gore, chaplain of the chantry of Laurence Shepey at the altar of St. Laurence in the church of St. Michael at Coventry, by consent of Sir Richard Notyngham, Prior of the cathedral church of St. Mary at Coventry, patron of the same, to Thomas Stone of Coventry, and Alice his wife, of a tenement in Gosford Street, extending from the highway to the ditch newly made. 43 Hen. VI.

Most of the others relate to tenements in Spon Street. In one of them mention is made of John Atte Welle, vicar of the church of Hampton in Arden (10 Ric. II.).

A bundle of ten ancient deeds relating to property at Langley, in the parish of Claverdon, co. Warwick. Among them is a grant by John de Twiford, Abbot of Bordesley, and the Convent of that place, to Gregory de la Hulle of Edston (Edricheston) and Matilda his wife, for their ives, of a tenement called Birch hurste, at Langley (Longgele), situate on the highway leading from Kington to Langley. Dated Thursday after Trinity Sunday, 1301.

A small bundle of ancient deeds relating to property at Studley.

A bundle of ancient deeds relating to property at Gorcote, near Studley co. Warwick. Among the persons mentioned are the following :—Richard son of Robert son of William de Wolverton (Wolwardington), Emma daughter of Rondulf le Harpur of Studley, relict of Henry de Burley, William Bretoun, knight, and Joan his wife. (48 Edw. III.)

A bundle of four ancient deeds relating to property at Moreton.

A bundle of miscellaneous ancient deeds. Among them are the following :—

Grant by Thomas Breton, son and heir of Guy Breton of Merston, to Sir Ralph Basset of Sapecote, knight, William de Catesby, William Breton, his brother, and Sir John de Bylneye, rector of the church of Hickeford, of all his lands at Merston, Wolston (Wolvericheston), Itchington, Bascote, and elsewhere, co. Warwick. 26 Edw. III.

Demise by Thomas Yonge, Dean of the collegiate church of St. Mary at Warwick, and the chapter of that place, to Robert Huggeford and Joyce his wife, of all their lands, etc., in Mulverton, for 100*s.* yearly. 10 Henry IV. Two seals attached.

H. C. MAXWELL LYTE.

## THE MANUSCRIPTS OF LORD BRAYE, AT STANFORD HALL, RUGBY.

LORD BRAYE'S
MSS.

THE manuscripts mentioned in the following pages have been found at different times within the last few years stowed away in no order in one of the lumber rooms at Stanford Hall. Since the date of my first visit to his house, Lord Braye has caused many of them to be arranged and bound in volumes. The collection may be said to consist of four parts, the Browne MSS., the Cave MSS., the Peck MSS., and the Stuart MSS., although this arrangement has not been observed in the calendar.

The Browne MSS. belonged formerly to John Browne, of Twickenham and of Eydon, co. Northampton, who was clerk of the Parliament during a great part of the seventeenth century. For some unknown reason, he retained for himself and his descendants a certain number of the official documents that passed through his hands, instead of depositing them among the archives of the House of Lords. Many of them were indeed transcribed by him into the Journals of that assembly, which have since been printed, but some interest attaches to the autographs. At Stanford are preserved various depositions and examinations with regard to the Earl of Strafford, Lord Digby's anonymous letter to Sir Lewis Dyves, which was produced as evidence against him, Sir John Hotham's letters to the Speaker of the House of Commons, concerning the King's attempt to enter Hull, the original of the Westminster Confession of Faith, the intercepted letter from the young Duke of York making arrangements for an escape from England, and various drafts and memoranda in the hands of Littleton, Williams, Pym, and other Parliamentary leaders of the time of Charles I. Many of the documents, however, have not been entered in the Lord's Journals, or otherwise printed. The first in point of date is an account of proceedings in the House of Commons in 1572. Soon after it come a number of letters to and from Laud, Bishop of London, concerning the mission of John Durye to the Continent for the purpose of effecting an union between the Lutherans and the Calvinists, between the years 1632 and 1636. The rest of the correspondence is still preserved in the House of Lords, as stated in the third Report of this Commission, and there is no evident reason for this separation of the papers. Under the date of October 1640 Lord Braye has a copy of a letter from York, giving particulars as to the negotiations then proceeding in the north of England. He has also a number of papers, some of which have not been printed, concerning negotiations between the English and Scottish Commissioners. A holograph petition from the Earl of Strafford, quoting precedents against the Bill of Attainder, although stated to have been read on the 5th of May 1641, does not appear in the Lords' Journals under that date. An original letter from Major Thomas Wade to Harbottle Grimston, written at Colchester in August 1642, gives a contemporary narrative of the attack on the residence of Sir John Lucas. Another letter, not original, furnishes an account of the siege of Sherborne in the following month. Particulars of the siege of Lyme Regis are given in copies of Col. Were's Journal and a letter from the Earl of Warwick. A series of elaborate notes taken from day to day during the trial of Archbishop Laud differ from the reports published by Prynne and Heylin. A letter from Sir H.

Cholmeley, Governor of Scarborough Castle, to Sir J. Meldrum, and the answer to it, are curious specimens of the controversial style of the time. The Historical MSS. Commission has more than once directed attention to the secret correspondence between Charles I. and Henrietta Maria, of which a portion only was published by the Parliament after the capture of the King's cabinet at Naseby. John Browne took copies of at least five of the letters from the King, and one of these has never been printed before. It is dated at Oxford on the 17th of April 1645, and it expresses hopes of military success and warm approval of the measures taken by the Queen. A long letter addressed to the English Parliament, in September 1645, states the views of the Scottish Commissioners upon the state of public affairs. A series of private letters from Thomas Margetts to John Browne gives many interesting details about the proceedings of Cromwell and Lambert in the north of England and their reception in Scotland in the autumn of 1648. The Browne MSS. of the time of Charles II. are not so important as those of the earlier period, but among them there are, a curious account of the death and funeral of Philip IV. of Spain, and narratives of naval actions between the English and the Dutch. The draft Journals of the House of Lords kept by Browne. after the Restoration do not supply so much information omitted from the formal Journals as those kept by him during the reign of Charles I. and those kept by his predecessor, Henry Elsynge, during the reign of James I., all of which are preserved at Stanford Hall.

The Cave MSS. consist chiefly of deeds and other legal documents, the earliest of which relates to the manor of Stanford in the 12th century. There is, however, among them a volume containing transcripts of letters concerning the military organisation of Northamptonshire in the early part of the reign of Charles I. Two letters from Rowland Berkeley to his father-in-law, Sir Thomas Cave, give contemporary particulars of the battle of Worcester, and some later letters contain notices of the battle of Oudenarde and the riots in London in 1710. Several bundles of letters and papers relate to Parliamentary elections in Leicestershire in the eighteenth century, and to the publication of Bridge's "*History of Northamptonshire.*" It is probable that some heraldic MSS. by William Burton, the historian of Leicestershire, and Robert Cooke, Clarencieux King of Arms, were acquired in the middle of the eighteenth century by Sir Thomas Cave of Stanford, who was much interested in antiquarian researches.

Sir Thomas Cave was certainly the purchaser of the manuscripts of Francis Peck, the author of the "*Annals of Stamford,*" and other historical works. They consist almost exclusively of transcripts, a holograph letter of Charles I. being perhaps the only exception. Peck made collections for a history of Grantham, a history of Lincolnshire, and other works. He also procured from his friend Dr. Zachary Grey a number of transcripts from the manuscript collections of Dr. John Nalson which were formerly in the possession of Dr. Philip Williams of St. John's College, Cambridge. Many of these transcripts are printed in Peck's "*Desiderata Curiosa,*" and some while ago, I made a calendar of the rest for the present report. As, however, I have since been so fortunate as to find the volumes of Nalson's collections, all of which had disappeared, in the house of another nobleman, I have kept back this calendar for collation with the original MSS., and probably for considerable enlargement. The only Peck MSS. noticed at any great length in the present report are copies of a number of

LORD BRAYE'S MSS. letters to and from John Mordaunt with regard to the royalist plots for the restoration of the House of Stuart to the throne. They supplement the correspondence printed in the "*Clarendon State Papers.*"

The Stuart MSS. now at Stanford Hall seem to have been overlooked a few years ago, when the late Miss Otway Cave presented to the British Museum the voluminous diaries and correspondence of Cardinal York, which had been purchased by her mother, Baroness Braye, at Rome in 1842, together with a number of portraits and other relics of the exiled house of Stuart. They have been arranged in chronological order, and bound in three volumes. Among them are two long narratives of the adventurous journey of the Princess Clementina Sobieski before her marriage to the Old Pretender, copies of letters relating to their subsequent separation, and many documents concerning the property of the Sobieski family, and the crown jewels of Poland. There are also many papers of Prince Charles Edward concerning his marriage, the reception of his wife at Rome, and the status of his illegitimate daughter. The correspondence of Cardinal York in the third volume relates chiefly to business, but it illustrates the relations that subsisted between him and the House of Hanover. Those of his effects which were not bought by Baroness Braye in 1842, were bought at the same time by the late Mr. Balfour of Townley Hall, where they are still preserved.

The Calendar of the Stuart Papers, and a great part of the remainder of the calendar of Lord Braye's Manuscripts has been drawn up by Mr. F. H. Blackburne Daniell.

I am also indebted to Dr. Stainer for assistance with regard to the old music. Lord Braye has himself afforded every facility for the examination of his manuscripts.

H. C. MAXWELL LYTE.

A great number of documents, ancient and modern, relating to the Cave family, and the parish of Stanford. One of them dates from the 12th century :—

Notification by R. Foliot to the Bishop of Lincoln, the Archdeacon of Northampton, and all men, that he has granted to the Church of St. German of Selby. (Salebi) and the monks thereof the manor of Stanfort, as he had it of Wido de Raimecurt or Richard, his son, and free from 4*l.* which Turstin Banastre claimed. Witnesses :— Richard de Curci, William de Curci the nephew (Willelmo nepote de Curci), and Master Peter his clerk, Henry de Otrincheam and Nicholas and Æbald his brothers, Jordan Fitz-Reiner Fitz-Count, and nine others named. Endorsed :—"Roberti Foliot de Stanford."

Grant by Elizabeth Vyell, daughter and heiress of Henry Vyell, late burgess of Bristol, to John Sutton, her cousin, son and heir of Henry Sutton, son of Thomas Sutton, burgess of Bristol, of her late father's lands in the counties of Northampton and Leicester, viz., at Swinford, Yelvertoft, Iseham, and Welton, mentioning her mother Agnes, wife of Thomas Burford. 22 Ric. II. Two seals, one that of the Town of Bristol.

A bundle of ancient deeds relating to property at Great Oakley, Little Oakley, and Geddington, co. Northampton. Among them are the following :—

Grant by William Argent, by consent of Sara, his daughter and heiress, to Alice daughter of Agnes his wife, of a messuage in his court (curia) in Oakley (Ocle) adjoining the house which the monks of Pipewell hold of him. Witnesses :—Seyr the parson of Childle, William de St. Maur, Alberic de Ocle, and four others named. Seal.  LORD BRAYE'S MSS.

Grant by John de Houby to Robert de Oseville, of a fourth part of the manor of Little Oakley, which he had of the grant of Matilda de Houby his mother. 13 Edw. II. Seal.

Grant by John Giffard of Cotterstock (Cotherstoke), clerk, to John Giffard his nephew and Isabel his wife, of a fourth part of the manor of Little Oakley and certain services in the vill of Newton, with successive remainders in tail to John Fitz-William of Lyveden, Ellen, niece of the grantor, and Joan and Joan (sic) sisters of Sir Luke Giffard, Rector of Cotterstock, 17 Edw. II. Two heraldic seals.

Settlement of the manor of Little Oakley and the advowson of the church on John Filiol, knight, and Margery his wife, and on Richard and John, sons of the said John, in tail. 5 Edw. III.

Release by Walter de Houby, knight, to Isabel, relict of John Giffard of Oakley, and William his son, of all his right in a fourth part of the manor of Little Oakley. Witnesses :—Sir John Engaine, Sir Simon de Drayton, knights, and seven others named. 9 Edw. III. Five heraldic and five other seals.

Release by John, son and heir of Roger Giffard, of Cotterstock, cousin and heir of John Giffard, lord of Cotterstock, clerk, to Henry Mulso of Geddington, of all his right in a fourth part of the manor of Little Oakley, with certain services in Great Newton. 35 Edw. III. Seal.

Grant by Henry de Geytington, clerk, and John Basset of Rushden (Rushenden), chaplain, to William Purly, of Oakley and Matilda his wife, of the fourth part of the manor of Little Oakley, called " Gyffards' place," which they had of the grant of Henry Mulsho. 42 Edw. III. Seal.

Grant by John Basset and Henry Drayton to Richard Erchebaud and Matilda his wife, for life, of the manor of Little Oakley and the advowson of the church, which they had of the grant of William Pirly, with remainder to Peter son and heir of William Pirly and the heirs of his body, and to William brother of the said Peter and the heirs of his body, and to the heirs of the bodies of the said Richard Erchebaud and Matilda his wife. 49 Edw. III.

A box containing six volumes of registers of the baptisms, marriages, and burials, in the following parishes, &c.—

Stanford, co. Northampton. A.D. 1607–1668.
Swinford, co. Leicester.     A.D. 1559–1632.
    „          „             A.D. 1706–1741.
Claybrook, co. Leicester.    A.D. 1563–1636.
    „          „             A.D. 1637–1664.
    „          „             A.D. 1664–1685.

A large roll of parchment containing copies of deeds of the fourteenth century relating to property at Northampton, Cotes, Hardingstone, Wotton, and Coddington.

A bundle of eleven ancient deeds relating to property at East Greenwich.

A bundle of ancient deeds relating to property at Inworth, Wolscote, Pillesgate, Bernack, Oudeby, Berugh, Tybynton, Rowley, Catthorpe,

LORD BRAYE'S MSS.

Ellesborough alias Eselborough, Olton, Keton, and Stornsworth, in various counties.

Subsidy Roll for the western division of the county of Northampton, A.D. 1628.

A bundle of letters and papers relating to Parliamentary elections in Leicestershire. A.D., 1710, 1714, 1716, 1741, 1762, 1768, 1774, 1775, 1790, and 1818.

A bundle of letters and papers relating the publication of Bridge's *History of Northamptonshire*. A.D. 1754–1768.

A volume of 22 leaves of paper (11½ × 8½ in.) in an old leather cover. It contains a curious account of Philip the Good and Charles the Bold, Dukes of Burgundy. The first part is headed :—"Sensuit en brief la declaracion de tous les haulx fais et glorieuses aventures de duc Phelippe de Burgoingne, cellui qui se nomme le duc et le grant lyon." The second part is headed :—"Icy apres que lacteur a fait mencion du pere mort ensemble parle du filz vivant, et commence en son regne." (Printed in *Œuvres historiques inédites de Sire George Chastellain*, 1837, pp. 502–511.) At the beginning and at the end of the volume are some verses in old French.

An oblong volume of 57 leaves of paper (6 × 8½ in.) newly bound in red, and lettered "Common-place Book." It contains music of the sixteenth century by, or in the style of, John Dowland. The following are the names of some of the pieces :—"The Kinge's Pavane," "A fancye of Francys Myllayne," "O God that art my ryghtuusnes," "The base of Spayne," "Fantazia Frauncis de Myllayne," "Marke Antonys Gallyarde," "Pardye, I sayde not soe," "Care who so wyll," "Philips song," "If care do men cause crye," "The hedgynge hay," "On wynters just retorne," "Quando claro, quando claro." Most of the pieces are dances, as pavans, galliards, a "saltrello," and the "antike." It appears that the first, or highest, string of the lute was tuned to E, the second to B, the third to F sharp, the fourth to D, the fifth to A, and the sixth, or lowest to E. The volume contains also verses of the sixteenth century, and recipes for cookery, a "remedy agaynst bytynge of a mad dogge or mad man," and other specifics.

An oblong volume of 89 leaves of paper (5½ in. × 7¾ in.) containing music transcribed at different dates. Among the earlier pieces are "The Queue's galliard," "Jhonsones paven," "Spannesche paven," "Allisuns galleard," "Robert Sprignell," "Pavan, Holborn," "Allysons Gal[iard] per Ro[bert] Spr[ignell]," "Gal[iard] Collyard per Ro[bert] Spr[ignell]," "Dowland, per Ro[bert] Sp[riguell]," "Cydippe, pav[an] per Ro[bert] Spr[ignell]," "Mr. Allisons Sharp pa[van] by Rob[ert] Sprig[nell]," "Doulandes Galliarde," "Ro[bert] Prime," "The L[ord] Souch (Zouche) his march," "Monsirs Almain," "Gal[iard] by Tho[mas] Sturgin."
Among the pieces in a later hand are "Phantazia, Thomas Robinson," "Moll Peddio," "The Queen's Coridon," "Wilsons wilde," "Tantara, or Lesbleys March," "Mr. Mulloynes Coranto," "Mr. Mulloyns antick saraband," "Bow bells," "An Almaine by Captaine Winn," "An Allmaine by Mr. Robinson," "Coranto by Captaine Winne," "Mr. William Lawes Elizium or faire Phidelia," "When the K[ing] enjoyes

his own again," "The L[ord] Chamberlaines maske," "Colonel Gerrards mistresse."

The book bears the name of Matthew Otley.

A small quarto volume of 109 leaves of paper, newly bound, and lettered—"Heraldic Notes. W. Burton." It contains tricks of several hundred shields, made by William Burton, the historian of Leicestershire. The following are the chief contents :—

f. 9. Arms of Lord Mayors of London in the fifteenth and sixteenth centuries.

f. 22. Arms of colleges at Oxford and Cambridge.

f. 45. Arms of German princes and nobles.

f. 50. Arms of English heralds in the sixteenth and seventeenth centuries.

f. 53. Arms of gentle families co. Leicester.

f. 63. List of English officers at the seige of Terouenne, with the badges of their respective standards. A.D. 1513.

f. 65. Arms of gentle families co. Stafford. A.D. 1583.

f. 68. Arms in the windows in the hall of Serjeants' Inn, London. A.D. 1599.

f. 71. Account of the coronation of James I. by H. Repingdon of the Inner Temple, who was present.

ff. 19, 41, 75. Arms of noble and gentle families in Ireland.

f. 81. Copy of a roll of arms of the time of Henry VI., beginning with Waterton and ending with Ralph Blaklow.

f. 86. Copy of a roll of arms of noble and gentle families in the county palatine of Chester in the time of Edward III., beginning with the Earl of Chester, and ending with Redley.

f. 89. Arms of noble and gentle families co. York. A.D. 1616.

f. 97. Arms of gentle families county Warwick, at a visitation taken in 1619.

f. 102. Arms of gentle families co. Lincoln.

f. 105. List of noblemen and gentlemen co. Lincoln. A.D. 1617.

f. 107. Extracts from the roll of John Rous of Warwick.

f. 129. Arms of gentle families co. Kent, about A.D. 1593.

f. 139. Arms of Scottish lords.

f. 141. Lists of Sheriffs of the counties of Stafford, Northampton, Salop, and York.

f. 194. Arms of gentle families co. Warwick.

The references given are according to the old pagination, which is unfortunately interrupted in places by the absence of several pages. Interspersed among the above contents are tricks of shields that were to be seen in many private houses in the reigns of Elizabeth and James I., as at Solihull, Shuckburgh, Meriden, Wolston, Edgbaston, Tanworth, Balsall, Haseley, Hillmorton, Whitley, Packwood, Castle Bromwich, Baginton, Arbury, and Elmdon, co. Warwick, Fawsley, Winwick, Horton, Newton, and Weston Favell, co. Northampton, Belgrave and Drayton, co. Leicester, Willesby and Foremark, co. Derby, Rotherfield and Tisted, co. Southampton. There are also notes taken in the churches of Higham Ferrers, Newton, Pitsford, and Easton Maudit, co. Northampton. Inasmuch as many of the shields tricked have impalements and quarterings, this volume would repay careful examination. It has a good index of names of families.

A folio volume bound in brown leather, containing pedigrees of different families in the counties of Buckingham and Stafford, with their arms tricked. Some of the pedigrees end with the year 1583 ;

others are brought down to the year 1605 in the same hand. The book seems to have been written by, or for, Robert Cooke, Clarencieux King of Arms. The following is a list of the pedigrees in the order in which they occur:—Lechingham, Hawtrey, Brudenell, Pigott, Belson, Wachell, Redman, Kingston, Cheney, Rufford, Lovett, Clarke, Norwood, Fowler, Collys, Pigott, Brightwell, West, Clanor, Foster, Longville, Ap-Rice, Ardes, Annesley, Fitz-Hugh, Chetwood, Bullock, Riseley, Porter, Purefoy, More, Mordant, Dormer, Sankey, Packington, Walweyn, Pigott, East, Duncombe, Wallinger, Meredith, Duncombe, Tyrill, Read, Riseley, Gedney, Temple, Woodford, Eyre, Puttman, Hawtrey, Brightinge, Jones, Bedenger, Woodward, Rookes, Hampden, Ruthall, Pigott, Packington, Hampden, Sandys, De Verdun, Arblaster, Wells, Hill, Endesore, Leigh, Grosvenor, Harper, Mowlisley, Whorewood, Leveson, Giffard, Broxton, Wrotesley, Colyar, Wirley, and Skrimsheire.

A thin folio volume of genealogical collections relating to the family of Temple down to the year 1702. It also contains pedigrees of the families of Beaufor, Grey, Spencer, Sandys, and Leveson, with trickings of their arms.

A small folio volume of 21 leaves of paper. It contains:—

f. 3. "Instructions for our cozen the Earl of Essex and the Lord Howard, our High Admirall, how to use themselves for execution of the commission given to them by us for some service to be done against the common enimie. Dated at Greenwich the 15th of May in the 38th yeare of our raigne, 1596."

f. 7. A paper beginning:—"There are two questions proposed. The first is if the government of a stranger be more to be desired than that of a home borne Prince."

f. 15. "An Epistle dedicatory of the Lord Henry Howarde in the beginning of a booke called, The Exhortations of Charles the fifth to his son King Phillipp, uppon the yielding up the goverment of his dominions to him. Translated out of the Spanish by the said Lord, and dedicated to her Majestie as followeth."

f. 20. A treatise "Of the five periods of 500 yeares through the course of our Englishe History from Brute to Queen Elizabeth."

A white volume entitled:—"A survaye made of the Castles, Fortes, Blockhouses and Platformes placed on eather side of Thames and Medway, and also of the Castles and Fortes with all their Fortifications along the Coastes of Kent, Sussex, Hampshire, and so onwards on the South Coast westward to the Land's End, including the Fortes of Cornwell, by Sir Richard Morrison, knight, Lieutenant of his Majestis Ordenaunce, Sir John Ogle, knight and Coronell, and Sir John Kay, knight, Surveyor of his Majesties said Ordnaunce, by vertue of certain instructions from the Lords of his Highnes most honourable Pryvie Councell, date 30th July, 1623."

Another white volume entitled:—"A survey in pursuite of his Majesties instructions, by Mountjoy, Earle of Newporte, Master Generall of his Majesties Ordnance, assisted by Alexander Hambleton, Collonell, and Francis Coningesby, Esquire; Surveyor of his Majesties Ordnance, of divers of his Majesties Castles and Fortes." Signed by them, and dated January 14, 1636.

A folio volume of 71 leaves of paper, newly bound, and lettered— "Historical Memoirs." It contains:—

f. 2. Life of Henry Stafford, second Duke of Buckingham.

f. 17.   Life of Edward Stafford, third Duke of Buckingham.     LORD BRAYE'S
f. 28.   "A discourse of passages between the Earl of Essex, Somer-     MSS.
sett, Northampton, the Countesse of Essex, Sir Thomas Overbury,
[and] otheres, with their risings [and] falls, togecher with diveres
otheres affayres as they occurred durcinge the late rayne of K[ing]
James, and also of the Duke of Buckingham, his first coming into
favour."

A folio volume containing transcripts of letters of the time of James
I. and Charles I.   The following are given, but not in chronological
order.
   (f. 43.)  May 31, 1620.  The Council to the Lord Lieutenant of
Northamptonshire.  Orders for a muster.  The beacons to be kept in
good repair.
   (f. 44.)  The Lord Lieutenant of Northamptonshire to his Deputy
Lieutenants.  Orders for a muster at Kettering on the 10th of August.
   (f. 47.)  June 11, 1623.  Whitehall.  The Council to the Lord
Lieutenant of Northamptonshire.  Orders for a muster.
   (f. 3.)  December 23, 1623.  Whitehall.  The Council to the
justices of the peace in Northamptonshire.  Orders for the strict
execution of the statute of Winchester concerning watches and wards,
and the statutes against rogues and vagabonds, and those concerning
" osteryes " (inns), alehouses, and drunkards.  Able-bodied watchmen
to be appointed in all towns and villages.  Search to be made at least
once a month for suspicious persons, rogues, and idlers.  The houses of
correction to be examined.  The price of corn being high in the
northern and western parts of the realm, all such alehouses as are not
needful are to be suppressed.
   (f. 49.)  December 31, 1623.  Hampton Court.  The Council to
the Lord Lieutenant of Northamptonshire.  Orders that the trained
bands be kept up to their full number as in past times.
   (f. 25.)  June 13, 1624.  Whitehall.  The Council to the
Lord Lieutenant of Northamptonshire.  The King has concluded a
treaty with the United Provinces, and consented to the raising of 6,000
voluntary soldiers for their defence against the Emperor and the Roman
Catholic league.  Assistance is to be given to the Earls of Oxford,
Southampton, and Essex, and Lord Willoughby, the Colonels deputed
by the ambassadors of the States.  The country will doubtless be " dis-
burthened " of many unnecessary persons who have no employment and
live lewdly and unprofitably.  Any persons who, after receiving " im-
presse money," run away from their captains or conductors, are to be
apprehended.
   (f. 29.)  October 29, 1624.  Royston.  The King to the Earl of
Exeter, Lieutenant of Northamptonshire.  Warrant for the impressment
of able men to serve in the war for the recovery of the Palatinate.
   (f. 30.)  October 31, 1624.  Whitehall.  The Council to the same.
Instructions as to the levy of three hundred men in the county of
Northampton.  They are to be of able bodies, and fit for employment,
but none of them are to be taken from the trained bands.  They are to
be in readiness at an hour's warning by or before the last of November,
to march from the place of levy to the port of Dover.  In respect of the
diversity of their habitations it is uncertain what amount of conduct-
money will be required to take them to the sea-side, the accustomed
rate being ½d. a mile.  The soldiers are therefore to receive their
ordinary pay of 8d. a day from the time of their assembly.  They will
be expected to march not less than twelve miles a day.

(f. 31.) November 2, 1624. St. Leonard's near Newark. The Earl of Exeter to his Deputy Lieutenants in the county of Northampton. He sends copies of the two preceding letters.

(f. 32.) November 3, 1624. Whitehall. G. Carew and four others, to the collectors of the subsidy in the county of Northampton. Order for the payment of money for three hundred foot-men at the rate of 8d. a piece per diem.

(f. 10.) November 30, 1624. Whitehall. The Council to the Lord Lieutenant of Northamptonshire. The King has given permission to the Earl of Lincoln to raise a troop of horse of three hundred voluntaries to serve in the expedition under Count Mansfield.

(f. 13.) December 7, 1624. St. Leonard's near Newark. The Earl of Exeter to his Deputy Lieutenants in the county of Northampton. He sends a copy of a letter from the Council. The Earl of Lincoln is thirsting for employment.

(f. 27.) May 5, 1625. Westminster. The King to the Lord Lieutenant of Northamptonshire. Warrant for the impressment of two hundred able men to serve in the war on behalf of the King's sister.

(f. 5.) May 6, 1625. Whitehall. The Council to the Lord Lieutenant of Northamptonshire. Instructions as to the levy of two hundred foot-soldiers in the county of Northampton. The place of their rendezvous to be at Plymouth on the 20th instant.

(f. 7.) May 6, 1625. St. John's. The Earl of Exeter to his Deputy Lieutenants in the county of Northampton. He sends a copy of the letter from the Council.

(f. 14.) May 13, 1625. London. The Earl of Exeter to ———. He enjoins obedience to the orders of the Council, especially on the part of the clergy who are " exceedingly refractory in his majesty's service." He orders musters at Northampton on the 8th of June, and at Kettering on the following day.

(f. 28.) August 13, 1625. Woodstock. The King to the Lord Lieutenant of Northamptonshire. Order concerning the militia.

(f. 9.) August 23, 1625. Beaulieu. The King to the Lord Lieutenant of Northamptonshire. Warrant for the levy of a hundred able men to supply the places of some who were dead, or discharged from Plymouth.

(f. 8.) August 23, 1625. Southampton. The Council to the same. On the same subject.

f. 37.) September 7, 1625. The Earl of Exeter to his Deputy Lieutenants in the western division of Northamptonshire. On the same subject.

(f. 45.) Lord Burghersh and seven other Deputy Lieutenants of Northamptonshire to their Lord Lieutenant. They have made a list of the persons whom they believe able to lend money for the King's service. Most of the chief gentry and men of quality live at the height of their means, spending a great part thereof in his Majesty's service. Many are already in debt. If they wished to borrow in order to lend they would not know how to get money, it being dangerous to have access to the city where the bankers are. Those of the inferior sort have been much weakened by the many frequent payments with which they have been charged, and also by the present stoppage of trade and commerce occasioned by the hand of God in the City of London and other places. A subsidy moreover is now being collected, and another is shortly to be raised. The sum that could be raised by loan would not be worthy of acceptance. Further directions in the matter are desired.

(f. 22.) October 24, 1625. Newark. The Earl of Exeter to his LORD BRAYE'S MSS. Deputy Lieutenants in the western division of the county of Northampton. He has received from them certificates of fit persons for privy seals. Their division is as large as the eastern, yet they are short by 300*l.* If they cannot amend this, they are to send him the subsidy-book. The sum to be lent in the eastern division amounts to 735*l.* To certify ciphers for figures will subject them and him to a sharp rebuke.

(f. 16.) January 13, 1625[-26]. Newark. The Earl of Exeter to his Deputy Lieutenants in the county of Northampton. He sends a letter which he has received from the Council, accompanied by two books of instructions about musters and arms. These are to be sent from one Deputy Lieutenant to another, and finally brought to him at Burghley.

(f. 1.) February 28, 1625[-26.] Whitehall. The Council to the Commissioners for the subsidy in the county of Northampton. They complain that whereas the subsidy in that country in the first year of Elizabeth yielded 1,615*l.* 11*s.* 11*d.*, that in the eighteenth of King James yielded only 897*l.* 14*s.* 6*d.* They are therefore to raise the assessment, beginning with themselves.

(ff. 40 and 56*b.*) May 21, 1626. Whitehall. The Council to the Lord Lieutenant of Northamptonshire. Orders for a muster of all the trained bands.

(f. 53.) May 24, 1624. Westminster. The King to the Council. (See Domestic State Papers, xxvii. 52.)

(f. 56.) June 11, 1626. Whitehall. The Council to the Lord Lieutenant of Northamptonshire. (See a similar letter in Domestic State Papers, xix. 70.)

(f. 56.) June 19, 1626. London. The Earl of Exeter to [his Deputy Lieutenants in the County of Northampton]. He sends copies of letters from the King and the Council.

(f. 56*b.*) Same day and place. The same to the same. Stringent orders for a muster of foot and horse on the 7th of September.

(f. 51.) July 7, 1626. Westminster. The King to the Justices of the peace in the county of Northampton. (See Domestic State Papers, xxxi. 30.)

(f. 52.) The same to the same. (See Domestic State Papers, xxxi. 31.)

(f. 54.) July 10, 1626. Whitehall. The Council to the Lord Lieutenant of Northamptonshire. The great and threatening preparations made in Spain and Flanders show that the King's enemies have some design upon his dominions. He has a great fleet ready to put to sea, and another fleet in preparation for the defence of the narrow seas. The arms of the trained bands are to be carefully examined, so that they may be complete according to the modern fashion. Soldiers are to be instructed in the exercise of their arms, in files, in squadrons, in whole companies, in regiments, and lastly in one body. Officers and soldiers alike are to take the oath of supremacy and allegiance. All able men between the ages of sixteen and sixty are to be enrolled. The number of horsemen is to be increased if possible. The arms of recusants may be taken and used on payment of their value to the owners. Minute instructions about munitions of war.

(f. 55.) July 13, 1626. St. John's, London. The Earl of Exeter to [his Deputy Lieutenants in the county of Northampton]. He commends to them the letter which he received on the previous day to the Council.

LORD BRAYE'S
MSS.

(f. 38.) September 25, 1626. Newmarche. The Earl of Exeter to his Deputy Lieutenants in the western division of the county of Northampton. He has charged the town of Northampton with four horses. He sends a list of the persons whom he considers not fit to undergo the charge of providing the arms charged upon Northampton, viz. Mr. Serjant the Mayor, Mr. Marten, Mr. Bradford, Mr. Cooper, and four others.

(f. 58 b.) February 9, 1626–7. The King to the Lord Lieutenant of Northamptonshire. He intends to send to his uncle the four regiments that are now in the Low Countries. The defects of these four regiments are to be made up in England, for which object one hundred men are to be levied in the western division of the county and fifty in the eastern.

(f. 55b.) February 10, 1626[-7]. Whitehall. The Council to the Commissioners for the loan in the county of Northampton. The returns made to his Majesty from most parts of the kingdom express the good affection of his subjects. From the eastern division of Northamptonshire he has received good satisfaction, but in the western he has found much contradiction. He lays the blame on those who have not only refused him in the country, but highly offended him in London. The coat and conduct money that was paid to the soldiers for the last voyage to Calais may be deducted out of the loan. The collection is to be hastened.

(f. 59.) February 28, 1626[-7]. Whitehall. The Council to the Lord Lieutenant of Northamptonshire. Orders for the levy of a hundred and fifty men, not drawn from the trained bands, to be brought to the port of London by the 25th of March. They are to receive 8d. a day apiece.

(f. 60.) March 2, 1626[7]. Whitehall. The Lord Treasurer and the Chancellor of the Exchequer to the Lord Lieutenant of Northamptonshire. Minute instructions about coat and conduct money.

(f. 59 b.) March 6, 1626[-7]. St. John's, London. The Earl of Exeter to [his Deputy Lieutenants in the county of Northampton]. He sends copies of the two preceding letters.

(f. 19.) March 14, 1626 [-7]. Whitehall. The Council to the Lord Lieutenant of Northamptonshire. Orders for a muster at Whitsuntide, a very convenient time.

(f. 20.) March 16, 1626 [-7]. St. John's, London. The Earl of Exeter [to his Deputy Lieutenants in the county of Northampton]. He sends a copy of the preceding letter.

(f. 60 b.) April 30, 1627. The Lord Treasurer and the Chancellor of the Exchequer to the Lord Lieutenant of Northamptonshire. Instructions about the payment of coat and conduct money.

(f. 58.) May 3, 1627. St. John's. The Earl of Exeter to [his Deputy Lieutenants in the county of Northampton]. He sends a copy of the preceding letter.

(f. 62.) June 24, 1627. St. John's, London. The same to the same. He reproves them for their slowness in the King's service, in the matter of the musters.

(f. 62b.) July 28, 1627. Westminster. The King to the Lord Lieutenant of Northamptonshire. (See Domestic State Papers, lxxii. 27.)

(f. 63.) July 31, 1627. Whitehall. The Council to the Lord Lieutenant of Northamptonshire. Orders for the levy of a hundred foot soldiers.

(f. 66.) August 24, 1627. Whitehall. The same to the same. (See Domestic State Papers, lxxiv. 90.)

(f. 61.) October 17, 1627. Worthrope. The Earl of Exeter to his Deputy Lieutenants in the western division of the county of Northampton. He sends a copy of a letter from the Deputy Lieutenants of the eastern division, which shows great care and respect for his Majesty's service. He demands accounts.

(f. 23.) November 30, 1627. Whitehall. The Council to the Deputy Lieutenants and Justices of the Peace in the county of Northampton. Many of the soldiers lately returned from the Isle of Rhé run from their colours. Diligent watches are therefore to be set upon all the usual roads adjoining the counties where soldiers are billeted. If runaways come in great numbers, as ten or twenty at a time, the leaders are to be examined and committed to the nearest prison for an example to others. The rest are to be sent back to their colours. If there be so many as cannot be ruled by the constables and their associates, the Deputy Lieutenants are to draw out the requisite number of men in the trained bands. Any vagabonds pretending to be soldiers are to be committed to prison.

(f. 66 b.) January 10, 1627[-8]. Whitehall. The Council to the ord Lieutenant of Northamptonshire. The King, understanding that many trained bands are very ill furnished, intends to take a view and muster of the horse of several shires. The horse of Northamptonshire are to appear before him at Hounslow Heath on the 21st of April. If any man shall appear with a borrowed horse or borrowed armour he will be proceeded against as a contemner of the royal commands.

(f. 67b.) January 23, 1627 [-8]. St. John's, London. The Earl of Exeter to his Deputy Lieutenants in the county of Northampton. He sends a copy of the preceding letter.

(f. 33.) January 1627. " The danger wherein the kingdome now standeth and the remedye, written by Sir Robert Cotton, knight and Barronet."

(f. 50.) February 10, 1627[-8]. Whitehall. The Council to the Lord Lieutenant of Northamptonshire. The soldiers billeted in the county of Buckingham are to be removed into that of Northampton, the greater part to be billeted in the western division thereof. Their charges, at the rate of 3s. 6d. a week for every man, will be repaid from the Exchequer.

(f. 49b.) February 11, 1627 [-8]. St. John's, London. The Earl of Exeter to his Deputy Lieutenants in the county of Northampton. He sends a copy of the preceding letter.

(f. 50b.) Same day and place. The same to the same. Concerning the muster of the horse in the presence of the King.

(f. 64.) February 13, 1627[-8]. Whitehall The Council to the Lord Lieutenant of Northamptonshire. (See Domestic State Papers, xciii. 23.)

(f. 65.) February 18, 1627[-8]. St. John's, London. The Earl of Exeter to his Deputy Lieutenants in the county of Northampton. He sends a copy of a letter from the Council.

(f. 41.) March 11, 1627[-8]. Whitehall. The Council to the Lord Lieutenant of Northamptonshire. The expense of billeting the soldiers is to be charged equally upon the two divisions of the county.

(f. 42.) Same day and place. The same to the same. No more voluntaries are to be billeted.

(f. 68.) March 13, 1627[-8]. Whitehall. The same to the same. Hearing that the troops in most counties are " so defective and in so ll equipage " that they cannot be made complete by the 21st of April, the King has adjourned the general muster until the 11th of June.

H 2

(f. 68. *b.*)    March 18, 1627[-8.]    St. John's, London.    The Earl of Exeter to his Deputy Lieutenants in the county of Northampton. He sends a copy of a letter from the Council.

(f. 69.)    April 7, 1628.    St. John's, London.    The same to the same.    The King expects that all Deputy Lieutenants will show their light horses on the occasion of the muster on Hounslow Heath.

(f. 69. *b.*)    June 12, 1628.    Whitehall.    The Council to the Lord Lieutenant of Northamptonshire.    (See Domestic State Papers, cvii. 9.)

(f. 70.)    June 15, 1628.    St. John's, London.    The Earl of Exeter to his Deputy Lieutenants in the county of Northampton.    He sends a copy of a letter from the Council.    He reproves them for not writing to him concerning the business of Wellingborough.    Complaint has been made at the Council table, and he can give no account of the matter.    He therefore desires speedy information.

(f. 70. *b.*)    July 18, 1628.    Whitehall.    The Council to ———.
The soldiers billeted in the county are to be removed to Portsmouth. Carts for them are to be charged at the rate of 2*d.* a mile.

(f. 71.)    August 15, 1628.    Whitehall.    The Council to the Lord Lieutenant of Northamptonshire.    Concerning the repayment of the charges for billeting soldiers.    The accounts will be carefully examined. "The exhausted state of his Majesty's revenue cannot possibly afforde that all which is dewe should be paied at once."    Sums due to particular billeters, keepers of victualling houses and people of the meaner sort are to be paid first.

(f. 11.)    1628.    "A copie of a letter that was found amongst some Jesuits that were taken lately at London, and addressed to the Father Rector att Bruxells."    About the calling of Parliament and its probable proceedings, the Duke of Buckingham, the spread of Arminianism, the Roman Catholics disguised as Puritans, the army, the high price of coal, &c.

(f. 47. *b.*)    1628.    "The Bishopp of Exeter's letter to the Parliament."

(f. 72.)    July 27, 1629.    Worthrope.    The Earl of Exeter to his Deputy Lieutenants in the western division of the county of Northampton. (See Domestic State Papers, cxlvii. 45.)

(f. 72 *b.*)    December 21, 1629.    Whitehall.    The Council to the Lord Lieutenant of Northamptonshire.    Minute instructions concerning musters.

(f. 73.)    December 28, 1629.    St. John's, London.    The Earl of Exeter to his Deputy Lieutenants in the county of Northampton.    He sends a copy of a letter from the Council.

(f. 73 *b.*)    January 20, 1629[-30.]    St. John's, London.    The same to the same.    He complains of the slowness of their proceedings, mentioning the " ill censure " which is already upon their county.

(f. 74.)    February 11, 1629[-30.]    Kettering.    The Earl of Westmoreland, Sir Lewis Watson, Sir Guy Palmes, Sir Thomas Cave, and William Lane, to the Earl of Exeter.    Since the musters have become almost annual, the muster-master has received a stipend of 50*l.* a year. The soldiers are able in the performance of their duties.

(f. 75.)    April 30, 1629.    Whitehall.    The Council to the Lord Lieutenant of Northamptonshire.    Instructions concerning musters.

(f. 77.)    May 15, 1629.    St. John's London.    The Earl of Exeter to his Deputy Lieutenants in the county of Northampton.    He sends a copy of a letter from the Council.    He orders a muster on the 1st of September.

(f. 77. *b.*) August 5, 1629. St. Leonard's, Newark. The same to the same. If the warrants have not been sent out, the muster may be deferred for a fortnight.　LORD BRAYE'S MSS.

(f. 79.) June 30, 1630. Whitehall. The Council to the Lord Lieutenant of Northamptonshire. Orders for a muster.

(f. 80.) July 24, 1630. St. Leonard's, Newark. The Earl of Exeter to his Deputy Lieutenants in the county of Northampton. He sends a copy of a letter from the Council.

(f. 79. *b.*) August 30, 1630. [The Deputy Lieutenants of Northamptonshire ?] to the chief constable of the Hundred of Guilsborough. Orders for a muster at Northampton Castle on the 4th of October.

(f. 81.) May 31, 1631. Whitehall. The Council to the Lord Lieutenant of Northamptonshire. Instructions for musters. The Captains are to put their companies in files and exercise them "upon holy dayes and otherwise when they commonly spend their time in drinking and unlawfull exercises."

(f. 83.) June 6, 1631. Certificate sent to the High Sheriff of Northampton. (See Domestic State Papers, cxciii. 34.).

(f. 82.) June 14, 1631. St. John's, London. The Earl of Exeter to his Deputy Lieutenants in the county of Northampton. He sends a copy of a letter from the Council. Some officers have been negligent concerning the last muster. They are to receive their ancient pay which is to be levied in the county. He hopes that the care of his Deputy Lieutenants in this year's service will "redeeme the old blemish of Northamptonshire."

(f. 84.) July 28, 1631. Whitehall. The Council to the Lord Lieutenant of Northamptonshire. Some refractory persons in several counties refuse to pay the rates at which they are assessed for the "entertainment" of the muster-masters, though they are no more than heretofore. The assessments are to be signed by the Lord Lieutenant or his Deputy. Persons who refuse to pay the rates are to be bound over to appear before the Council.

(f. 85.) August 6, 1631. The Earl of Exeter to his Deputy Lieutenants in the county of Northampton. He sends a copy of the preceding letter.

(f. 86.) September 7, 1631. Worthrope. The Earl of Exeter to his Deputy Lieutenants in the western division of the county of Northampton. He sends a draft of a warrant for the money for the musters. Their division is much in arrears towards the muster-master.

(f. 86.) Same day. The same to the chief constables of the Hundred of Wimmersleigh. On the same subject.

(f. 87.) Draft warrant for a muster.

(f. 87*b.*) February 11, 1631[-2]. St. John's, London. The Earl of Exeter to [his Deputy Lieutenants in the county of Northampton ?] The Council are very well pleased with their care and diligence in the King's service. He sends instructions about the payment of the officers.

(f. 88.) February 28, 1631[-2.] Whitehall. Order made after the examination of William Waters, High Constable of the Hundred of Towcester before the Council.

(f. 89*b.*) March 2, 1631[-2.] Whitehall. Order made after the examination of Matthew Selby, Mayor of Northampton, before the Council.

(f. 88*b.*) April 10, 1632. St. John's, London. The Earl of Exeter to his Deputy Lieutenants in the county of Northampton. He sends copies of the two preceding orders.

(f. 89.) April 30, 1632. Whitehall. The Council to the Lord Lieutenant of Northamptonshire. Order concerning musters.

(ff. 48, 60b, 61b.) Undated letters concerning musters and assessments.

(f. 57.) N.D. [1624?] Richard Knightley, Thomas Cave, and Thomas Elmes to the Earl of Exeter, and also to the Countess. They desire that Sir William Spencer should be re-appointed a Deputy Lieutenant.

(f. 57b.) N.D. [1625 or 1631?] H. Farmor, Thomas Cave, Richard Knightley, and Thomas Elmes, to the Council. On Monday the 31st of October they went to the house of Mrs. Elizabeth Vaux accompanied by the Under-Sheriff of the County. They showed their authority to Lord Vaux and his mother and then made search for arms. Mr. William Vaux, a Romish recusant, brother to Lord Vaux, complained that they could not be treated worse unless their throats were cut. Mr. Knightley admonished him to forbear swearing, but he only redoubled his oaths. Mr. Knightley desired that Mrs. Vaux or Lord Vaux should satisfy the penalty of the statute for him, and, on their refusal, sent for a constable of the town to distrain any of the goods of Mr. William Vaux. When they all returned to the hall of the house, Lord Vaux pushed Mr. Knightley out, saying that had no longer any business there. When he refused to leave Lord Vaux struck him several times with his fist, and knocked down his servant with a cudgel.

A folio volume of 75 leaves of paper, newly bound, and lettered— "Proceedings against Strafford and Laud, 1641–1644."

f. 1. "The proceedinges against Thomas, Earle of Strafford, Lord Leiutenant of the Kingdome of Ireland, in the English Parliament, 1641." There is in the library of the House of Commons a printed copy of this tract, entitled—"A briefe and perfect relation of the answeres and replies of Thomas Earle of Strafford, to the articles exhibited against him on the thirteenth of Aprill, An. Dom. 1641. London. Printed 1647." There are, however, many verbal differences. the text of this manuscript being better than that of the printed tract The manuscript also contains verses, beginning—

"Great Strafford, worthy of that name, though all,"

and the Epitaph beginning—

"Here lies wisdom, courage, wit,"

(Both of these are printed, with some variations, in Somers's *Tracts*, vol. iv., pp. 296, 297. A great part of this tract is reprinted, without acknowledgement, in Nalson's *Impartial Collection*, vol. ii.)

f. 29. "Originall papers in Parlament att the tryall of the Archbishopp of Canterbury." These are elaborate notes taken from day to day by a person present at the trial of Archbishop Laud. They differ from those published by Prynne and by Heylin. On f. 30 there is a note—"December 1, 1676. Memorandum. I have some loose papers of Mr. Browne's relateing to this business, which being att my chamber att the other end of the Towne, I cannot goe my selfe now for them, by reason of a bruise I received by a fall this slippery weather : but I will deliver them to Mr. Browne him selfe, when hee comes to Towne. Jo. Rushworth."

A folio volume of 145 leaves of paper, newly bound and lettered—
" Westminster Assembly of Divines. 1644-1646." It contains:—
" The humble advise of the Assembly of Divines now sitting by
Ordinance of Parliament at Westminster, concerning Church Govern-
ment." Subscribed by William Twisse, Prolocutor, Cornelius Burges
and John White, assessors, and Henry Roborough and Adoniram
Byfield, scribes. Endorsed :—" Received 11° Dec. 1644."
" The humble Petition of the Assembly of Divines now sitting by
ordinance of Parliament in Westminster." Subscribed by John White,
Prolocutor pro tempore, Henry Roborough and Adoniram Byfield,
scribes. Endorsed :—" 4 Augusti 1645."
" The Answere of the Assemblie of Divines by authoritie of Parliament now sitting at Westminster unto the Reasons given in to this
Assemblie by the dissenting Brethren of their not bringing in a modell
of their way, and since published in print under the title of A Coppie of
a Remonstrance." Subscribed by Cornelius Burges, Prolocutor pro
tempore, and Adoniram Byfield, scribe.
" The Reasons of the dissenting Brethren against the Third Proposition concerning Presbiteriall Government." Certified by Adoniram
Byfield, scribe, as a true copy of the original document subscribed by
Thomas Goodwin, Philip Nye, Jeremiah Burroughes, Sydrach Simpson,
William Bridge, Willsam Greenhill and William Carter.
" The Answere of the Assembly of Divines to the reasons of the
dissenting Brethren against the 3rd Proposition concerning Presby-
teriall Government." Subscribed by Cornelius Burges, Prolocutor pro
tempore, John White, assessor, Henry Roburgh and Adoniram Byfield,
scribes.
" The humble Advice of the Assembly of Divines now sitting at
Westminster, by authority of Parliament, concerning a Confession of
Faith, which is here presented whole and entire." Subscribed by
Charles Herle, Prolocutor, Cornelius Burges and Herbert Palmer,
assessors, Henry Roborough and Adoniram Byfield, scribes.

A folio volume bound in white, being a Common-place book of John
Browne. It contains:—
f. 10. Speech of James I. in Parliament. April 5, 1614. (*Parliamentary History*, vol. i. c. 1149.)
f. 13. Commission from James I. to Sir John Digby. April 16.
1617.
f. 15. The heads of the charge against the Earl of Oxford.
f. 16. Proceedings at the Court. Jan^y 15. 1620.
f. 17. Sir Edward Sackville's speech in Parliament. 1621.
f. 23. Sir Edward Cecil's speech in Parliament. February, 1620
[-1].
f. 29. Sir James Perrott's motion in Parliament. June 4, 1621.
(Part given in *Parl. Hist.* vol. i. c. 1293.)
f. 33. Letter from James I. to the Speaker of the House of Commons.
December 3, 1621 (*Parl. Hist.* vol. i. c. 1326.)
f. 35. Petition to be sent to the King at Newmarket on the 8th of
December, 1621. (*Parl. Hist.* vol. i. c. 1323.)
f. 41. Petition sent to the King on the 8th of December, 1621.
(*Parl. Hist.* vol. i. c. 1333.)
f. 46. Heads for a petition for the better execution of the laws
against seminary priests and Popish recusants.
f. 48. Answer of James I. to the apologetic petition of the Commons.
(*Parl. Hist.* vol. i. c. 1338.)

f. 151. The Lord Keeper's speech. February 19, 1623.

f. 152. The Duke of Buckingham's relation to both Houses. February 24, 1623.

f. 165. Speeches of the Speaker and the Lord Keeper. February 21, 1623. (A different version given in *Parl. Hist.* vol. i. c. 1376).

f. 176. Conference between the two houses. March 2, 1623.

f. 181. Reasons offered by the Commons for breaking off the treaty for the Spanish match, and that for the Palatinate.

f. 183. Letter from the King of Spain to Conde Olivares. November 5, 1622. (English).

f. 184. Answer of the Conde Olivares. November 8, 1622. (English).

f. 188. Collections out of Sir Richard Weston's report to the Commons. March 4, 1623.

f. 191. Collections out of Secretary Cottington's report.

f. 194. Message of both Houses delivered to the King at Theobald's by the Archbishop of Canterbury. (*Parl. Hist.* vol. i. c. 1387.)

f. 195. The King's answer thereto. March 5, (*sic*) 1623. (*Parl. Hist.* vol. i. c. 1387.)

f. 200. The Prince's speech to a Committee of both Houses. March 11, 1623.

f. 202. Speech of James I. at Whitehall. March 14, 1623. (*Parl. Hist.* vol. i. c. 1395.)

f. 207. Speech of the Duke of Buckingham to both Houses in the Painted Chamber. March 15, 1623, or Wednesday, March 17, 1623.

f. 210. Letter from the King, read in Parliament by the Lord Keeper on the 17 of March, 1623.

f. 211. Articles to be seen into speedily.

f. 212. Petition from both Houses to the King. March 23, 1623. (*Parl. Hist.* vol. i. c. 1398).

f. 214. The King's answer thereto. (A different version is given in *Parl. Hist.* vol. i. c. 1403.)

f. 216. Speech of Sir Thomas Crewe. May 28, 1624. (*Parl. Hist.* vol. i. c. 1498.)

f. 223. Articles of the league between the Kings of France and England, the Commonwealth of Venice and the Duke of Savoy.

f. 225. The Earl of Northumberland's discourse of the proceedings between himself and Sir Francis Vere.

f. 231. Letter from Anne Boleyn to Henry VIII. found among Cromwell's papers. Dated from the Tower, May 6 [1536].

f. 234. Message from Queen Elizabeth to certain members of the House of Commons. May 27, 1571.

f. 235. Proclamation for calling in Dr. Cowell's *Interpreter.* March 25, 1610.

f. 237. Letter from Sir John Maynard to one about the King, concerning the state of affairs in London. August, 1648.

f. 239. Paper given by Charles I. to the Princess Elizabeth when she came to take leave of him, containing the speech which he would have made in Westminster Hall on Monday the 22nd of January 1648[-9], if he had been allowed to speak further about his reasons.

f. 243. Queries propounded by sundry clergy of the diocese of London concerning the oath enjoined by the 6th Canon.

f. 247. Extracts from a book in the hand of Anderson, Lord Chief Justice, concerning commitments without cause shown.

f. 252. Declaration by the Assembly of Divines, and by authority of Parliament, against the blasphemous opinions in Mr. Archer's book.

f. 256. Protestation of the Doctors of Divinity at Oxford concerning the oaths of supremacy and allegiance. February 16, 1641.

f. 257. Protestation of Queen Henrietta Maria at her departure from Scheveling. February 25, 1643. (Rushworth's *Collections*, part iii., vol. ii., p. 163.)

f. 259. Answer from both Houses to the King. April 1643. Intended, but not sent.

f. 264. The oath of the Clerk of the Parliament.

f. 264. Proposals sent by the General and Council of the Army to the Commissioners of Parliament. 1647.

f. 277. Commission to Lord Inchiquin to be President of Munster. January 14, 1644.

f. 280. Instructions for the President of Munster.

f. 289. Manifesto of Charles I. concerning the Palatinate.

f. 288. Propositions of the Commissioner of the Queen of Sweden to the English Parliament. March 31, 1645.

f. 292. Answer of the Parliament thereto. Same day.

f. 296. Letter from the Commissioners for the Parliament of Scotland to the Speaker of the House of Peers. January 24, 1645.

f. 303. Forms of direction for royal letters.

f. 304. List of cathedral and collegiate churches in England and Wales.

f. 306. Act for erecting a High Court of Justice for the trial of James, Earl of Cambridge, Henry, Earl of Holland, and others.

f. 308. Warrant for the execution of the Earl of Cambridge. March 6, 1648.

f. 310. Instructions for Viscount Falkland, Lord Deputy of Ireland. August 4, 1622.

f. 321. Statutes of the Order of the Garter, as reformed by Henry VIII., with additions by Philip and Mary.

f. 355. Grant by Charles II. to Sir Richard Browne, Bart., of the office of Muster-Master General. March 30. 13 Car. II.

f. 356. Table of the revenues and tenths of the different bishopricks in England and Wales.

f. 358. Notes concerning proceedings in Chancery.

f. 361. Queries concerning Convocation.

f. 364. Letter from the King of France to the Pope. August 30, 1662. (English.)

f. 364. Letter from the same to certain Cardinals. Same date.

f. 366. Challenge sent by the Earl of Middlesex to the Earl of Bridgewater. 1663.

f. 367. Propositions delivered to the King by the Earl of Strafford for securing his estate and bridling parliaments.

f. 379. Letter from Sir Walter Raleigh to James I.

f. 381. Sir Walter Raleigh's protestation at his death.

f. 382. Letter from Gilbert, Archbishop of Canterbury, to the Bishop of London, concerning conventicles. June 8, 1669.

f. 383. Letter from Humphry, Bishop of London to the Bishop of Peterborough, concerning the same. June 20, 1669.

Instructions concerning conventicles. July 7, 1669.

f. 385. Letter from the King of France to the Pope. August 30, 1662. (English.)

f. 386. Paper brought into the House of Lords from the French Ambassador. January 25, 1673.

f. 401. Letter from the Duke of Monmouth to the Vice-Chancellor of Cambridge.

f. 402. Heads of the articles between the King of Great Britain and LORD BRAYE'S MSS. the States of Holland. 1673.

f. 405. Petition to the Queen, for association in religion.

f. 419. Letter to the Bishops (temp. Elizabeth).

f. 435. The case of M. de Luzancy, a French preacher newly converted to the Protestant religion as established in England. 1675.

f. 440. Letter from the Earl of Manchester to his son, Walter Monntagu. 1635.

f. 450. Speech of Lord Lucas in Parliament, concerning a subsidy.

f. 453. Speech of the Duke of Buckingham in Parliament, concerning Protestant dissenters.

f. 455. Letter from the Earl of Shaftesbury to the Earl of Carlisle.

f. 456. Retrenchments in the King's expenditure.

f. 457. Commission from Charles I. to Thomas, Earl of Arundel, K.G., to be General of the army to be sent into the north.

f. 460. List of Peers in the commission for the trial of Lord Cornwallis. June 30, 1676.

f. 461. Speech of the Earl of Shaftesbury in the Court of King's Bench. June 29, 1677.

f. 463. Information of Sir Robert Heath, Attorney-General, against Sir Robert Cotton, and others.

f. 470. The Scots' reasons against the Book of Common Prayer. Edinburgh. August 1637.

f. 472. Narrative of the life of John Packer, Esq., who was born at Twickenham, November 12, 1572, and died February 9, 1648.

f. 478. Petition of Gilbert, Archbishop of Canterbury to the King, against toleration of Popery. 1663.

f. 479. Petition of the Irish Bishops to Parliament, against toleration of Popery.

f. 480. Declaration by John, Bishop of Worcester.

f. 481. Speech of the Earl of Shaftesbury in Parliament in a debate on the King's Speech. Begins—" In this grate debate." Ends—" take counsel as he thinks fit." 1681.

f. 486. Address from the Presbyterian ministers in London to the King. April 30, 1687.

f. 486. Address from the Quakers to the King.

f. 488. Declaration of Liberty of Conscience. April 4, 1687.

f. 492. Letter from the Earl of Rochester to Dr. Burnet, written on his death bed. June 25, 1680.

f. 493. Reasons of the House of Commons against toleration. Friday, February 27, 1662.

f. 496. Petition of Roman Catholics to the House of Lords. June 10, 1661. Orders of the House concerning the same. June 11–28.

f. 499. Speech of the Earl of Essex at the delivery of the petition from certain Lords. January 25, 1680.

Petition of the Duke of Monmouth and fifteen other Lords.

f. 502. Letter from Mercy Povey, in Lime Street, London, to Staffordshire, concerning the dissenters' complaint of their persecution.

f. 506. A letter from M. Fagel, Pensioner of Holland, to James Stewart, Advocate, giving the views of the Prince and Princess of Orange concerning the repeal of the penal laws, etc. November 4, 1687.

f. 513. Letter from a Jesuit in London to the College at Liège, intercepted and carried to the Prince of Orange.

f. 516. List of penal laws, etc. (continued from f. 498).

f. 520.   Letter from Father Petre to Père la Chaise.

f. 526.   Lines to the haters of Popery (by Partridge ?)   Begin :—
"Thus t'was of old when Israel felt the rod."

f. 527.   Astrological notes for the year 1688.

f. 539.   Letter from Père la Chaise to Father Petre.   Dated at Paris,
July 8, 1688.

A small 4to volume bound in white, and entitled "Some Parliament
Passages, annis 1621 et 1625." It contains a copy of the Latin treatise
"Modus tenendi Parliamentum," and 67 other pieces, all, or almost all,
of which are also transcribed in the folio Common-place book last
mentioned.

A small 4to volume bound in brown.   It contains :—

f. 1.   An Act declaring and settling the Government, A.D. 1654.

f. 45.   Report from the sub-committee of the full value of the
revenues of the Commonwealth.

f. 55.   Proposals made to the Parliament by a member thereof.
September 7, 1655.

f. 57.   Observations upon the proviso in the indenture of elections and
upon the Protector's engagement imposed upon the Parliament the 12th
of September, 1654.

f. 65.   Remonstrance brought into Parliament by Alderman Pack.
A.D. 1656.

f. 79.   Conference with the Protector concerning kingship.   April
9 and 11, 1657.

f. 117.   The Protector's answer at the Conference of April 13, 1657.

f. 137.   Further proceedings at the Conference, April 16, 1657.

A folio volume, bound in white, entitled " The Habeas Corpus, or the
proceedings att the King's Bench Barr betweene the Kinge and divers
of his subjects imprisoned in Michaelmas Terme in the third yeare of the
raigne of our soveraigne Lord King Charles, Anno Domini, 1627."

A folio volume, bound in white, containing a few precedents for
impeachments, &c.

A folio volume, bound in white, containing copies of the Petition of
the Commons, the King's answer, &c.   A.D. 1610.

A thin folio volume, bound in white, containing—

(1.) " The State of the publicke accounts presented to the Lords in
Parliament by the Commissioners that sat at Brooke House.
Oct. 25, 1669."

(2.) " An Act for the illegitimation of the children of the Lady
Anne Roos, 18 & 19 Car. II."

(3.) " An Act for John Manners, called Lord Roos, to marry again.
22 Car. II."

A folio volume bound in white.   It contains "The tytles of all the
pryvate Actes of Parlyament with notes what personnes and landes are
towched in the same, from the begynninge of the reigne of King
Henry 8th, untyll the 32nd yere of our Sovereigne Lady Elizabeth."—
(ff. 1–71, and 3 ff. of " Index Nominum.")   Inscribed " This booke
belonges to the Parliament Office.—Henry Elsynge."

A collection of drafts of the Journals of the House of Lords in the
seventeenth century, being for the most part much briefer than the

formal Journals which have been printed, but giving in many instances the names of movers of resolutions and other particulars afterwards omitted from the formal Journals :—

First drafts of the Journals of the House of Lords, by Henry Elsynge, in five folio volumes bound in white. (See a list of somewhat similar works at Crowcombe Court in the 4th Report of the Historical MSS. Commission, App. p. 369.)

(1.) March 12, 1620-[1], to March 27, 1621.
(2.) April 17, 1621, to May 18, 1621.
(3.) May 19, 1624, to March 15, 1624[-5].
(4.) March 17, 1627[-8], to April 30, 1628.
(5.) May 1, 1628, to June 26, 1628.

First drafts of the Journals of the House of Lords, by John Browne, in ten folio volumes bound in white.

(A.) April 13, 1640, to May 5, 1640.
(1.) November 3, 1640, to February 9, 1640[-1].
(2.) February, 1640[-1], to April 8, 1641. (The contents of this volume have been torn out.)
(3.) April 9, 1641, to June 14, 1641.
(4.) June 15, 1641, to June 29, 1641.
(5.) June 30, 1641, to October 23, 1641.
(6.) October 25, 1641, to January 14, 1641[-2].
(7.) January 15, 1641[-2], to March 2, 1641[-2].
(8 ) March 4, 1641[-2], to April 1, 1642.
(9.) April 2, 1642, to April 28, 1642.

First drafts of the Journals of the House of Lords, by John Browne, in parts, not bound.

May 8, 1661, to February 20, 1661[-2]. (5 parts.)
April 3, 1662, to May 19, 1662. (2 parts.)
February 8, 1662[-3], to May 11, 1663.
July 8, 1663, to July 27, 1663. (2 parts.)
March 16, 1663[-4], to May 13, 1664.
September 18, 1666, to February 8, 1666[-7]. (3 parts.)
October 19, 1669, to December 11, 1669.
February 14, 1669[-70], to April 11, 1670. (3 parts.)
October 24, 1670, to April 7, 1671. (3 parts.)
March 24, 1672[-3], to April 26, 1675. (2 parts.)
October 13, 1675, to November 22, 1675.
January 15, 1677[-8], to March 6, 1677[-8].
October 21, 1678, to November 16, 1678.
December 19, 1678, to April 9, 1679. (2 parts.)
May 12, 1679, to November 20, 1680. (2 parts.)
June 29, 1685, to November 20, 1685.
January 22, 1688[-9], to March 4, 1688[-9].
April 24, 1689, to January 26, 1689[-90]. (5 parts.)

Other parts may perhaps be found hereafter at Stanford, to fill up the lacunæ.

A folio volume, newly bound in red, and lettered " Letters and State Papers, 1572—1636."

May, 1572. Paper containing three distinct parts.—I. Notes of the proceedings of the House of Commons on May 24, 29, 30, 31, mostly agreeing with the entries in the Journals, i. 98, 99, under those dates. In some cases, however, the names of the speakers for and against some bills, and a summary of their speeches, are given, especially on the motion for the speedy execution of the Duke of Norfolk, the most remarkable of which are as follows :—

On the 29th, Saint Leger said, " Since the Queene's majesties will and pleasure is that we should not proceede nor deale with the firste bill against the monstrous and huge dragon and masse of the earth, the Queene of Scottes, yet my conscience urgeth and pricketh me to speake and move this house to be in hande with her Majestie with the execution of the roaring lion, I meane the Duke of Norfolk. And although her Majestic be lolled asleepe, and wrapped in the mantle of her owne perill, yet for my part I cannot be silent in uttering of my conscience, and alleaged the text of wicked Hamon, whom he applied to the Duke, and of the godly Queen Hester to the Queene's Majestie." On the 31st, Sir Francis Knowles said, " I perceave your intent is to make motion for the execution of the Duke, which I perceave proceedeth of veric love and care you have to the Queene's person (which is the marke whereat all good subjectes shoot at). And although I doo know nothing more convenient and needfull then execution, and that with speede, yet I knowe the disposition of princes is rather of themselves to doo such thinges then by way of pressing and urging. It may be, and it is like enough, her Majestie is of herselfe already disposed sooner to doo it then you doo perhaps think or beleve. And I would not wishe we should attempt her of his hastic execution, for that I knowe alreadie her minde partly therein. The execution will be more honourable to her Majestie, if the doing thereof come of her free minde without our motion. The woordes that I speake, I speake upon good reason, and I would wishe you all to consider what moveth me thereunto, and what may cause me to have and use this speeche. I pray you all let us stay; I trust we shall not repent it. If you go on with this attempt alreadie in hande, you may perhaps delay the thing you secke to further."

II. "A briefe note of the Acte concerning Marie, daughter of James the Fifth, late King of Scottes, called the Queen of Scottes." This bill passed both houses but never received the royal assent. The preamble charges her with having claimed the present possession of the crown of England, with withdrawing the Duke of Norfolk from his allegiance by contracting marriage with him, with assisting in the late rebellion in the north and procuring relief for the fugitive rebels from the Duke of Alva, with designing a new rebellion by aid of strangers landing at Harwich, with publishing certain books which asserted that she was entitled to the crown, and that Elizabeth was a usurper, and with intending a disturbance of the last Parliament. The enacting part declares her incapable and unworthy of all such title and interest to the crown as she with her adherents upon a vain and uncertain hope, founded upon uncertain and doubtful causes, should imagine her to have, sentences any person thereafter advancing such claim to death, as in cases of high treason ; declares that if she or any of her adherents should by any ways advance the said claim, she and they should abide such trial of the law as the heinousness of such a fact should require, with a proviso that her trial is to be by the peers of the realm ; finally that if for her sake and in her name any tumult or insurrection be raised without her knowledge or consent, she is to abide the same trial as if she had been the deviser thereof, and if any person should attempt to dispatch and destroy her, he should not be troubled or impeached for the same. A proviso that nothing in the Act should be interpreted to allow or confirm any right touching the succession to the crown of any person whatsoever. Subjoined arc summaries of the speeches of Sir F. Alford and Mr. Norton. The former objected to the provisions that she should be triable, if any LORD BRAYE'S MSS. tumult was raised even without her consent, and that any person might lay hands on her. " I thinke her to be as vile and naughtie a creature as ever the earth bare, and am as strongly persuaded of her lewde demeanour as any man in this companie, yet can I not see howe it can stand with the honour of England for the avoiding of forcine slaunder either to condemne her unheard, or to towche her in life for that she never knewe of." Again he did not wish any man to inure a subject's hands with prince's blood, it being a perilous precedent. He then instanced the case of David's sparing Saul.

III. The protestation of the Queen of Scots. (The substance is in Kennet ii. 442.)

June 30, 1601. London. Richard, Bishop of London, to ——. You are appointed to preach at Paul's Cross on the 9th of August next, by the discreet performance of which duty you shall do good service to God, her Majesty, and the State, and receive thankful commendation. These are therefore to require you in her Majesty's name to keep the day appointed, all excuses set apart. Whereas the malice of our Romish adversaries doth still increase, I desire that you avoid all domestic controversies, and discover to the auditory the absurdities and falsehood of Popery. Hereof fail not to send your direct answer in writing, and fail not to be ready at the time and place appointed, as you will answer the contrary at your peril. Endorsed :—" The fourth time of my preaching at St. Paul's Cross. 9 August, 1601."

[May 29, 1624.] " My conclusion speech to King James at the first session, when he gave his royall assent." (This is the speech *in extenso* of Sir Thomas Crew, Speaker of the House of Commons, which is reported in a condensed form in Rushworth i. 146, and *Lords' Journals*, iii. 423.)

[April 1625.] " A discourse of passages between the Earls of Essex, Somersett, Northampton, the Countess of Essex, Sir Thomas Overbury and others, with their risings and falls, together with diverse other affayres as they occurred during the late raing of K. James, and alsoe of the Duke of Buckingham his first coming into favour." (A transcript in the handwriting of Mr. Browne from the volume referred to on page 110 as "*Historical Memoirs.*" Apparently the only new fact it contains is a statement that the girl said to have been examined by the jury of matrons in the Essex divorce case was one of Sir Thomas Mounson's daughters.)

1626. A number of original petitions of the Earl of Bristol dated respectively (i.) March 22nd, April 19th (including an original letter from Lord Keeper Coventry with the Earl's answer), May 8th (2), June 8th, June 10th, June 14th, (ii.) June 9th, 12th, (iii.) May 15th. The first are printed verbatim in *Lords' Journals*, iii. 539, 563, 588, 589, 669, 672, 680, except that the last clause of the last petition is omitted (Cf. *Lords' Journals*, iii. 681). It is as follows :—" That forasmuch as the Earle hath great reason to believe the copie of the King's letter read in this House by the Duke of Buckingham is not a true coppie, and the letter itself surruptitiously gotten. That that coppie soe read by the Duke may be brought into the House, and that the Earle having already the Kinge's leave by a letter written by the Lord Conway to speake to that letter may be by your Lordships' favour admitted thereunto." Of the second the effect is given in *Lords' Journals*, iii. 655, 671, 673. The remaining petition is a formal one relating to the appointment of counsel, and praying that Mr. Maxwell may be ordered to transmit any further petitions he may present.

April 29, 1626. Draft Report of the Committee of Privileges. (Printed in *Lords' Journals* iii. 574.)

May 17, 1626. Draft message from the King. (Printed in *Lords' Journals*, iii. 629.)

June 30, 1627. Whitehall. The Council to the Commissioners for the Loans in the County of Northampton. There has been much slackness in the collection of money during the last term, and his Majesty imputes the fault to you, rather than to those who are to lend, for they have shown good affections in paying and promising. Many of the Commissioners absent themselves from the sittings. You are required to furnish an account of your proceedings before the 15th of July next. All the money collected upon these loans, with much more of the King's own treasure, is employed for the defence of the realm, for the succour of his Majesty's allies, and for the maintenance of the cause of religion.

November 27, 1627. A long list of persons to whom gowns and cloaks were given, on the occasion of a funeral in London. Lord Noel, and Richard Crashaw, the poet, are among them. The deceased seems to have been connected with the Merchant Taylors.

June 4, 1628. "The effect of Mr. Pym's speech at the conference betweene both Houses" in the case of Doctor Mannering (*sic*). (This is a fuller report of the speech than those printed in *Parliamentary History*, ii. 390, and Rushworth, i, 595.)

June 9, 1628. A paper in Mr. Pym's handwriting with the names of the witnesses he desired to call in support of his case against Dr. Manwaring. (The names of those sworn are given in *Lords' Journals*, iii. 846, 847, except that Sir Francis Annesley is called Sir Francis Onslow. In addition to the persons there mentioned as sworn, three more are included in the list, Sir Thomas Darnell, Mr. Porter, and Mr. Howland.)

June 10, 1628. Original Depositions of Abraham Speckart, Sir Thomas Conye, Matthew Howland, Laurence Whittaker, Sir Francis Annesley, Sir William Lytton, Sir George Hastings, Hamond Claxton, John Shelbery, John Knight, Sir Francis Darcy, and Sir Daniel Norton, in Dr. Manwaring's case.

June 11th, 1628. A paper containing passages from Dr. Manwaring's sermons adduced in support of the charge against him. (Cf. *Lords' Journals*, iii. 848.)

June 14, 1628. Draft of the sentence on Dr. Manwaring. (Printed in *Lords' Journals*, iii. 853.)

June 21, 1628. Original submission of Dr. Manwaring. Signed— Roger Maynwaringe. (Printed in *Lords' Journals*, iii. 870.)

December 30, 1629. Copy of the King's Instructions to the Archbishop of Canterbury. (Printed in Rushworth, ii. 30, except the first two clauses, which are as follows:—

1. "That the Lordes the bishops be commanded to their severall seats to keepe residence exceptinge those which are in necessary attendance at Courte.

2. "That none of them reside upon his lande or lease that he hath purchased nor on his commendam if he hold any but in one of his episcopall houses if he have any and that he wast not the woods where any are left.")

Hilary term, 5 Car. I. (January 1629–30.) Report in Law French of the trial in the Star Chamber of Walter Long, Esq. (Cf. Rushworth, i, 684.)

1632—1636.  A number of letters and papers relating to John
Durye's mission to the Continent for the purpose of effecting an union
between the Lutherans and the Calvinists.   (Others of the series are
among the MSS. of the House of Lords.   See *Report of Commissioners on Historical Manuscripts*, iii. 1, 2.)

LORD BRAYE'S
MSS.

November 1, 1632.  Hanau.  Latin letter to Laud, then Bishop of London,
from some Calvinist ministers there, two each from the churches of
France and Germany, one from the Belgian, one from the Flemish, and
one, Conrad Ammonius, being Court preacher.  Expresses their wish
for an union.  If a complete one be impossible, perhaps a syncretism,
such as in Poland, may be attainable.  In a hurried P.S. " When we
signed this we expected nothing less than the death of the Most Serene
King of Sweden, who was the thunderbolt of Anti-Christ, and he has
perished, Ah, proh dolor !  God thus punishing our sins." Seal of arms.
Endorsed in Laud's handwriting.  " Rec. Novemb. 11, 1633.  Hannoviæ
Calend. Novemb. 1632.  De Conciliatione Evangelicorum."

March 7, 1632[-3].  Hanau.  Latin letter to George [Abbot], Archbishop of Canterbury, and William [Laud], Bishop of London, from Paulus
Tossanus, D.D., Assessor of the Synod of the Lower Electoral Palatinate.
Writes by the command of Louis Philip, Guardian and Administrator
of the Palatinate, whose brother, the late King of Bohemia, a few
weeks before his death, had desired the writer to write to the chief
bishops of England, to express his desire and that of all the ecclesiastics
and theologians in the Palatinate for peace between all the Evangelicals
in Germany.  The Prince wishes to tread in his brother's footsteps.
Seal of arms.  Endorsed in Laud's hand, " Rece. Novemb. 11, 1633.
Paulus Tossanus, nomine Administratoris Palatinatus Electoralis &c.
De Concordia Evangelicorum."

October 15, 1633.  Zurich.  Copy of a Latin letter endorsed in
Laud's hand, " Rece. Apr. 26, 1634.  The copye of a Latin letter from
the churches of Helvetia to Mr. Jo. Durye about the pacification."
They not only will not hinder any attempt made by anyone to bring
about either union or mutual toleration, but greatly desire it.  They
are however apprehensive that such an attempt may be made
inopportunely, and at the expense of Catholic truth, merely for
political reasons.  Perhaps there would be more hope of it, if, during
the war, each party would refrain from abusing, attacking, and placing
false interpretations on the proceedings of the others.  They think that
the conclusion of peace would be the most favourable moment for
effecting a religious reconciliation.

February 7, 1634.  Alba Julia (Karlsburg in Transylvania).  Latin
letter to George [Abbot], Archbishop of Canterbury from Stephen
Katona Geleji, bishop of the orthodox Hungarian churches in Transylvania and of Alba Julia, and three professors there.  Compares Charles I.
to a new Jason, who is leading Kings Princes and Republics, as he
led his 54 companions, to win the Golden Fleece of union.

Same date and place.  Enclosed is a long paper (15 pages) on an
union between the Evangelical churches, the method of effecting it,
and the points of controversy.  Signed as the last, and also subscribed
by fourteen other ministers and pastors of different places in Transylvania,
among them Klausenburg, Vasarhely, and Fogaros.  They promise that
their Prince [Ragotzky] will not fail to do his part.  This letter and
paper were apparently in reply to a letter of Durye's.  Seals of arms.
Endorsed :—" Rece. Oct. 21, 1634.  Responsa Episcopi Alba-Juliensis
necnon trium Professorum aliorumque Ministrorum Transilvan. circa

negotium de Unione Ecclesiarum Lutheranarum et Calvin. 1, Ad
Quæstiones Parasceuasticas 4. 2, ad Problemata de Pacis Ecclesiasticæ
Consiliis Capessend. 5. 3, De Mediis agendique modo 3. 4, De Contro-
versis Capitibus 3." Shorter endorsement on letter.

February 28, 1634. Copy of a Latin letter to Durye from George
Richter in the name of the Free City of Nuremberg. Endorsed in
Laud's hand : "Rece. April 13, 1634."

March 7, 1634. Copy of a Latin letter to Durye from the Dean,
Seniors, and Professors of the Theological College in the Academia Julia
at Helmstadt. Mentions that their Sovereign, the Duke of Brunswick, is
wholly in favour of the Union. Endorsed in Laud's hand : "Rece.
April. ult. 1634."

March 9, 1634. Westminster. English letter from Durye to Laud.
Discusses whether, if he should go again, he should do so as a messenger from England, or as one that is but allowed to negotiate still in
private, as he had formerly done. His intentions in going again, if he
does so. Thinks it necessary he should be more public than before, and
have a warrant to show, if need should require, that he is entrusted by
Laud and sent hence to negotiate with them, and to declare to them the
pious affection of the Church of England. The two objects he aims at
are to bring the different parties first to a ratification of the Conference
of Leipsic, and then to a more absolute agreement in some fundamental
confession and Common Liturgy to which all sides should give their
approbation. Wishes to be supplied with a Latin translation of the
Liturgy, Canons, and Articles of the Church of England, to be communicated to such as should be inclinable to use them. The only means
of opposing a threatening growth of Socinianism is to be found in a
general agreement and uniformity among themselves, of which the only
perfect pattern is in the Church of England. Among the collateral
advantages of his mission, he might induce them to send their sons to
English Universities, he might observe the causes of their evils and con-
fusions, finally, by collecting their different forms of liturgy and Church
government and comparing them with those of the English Church, he
might show the homebred Puritans their madness in esteeming more of
foreign disorder than domestic order. For his mission he will require
at least two attendants, one a scholar, knowing German, able to copy
writings and to go errands to persons of quality, and the other a servant, and at least three, if not four, horses. The charges at German
inns to maintain himself and these will be as follows :—

|  | s. | d. |
|---|---|---|
| For a horse, lodging and diet, day and night, one rix dollar, that is | 4 | 6 |
| For my own diet, every meal one German guilder, that is | 3 | 0 |
| For a serving man's, every meal half a German guilder, that is | 1 | 6 |

Thus three men's and four horses' meat daily, without any extraordinaries, will come to thirty shillings sterling (marginal note in Laud's
hand, "5 17 li. a year"). What the ordinary charges of letters will come
to is uncertain ; the postage in Germany is full as dear as here. All
other things "resent the desolations of the countrie," and in most places
are scarce to be had for money. Had he not found extraordinary friends
of his own country when he was last in those quarters, it would have
been impossible for him to have subsisted. Endorsed in Laud's hand :
" Rece. Mar. 10, 1633. Comp[utatione] Ang[lica]."

March 28, 1634. Dresden. Latin opinion of Dr. Hoe. Headed in LORD BRAYE'S MSS. Laud's handwriting : "Whether it be lawful to unite with Calvinists for the defence of Religion," which he decides in the negative. (See letters of July 24 and Aug. 4, 1634.) Endorsed by Laud : "Rece. July 19, 1634. Dr. Hoe's opinion delivered about the Lutherans having peace with the Calvinists. Sent from Franckfort 30 June 1634, by Sir Robt. Anstruither, embassador in Germany."

A copy of the same.

[March or April 1634.] English letter from Durye to Laud, enclosing the copy of that of February 28, 1634, from Nuremberg. As the Diet has begun at Frankfort, and the deputies are charged to effect an ecclesiastical pacification, he asks for a letter of recommendation from Laud or from the King's Minister at the Diet, and that the latter should encourage the work as he shall think most expedient. Endorsed by Laud : "Rece. April 13, 1634. Mr. John Durye's demand about this pacification."

April 8, 1634. Bulwick. Sir Thomas Rowe to Laud. Thanks him for his kindness to Mr. Durye, and desires that countenance and support may be given him at the approaching Diet. Has received a very kind letter from the Chancellor of Sweden [Oxenstiern] recommending to him his son's employment to his Majesty, "mistaking my condition in Court, but being in a retyred life I have not what to answere, nor will I presume to enquire into the secretts of State ; I remember Pentheus' punishment. I will see but one sunne and one Thebes, my master and his service." Hopes the Ambassador [Oxenstiern's son] has opened himself to Laud in this point of pacification. Endorsed by Laud : "Rece. Apr. 13, 1634. Concerninge Mr. Durye and the Diett at Frankford from Sir Thomas Roe."

April 22, 1634. Paper endorsed by Laud "April 22, 1634. The copye of my leters to Sir Rob. Anstruder by Mr. Durye, how to carye himselfe in the reconciliation of the Lutherans and the Calvinists &c." Mr. Durye has endeavoured to get letters from his Majesty to declare himselfe in that business and to make himself a chief mediator in the pacification. Though most English Divines, especially those of note, would be very glad to hear of so happy a peace, his Majesty (though also very well affected to it), does not conceive the business is so ripe as yet, as that it is fit for him to mediate in a public way. As no prince either Lutheran or Calvinist has yet declared himself publicly, it cannot be reasonable for him to come forward publicly, as he believes that were it really intended some of the Princes on the place would have showed themselves before this. As Mr. Durye's intentions are very pious, and would probably produce much good, could they be carried out, Sir Robert is to take knowledge of him and his Christian endeavours privately, but not to engage the King or use his name without his express warrant.

July 24, 1634. Frankfort. Durye to Laud. Gives an account of the proceedings of the Diet at Frankfort, and encloses a copy of his petition to them. Refers to the writing said to be Dr. Hoe's, but thought to be Dr. Wolff's of Darmstadt, given out as an answer to a case of conscience concerning the League of Heilbronn, and showing that it was unlawful for Lutherans to join in such a League with Calvinists. Mentions that Grotius was then at Frankfort, and that Ratisbon had been taken on the 15th instant by the King of Hungary. Endorsed, " Recev. August 8, 1634. Mr. Durye's letters from Frankford about the Reconciliation &c. Item, his petition put up to the Princes at Frankford."

August 4, 1634. Bulwick. Sir Thomas Rowe to Laud. Refers to "the libel supposed to be written by Doctor Hoo and directed to the Elector of Saxe," of which a copy is enclosed. "It is the perfect dialect of Rabshekah, without learning, or proofe, but by bitter invectives, and rayling presumptions of his own authoritye ; the question being alway begged and then concluded." Suspicion that he is either corrupted by the Imperial party, or by the Landgrave of Darmstadt and his Chancellor Wolfe, the only two that may lose by unity. His own opinion is that it is made by concert of the Elector [of Saxony] and Hoe, not for care of religion but to cover his false intentions towards an untimely peace under the vail of conscience and religion, as he has ever been wavering. Is thinking of writing an answer to it. Endorsed, "Recep. Aug. 23, 1634. Sir Thomas Roe's letter concerning Dr. Hoe's Invective against the Reconciliation &c."

August 25, 1634. Paper endorsed, "Aug. 25, 1634. The copye of my letter to Sir Thomas Roe about Dr. Hoe's opinion concerning the Reconciliation &c." His letter of the 4th came not to hand till the 23rd, and then was left at an inn. Has had a little (and but little) leisure these three weeks, and now that his Majesty is returning, he must fall to grinding again. Has already received a copy of Dr. Hoe's pamphlet with letters from the Ambassador and Dr. Durye. "I have in my time read much bitternes, but hardly have I seen more gaule drop from any man's penn. If it please God, see much good may come of it as you mention, that is to make moderate men unite." Does not consider either the man, or the thing, deserves an answer. Thinks it improper for Sir Thomas, who has been publicly employed in those parts, to undertake the quarrel, and finally is uncertain whether any answer at all is wise, as the consequence would be an angry controversy, which would destroy all hope of pacification.

October 14, 1634. Leyden. Durye to Laud. Since the Evangelical confederates at his solicitation made a public Act at the Diet to undertake the business, he resolved to return to England to give Laud a full account personally. Has therefore not written before, but now does so, as he is waiting there in order to give and receive further satisfaction to the chief Divines of these parts. Seal of Arms. Endorsed by Laud, "Rece. Novemb. 9, 1634. Mr. Durye about the success at the last Diett at Frankford."

February 17, 1635 (new style). Durye to Laud. A long narrative of his proceedings since he sailed from Gravesend on the previous 2nd of May to Hamburgh, where he negotiated with the divines. They were about to hold a synod with those of Lubeck and Luneburg, to settle a course of uniform proceeding with the Socinians, the Swenckfeldians, and a new sect of ecclesiastical prophets. Thence he travelled with Sir R. Anstruther to Frankfort, arriving on June 19. Refers to Dr. Hoe's reputed pamphlet. The Ambassadors of the Reformed [Calvinist] princes, viz., Palatinate, Brandenburg, Deux-ponts, Anhalt, Mecklenburg, and some Earls of the Wetterau and Westerwald, who were present in person, consequently met at the Landgrave of Hesse's, to consult with him as to mutual assistance and closer alliance between themselves and with neighbouring States, in case the Lutherans should not be faithful to the League of Heilbronn, but betray them to the Papists. Both the meeting and its result were kept very secret. His theological proposition or Petition to the Diet. Much delay in

answering it, as the Chancellor of Sweden, as director of the four Upper Lord Brave's Circles, was then negotiating a treaty with the two Saxon Circles. A MSS. committee of sixteen however was appointed on August 16. His speech before them, and the result. His dealings with the Saxon Ambassadors, to whom he was introduced by those of Weimar and Onoltzbach (Anspach). Mentions that he had just cause to rely on the King of Sweden during his life by reason of his special promise of assistance, made by his own mouth to him. The Committee in the meantime agreed on a decree (September 1), which he immediately translated from German into Latin, and sent copies by the merchants from Frankfort to all foreign churches that had approved of the work. Left Frankfort the end of September, and having taken leave of Oxenstiern at Mentz came down the Rhine through many dangers at the same time when the Cardinal Infanta (sic) was come through the Wetterau to pass the Rhine at Andernach, arriving at Amsterdam about October 17. Having met there M. Maureis, the chief French preacher, he went to Leyden on the 22nd, and stayed there to open the matter to the chief divines of Holland. The state of the Church there. His consequent resolution. He resolves to begin with the professors of Leyden. His speech to them. He is advised to address the ministers at Leyden, and also Mr. Ghysius, the Deputy of the Provincial Synod of South Holland, and Dr. Begermannus. His proceedings with the Consistory of Leyden. At the Hague acquaints Sir Wm. Boswell, the English Ambassador, the Swedish Ambassador, the Queen of Bohemia, and the young Elector Palatine with his business. Meeting of the Deputies of the Synods of North and South Holland on November 15. His speech to them. Their answer and his reply, and their further reply. They decline to give any answer, their powers being limited, though approving of his zeal and good intentions. His second meeting with the Leyden professors. Their delays caused by Dr. Begermannus. Their final meeting on December 26, when they decide they can do nothing till the Synods have met. Intended to embark on January 8 from the Brill, but was frozen in till February 7, when he set sail and reached Gravesend the 11th. Asks leave to go to Holland and Germany again to continue the work, and asks Laud to confer on him the place which Mr. Elborough, the late preacher of the Company at Hamburgh is leaving. (Note by Laud. "He stayed thar, see this could not be granted to Mr. Durye.") Annexed are—
(i.) Copy of the Decree of the Diet dated September 1, 1634.
(ii.) Copy of Durye's letter to the Synods of Holland.
Endorsed by Laud, " Recc. Mart. 12, 1634. Comp. Aug."

May 31, 1635. Draft testimonial in Latin from Laud in favour of Durye. Some corrections in Laud's handwriting.

August 4; Sept. 1–4, 1635. Copy of the respective replies of the Synods of South Holland and Utrecht to Mr. Durye's proposals. They commend his zeal and good intentions, but state that only a National Synod is competent to deal with them.

January 14, 1636. Copy of the Reply of the Leyden Professors. They approve of Durye's intentions, but can do nothing without the consent of the Synods.

January $\frac{18}{28}$, $\frac{1635}{1636}$. Amsterdam. Durye to Laud. Had crossed to Holland in July. After giving some information about his plans to the Deputies of the Synod of South Holland, and to the States of the Province, he went into Zealand. In the middle of August, he went to the Synod of North Holland, where he found much prejudice against him and the work. They had predetermined not to disagree from the resolution of the Synod of South Holland held while he was in Zealand. Their shift was to declare that the consideration of his proposals belonged to a national Synod of all the provinces. The root of all the opposition is in two or three in the Synod of South Holland. His dealings in September with the Synod of Utrecht, who were rather more favourable. The real aim of some was on this ground to get leave from the States General to convene a National Synod which they desired for other purposes. In Friesland the consideration of his proposal was deferred till the next year's Synod ; in Overyssel copies of his letters were given to each church ; in Groningen the matter had not yet been laid before the Synod, while that of Gelderland could not meet that year on account of the war. He then applied to the Universities. The plague prevented his going to Leyden at once, so after staying a while at Amsterdam he visited the Queen of Bohemia's Court at Rhenen. About a month ago he went to Leyden, and procured the declaration of the Synod of South Holland and the judgment of the Professors. Endorsed, "Recep. Febr. 13, 1635. Mr. Dury his accompt concerning the Busines of Reconciling the Protestant Churches beyond the Seas &c."

A folio volume, newly bound, and lettered "Letters and State Papers, 1637–1641 :"—

July 11, 1637. Oriel College, Oxford. The Provost and Fellows to Sir Thomas Cave, of Stanford. You studied here in your youth, and you are accounted one of our benefactors. We are always glad to receive alms, but we are sorry to have to beg. You formerly gave us a gilded cup. Our walls are now tottering. (Latin.)

August 25, 1637. Edinburgh. "The Scotts' Remonstrance, and theire Reasons aganist the Booke of Common Prayers."

July 18–24, 1637. Copy of the proceedings in the High Commission Court against Williams, Bishop of Lincoln, for enforcing the sentence of suspension pronounced against him in the Star Chamber. Annexed is a copy of the judgment in the Star Chamber. (57 pages folio. As the first page is numbered 6 the first five pages are apparently lost.)

1638. Copies of assessments made in 1614 and 1615, and of two letters written in 1616 and 1638, relating to the assessment on the parishes of Twickenham and Whitton of four loads of hay, which according to a composition they had to supply to the King's stables. They include a particular of the parcels of meadow in those parishes, and the names of various residents. Strawberry Hill is called Strawberry Hall.

[1637 or 8.] John Crewe to [John Browne ?]. I went yesterday to Preston to meet one who had power from Sir W. Spencer to sell Rads[t]on. As you may perceive by their particular at 19 years purchase with the present value of the wood, it comes to above 10,000*l.*, but then the 25*l.* per annum, which the curate hath, was reckoned, which could not be justified. I stuck hard at 9,000*l.*, or 9,500*l.* if they would make good the particular ; but neither of those offers would do. Mr. Prescot swore I should have it for the tenants' sake 200*l.* cheaper than another. That night we could not agree, next morning after we had slept upon it, we agreed, as you may see in the note enclosed. Reckoning in the 50*l.* which Mr. Prescot must have, and 5*l.*, which one Glover another of Sir W. Spencer's servants will expect, it will cost you near upon 9,400*l.*

[1637 or 8.] The particular of the rents for the half year ending Lady Day 1637 or 1638.

1639. Paper containing:—1. A copy of the instrument dated LORD BRAYE's
January 24th, 1639, by which Alexander Leslie, minister of St. MSS.
Maldoes, dimitted quitted claim and overgave his "pretended office of
episcopacy as pretended bishopp of Dunkeldon."

2. Reports of some of the proceedings of the General Assembly at
Edinburgh in August 1639. " In the sixteenth sessions the Moderator
regrated that this Nationall Kirk, and many honnorable members thereof,
doe suffer under a declaration fathered upon the King's Majestie, but most
of all that his Majestie suffereth being made the speaker of the whole
stories, which could not come to his Majestie but by a report, and
therefore desired they would consider how the King's honnor might be
repaired, and everything donne in this buisnes as becometh a grave
assemblye. The Commissioner desired, since the Declaration caried the
title of the King's name, that the assembly would walk so circumspectly
as might testifie that they tender his Majesty's honnor. The Moderator
answered, It shall be our endeavour to tender his Majestie's honnor as
the apple of our eye. The Commissioner said, Since I understand it
concernes my master so near, I desire before you bring it any more in
publique that some may speake with me in private. The Earle of Rothes
said, It becomes us to speake very tenderly of that which is really done
by the King, but for that which hath come by misinformation we must
cleare that to the full. The Moderator desired that some might be
appoynted to revise the book. Mr. Allex. Henderson said, Truly for the
matter itselfe it is very necessary, and I think it will give noe offence to
the Kinge's Majestie that the buike be examined ; for in truth I thinke it
were a dishonor to his Majestie to be King over such subjects as are
described in that booke. Again, I herd his Majestie say many things
contrary to that booke, and I beleeve it is not written by his particular
direction, nor is he acquainted with the particulars of it." The assembly
then referred the book to a Committee.

In the twentieth session, the Moderator showed to the Commissioner
that the assembly were longing to have his Grace with them under one
covenant and word. The Commissioner acknowledged they had reason
to press that matter, but in regard the Covenant is made up of two
bodies, to wit, the confession and bond, he' behoved to be well advised
thereanent ; for the confession, he had no scruple at all, neither as it is
literally set down, nor as it is explained, and if there be any mistake it
was about this bond, yet he thought if in form and matter some things
were rightly understood sovereignty would receive satisfaction. The
Moderator answered, We have still been, and are ready to give satisfaction
in all things that might require the due estimation of good and loyal
subjects. As for the bond, we think it so well conceived that if it were
to be done again we could not light on so happy expressions ; nevertheless we are content that your Grace use all means to receive
satisfaction.

In the twenty-first session when the Moderator repeated his speech
to the Commissioner, the latter said that he and the council were
satisfied, both anent the matter and form, and that for authorising
thereof he and the council thought fit that the council should follow a
precedent of former times, to wit, that they would give in a supplication
to the council, desiring that as the assembly had added their ecclesiastical
authority, so they would add their civil sanction, willing all to subscribe
the same. He declared he was willing to subscribe the whole covenant,
but only desired to prefix a declaration to his subscription, which he
hoped would reconcile all. The assembly applauded thereat as a matter
of great thankfulness, and more than they had expected. (Then follows

the supplication, which is printed with some small variations in Rushworth, ii. 961.)

In the twenty-third session, the Committee on the Declaration having presented their report, and the Moderator having asked the opinion of some of the brethren, Mr. Andrew Cant said, " That booke is so full of grosse absurdities that I thinke hanging of the authors should prevent all theire censures. The Moderator answered that punishment is not in the hands of kirkmen. The scherif of Tividaill [Sir William Douglas of Cavers] said, Truly I would execute that sentance with all my hart, because I am better acquainted with hanging. My Lord Kirkcudbright said, It is a greate pity many honest men in Christendome for writting little pamphletts should want the eares, and false knaves for writting such volumes should brooke(?) heades." The assembly then drew up the supplication. (Printed in Rushworth, ii. 960.)

August 1639. Report of " The most considerable passages of the late General Assembly at Edinburgh." Imperfect, ending abruptly with page 32, pages 21–28 being missing. (Parts of it are printed in Rushworth, ii. 957, 958.)

[1639.] " To the King his most excellent Majestie. The humble petition of the Bishopes of the Church of Scotland, most humblie showeth. Whairas ane act of oblivion and pacification is socht in this parliament with exception of your Majesteis petitioners furth of the same, your Majestie may be gratiouslie pleased to give order that the parliament may tak notice of the petitioncres interest and heir thair reasons aganest the said exception. And they sall evir pray, as they are bund, for your Majesties long and prosperous raigne." Endorsed by Charles I.—" C.R. I remitt this to the Parlament."

April 24, 1640. Two propositions voted in the House of Lords, probably in the hand of the Lord Keeper, Sir. E. Lyttelton. (Printed in *Lords' Journals*, vol. iv., p. 67.)

April 25, 1640. " The heads of what I was commanded by the Lords to speake to the House of Comons at the Conference," probably in the hand of the Lord ·Keeper, Sir E. Lyttelton. (An abstract is printed in *Lords' Journals*, vol. iv., p. 68.)

April 28, 1640. Speech of Mr. Pym at the Conference. (An ·abstract is printed in *Lords' Journals*, vol. iv., p. 72.)

May 1, 1640. Speech of the Lord Keeper to the House of Commons, in the Painted Chamber. (Printed in *Lords' Journals*, vol. iv., pp. 75–77.)

July 13, 1640. Whitehall. The Council to Henry Kyme, one of ·the messengers of his Majesty's Chamber. Warrant for the arrest of —Hamilton,—Kep, and forty-five other inhabitants of Hampton,Tedding-.ton, Hanworth, East Bedfont, Feltham and Sunbury. Signed by the Archbishop of Canterbury, the Earl of Strafford, and eight others. Seal affixed.

October [1640. York.] — to —. Yesterday, being Sunday, there came hither from Ripon, from their fellow Commissioners, the Lords Hertford, Holland, Bristol and Mandeville. The third of these, in a full assembly in the afternoon, gave an account of what they had done. They had agreed that 50,000*l.* should be paid to, the Scots, as a contribution for two months to begin on the 16th instant, by the town of Newcastle, the Bishopric [of Durham], Northumberland, Cumberland and Westmoreland, nothing being now wanting to a cessation of arms but security for the payment of this sum. The Scots said that for LORD BRAYE'S MSS. want of this they would be forced to deal hostilely with the country, which in a time of cessation would make them and their cause odious. They also said that this sum was not sufficient to maintain them, but that they did not wish to appear unreasonable. For security, they demanded that of those great Lords who had lands in those counties. Lord Bristol said that though these terms were not so honourable for his Majesty and this kingdom as he might have wished, the Commissioners had done no disservice to them. The question of security was referred to the Lords. The Lord Lieutenant [Strafford] in reply declared that he could not agree to making provision for the Scottish army for two months, while the King's army had not provision for half that time. The King pressed the Commissioners to take the whole affair on themselves, but they desired to be excused, and all resolutions were deferred until to-day. The King complained that the Londoners had spread a report that he had changed his demeanour as soon as he had obtained a promise of money, which report all present declared to be groundless. He also desired them to press the Londoners with a new letter, inasmuch as they had grown extremely backward even in making good their own undertakings, but the drawing up of the letter was deferred. To-day they met again in the afternoon. Lord Bristol declared that those were most to blame who had led the King to think that he' might have three armies in the country of the Scots, who instead had one in ours. The Lord Lieutenant answered that he could not but see that he was pointed at, and that for a long time he had ten thousand men ready in Ireland, who might have been brought over at once if the King had but provided the ships. The Marquess Hamilton said that he was not answerable, inasmuch as he had not had the army which was to have been under his command. The King said that the design was not to be blamed because money had failed, to which Lord Bristol replied that wise men ought not to enter into an undertaking without equal certainty of the means. They then turned to the question of the security for the contribution. Some persons of Newcastle, of the Bishopric, and of Northumberland were admitted, and, being examined as to the ability of those places, they did not make good so much as the Lords had expected of them, viz., the money for the first month. After much dispute, Lord Bristol said that he remembered that the Lord Lieutenant had said that if the Scots marched without a battle (which he then confessed it was inconvenient to venture), he could not keep them out of Yorkshire. He therefore thought that that country ought to join in the contribution. The Lord Lieutenant answered that Lord Bristol had remembered a part only of what he had said. He had spoken of their marching with their whole army, which, by reason of the increase of winter, he was confident they could not do, and with 18,000 foot and 2,400 horse, he could easily make the country too hot for any small parties that might be sent to plunder it. After much discourse, the Lords resolved to take the burden of securing the contribution from their own shoulders and to lay it upon those of their Commissioners, to whom they again gave power to obtain it from as many persons as possible. The Lord Lieutenant seemed displeased with this resolution, saying that when he had proposed that all countries should be asked to contribute to the King's army, he had not been listened to. Much less therefore could he consent to using this course for the maintenance of rebels. The Council however did not heed him, and the resolution was passed. To-morrow the four Lords return to Ripon, where I shall wait upon them, ready, upon the first resolution of the cessation, to take post, and, by the advantage of a shorter cut than

York, bring the news of it to London before the King's letters. Of the Lords' letters to London, I do not hear that any draft was made to-day, perhaps for want of leisure. (Copy in Browne's hand. Cf. Hardwicke's *State Papers*, vol. ii.)

November 5, 1640. Report of the speech of Lord Keeper Finch, approving the choice of Mr. Lenthal as Speaker.

November 14, 1640. "An Order mended with the Lord Keeper's owne hand." (Printed in *Lords' Journals*, vol. iv., p. 91.)

November 27, 1640. Original paper stating the practice of the Court of Star Chamber with regard to (1) Examination of witnesses by commission, (2) Examination of witnesses in court, (3) Examinations to shake the credit of witnesses, (4) Publication of the depositions. Signed Henry Jones, Jo. Haker, Robt. Paley, Hen. Hudson, Jo. Arthur, Registrar.

November 30, 1640. Holograph petition of the Earl of Strafford, concerning Mr. Darley. (Printed in *Lords' Journals*, iv. 102.)

December 1640. The particular note under the hand of the Lieutenant of the Tower, (referred to in *Lords' Journals*, iv. 106,) giving the names of the persons who had visited Lord Strafford. On the same paper are the minutes from which the order for the safe keeping of the Earl of Strafford (printed in *Lords' Journals*, iv. 106) was drawn up.

December 9, 1640. The reply of the English Commissioners, on behalf of the King, to the fourth demand of the Scottish Commissioners touching incendiaries. " His Majestie conceaveth he hath no such about him. And as he cannot but in honor give all just protection to his servants, so he holdeth it an act of his royall justice that whosoever shall upon a fayre and equall tryall and examination be found by the estates of either of the two Parliaments (they judging against the persons subject to their own authoritie) to have been in any sort the authors or causers of the late and present troubles and combustion shall be lyable to the censure and sentence of the said Parliaments respectively." Cf. Rushworth, iii. 1365.)

December 15 and 16, 1640. Three original papers of the Scottish Commissioners, signed by Adam Blair. The first is a demand that money be immediately sent down for the supply of their army according to the armistice of Ripon (Cf. Nalson i. 680), the second and third are the charges against the Archbishop of Canterbury and the Earl of Strafford. (Printed in full, Nalson i. 681, 686. Extracts in Rushworth iii. 1. 1370, and *Trial of Strafford*, 769.)

December 23, 1640. Copy of the reply of the Scottish Commissioners to the answer to their further demand concerning incendiaries. (Cf. Rushworth iii. 1. 365.)

January 8, 1640[-1]. Schedule of records and pleadings in the Star Chamber, delivered by the registrar to Mr. Browne, Clerk of Parliament, pursuant to an order of the House of Lords, concerning Sir Richard Wiseman. (Cf. *Lords' Journals*, iv. 124.)

January 14, 1640[-1]. Report of the conclusion of Lord Falkland's speech on the impeachment of Lord Keeper Finch. (Printed in Nalson i. 726. " I shall not need to say, &c.," where " computation " is a misprint for " complication.")

February 3, 1640[-1]. Paper in the handwriting of Williams, Bishop of Lincoln, being a statement on the question whether the bishops should speak or vote on the impeachment of the Earl of Strafford. (The LORD BRAYE'S concluding words are printed in *Lords' Journals*, iv. 150.) MSS.

February 16, 1640 [-1]. Draft of instructions to the Lord Keeper for a vote of thanks to the King. (*Lords' Journals* vol. iv. p. 164.)

Copy of the protest of the Lords spiritual and temporal of Ireland touching part of the preamble of the act of four subsidies (15 Car. I. c. 13 Irish Statutes, which is printed in Nalson, i. 280,) read on March 23rd, 1640-1 (Cf. Rushworth, *Trial of Strafford*, 113). After reciting the aforesaid part of the preamble, they state that the act had only been read after the Earl of Strafford had by declaring there was imminent danger of a Scotch invasion procured the grant of four subsidies, and the delay which would have been caused by the transmission of the bill to England under Poyning's Act, while, as they believed, a Scotch invasion was imminent, was the only cause which had prevented exception being taken to the said part of the preamble, which had indeed been purposely inserted by the Earl to anticipate the just and universal complaints of the subjects of that kingdom. They further protest and declare that this kingdom was in a flourishing and happy state when Lord Strafford assumed the government, that since then he and his ministers have changed the face of the government by introducing a new unlawful arbitrary and tyrannical government, by the determination of all or most causes by paper petitions and other unjust and unwarrantable proceedings, to the particular profit of himself and his ministers, tending to the impoverishment and destruction of his Majesty's subjects in their lands, goods, lives and just liberties, and to the subversion of the former laudable, mild, and loyal government for many ages past. They accuse Strafford and his ministers of having advanced and enriched themselves by all sorts of extortion and injustice. They declare their conviction that his Majesty's intention in appointing him was that he should demean himself as an upright and equal governor according to the laws of the kingdom, but that he and his ministers had managed the affairs of the kingdom directly contrary to his Majesty's pious intention. They declare their approval of the rest of the act and the grant of the four subsidies, and pray that an act may be passed for removing from the Records of Parliament the part of the preamble against which they protest, that Strafford and his ministers may henceforth have nothing to do with the government and the affairs of this kingdom, and that the contrivers and advisers of the said part of the preamble may be impeached and punished. (Copy by Philip Percival, Clerk of the Parliament.)

March 6, 1640[-1]. Message of the House of Commons concerning the Earl of Strafford. (Printed in *Lords' Journals*, iv. 177.)

March 9, 1640[-1]. The Index of the remanent heads contained in the eighth demand of the Scottish Commissioners for establishing of a firm and durable peace. (Cf. *Lords' Journals*, iv. 216.)

March 15, 1640[-1]. Copy of the answer of the English Commissioners to the Scottish Commissioners. (Cf. *Lords' Journals*, iv. 216.) It concludes thus—" His Majestie expects that according to your many professions and of that which is contayned in your owne paper you will not intermeddle with the Reformation in England but leave the care thereof to the King and kingdome. As likewise that you should not publish or divulge any discourses by which the subjects of this kingdome should be stirred up against the established lawes of the kingdome but that you should acquiesse with this answeare."

March 15, 1640[-1]. Answer of the Scottish Commissioners. They acknowledge that no reformation can be expected but from the wisdom and authority of the King and the Houses of Parliament. Their motive for giving their reasons for considering that the peace without uniformity of church government will be less durable than they wish. A difference should be made between discourses to stir up the people against the laws of the kingdom and the presenting in a humble and peaceable way to the King and parliament such things as are judged necessary for a permanent peace. As they had exhibited the heads of their 8th demand only by way of Index, they had deemed it incumbent on them to " propone " their meaning in so many of them as concerned both nations. They entreat the English Commissioners, as they have showed their desire concerning this mean of peace to the King, they will also show the same to the Houses of Parliament.

[1640-1]. Paper containing notes of the manner in which the trial of the Earl of Strafford is to be conducted.

—— to ——. During the assize week the gentry and clergy of Devonshire have taken great pains to frame a petition against the oath in the new canons. Lord Bath first " firmed " it, and then most of the gentry and clergy. It is said that Mr. Wise and Mr. Seymour our Knights in Parliament have undertaken to deliver it. Very few in the country will take the oath. Copy of the seven exceptions to the oath, and of the petition of many gentlemen of the county of Devon, to the Lords of the Privy Council. (Copy by J. Browne.)

April 2, 1641. Original petition of Sir Thomas Aston, Baronet, on behalf of the County Palatine of Chester, against a libel printed as a petition in the name of the said county against bishops, asserting among other things that they are only of ethnical or diabolical institution, read on the above date. (Cf. *Lords' Journals*, iv. 204 ; Nalson i. 795.)

April 10, 1641. Reasons for the order touching the examination of new witnesses in Lord Strafford's trial. (Printed in *Lords' Journals*, iv. 212.)

[April 12, 1641.] Paper containing apparently notes of what passed at the conference of that date of the Committee of both Houses. (Cf. *Lords' Journals*, iv. 215 ; Nalson, ii. 103.)

April 12, 1641. Copy of the answer of the English to the Scottish Commissioners touching unity of Church Government. " That his Majestie commandeth us to adhere to his former answeare, and conceaveth it most just you should acquiesse therewith."

April 26, 1641. Report of Mr. Hyde's speech against the President and Council of the North. (Printed in Nalson, i. 801 ; Extracts in Rushworth, ii. 2, 1336.)

May 1, 1641. The Heads of the King's speech concerning Lord Strafford. (Printed in Nalson, ii. 186, and Rushworth, *Trial of Strafford*. This report agrees substantially with the printed copies which conclude with the word " misdemeanor," but contains in addition, " Now I cannott lett you go without putting you in mynd what I said the last day in the Bancketting House at Whitehall. The summe of it was to show my earnest desire and crave your assistance for disbanding all armyes soe that now not only having my consent but desired (*sic*) your assistance for disbanding the Irish army and all others all the world shall see it is not my fault if this be not speedily done, and I shall not be wanting on my parte for restoring a happy peace and tranquillity.")

1641. Deposition of Eus[eby] Andrewes. On Monday the 3rd of May [1641] instant he was in discourse with Francis Littleton and John Lylborne. He asked the latter the meaning of the numbers of people then gathered together. Lylborne answered they came for justice, and Lord Braye's MSS. were about the number of 6 or 7,000, and that there would be 40 or 50,000 the next day, and that they came then with their cloaks, but that the next day they would come with their swords by their sides and armed. He then asked what would be the end of this business, or what their meaning was in so doing, to which Lylborne answered there was a report or rumour that they will either have the Deputy or the King. "And being by mee procured to be brought into the messinger's custody the said Lylbon recollected the wordes of his own accord and confessed them."

[May, 1641.] "To the Lords spirituall and temporall in this present Parliament assembled. The humble petition of Thomas Earle of Strafforde. Besecheth your Lordships that wheras ther was much new matter alledged by the honorable house of Commons in matter of law, as concerning the bill of Attaindure past ther aganst him, to his grate greefe.

That your Lordships would be pleased to admitt him a time to be hearde therin by his Counsell, or otherwise in writing to offer such an humble defence therin, as your humble petitioner conceaves avaylable for him, and that the rather, for that records themselves vewed will be founde (he trusts) to containe matter very necessary by your Lordships to be informed of before itt willbe fully prepared for your judgments therein.

Which as your petitioner conceaves, amongst other, will appeare by the following instances." Examines the cases of Savage, in 5 Hen. IV. c. 6; Gomines and Weston, in 1 Ric. II.; the Ambassador of Genoa; the statute 11 Ric. II. c. 3; Sir John Mortimer, in 2 Hen. VI.; the statute of 22 Hen. VIII. c. 9; Elizabeth Barton, in 25 Hen. VIII. c. 12; Sir Thomas Seymour, in 2 & 3 Edw. VI. c. 18. "Soe that under favoure your Petitioner humbly conceaves, not any president was produced for an offence not capitall by law, made capitall by acttes of Parliament, and the party punished by the same acttes. Humbly beseeching your Lordships to consider the statutes of E[dward] 6 for two witnesses.

And your petitioner shall humbly pray long to continue your Lordships with all increase of honour and happinesse. Strafforde." (Holograph, 4 sides. Probably dictated by a lawyer. Endorsed "Lecta 5°. Maij 1641.")

May 5, 6, and 7, 1641. Copy of the Resolutions of the House of Lords upon which the judges gave their opinion about the Earl of Strafford. (Printed in Nalson ii., 192, and *Lords' Journals*, iv. 239.)

1. Resolved upon the question, that going by way of Bill in the discussing of the matter of fact in this whole cause the rule shall be only the persuasion of every man's conscience.

2. That the Earl of Strafford gave warrant for cessing of soldiers upon men's lands in Ireland, and the same was executed accordingly.

3. That the cessing of soldiers was done for the disobeying of the Earl of Strafford's orders made upon paper petitions between party and party against their consents.

4. That the cessing of soldiers was with arms and officers in a warlike manner.

5. The same with a verbal alteration.

6. That the Earl of Strafford did counsel and advise his Majesty that he was absolved from rules of Government.

7. That the Earl of Strafford said unto his Majesty that in cases of necessity and for the defence and safety of the kingdom, if the people did not use to supply the king the king is absolved from rules of government

and that everything is to be done for the preservation of the king and
his people, and that his Majesty was acquitted before God & man.

8. Similar to the last in different words.

9. That the Earl of Strafford said to the King these words : You have
an army in Ireland which your Majesty may employ to reduce this
kingdom, or words to that effect.

10. That these words (to reduce this kingdom) were spoken of the
kingdom of England.

11. That the Earl of Strafford hath by his words counsels and actions
endeavoured to subvert the fundamental laws of the kingdoms of
England and Ireland, and to introduce an arbitrary power.

12. That the Earl of Strafford hath exercised a tyrannous and
exorbitant government above and against the laws over the lives
liberties and estates of the subjects.

13. Resolved by vote that this question be put to the judges : That
upon all that the Lords have voted to be proved that the Earl of
Strafford doth deserve to undergo the pains and penalties of High
Treason by law.

May 4, 1641. Original Examination of Elizabeth Nutt, Anne Bardsey,
and Anne Vyner. (Printed in *An Exact Account*, King's Pamphlets,
British Museum, E. 241, p. 236, being one of the documents annexed
to the Remonstrance of the Lords and Commons of May 19, 1642.
This will be hereafter referred to simply as *Exact Account.*)

May 11, 1641. Original Examination of John Lanyon. (Printed,
*Exact Account*, p. 234.)   Subscribed—John Lanyon.

May 11, 1641. Original Examination of Captain James Chudleigh.
(Printed, *Exact Account*, p. 220.)   Subscribed—James Chudleigh, and
attested by the signatures of the Earls of Essex and Warwick, Lord
P. Howard, Lord W. Howard.

May 18, 1641. Original second Examination of Captain James
Chudleigh. (Printed in *Exact Account*, p. 223.) Subscribed—James
Chudleigh, and attested by the signatures of the Earls of Essex and
Warwick, Lords Say and Seale, and Howard.

May 18, 1641. Original Examination of Captain William Legge.
(Printed, *Exact Account*, p. 224.)   Subscribed—Will. Legge.

May 29, 1641. Original Examination of Colonel Vavasour
(Printed, *Exact Account*, p. 227.) Subscribed—Will. Vavasour, and
attested by the signatures of Viscount Mandeville, and Lords Wharton
and Howard.

June 2, 1641. Original Examination of Sir W. Balfour, Lieutenant
of the Tower. (Printed, *Exact Account*, p. 232.) Subscribed—W.
Balfour, and attested by the signatures of the Earls of Essex and
Warwick, Lord Wharton, Lord Howard and Viscount Mandeville.

June 19, 1641. Original Examination of Colonel Goring. (Printed,
*Exact Account*, p. 215.)   Subscribed—George Goring.

Copies of a number of orders made by the Lords' Committee for
petitions, the first in order being dated June 6th, 1641, but the earliest
in date being dated February 4th, and the last August 29th, 1641. The
only one containing anything of interest is dated June 9th, on the
petition of Dr. Robert Metcalfe, late Professor of Hebrew in the
University of Cambridge, stating that on relinquishing his professorship
he ought to become Fellow of Trinity College, which though the Masters
and Seniors had granted, yet the seniority among the Fellows to which
he was entitled by the Statutes was denied him.

May–July 1641. Document endorsed "Instructions for taking the
Protestation," but really a draft or copy of the Bill imposing it.   (In J.
Browne's hand.)

July 19, 1641. Original Report on the quarrel between the Lord
Chamberlain (the Earl of Pembroke and Montgomery) and Lord Mowbray and Maltravers.   "The committee havinge mett about the Jurisdiction of the Lords howse in matters of law betweene party and party
tryable by a jury, there was a desyre of divers of the Lords to heare the
Stat. of 4$^{to}$ Hen. IV. read, which was vouched at the Barre by one of the
counsel in the case of Sutton Marsh, which was done accordingly.
Then my Lord Duke of Lenox beinge newly come in demanded
whither the readinge of that statute had relation to Sutton Marsh, to
which the Lord Seymour answered, This is read onely as concerning the
generall Jurisdiction of the howse. Whereupon there havinge bine some
former discourse of Sutton Marsh, my Lord Chamberlayne sayd, lookinge
towards my Lord Matravers and pointing with his staff — No
man named Sutton Marsh till you named it, to which my Lord Matravers replyed I never named it till you named it first, and I appeale to
the Committee.   To which my Lord Chamberlayne sayd—But you did.
The other answered—I did not; and soe twise or thrise to and fro.
Then said my Lord Chamberlayne—My Yea is as good as your No, to
which my Lord Maltravers—And my No as your Yea, and further sayd
that he would maintayne that he had named it 20 tymes this day.   To
which my Lord Chamberlayne sayd that he durst not maintayne it out of
that place.   Then my Lord Matravers sayd, That he would maintayne it
in any place, for it was true ;  To which my Lord Chamberlayne replyed
that it was false.   My Lord Matravers said You lye.   Whereupon my
Lord Chamberlayne reached out his white staffe and over the table strok
him on the head.   Then my Lord Matravers took up the standesh that
was on the table before him, and my Lord Chamberlayne goinge farther
from him, he threw it after him but misst him.   Then my Lord
Chamberlayne came towards him agayne and over the table gave him a
second blow with his white staffe.

| | |
|---|---|
| D. of Lennox (sic)   · | Ld. Mandevill, |
| E. of Bathe, | Ld. Andevor, |
| E. of Barkshyre, | Ld. Savill, |
| Ld. B[ishop] of Lincolne, | Ld. Seymaur, |

out of whose relation this was sett downe."

July 21, 1641. Original Petition of the Earl of Pembroke and Montgomery to the House, apologizing "for his miscarriage towards Your
Lordships." Subscribed—Pembroke and Montgomery.

July 22, 1641. Original Petition of Lord Mowbray and Maltravers
to the House apologising for having been "transported to an excesse
which in respect to your Lordships and that place he should have
foreborne." Subscribed—Mowbray and Matravers.

July 24, 1641. List of the Lords' Committee appointed to draw up
the submissions of the Earl of Pembroke and Montgomery and the
Lord Mowbray and Maltravers.   (Cf. Rushworth, iii. 1. 350.)

August 16, 1641. Original Examination of the Earl of Pembroke
and Montgomery before the Committee for taking examinations concerning Incendiaries.   (For the circumstances under which the Committee was appointed before whom this and following five depositions of
the same date were taken, see Lords' Journals, iv. 365, 366 ; Nalson, ii.
444, 447.)   Subscribed—Pembroke and Montgomery, and attested by the
signatures of the Earls of Warwick and Dover, and Lord Mandeville.

Same date. Original Examination of Lord Mandeville before the same Committee. Subscribed—Mandeville, and attested by the signatures of the Earls of Warwick and Dover, the Earl of Loudoun and Lord Howard (of Escrick).

Same date. Original Examination of the Earl of Stirling before the same Committee. Subscribed—Sterling, and attested by the signatures of the Earls of Warwick and Dover, and Lord Howard.

Same date. Original Examination of Robert Young, Printer, before the same Committee. States that he and Richard Badger printed the declaration, and that the original was delivered to them by Mr. Secretary Windebank, who declared it was his Majesty's pleasure that it should be printed. That the prototype or first draught of the said declaration was all in the same hand. That he printed the declaration concerning the proceedings of the subjects of Scotland since the Pacification which was published in 1640. Finding some doubtful expressions in the copy he took it to Mr. Robert Reade (in whose handwriting it was) who told the deponent that he could say nothing till he had seen Traquair, whose business it was, for it is he that doth all the work. The proclamation was printed by him by command of Mr. Secretary Windebank and was in the handwriting of Sir John Hayes. Subscribed—Robt. Young, and attested by the signatures of the Earls of Warwick and Dover, the Earl of Loudoun and Lord Howard.

Same date. Original Examination of Robert Chapman, composer (compositor). Subscribed—Robert Chapman, and attested as the last.

Same date. Original Examination of William Warriner. Subscribed William Warriner, and attested as the last, except that it is also attested by Lord Mandeville.

August 31, 1641. Draft of a letter to the Lords Justices of Ireland, in the handwriting of Williams, Bishop of Lincoln. (Printed in *Lords' Journals*, iv. 387.)

September 3 and 6, 1641. Original Informations of George Carpenter and other servants to the French Ambassador, concerning the riot at his house in Lincoln's Inn Fields. " After the ambassadour hadd dined his porter (as his manner was) went to the doore to distribute the broken meat and such alms as hee was appointed to to the poore that resorted thither, and in that distribution he having more respect to relieve the aged and impotent poore before the younger sort, one Roger Gardner, a disorderly young fellow, contending with the porter about the almes, the porter gave him a blow with a cane, whereupon the said Gardner did throw stones at the ambassador's windows." Subjoined are the names of the accused and their examinations attested by the signatures of George Long, John Hooker, and Thomas Sheppard, the justices before whom they were taken. (Cf. *Lords' Journals*, iv. 382, 389.)

October 29, 1641. Original examination of Sir Jacob Astley before the Committee of the Lords. (This and the following four examinations are printed in *Exact Account*, pp. 232, 232, 230, 231, and 228.) Signed—Jacob Asteley.

Same date. Original examination of Sir Fulke Huncks before the same Committee. Signed—Fulke Hunckes.

Same date. Original examination of Sir John Conyers before the same Committee. Signed—Jo. Conyers.

October 30, 1641. Original second examination of the same.

Same date. Original examination of Captain William Legge before the same Committee. Signed—Will. Legge.

December 20, 1641. A. Fullarton to ———. It is now twenty days LORD BRAYE's MSS. since we came hither, and a fortnight since we began the treaty. No answer however has been given to any of our propositions. In case of further delay we demand that we may have entertainment for the 2,500 men whom we have kept up for this service. (Copy.) Endorsed, " 8th paper of the Commissioners of Scotland."

A folio volume, newly bound and lettered " Letters and State Papers, 1642-1647."

January 20, 1641[-2.] Middleborough—[Lord Digby] to Sir Lewis Dives, Knt., at the Earl of Bristol's house in Queen Street, London. (Original. Printed in *State Trials*, 1809, vol. iv., p 137.)

March 22, 1641[-2]. Copy of the examination of Hugh Macmahon upon the rack. Sir Phelim O'Neale, Lord Maguire and Philip McHugh O'Reilly were the first complotters and contrivers of the Rebellion in Ireland. They had told him that all parties who were Parliament men at the session of Parliament holden about May last, that were Papists, knew and approved of the said rebellion. O'Reilly further had told him in Dublin about May last that the Committee or Agents who were employed into England by the Parliament would procure an order or commission from the King to authorise the Papists of Ireland to proceed in their rebellious causes, and that the said O'Reilly did also tell him the same again in the county of Monaghan a little before the 23rd of October. Colonel McBryan Macmahon told him on the 20th of October last at his own house that the King had given a commission to the Papists of Ireland to seize upon all the garrisons and strongholds in Ireland, and that he should see the said commission at his coming to Dublin, and that Captain Brian O'Neale, grandchild to Sir Turloe McHenry should bring him to the agent who was one of the committee that did bring the commission out of England, but the agent named, the said Colonel McBryan, did not or could not tell him. That his nephew Philip McHugh O'Neale meeting him at Finglas near Dublin, on the 22nd of October last told him that there would be twenty persons out of every county in the kingdom to assist in the taking of the Castle of Dublin. That Art McHugh Oge Macmahon came in his company to assist in the taking of the Castle of Dublin. That Colonel Mac Brian Macmahon did procure Rory Oge Mac Patrick Macmahon to persuade Patrick McArt Macmahon and Patrick McOwen McMahon Mc Patrick Macmahon and two other Macmahons whom he knows not, and Donogh O'Finehy to come to Dublin to assist in the taking of the Castle of Dublin, who were all apprehended in the same house in Dublin as himself. (In J. Browne's hand.)

April, [1642], Hull. Sir John Hotham to William Lenthall, Speaker of the House of Commons. (Original. Printed in *Lords' Journals*, vol. v., pp. 28, 29.)

May 16, 1642. Memoranda taken at the conference between the Houses to keep correspondency and to prevent dangers. (Cf. *Lords' Journals*, v. 67), noting what papers were read thereat.

May 19, 1642. List of papers delivered to Joseph Hunscott and John Wright with their receipt for them and an undertaking to return them in 8 days. (The List is printed in *Commons' Journals*, ii. 573. Most of the original documents are in this collection.)

[May, (?) 1642.] Memorandum " that the substance of his Majesties proposition consisted in these two particulars :—(1.) To know whether wee would defend his Majesties royall person from violence, or noe ;

accordinge to our dutie. (2.) To have our advise concerninge his Majestie being not admitted into his Towne of Hull; and how his Majestie may be vindicated in his Honor, for the affront, and how hee may bee putt into the possession of his owne. May it please your sacred Majestie wee shall bee ready to defend your Majesties person from violence by all such wayes as the lawes and our dutie bindeth. And for the meanes to vindicate your Majesties Honour, and to putt you into possession of your owne, wee conceive the best advise that wee can offer to your Majestie is humblie to desire you to hearken to the Councell of the Parliament, who, wee assure ourselves, will bee carefull of your Majesties person and Honor, and to whom your Majestie hath already beene pleased to direct a message." Endorsed, "The King's Propositions to the Gentry at Yorke."

June 10, 1642. Original Deposition of Herbert Finch. Printed in *Lords' Journals*, v. 124.

June 17, 1642. Westminster. James Prymerose, for the Council of Scotland, to the Houses of Lords and Commons. (Printed in *Lords' Journals*, vol. v., p. 146.)

June 20, 1642. Burghley. The Earl of Exeter to Lord Wharton. Inasmuch as some of his Deputy Lieutenants are in London, he desires to be given further time for the execution of his orders. Signed. Heraldic seal affixed. (Cf. *Lords' Journals*, vol. v., p. 141.)

June 28, 1642. The King to the Earl of Warwick. Signed— "Charles R." Seal attached. (Printed in *Lords' Journals*, v. 178.)

July 2, 1642. Resolution of the Commanders of the Fleet. (Printed in *Lords' Journals*, v. 179.) All in apparently the same handwriting except the signatures of Richard and William Swanley.

Same date. Four original letters with seals from Captains Robert Slingsby, Richard Fogg, Baldwin Wake and John Mennes, to the Earl of Warwick. (Printed in *Lords' Journals*, v. 179, 180.)

July 13, 1642. Hull. Sir John Hotham, Peregrine Pelham, and John Alured, to William Lentall, Esq., Speaker of the House of Commons. (Printed in *Lords' Journals*, vol. v., p. 217.) Seal affixed.

July 21, 1642. Draft of the Declaration of both Houses of Parliament to the General Assembly in Scotland. (Printed in *Lords' Journals*, vol. v., p. 229.)

August 5, 1642. Original letter (unsigned), written from Burlington aboard the Unicorn to Sir John Hotham, Governor of Hull. (The substance and in parts the wording is the same as that of the letter dated the previous day from the same place from Thomas Trenchfield to the Speaker of the House of Lords, which is printed in *Lords' Journals*, v. 314.)

August 22, 1642. Colchester. Major Thomas Wade to Harbottle Grimston, Recorder of Colchester, and a Member of Parliament. On Saturday there was a report in our town about a store of arms that were taken from Humerstone, one of our carriers, belonging to Sir John Lucas, which were packed up to be sent to his house in Colchester. This bred in the common people such fears and jealousies that they wanted but an opportunity to search his house. Yesterday at noon Captain Langley came and told me that he was credibly informed that Sir John Lucas intended to send some horses to the King this day, and at night Mr. Coxe, the High Constable, came and told me the same. I therefore desired him to set a watch on Sir John Lucas's house, which he did. About twelve o'clock the watch discovered some horses coming out of a back gate and stopped them. Presently word was brought into the LORD BRAYE'S MSS. town that there were a hundred men in arms at Sir John's. The drums thereupon beat up, the town got into an uproar, and the trained band and volunteers presently beset the house. There are gathered together, besides the bands, five thousand men, women, and children, which I feared might do some hurt. I therefore, being accompanied by some other justices and aldermen, made proclamation in several places where the tumults were, at one o'clock in the night and several times since, charging the people to depart. They however regarded us no more than they do a child, and then we charged the bands to keep careful watch about the house. This they did until day light, and then the rude sort of people broke into Sir John's house, and seized upon his horses, some 8 or 9 in number, which I have caused to be kept until I hear from you. They have also found much armour and many new pistols and carbines ready charged, new great saddles and other warlike furniture, part of which they have brought up to the hall. Nothing would satisfy these tumultuous people but that Sir John Lucas, his mother, and his servants should be committed. I therefore desired Sir John to go to my house for safety, and he and his lady mother and his sister went there. When the people knew that they were not committed, they came in great numbers and told me to my face that they would pull down my house upon my head. Sir John, his lady mother and sister then went to the Moot hall, in order to save my house, and they are now in the hall. One of Sir John's men is said to have confessed that twelve horses were to have gone to the King last night, Sir John riding one of them and Mr. Newcomen, clerk, another. The rude people do much abuse themselves and Sir John also in rifling his house, spoiling his goods, and carrying away his plate, money, books, boxes, writings and household stuff. They are come to such a head being a mixed company of town and country, that we know not how to quiet them. Believe we could not repress them if we had five trained bands, unless they were killed. We fear they will not stay here, for they say that they will go to Lady Savage's at St. Osith, and to some other places about the town. I pray you to acquaint the house with those things and to send me directions with all speed.

September 6, 1642. Copy of a letter from Sherborne to the Lord General from the Earl of Bedford, Col. Denzil Hollis, and Col. Essex. We have been three days and three nights in arms before Sherborne and with as much sufferance to ourselves and little hurt unto the enemy as ever any thing that had the name of an army was, our number of men having been rather the show of an army for muster than an army to fight, for there is neither officer or soldier amongst them except it be two or three captains and as many lieutenants and serjeants that will do any duty themselves then much less the soldiers, and for all the rest even through the whole army when any alarum is, as very many we have in the nights, we cannot for our lives draw the companies into battallia. Very few officers are there to be found nor will they go upon any action when they are commanded. If a bullet come over their heads, they fall flat upon their bellies, and some four or five being slain hath made about half of them run away and we are confident half of those that are left will follow; so that of four and twenty hundred that came with us out of Somersetshire and nine hundred that came out of Dorsetshire and Devonshire, we have not twelve hundred left, and God knows how many may slip away this night. The Deputy Lieutenants and Prime Gentlemen of the country which are with us are willing to do anything they can, but your Excellency well knows it is not in their way, and they presumed upon the country people who have deceived them. The short of all is we have no army, nor can possibly with these men do this work. We much doubt if we shall be able to make good our quarters, for the cannon out of the castle shooting compass reaches it, hath hurt some men this afternoon, broke the leg of one and arm of another, and they run away upon it, so as some regiments are not so strong as a company, and we cannot make them perfect their entrenchment, which we have been a whole day and a half about, whereas it should have been done in four or five hours upon the first sitting down. The whole business lies upon the hands of two or three who must do the officers of all the particular offices of every regiment down to that of a serjeant. The Castle is strong, that our cannon which is but demiculverin works no effect upon it. What number of men they have in it we cannot certainly learn, but this we are confident, that to do good upon it, there must be three several quarters made about it, and we are not able now to make good one, and they in the Castle are at liberty to take in what fresh supplies they will. My Lord, you must send us down more forces, 3 regiments of foot and 3 troops of horse, for these horse which are our only safety are clean worn out with being continually in arms and cannot hold out, and should they fail us all were lost. We have no engineer or quartermaster nor workbase, though we have several times writ for some, and certainly our letters have been intercepted, else your Excellency would not think we had neglected writing. The messenger whom we last sent, who is servant to Mr. Popham, in his return was taken and is yet a prisoner in Sherborne so as we know not what answer was sent us. We only know this, that we have done and will do what lies in us, but our army deserting us, it was not to be done by us alone.

So much of this letter was written yesternight, and this morning we find so many more men gone, that we are necessitated to rise and upon mature deliberation with all the colonels and prime gentlemen we have taken this resolution ; to march presently away with the whole body to Dorchester and there stay three or four days to refresh man and horse, then the Somersetshire troops to return into Somersetshire with two troops of our horse to convey them to secure Bridgwater and Taunton, we to stay at Dorchester with our horse and what force that country will afford to secure all those parts and all along the sea coast especially Weymouth, which is a considerable place and a little doubtful, and be ready when the supplies shall come from your Excellency to fall upon Sherborne, but we must of necessity have some whole cannon, two at the least. We shall humbly beseech you to consider the great consequence of this action that upon the reducing of this castle and the scattering these malignants who are in it, depends the good or evil of the whole business of the kingdom. We for our parts will gladly lay down our lives for the well effecting of it, but truly we would die like men and with men and not like fools in the company of heartless beasts, with whom we had no more wit than to engage our honours and lives. Your Excellency will pardon this long and unpleasing relation and the untoward expression of it for this is the fourth extreme cold night we have been without any sleep that never were men more dazed than your Excellencies most obedient servants.

A postscript recommends the bearer Lieut. Smyth, who is newly come out of Ireland. (Cf. Rushworth, iii. 1. 685 ; *Commons' Journals*, ii. 758 ; *Lords' Journals*, v. 343.)

September 17, 1642. Copy of a letter to the Lord General from John Fielden, Sir William Lewis, and Richard Norton, from Stubbington, giving an account of the surrender of Portsmouth. Some of the forces here being commanded to provide for the surprise of Southsea Castle had so good success on Saturday night last as to take it without any loss of blood on either side or any great difficulty, which became such a disadvantage to Portsmouth in seconding a battery we had at Gosport that our ordinance from both places played so on the town as it occasioned a meeting there and brought Col. Goring on Sunday to write to Sir W. Waller for a parley which was begun on Monday last and ended this day in the articles enclosed for which we have great cause to pray God considering the great terror the designs there menaced not only those parts with, but the rest of the kingdom. The particulars in this action, the bearer having had so great a share in, he is so well able to give your Lordship an account of, that we will not hereby trouble you therewith.

Same date. Copy of the articles for the surrender of Portsmouth. (Cf. Rushworth, iii. 1. 683.)

October 10, 1642. Copy of a letter to Sir John Bankes, Chief Justice of the Common Pleas, from the houses of Parliament, enclosing the treaty agreed between the Commissioners of England and Scotland, to be presented to the King.

November $\frac{22}{12}$, 1642. The Hague. —— to [Edward Nicholas]. (Printed in *Lords' Journals*, vol. v., p. 461. See also *Commons' Journals*, vol. ii., p. 865.)

December 29, 1642. Selby. Lord Fairfax to ——. (Printed in *Lords' Journals*, vol. v., p. 527.)

December 31, 1642. Copy of a commission given at Kilkenny from the Supreme Council of the Confederate Catholics in Ireland, appointing Captain Francis Oliver, a native of Flanders, captain of the ship called *St. Michael the Archangel.* (Cf. *Commons' Journals,* iii. 99.)

March 15, 1643. Oxford. Charles I. to the Marquess of Newcastle. (Holograph from the Peck Collection. Printed in Peck's *Desiderata Curiosa*, p. 343.)

March 17,1642[-3.] Draft in John Pym's handwriting of the preamble and conclusion of the articles of Cessation. (Printed in Rushworth, iii. 2. 173; *Lords' Journals*, v. 653; *Commons' Journals*, iii. 75.)

[March, 1643. Oxford.] Copy of a letter to the Speaker (?) Omits circumstances relating to the Commissioners' arrival and entertainment as having been presented to the House on Saturday last. On Monday morning according to the King's appointment the Commissioners met at the Schoolhouse appointed for the treaty. When their commission was read expressing their power to treat, the King said, "The word Treate was a good word." Then the Earl of Northumberland delivered the King a paper expressing the method they were to observe in treating upon the propositions in order and after another and not all together, and how they were enjoined to deliver all their demands and to preserve his Majesty's answers in writing, which latter clause with which he was well pleased and said they had prevented him, for it was in his thought to have desired it of them. Upon this the King and his counsel withdrew, and within half an hour brought in 3 papers, the first desiring copies of the Commissioners' instructions and of the propositions, the second declaring that no agreement put in writing should be binding on either side till the conclusion of the whole treaty and the third desiring that the Scots might be called to procure their own, and to settle our peace, and not (by any omission) be left to sow seed of future trouble. To the first the Commissioners answered they had no warrant to show their instructions nor to deliver any copy of propositions as the subject matter of the Treaty, yet notwithstanding upon the King's importunity they caused a copy of them which they had prepared for their own use wherein the Scots' interest was left out to be delivered to the King with this salvo that it was not that they were to treat on but to give his Majesty satisfaction. This the King gave them thanks for. The second needed no answer, and the third upon four hours' debate was recalled. After this a second paper was delivered by our Commissioners containing the proposition for recalling of oaths and declarations &c. which the King will consent unto, but not as to the preamble, which was all yesterday in debate, and it's to be the subject of this day's meeting. This the King at present will not agree unto, and used these arguments. That first it will be binding *ad semper.* Second he shall therein condemn himself, which he will not do, though he be very desirous to justify them, and to give them all the security that possibly can be imagined. This great debate was chiefly managed by Sir Henry Vane, and Mr. Pierpoint and Mr. Browne, who did it with much clearness and ingenuity, as the King himself was pleased to confess. This morning I had carried another paper to Sir Edward Walker from the Commissioners, insisting upon the preamble, which is all the account I shall trouble you with at present. (Cf. *Lords' Journals,* v. 654; Rushworth, iii. 2. 195.)

May 6, 1643. Letter from the Scotch Commissioners at Westminster, (Printed *Lords' Journals,* vi. 45.) Subscribed—Ja. Prymerose.

May 16, 1643. Letter from the Houses of Parliament to the Secret Council of Scotland and the Commissioners for Peace. (Printed in *Lords' Journals,* vi. 45.) Signed—Manchester, W^m. Lenthall.

[Close of 1643 ?] "A callender of the severall impeachments and charges against severall persons brought up from the House of Commons and how far they have bin proceeded upon." The latest date mentioned in it is November 13, 1643, the date of the Archbishop of Canterbury's answer.

December 21, 1643. Arundel. Copy of a letter from Sir William Waller to the House of Lords. (Part printed in *Lords' Journals,* vi. 350.) It continues thus : " Likewise the Kentish foote are not come upp, and I expect them not these two dayes. The last night I receavid an advertisement from Winchester that Prince Rupert was expected that night theare, and there were 120 cartes sent out for his trayne and baggage. All the country there is sumoned to come in with their armes. My neighboures of Pettersfeild, when they quitted that quarter, uppon the allarum at Alton, left many of their armes behind them, which on Tuesday were fetched to Portsmouth. If I had had some fresh horse, I might easily have cutt off ten or twelve troopes of the enemie's horse that are quartered betwixt this and Braintree, but being soe weary and in soe weake a condition I am forced to keepe home for a whyle, and to watch the nine that are in the Castle. I sumoned them, but they refused either to give or take quarter, soe confident they are of succors; my trust is in God.

P.S.—I humbly desire my commission may bee forthwith sent downe, for without it I shall not bee able to settle theis countyes."

December 29, 1643. St. Albans. The Earl of Bedford to [the Speaker of the House of Peers]. (Printed in *Lords' Journals,* vol. vi., p. 356.)

February 17, 1643–4. John Cheislie, for the Scottish Commissioners, to the Houses of Parliament. (Printed in *Lords' Journals*, vi. 460.) LORD BRAYE'S MSS.

February–May, 1644. Copy of Col. Were's journal of the siege of Lyme Regis. (Most of it after April 20th is printed in Rushworth, iii. 2. 677–680, but the MS. is fuller and differs in parts from the printed copy. The beginning, which is not printed, is as follows :—)Feb. 21. Col. Were landed at Lyme Regis. 22. All his forces with the garrison of the town were drawn forth upon Lyme Hill, from whence a party was sent to Studcombe House, and Axmouth, under the command of C. Pey to secure those places. 23. Col. Were with his officers and 300 foot advanced to Studcombe house with a resolution to have fallen upon Colyton, but was commanded back by the Governor of Lyme, as by his letter will appear. March 3. Capt. Townesend drew out by command of the Council of War 100 firelocks and fell upon Bridport where he surprised 130 horse and met with his Colonel and C. Pyne at Chidiocke hill, where they were with horse and foot to secure his retreat. 4. Several messengers came out of Devonshire to inform us that the country was in arms, and desired assistance from the Council of War at Lyme of horse and ammunition which by a general consent was granted unto them, Major Butler being Commander-in-Chief and some other Captains sent with him. They advanced to Hemiocke, where they were set upon by Major Carre, who lost his life and divers of his soldiers. 5–6. The enemy drew out of their garrisons of Axminster and Colyton, Chard, Exon, Taunton and Bridgewater what forces they could to fall on Hemiocke. 9. Col. Were, to divert their besieging of Hemiocke, fell upon Collington with 300 men and took that town, 300 arms, 250 prisoners, all their magazine, their colours, 12 drums, besides divers persons of note, and was advancing to the relief of Hemiocke, but met with the ill news of his officer being surprised before, which hindered his resolution, and caused him to retreat to Studcombe House again where he continued till April 20, every day or night having an alarm or fight with the enemy and was called three times to give assistance to the town of Lyme Regis, and to have fallen upon a quarter of the enemies, which was accordingly performed through tedious marches by him and his soldiers, though little use made of them when they came there, which was no small discouragement to the soldiers.

[1644 ?] Declaration by the Marquis of Montrose, his Majesty's Lieutenant General of the Kingdom of Scotland.—Whereas this traitorous faction of hollow-hearted rebels, who have been a raging within this kingdom these many years bygone, contrary to all laws divine and human but what they themselves have framed for the accomplishment of their desperate and unheard of treasons and cruelties, have put out sundry scandalous pasquils contrary to the conscience and justice of his Majesty's service to deceive the weak and ignorant multitude, whom they have hitherto so pestered and enslaved to the ruin of this whole kingdom and the utter destruction of those poor souls whom they have so invincibly blinded, as I could not, though I had much patience, enduring their abominable lies and calumnies from my duty to his sacred Majesty, the world, and mine own honour, but declare the raging fury of those desperate rebels contrary to the religion and equity of his Majesty's commands, for withal thay had granted to them even all their vast and endless desires, have been so far from being thankful to the goodness of God and justice of their native king, and enjoying of those happy blessings while none was stirring their peace, as most contrary to all, have out of wantonness, wicked ends, and base ingratitude waged a war by assisting a faction of foreign rebels and most bloodily pursued the

LORD BRAYE'S
MSS.

Prince's ruin in a strange nation. And now that his Majesty hath been by all reason and necessity at last constrained to set his service afoot in this kingdom to disappoint or oppose the extreme evils of his own imminent ruin, this they term Rebellion, and those whom his sacred Majesty honours with commission in it traitors to the estate, and though all the world may see the brasen face of those impudent rebels now so clearly unmasked as they are without all excuse, yet there being perhaps many innocent and well meaning people have been involved in their intricate courses, who his Majesty from his wonted goodness and piety is rather willing to reclaim than punish, I do by these in his Majesty's name offer a free pardon to all and everyone so engaged, who upon the present publishing hereof shall repair to us and join with his Majesty's force. Notwithstanding their masters and superiors may be perhaps engaged in this present rebellion, I do likewise in his Majesty's name give them all certainty and assurance to be well and safely protected as good countrymen and faithful subjects.

May 22 [1644]. Lincoln. The Earl of Manchester to [the Speaker of the House of Peers?] I have four regiments of foot with me, and four more at Gainsborough, Torksey Bridge, and Saxelby, in readiness to march towards the Scottish army, upon certain notice of Prince Rupert marching that way. Most of my horse are already joined with the Scottish horse, and lie quartered on the other side of the Trent. The Derby and Nottingham horse intend to join them. Those on the other side of the Trent will make nearly 6,000 horse and dragoons. On this side I keep 1,200 horse with my foot. The Scottish army before York and mine will not draw near each other unless Prince Rupert appears. Col. Whyte will give a full account of the Scottish army. The great rains have so raised the Trent, as to hinder my marching.

June 5, 1644. Original examination of Lord Conway. (Printed in *Lords' Journals*, vi. 578.) Subscribed—Conway, and attested by the signatures of the Earls of Northumberland, Stamford and Salisbury, Viscount Say and Sele, and Lord Grey of Wark.

June 15, 1644. Copy of a letter from the Earl of Warwick to the Parliament about the raising of the siege of Lyme. Has remained there since his last letter. The enemy have in the five days last past shot many vollies of great and small shot into the town which the besieged have received and answered with equal courage as before. On the 12th instant I furnished the town with ten barrels of powder, their store being near exhausted. On the 13th they took a prisoner who gave the information that the Lord Hopton had been in the leaguer last Sabbath day and demanded five men out of every company which he promised to make good by an equal number of pressed men, but they were denied him. From thence (as I heard by one of the Frigates that came from the West on Wednesday last) he went to Dartmouth whither he came in on Tuesday night with seven horse giving out that he was to raise an army of 15,000 men. The said 13th instant upon desire from the Council of War in Lyme I resolved to send the boats and small vessels here to give an alarm on the East part of Lyme for distracting of the enemy and drawing him off from the town (notice being given of the soldiers' affreightment with what was formerly done of the like kind) which was yesterday put in execution accordingly, the seamen landing and marching up into the country, which caused the horse and foot that came down to attend them to fly to the hills and gave the seamen opportunity to converse with many of the country people; who appeared generally well affected to the parliament in respect of the great pressures laid upon them by a beggarly and cruel enemy. By some of them I received notice that the Lord Hopton had two days before commanded all thereabouts from 16 to 60 to repair forthwith to Dorchester with such arms as they could provide, as also with victuals and money, to withstand some forces expected there suddenly under command of his Excellency or Sir William Waller, and that some hundreds of men had been pressed for his service, who had near all of them made an escape. Yesterday there came aboard me one Lieut. Parre of the Lord Broghill's regiment, and his ensign, who had the night before come into Lyme with 22 of the soldiers under his care. By him I received intelligence that Prince Maurice had notice of some forces coming to Dorchester, that the Queen was about 10 days ago brought to bed at Exeter of a boy, that many of the Prince's army were ready to come into Lyme as soon as they could gain a convenience. This morning about 2 of the clock our boat came from the town with advice that the enemy was drawing off his great guns and raising his siege which by letter received this day from the Governor was confirmed, the Prince withdrawing himself last night about 5 of the clock and his army starting away about 2 of the clock this morning. Mentions that he landed and viewed the works, those of the enemy being of great strength, but those of the townsmen so slight that it was near a miracle they should hold out so long against so violent and resolved an enemy. Commends the officers and soldiers and backs their request for a supply of money, and forwards the request of the garrison of Plymouth for some money and a governor. Mentions a report that Weymouth has been surrendered to the Parliament and another that Prince Charles was lately there. (Cf. *Lords' Journals*, vi. 595.)

August 6, 1644. Paper purporting to be a copy of instructions from the King to Richard Harding, Esq. He is to accompany Lord Beauchamp to the Earl of Essex as secretly as possible and deliver to him the King's letter informing him that the credence therein relates to himself, and if possible induce the Earl to join the King with his forces in order to effect a general pacification. (Cf. Rushworth, iii. 2. 710.)

August 15, 1644. Original paper from the Commissioners of the Church of Scotland. (Printed in *Lords' Journals*, vi. 674.)

September 1644 (?). Copy of the examination of Anthony Nicoll, deposing to conversations with Major-General Skippon, Col. Tyrill, Sir Philip Stapleton, and the Lord General concerning the alleged instructions from the king and the conduct of Col. Butler.

September 23, 1644. Copy of the examination of Col. Tyrrill.

September 24, 1644. Copy of the examination of Col. Barclay.

September 26, 1644. Copy of the examination of Richard Deane, controller of the ordinance. (The last three all relate to the same subject as the examination of Anthony Nicoll. Much of the matter is given in Skippon's Examination, printed in Rushworth, iii. 2. 710. Cf. also the rest of pages 710, 711.)

October 14, 1644. (N.B. The month is apparently October, but in the letter of the 8th April following the date of this letter is given as *September* 14th.) Original paper from the Scotch Commissioners to the English Commissioners concerning the Army. Subscribed—Jo. Cheislie. They complain that divers letters and papers have been presented to the Houses of Parliament by their Commissioners with the Scotch army without the answers of the Committee of the Scotch estates, and also that directions received from the Committee of the Scotch Estates with the army had been directly referred to a Committee of the House of Commons, at which the Scotch Commissioners could not be present. The English Commissioners had been appointed as the authorised organ of communication with the Scotch Commissioners, who now represent that mistakes and differences will arise if this arrangement is abandoned and they therefore urge the English Commissioners to press upon the Houses that all doubts and objections which may arise about the Scotch armies should be referred to them to discuss with the Scotch Commissioners and then report to the Houses. They further complain of the granting of commissions for levying Regiments in the County of Northumberland and the Bishopric of Durham to persons who live on free quarter, without doing any service, which is a great burden to the country, and a prejudice to the Scotch armies by lessening the assessments. They therefore request that these Colonels be called into Yorkshire for the defence of that county.

Referring to their paper of the 9th of September concerning the assessments of the County of York and Northumberland, and the Bishopric of Durham, they request that the Houses of Parliament will take into their serious consideration the ascertaining the entertainment of the Scotch armies out of such ways and means as they shall think fit, and those armies may depend upon. With regard to complaints to the Houses by those counties charging several disorders upon the Scotch armies, they answer that general complaints can have no answers but of the same kind, and, admitting that some of the inhabitants may have had just reason to complain, they assert that no complaints in particular have been made known to the Committee of Estates on the Lord General without redress and punishment of the offenders.

With regard to the paper of August 16th desiring that all the officers and soldiers of the Scotch army should be informed of the articles of the Treaty between the kingdoms, the Committee of the Estates had unanimously decided that these articles were already known to most of the officers, and that it was neither necessary or fitting they should be divulged to our common soldiers, or published to the world.

With regard to the other paper of the same date desiring that tickets should be given to all inhabitants of all such officers and soldiers as take up billet upon free quarters, and that no officer should assume to impose any taxes or assessments upon the people without the consent of the Committee of both kingdoms, they answer that the Lord General immediately renewed his former command to the officers and soldiers to observe the several orders of the Committee of both kingdoms, and of the Committee of Estates which had been intimated upon the head of every regiment against taking anything in the country without ticket, or imposing taxes at their own hands.

With regard to the other part of the last paper desiring the concurrence of the Committee of Estates in the operation of the ordinances of excise and sequestration, they declare that they always been ready and willing to do so, but with regard to Stockton and Hartlepool the Committee of Parliament having caused a ship to be seized and sent to London contrary to the capitulation of Hartlepool, the Earl of Callendar, until the pleasure of the houses of Parliament concerning the same should be known, thought it necessary for the vindication of the honour of the Scotch army and nation by some act to manifest their resolution to perform the said capitulation, for which it was desired that the uplifting of excise and sequestrations in Hartlepool and Stockton might be for some short time respited.

(The order of the House of Commons made upon this paper on October 17th is printed in *Commons' Journals*, ii. 688.)

October 25, 1644. Letter from A. Johnston and J. Crewe, the Commissioners with the army, to the Houses of Parliament from Buckleberry Heath. "My Lord General quartered last night at Bradfield six miles from Reading. My Lord of Manchester's forces, which had the van, quartered at Buckleberry upon intelligence if the King's army continued at Newberry. This morning, about ten of the clock, the horse and foote are all drawne out upon Buckleberry Heath, 4 miles from Newberry, great bodies of the enemyes' horse are in viewe, but whether to fall on engage we know not; ours resolve if they will not stand their charge to pursue them.

LORD BRAYE'S MSS.

My Lord General hath had upon him some indisposition for divers dayes which hath ben much increased by his striving with it. He would not be persuaded from marching yesterday, and was resolved to have marched to-day, but not taking his rest last night he is growne feverish, and was forced to goe back to Reading on a feather bed layd in his coach; here will be much want of his presence. We shall conceale his absence as much as we can, and hope that those which are here will make all the supply that they can by extraordinary dilligence.

Postscript. Since the writing this letter, it was thought fitt at a councel of warr held upon the Heath that we should march to Thatcham, 2 miles from Newberry. We now have intelligence that the enemies' horse and foote are drawn up between Newberry and Donnington Castle. This night we are to march beyond Thatcham either to the right hand or left, as the field shall be most advantagious; our officers continue very unanimous, and our souldiers are very cheereful upon their going on towards the enemy."

January 24, 1644[-5.] Letter from the Houses of Parliament to the States of Holland. Subscribed: Grey of Wark, Speaker of the House of Peers pro tem., and Wm. Lenthall, Speaker of the Commons' House in the Parliament of England assembled. (Printed in *Lords' Journals*, vii. 155.)

February 3, 1644[-5]. "Instructions for the Committees of both Houses." (Printed in *Lords' Journals*, vol. vii., p. 261.)

February 26, 1644–5. Sir H. Cholmeley [governor of Scarborough Castle] to Sir John Meldrum. " I confesse noe man hath more reason to upbraid mee with my incapacity than you, for though I have taken tyme enough to consider your letter, I cannott find that it affords more than these two parts, one that I understand nott att all, another that I doe (though with difficulty), it beinge the stile of conquerors alone. To that I understand nott you will nott expect much answeer, only I shall say that before there can bee a good and a true understanding betweene us (at cearme soe much spoken of, and desyred by those that seeme more moderate of both parties) there ought to be an understanding simply, which I conceive your phrase endeavours nott. To the rest I had returned answere before this time, but that I do not please myself in raylings and personall recriminations, nothinge else beinge suteable to those I receive from you, though you seeme to sett me out bounds and limits to govern my language as a man in affliction by tellinge me that one of common sense would nott irritate you, noe more perhaps would one of common spirit. But for my part I cannott imagine a condition soo lowe shall force a newe dialect uppon me or anythinge incompatible with the resolution of a gentleman, and the office I bear. Admitt my case weare miserable as you call it, yet I should presume a fair confidence were more noble in my condition than insolence in yours. 'Tis well known I always abhorred whatsoever tended toward tirrannie. And though I daily heare of impositions upon men's consciences and personall liberties by your party, yett

LORD BRAYE'S
MSS.

certainly itt's a point unpractised untill your tyme to prohibite a generous
mynd from a due resentment of injuries and from seekinge defence from
the same sort of weapon, with which it is assaulted. And that I may
performe this duty to myselfe I must call to your memorye a clause wherein
you attribute much to the Grace of the kingdome, a forme of speech never
before heard of in England nor any monarchye, all acts of Grace being
inseparable from the sovereigne power, of which you cannott be ignorante,
though perhapps unwillinge to name the kinge, lest men shoulde make
observations upon your ingratitude, as alsoe upon the dazeling lighte of
Reformation you boast of, all men knowinge what lights you study to
preserve, which not like seamarks have directed but like ignis (*sic*) fatui
have misled you out of the way of obedience. For the churchyard you
bragg of make your boast of it, which I doubt nott will prove only usefull
to you to bury your dead in, though I finde you make no more scruple of
that decency than other things befittynge the consideration of Christians.
To the violation of faith and articles which you apply to yourselfe I
confesse ingeniously I charged you nott, neither doeth my letter pointe
more particularly than that conditions have been frequently broaken, and
this I thinke a truth you will neither deny nor excuse. By this tyme
Sir, I shall hopeyou will bee as far from expectinge to fright me to any ende
you have upon me as I am from courtinge you to any other waies of
correspondence. I shall therefore desire you to leave this manner of
style, crosse to my nature, as not agreeable with gentlemen or men. And
when you have busines to which you intend to have answeers from me,
lett it be so qualified as may become you to write and me to receive,
wherby you may assure yourselfe of a return of all civillities from
Hugh Cholmeley."

February 27, 1641–5. Answer of Sir J. Meldrum to the last.
This draught of a letter, I had resolved to have sent to you, will free
me from the guilt of aiming at your blood (intimated by your last note),
unless your lofty and impertinent answer to my summons had altered
my resolution. If you have not a better reply to that part of my letter
pressing that a reformation doth dazzle your eyesight than to fall very
impertinently upon my lights, I must answer you that such a poor and
weak repartee doth argue some defect which I shall forbear to express,
it being very well known that those lights have done more service to
the kingdoms and to all the navigation in Europe where use was to be
made of them, than the breaking down of many fair bridges which (if
you had continued constant to your party) might have been reputed
good services : If you had not begun in that railing way (as you are
pleased to call it) you should never have heard more of me, but in the
following of my point which was and is (by God's assistance) to bring
you out of that hold you seek to enthrall the kingdom by : The maintenance whereof will require better forces than you can expect from the
Queen, out of France, from Oxford, or from Newark, or from the issue
of the treaty, which (at the best) hath as yet produced no other effect
but the surprisal of Shrewsbury by that worthy and valiant gentleman
Colonel Mitton, with whom if you had kept a better correspondency
than with Sir Marmaduke Langdale you had not been in so sad a condition as you are in ; you can lose nothing by any act of courtesy (though
by your own expression it was done for Colonel Bethel and not for me)
in sparing of the trumpet. Your Newark messenger, as a spy sent to Sir
Marmaduke Langdale and the governor of Newark might have more
justly suffered than the trumpeter : I look for no grace from the king
but from the kingdom, so long as the beams of his sun doth shine upon
a viperous brood that have sought to destroy their own mother that

bred them: and that he is misled by such pernicious counsellors, who
have brought him and his posterity to so low an ebb: nor can I find a
more proper means to supply the defects of nature than by grace which
you very wittily would make inseparable from monarchy : If you mean
a moderate and well tempered monarchy I shall not much dissent from
you, but of a Straffordian I have ever and ever will be of opinion that
it is at least cousin german if not worse than anarchy itself.  Those old
rotten tenets are out of date where the power of monarchy hath been so
irregular that you and such others of your tempers have been rather led
on by the Ignes fatui of the time to the destruction of the kingdom,
than my lights have led me out of the way of my obedience to the king.
I have no other end upon you than by fair means to persuade you to
render up the Castle of Scarborough with all kind of ordnance, ammunition, and other provision for the king and parliament whereunto if I
find you inclinable you may look for the real accomplishment of the
conditions offered in the summons to you and your associates, which you
may expect in vain, if the kingdom be put to the trouble of bringing
great ordnance whereby I will endeavour to make your strong walls
spue you out at the broad side, and as you did first begin this kind of
stile I would not have you think but that you must be the first that
shall forbear it : none shall go beyond me in point of civility, so long as
your epithets of conqueror, commander of the world, violator of articles
and conditions, railer, ingrate, insolent, and the ignes fatui wherewith you brand me shall not enforce me to pay you in your own coin
though in a different manner, the one being grounded upon manifest
truths the other upon chimeras ; but if you think yourself to be in a
condition rather to give the law than to take it the issue will bear wit-
ness which of us have been most out of square, which is all and the last
time I intend to trouble you with my pen.

January 2, 1644-5.   Oxford.   Charles I. to Henrietta Maria.
Copy by J. Browne, endorsed, " Copie to my wyfe . . . by P. A."
(Printed in Halliwell's " *Letters of the Kings of England,*" vol. ii., p.
358.)

February $\frac{24}{16}$, 1644-5.   Oxford.   The same to the same.   Copy by
J. Browne, endorsed, " Copie to my wife . . by P. A." (Printed
in Halliwell, p. 365.)

March 3, 1644[-5].   John Cheislie, for the Commissioners of
Scotland, to the House of Lords.  (Printed in *Lords' Journals,* vol. vii.,
p. 261.)

March 13, 1644-5.  Oxford.  Charles I. to Henrietta Maria.  Copy
by J. Browne, endorsed, "To my wife . . . by P. A." (Printed
in Halliwell, p. 368.)

March 30, 1645.  Oxford.  The same to the same.  Copy by
J. Browne, endorsed, "To my wife . . . by Petit." (Printed in
Halliwell, p. 347.)

April 8, 1645.  Two original letters from the Scotch Commissioners.  Subscribed—Jo. Cheislie.  (Printed in *Lords' Journals,* vii. 311,
312.)

April 11, 1645.  Original letter from the Commissioners of the
General Assembly of the kirk of Scotland.  Subscribed—John Donn.
(Printed in *Lords' Journals,* vii. 317.)

Thursday, April 17, 1645.  Oxford.  Charles I. to Henrietta
Maria.  " Deare Hart.  The last weeke I wrott thrice to thee, by two
severall messengers, besides this usuall way, since when no action of

moment hath hapned. Preparations on both sides hath been slower then was expected, but now I being certaine to have all those things before Sunday next which was my only stay, I am confedent to be in the field much sooner then the Rebells (there distractions rather yet encreasing then deminishing) and by my next I dare promise thee to name the day of my setting forth, albeit I was somewhat mistaken in this particular when I last mentioned it to thee. Warwicke hath fullfiled my profesy of him, but he could not doe otherwise, not having command of the Sea Captains. Since mine by Petit I have not hard any more of that Proposition I then advertised thee of, concerning the renewing of the Treaty for Peace, and I can now only tell thee, that it came to Secretary Nicholas (who was the honnest servant I then mentioned) from the Duke of Richmond's Webb, whom I estime to be such an apochriphall author, that it much confirmes me in my opinion that it will come to nothing. For Scotts newes, I was in good hope to have given thee a perfect account by this, one of my expresses being returned from thence, but he being unluckely taken, not farr from hence, I can only say that those who spake with him assure me from his relations, that Muntrosse is about St. Johnstowne, very strong, and maister of the field (I doubt they overnumber his army, for they call it 10,000 foote and 1,500 horse) and that if he had store of ammunition, he would reduce all Scotland to my obedience, to supply which I finde by the Lord Jermin's last dispatch thou hast taken some care, for which I much commend thy judgment, which indeed is answerable to the rest of thy proceedings in order to my assistance, and likewise to every circumstance of expressing thy kindnesse to me, wherein thou hast rather exceeded then falen short of my expectation. Only I thought to have ben encouraged in my proceedings by thy approbation, more then yet thou hast done, for if you knew the difficulties I have wrestled with (which now, I thanke God, is pretily over) by the follies of my owen party, thou would have thought it just and fitting to have hartned me by comending at least my patience and constancy, but I confesse when I remember what company I have (in a manner) been forced to waite upon thee, I then pittie thee for the trouble those people bring upon thee, and no more wonder that those sometymes mistakes my proceedings, but rather it joyes me that thy affection (even through those mistakings) is most visible to him who is eternally thyne. The expresse is newly escaped who confirmes what I have said concerning Muntrosse, only he left him Murray land insteede of St. Johnstowne." Endorsed, " To my wyfe." (Copy in the hand of J. Browne.)

June 26, 1645. Original paper from the Scotch Commissioners. Subscribed—Jo. Cheislie. (Printed in *Lords' Journals*, vii., 464.)

July ?, 1645. Original paper from the same, subscribed as the last. (Printed in *Lords' Journals*, vii., 475.)

July 3, 1645. Original letter from Derby House from A. Johnston and R. Barclay, to the Speaker of the House of Lords, enclosing the last paper. Seal. (Printed in *Lords' Journals*, vii. 464.) In the original is the following postscript : " While wee were despatching this paper to your Lordships, Mr. Broun, Clerk to the House of Peeres, came hither with those letters, but told us that in respect they were to bee communicated to the City in the afternoone, he could not stay nor leave them with us till wee perused them."

July 4, 1645. Duplicates of a paper from the Scotch Commissioners, both subscribed—Jo. Cheislie. (Printed in *Lords' Journals*, vii., 479.)

August 11, 1645. The camp before Hereford. The Earl of Lothian Lord Braye's and John Corbett to the Committee sitting at Derby House. (Printed in MSS. *Lords' Journals*, vol. vii., p. 538.)

August 11, 1645. "The Leager before Hereford." The Earl of Lothian to the Scottish Commissioners. (Copy. Printed in *Lords' Journals*, vol. vii., p. 539).

September 3, 1645. Draft of letter to be sent to Sir Thomas Fairfax. (Cf. *Lords' Journals*, vol. vii., p. 565.)

[After August 15, 1645.] A paper of Latin Chronograms upon the battle of Naseby, the battle of Langport, the taking of Bridgewater, and the taking of Sherborne Castle.

September 4, 1645. Copy of a letter from the Derbyshire Committee at Derby to the Committee at Derby House. "Wee are bould to represent the sad and suffering condition of our distressed County, being the Theatree whereon the guarrisons of Newarke, Lichfield, Ashby, Titbury and Welbecke (which hath its onely subsistence from this county) doe dayly exercise there barbarous crueltyes by imprisoning our honest countrey-men, by imposing insupportable taxes upon them, by sweeping away there cattle, against which mischiefes the onely meanes to oppose and to protect ourselves is our horse, fower hundred of which your Lordships have comanded to Generall Poynts by your letter of the 30th of August to Sir John Gell ; which in there last march after the king are much worne and decayed, and wee unable to recreate them, soe that upon advance of fower hundred of our horse (wee having but about five hundred, and fower guarrisons to maintayne therewith), wee shall be rendered unable to defend our county, and are confident that the enemy will take this opportunity to infest the same by there dayly incursions all which wee humbly remonstrate unto your Lordships, hopeing that in your wisedomes you will please to spare our horse for the necessary protection of our expiringe countrey, which is the ardent desire of your Lordship's humble servants, Nich. Leek, H. Lleigh, Nath. Hallowes, Joh. Isbunds, Rob. Eyre, Fr. Revell, Row. Morewood, Edw. Charlton, Ra. Clarke."

September 8, 1645. Letter from the Committee at Derby House to the Houses of Parliament, enclosing the last letter. (Printed in *Lords' Journals*, vii., 572.)

September 10, 1645. Original letter from the Scotch Commissioners to the House of Lords. Subscribed—Jo. Cheislie. (Printed in *Lords' Journals*, vii., 575.)

September 12, 1645. Original letter or paper from the same to both Houses of Parliament. (Cf. *Commons' Journals*, iv., 273.) It hath pleased the Lord our God, who worketh all things according to the counsel of his own will, in his wise and righteous providence so to dispose at this time upon the affairs of the kingdom of Scotland that they are upon the sudden brought to a lower and more deplorable con-dition than could in any probability have been expected or the enemy himself in his pride could have presumed. We speak not of the devour-ing pestilence, which in many parts of the land, especially in and about the chiefest city, hath raged for a long time in many degrees above any-thing that either ourselves or our predecessors have ever known, and hath taken away many thousands of the people. This (although it hath been a great advantage to the enemy and no small discouragement and hindrance to the opposing of his power), we acknowledge to be a plague from the more immediate hand of God, against which there is no remedy from man but the fervent prayers of the people of God, which we earnestly desire may be here continued as they are piously begun till the Lord be entreated for the land.

Our desire is to represent what the sword of the enemy hath done; after many conflicts in divers places in the North of the kingdom, whereby great numbers hath fallen, and the enemy, despicable in the beginning, hath increased in strength and boldness, at last in the very bowels of the kingdom he hath so far prevailed, that not only thousands of the best affected have loosed their lives, and divers of them taken prisoners, but also our whole army and forces are put to the worse and scattered : such as were most zealous for the covenant and cause of God (having no army on foot to join with nor garrison towns for places of refuge) are forced to fly for their lives and to leave their habitations, possessions, and all that they have in this world to the cruelty and spoil of the enemy. Many of the common sort are drawn away by his flatteries and promises by the proclamations which he maketh and the declarations which he emitteth, at his pleasure offering unto them protection to their persons and estates, freedom and exemption from all the taxes, impositions and burdens which they are pressed with for the maintenance and supply of their armies in England, Ireland, and at home in their own country, together with the liberty of their religion, according to their National Covenant and all other liberties and privileges formerly established with his Majesty's consent ; upon condition that they will renounce their covenant with England, and take an oath that they shall no more lift arms against the king and his assistants. Some of place and power who formerly were either professed enemies to Religion, or never took Religion to heart have dealt falsely in the covenant and presuming upon the success of the enemy and waiting for such a time as this is, have joined with him against their country. The most faithful of the ministry by the principal enemy and by malignants in their own congregations are driven from their stations and forced to seek shelter for the saving of their lives, whereby the people left behind are laid open to all sorts of temptations and Religion itself is in no small danger. As we are not willing to conceal or extenuate their miseries, in this day of the Lord's visitation, so are we not able sufficiently to express them ; the yoke of their transgressions is bound by his hand, they are wreathed and come up upon their neck, he hath made their strength to fall, the Lord hath delivered them into their hands from whom they are not able to rise up. In this their extremity the Committee of the notables of the kingdom being for the present put out of all hope of any succours from their forces in Ireland, and knowing no other means of help, found it necessary, unless they would lose the kingdom and lie still under such miseries, as are more intolerable than death, that the Scottish army in England should move Northward, to the end that (if God in the present time did provide no other way) they might come to their relief and deliverance, and withal to implore the affection counsel and assistance of their brethren of England, and therefore to send the Lord Chancellor for representing their distresses and desires to the honourable houses.

Concerning the speedy march of the Scottish army Northward for their relief, they supposed that Charity would move the honourable houses and all charitable Christians to consider that in the time of extreme trouble, natural affection on both sides, in calling for and giving of help is unresistable, and that there was no liberty left in such a case, when both the public and every man's private was in hazard and well near lost either for the Committee or for the army to consult or to choose what to do. That their justice would bring to their remembrance that this army (as is contained in the treaty) was levied and came into England LORD BRAYE's MSS. for the pursuance of the ends expressed in the covenant, which were the safety of both kingdoms, and their mutual defence against the popish, prelatical, and malignant party, their adherents in both kingdoms, and that they were to be employed where they might be most useful for the common cause and for opposing the enemy, where his power and the danger was greatest. In this notion was their marching to the North, when the King went Northwards, looked upon, and now when his forces have so far prevailed in Scotland their marching thither is to be interpreted to no other sense. They supposed also that the wisdom of the honourable Houses would make them see that this expedition might by the blessing of God not only be a means of deliverance to Scotland, but also prevent the invading of England by a new army, which, if Scotland be altogether subdued, may be certainly expected. The timeous prevention of such an invasion may prove no less favourable for the good of the cause and to the kingdom of England than the present opposition of any hostile army within the kingdom of England.

As those necessary considerations have moved the Committee of the estates of Scotland to desire the marching of their army Northward, so are they confident the honourable houses will rest satisfied therewith, and do expect from them and from all the well affected in England, a brotherly compassion and Christian fellow-feeling in their bitter sufferings, all necessary assistance and seasonable supply of arms, ammunition, and money, and in due time such forces as may be spared, if thorow the increase of their troubles their need shall require, and call for them. It shall not be necessary to multiply arguments to this purpose : the wisdom of Parliament can call to remembrance the expressions in their own declaration of the 7th November 1642, and in the papers delivered in by their Commissioners in their names to the Convention of the Estates of Scotland, August 12th, 1643, together with the treaty and the Solemn League and Covenant. It will never be forgotten by our brethren of England that when our country was in great quietness and the greatest assurance that was possible was offered for our future security, we choosed rather than to enjoy our own peace without the peace of this kingdom, upon the reasons contained in the declarations of the kingdom of Scotland, to come with an army into England, against all discouragements, that might arise either from the stormy winter season, or the power of a mighty army in the North of the kingdom ready to encounter us. What the endeavours, the actions, and the success of that army were, let the enemy before that time prevalent, from his own sense give testimony.

When the kingdom of Scotland had layed forth their strength for the recovery of Ireland and defence of England, and promised unto themselves security from foreign invasion, especially from Ireland, upon the grounds contained in the large treaty and in the propositions made by Commissioners sent from both houses, and particularly by the ships, which according to an article of the late treaty were to be employed for defence of the coast of Scotland ; an enemy nevertheless from Ireland entered the kingdom of Scotland, having no other controversy nor pretending any other cause against them but their treaty and covenant with England and their assistance following thereupon, and have prevailed so far, as hath made this sad remonstrance necessary at this time.

It is no matter of great difficulty (unless we will shut our eyes and hide from ourselves our own danger and threatened ruin), to discern and determine what is the great and main design of the enemy now waxed proud and insolent by the afflictions which the Lord hath brought upon

U 24962.                                                                 L

LORD BRAYE'S
MSS.

the kingdom of Scotland : when he hath brought all these under his power, a work, which through the malignancy of some open and many formerly secret enemies now appearing and joining with him, through the sufferings, calamities and hatred brought upon the best affected, and such as hath been most active and instrumental in this cause, and through the discontent and distempers of the multitude, for the loss of their means and friends in the war at home and abroad, he presageth to be more easy and feasible, than what he hath already brought to pass; his second expedition is against the parliament of England, which is not any uncertain conjecture, but his own professed resolution and confidence; but is too apparent, that unless he be speedily suppressed he may through the concourse and combination of the malignants of Scotland and of the Northern Counties of England grow to a greater strength (especially if he join with the King and his forces, which he is also very confident of) than can be afterwards safely opposed; and thereby may reduce these kingdoms to a more miserable condition, in respect both of religion and liberty (beside all their intervening sufferings) than they were in before the beginning of this unhappy war.   We know the cause is the same which it was at the first undertaking, that the Godly in Scotland, who loved it from the beginning, are resolved to live and die in it; that the conjuncture of the two kingdoms which the enemy labours to divide and so to overcome, is no less beneficial to both than it was formerly conceived to be ; that the Popish and prelatical faction in foreign parts as well as in His Majesty's dominions, upon the union of these kingdoms, are more strictly and powerfully combined than they have been at other times; that the reformation of religion and the common interest of all the reformed Churches in Christendom groaning so long under the Cross is as much to be looked into as ever, and who knoweth but the Lord in His wisdom and justice is at this time putting both kingdoms to a further trial, the one by suffering, the other by doing, that it may be known whether they have been seeking their own peace and preservation, or the honour of his name and good of Religion.

We may without giving the least cause of offence in this conjuncture of time make use of the words of the declaration of the convention of Estates of the kingdom of Scotland to the subjects there concerning their expedition into England for the assistance of their brethren, only changing the persons, and if they were not extant in that declaration we would have expressed ourselves in another manner : The Lord save you from the curse of Meroz, who came not to help the Lord, to help the Lord against the mighty, when we look upon the cause which Scotland maintaineth, the prayers, tears, and blood which they have poured forth and the insolencies and blasphemies of the many, we cannot doubt but inlargement and deliverance shall arise unto Scotland, but England hath reason to fear, if upon so fair a call they sit still and hold their peace, they shall perish by the hand of the same enemy and there shall be none to deliver them.   We have many grounds of assurance that this cloud shall pass over and after the Lord hath proved and tried the constancy of his servants, the malignancy of hypocrites, and the fellow-feeling of our brethren his face will again shine upon us and his hand will raise us up and ruin our enemies, our desire and expectation is that in the day of our rejoicing our brethren may rejoice with us and be comforted ·in this testimony that they did not forsake us in the day of trouble.

We cannot deny but during the sitting of the parliament, and divers times before, this kingdom hath laid to heart the dangers of the kingdom of Scotland, nor can it be denied that the kingdom of Scotland hath of late given abundant testimony of their affection and faithfulness to this kingdom, in departing the kingdom after such a manner in the year LORD BRAYE'S MSS. 1641, which we mention, because of the many sinister suspicions and unjust calumnies vented to the contrary, and by their coming again into this kingdom at such a time for such ends and against so many impediments. If any discontent, differences, or jealousies have been raised, which were nothing strange, because very ordinary and incident in the time of war, a time that useth to produce many and great difficulties, we desire that they may be all mutually forgiven and forgotten, that the war be managed in Scotland as in England by the joint committees of both kingdoms, and that in everything a right understanding and a strong mutual confidence may be revived and renewed that either kingdom may help the other in the time of trouble as if they were but one kingdom, and the Lord may delight to bless them both.

September 19, 1645. Draft report of the Committee on Lord Hunsdon's case. Probably in the handwriting of Lord Roberts. (Printed in *Lords' Journals*, vii., 584.)

September 25, 1645. Original letter to the Speaker of the House of Commons from Major-General Poyntz announcing his victory at Rowton Heath. (Printed in *Lords' Journals*, vii., 608.)

September 26, 1645. Original letter, with heraldic seal, from Colonel Norton, Governor of Portsmouth, to the Committee of both Kingdoms. When your order for my drawing towards Sussex in respect of the clubmen come into the county, I was then waiting upon the General to desire some assistance of him both for the reducing of Winchester Garrison and the subduing the clubmen in our county [Hampshire]. I prevailed with the Lord General for a regiment of horse to effect the latter, which by God's blessing I hope is done, for upon Wednesday last they were all assembled at one place, and I drew up all our horse round them and then demanded some of 'the chief of them and their arms. The first though unwillingly they yielded to, the latter we forced them to, but though they had granted the first some of our Committee being there (unknown to me) while I was busy in disposing the horse had given their words to them that they should go off without prejudice, which in regard one of them was a Parliament man I was forced to yield unto, but I hope I shall get them again. There were only two towns that resisted us, which were very ill affected, and it pleased God to separate them from the rest before they gave us occasion to fall on them. I believe we took from them above 500 arms, their colours and drums. I hope this will be a warning to Sussex ; if not, we shall be ready to serve them the like trick. Truly it was high time, for it is evident by the heads of them that they intended mischief, and I am persuaded it is the last and most devilish plot that the enemies of God and good men have left them. I have three of the most notorious rascals prisoners though they are not chief men, and I hope to get the rest. I wish I might know what to do with them, and wish I might have power to hang some of them if they rise again. In the mean time while I am serving the country abroad I am suffering at home. I wrote to the Lord General concerning my garrison. Truly I have not a penny to pay them on Monday sevennight, and if I am not supplied by the excisemen I am sure they will all mutiny here, for I am confident there is not a more disorderly soldiery in England. Therefore I most humbly beg that I may have a power of martial law, my Lord General gave it for Hampton. (Cf. *Commons' Journals*, iv. 279, 280.)

October 14, 1645. Original letter from the Scottish Commissioners to the Speaker of the House of Lords. (Printed in *Lords Journals*, vii. 637.) Heraldic seal affixed.

October 21, 1645. Order in extenso to Mr. Browne to deliver up to Mr. Leicester Devereux the deeds and writings therein mentioned. (An abstract of the order is printed in *Lords' Journals*, vii. 654.) At the foot is a receipt for them dated November 7th, and signed Lees. Devereux.

February 11, 1645[-6]. Copy of an Act of the Common Council of the City concerning a letter received from the Parliament of Scotland, dated at St. Androis, January 27th, 1646 (new style). (The letter of which a copy is annexed is printed in Rushworth, iv. 1, 232. Cf. *Lords' Journals*, x. 104.)

March 14, 1645[-6]. Lincoln. The Earl of Rutland and Lord Mountagu to the Speaker of the House of Peers. (Printed in *Lords' Journals*, vol. viii., p. 220.) Heraldic seal affixed.

[July, 1646.] Original paper from the Commissioners of the Parliament of Scotland, signed—J. Cheislie.

They had received on the third of this instant July a declaration of the Parliament of England concerning the distinct and divided interests of the two kingdoms in the propositions of peace agreed on by both kingdoms to be sent to the king, and concerning the distinct legislative powers in each kingdom, to continue, repeal, or alter any law that shall be made upon the said propositions. While the Commissioners admit the distinct legislative power of both kingdoms and have no thought of the dependency of one upon the other and concede that there are matters in the propositions which concern England alone, they assert there are others of the highest importance which are of common and joint concernment to both kingdoms. A league between two kingdoms cannot be altered without the consent of each. They cannot therefore acknowledge without distinction that the interest of both kingdoms is divided in the propositions for the Covenant itself and the treaties between the kingdoms on the matter of divers of the propositions. They must therefore expect from the justice and wisdom of the Houses, that as regards matters of joint concernment they will never conceive themselves to be the sole judges, or to have power of continuing, altering, or repealing them, as they shall think good, without the consent of the kingdom of Scotland. They support their argument by the late declaration of both Houses that they are fully resolved to maintain the Solemn League and Covenant and the treaties between the kingdoms, and also by the declaration made divers months ago by both Houses to the States General [dated August 5th, 1645] showing why the mediation of the Dutch Ambassador could not be accepted without application to the kingdom of Scotland. (Cf. *Lords' Journals*, viii. 414.)

July 10, 1646. Copy of an Act of the Common Council of the City concerning a letter received from the Church of Scotland dated at Edinburgh, June 18th, 1646. (The letter of which a copy is annexed is printed in Rushworth, iv. 1, 307. Cf. *Lords' Journals*, x. 104.)

[Before September, 1646.] A list of the subscriptions of nineteen lords in the Long Parliament.

October 14 and 15, 1646. Copies of the examinations of Lawrence Chapman, Samuel Pecke, and Anne Griffin touching the printing of the three speeches of the Earl of Loudoun and copy of the warrant from the Earl dated October 13th but written on October 14th. (For the substance of these examinations see *Commons' Journals*, iv. 693, 695. Cf. also Rushworth, iv. 1, 336.)

December 1, 1646. Worcester House. The Scottish Commissioners to William Lenthall, Esq., Speaker of the House of Commons. We

have received your letter with some sealed papers, which, you say, LORD BRAYE'S
contain the answer of the House of Commons to our paper of the 20th MSS.
and letter of the 24th of October. Although we very much esteem any
thing that comes from that honourable House, yet we have been sent
hither from the Parliament of Scotland to both Houses. The papers
relate to the disposing of the person of the King, and all our former
conferences, etc. have been with both Houses. We cannot accept an
answer from either of the Houses alone, and we therefore return the
papers, sealed as we received them. (Copy.)

January, (?) 1646[-7]. Copy of a paper from Sir Thomas Wharton
and Major Richard Salway presented to the House of Lords giving an
account of the proceedings of themselves and their fellow Commissioners
in Ireland. They left London on October 26th and reached Chester on
the 30th, but found the provisions and shipping were not ready. On
the 7th and 8th all the horse that had shipping and most of the foot were
shipped at Helbry and Liverpool, and the Commissioners that evening
came to the waterside but found the men that were shipped in a mutiny
not suffering any muster-master or officer to be on shipboard or the seamen to do their duty. The remainder on shore being about 120 stood
upon their guard, and would not be shipped, not suffering any officer to
come near them, being a very great part Irish or disaffected to the
Parliament and under no discipline, and therefore the Commissioners
hope to be excused for not prevailing with such men to forbear the 10s.
which was formerly promised to each of them upon their transportation,
although such forbearance was expected by the Committee for Irish
affairs, whose letter to that purpose was not received by the Commissioners till they were going on shipboard. The next day the wind was
contrary and on the 11th it was necessary to unship the horse, but on
the 12th the wind became fair, they sailed, and got into Dublin Bay on
the 13th at about four in the afternoon, and sent to the Marquess of
Ormonde for a safe conduct, and on the 14th the shipping weighed and
came over the bar, not being able to ride in the road. Upon the 15th
at 9 a.m. the treaty began. Subjoined are copies of the safe conduct
and accompanying letter referred to in the last.

January, (?) 1646[-7]. Copy of a second paper from the same to the
same. Mentions that on Thursday the 17th one of the ships having
about 240 men on board having the day before been in collision with
another was forced to run aground to save the men, and most of the
rest of the soldiers having come into the town (notwithstanding strict
orders to the contrary) and many the soldiers from their bad accommodation on board and want of provisions having fallen sick, the Commissioners asked Lord Ormonde's permission to land the soldiers
which was accordingly permitted. Subjoined are copies of the Lord
Lieutenant's letters promising to allow the soldiers landed to re-embark,
and of the Commissioners' engagement that the soldiers disembarked
and to be quartered at Ringsend, Lowsy hill and Bagotrath should do
no injury to the people of those places or the city of Dublin.

January, (?) 1646[-7]. Copy of a third paper from the same to the
same stating that the treaty not succeeding the Commissioners thought
it best that a quorum of them should accompany the forces to Belfast.

January 11, 1646[-7]. Copy of the narrative of Sir Thomas
Wharton about the cipher agreed upon between the Marquess of
Ormonde and the Commissioners. When the negotiations were at an
end he expressed his sorrow at their failure, and his intention of attacking Owen Roe O'Neale, and would communicate the time of doing so to

the Commissioners in Ulster, and would use all his influence to gain the King's consent to surrendering the garrisons and forces to the Parliament, and would communicate the King's answer to the Parliament and the Commissioners in Ulster. It was solely for these purposes that the cipher was agreed upon. Subjoined are copies of the only two letters for which the cipher was used.

January 27, 1646[-7]. Draft of a letter to the Parliament of Scotland. (Printed in *Lords' Journals*, viii. 691.)

February 8, 1646[-7]. Paper presented by the East India Company to the House of Lords. With regard to certain points they refer to their petition presented to Parliament some years before [in 1628, and printed in 1641] while with regard to the new objection against the pursuance of the East India trade by one joint stock they justify their practice by the following arguments:—

1. They had to encounter the Portugals and Hollanders as their competitors, from whom in their united condition they had sustained many assaults injuries and indignities; if weakened by division they feared on the first occasion of dissension to be utterly crushed and destroyed.

2. In the infancy of the trade it had happened that three ships for as many distinct stocks had arrived to load at the same port, and the natives, knowing that if they did not load while the monsoon served they would be detained six months, and observing this competition took advantage of it to buy cheap and sell dear.

3. The voyage being so long and exposed to so many casualties such as death of men, loss of rigging and provisions, &c. a joint stock takes care of all, and all their outward bound ships carry supplies to relieve such distressed shipping as they may meet homeward bound, and for this a rendezvous is appointed. This has been the preservation of many ships of great value. The contrary has been the cause why so many have miscarried in Mr. Curteene's employment.

4. The trade of East India is now settled in the dominions of 14 sovereign Princes, in which they maintain 23 factories, and 92 English factors of all conditions, upon which factories depends the employment of 20 ships, a great part of which are employed from port to port in collecting merchandise to be ultimately shipped to Europe. This can be managed only by a joint stock.

5. By their treaty with the people in all places of India they are bound to make satisfaction for all injuries committed by Englishmen. They cannot adventure their estates to the mercy of other men, in whom they have no interest and over whom they have no control. They mention the instances of Cobb and Ayres in the Red Sea and of Captain Weddall in China and at Messulapatan.

Lastly the East India Company having tried all other ways and finding by long and dear experience that one joint stock is the best and only way to carry on this work with honour and profit to this nation, they humbly beseech their Honours to believe that they are not so prodigal of their reputations, nor so treacherous to their own or other men's estates, as to propose the managing of them in a known way of prejudice, nor have they any such interest in the present government as doth perpetuate unto them the least particular advantage. They all shall be out of office in July next, and so shall continue to be, except they be chosen anew by the generality of adventurers. They therefore humbly beseech their Honours to believe that it is not for selfish or indirect ends they sollicit their countenance and encouragement to support the trade which they hope will become a national one. Notwithstanding their title to it they are ready to admit any man to join for a very small consideration by way of acknowledgement. LORD BRAYE'S MSS.

Another copy of the last with the reasons delivered on February 13th by Alderman Fowke by order of the Lords' Committee to show that a general joint stock is not the best way for the carrying on of the East India Company.

(A copy of the Remonstrance and petition above referred to, being a printed pamphlet, is among Lord Braye's papers.)

[January or February, 1646[-7].] Copy of a letter from one of the Irish Commissioners to the Speaker of the House of Lords. Defective in parts. This is the fifth time I have written to you, since my landing in the North of Ireland. I will not repeat anything again saving the short paper that [came] from my Lord of Ormonde. It was sent from —— Robert Ward at Dundalk a notable malignant. [It] was directed to Sir John Clotworthy, and Ward's letter only signified it came from a friend to whom he would return answer if it required it. The words of the paper were as follows :—I have prevailed with my Lord Digby, and am more than hopeful you shall hear from me shortly to your content. These words were written in Character, and Sir John produced a Clavis left with him by Sir Thomas Wharton, which he said would open it, but upon trial it would not do. However in regard I thought there might be something of moment in it I gave it not over till I had almost made it out and then with Sir John's help we completed it. It had no date nor any direction upon it. To whom it was meant I know not, but this I am sure of; there was no reason to write to us of prevailing with my Lord Digby for I expect no good of anything his counsel is in.

May 11, 1647. Holmby. The examinations of John Brown and Mrs. Mary Cave. (Copies. Printed in *Lords' Journals*, ix. 190.)

May 12, 1647. Holmby. The Earl of Denbigh and Lord Mountagu, to ——. (Copy. Printed in *Lords' Journals*, vol. ix. p. 189.)

June 12, 1647. London. The Mayor, Aldermen, and Commons, to the Commanders of the Army. (Printed in Rushworth's *Collections*, part iv. p. 557.)

June 23, 1647. St. Albans. Sir Thomas Fairfax to Alderman Warner, and the rest of the Committee sent from the City of London to the Army. In order to keep a right understanding with the city, we desire that some of your number may stay with us at head quarters. I shall, as I told you, remove my head quarters to Berkhamsted, and I expect to hear from you to-morrow night. (Copy.)

September 22, 1647. Paper under the hand of Thomas Andrews, Alderman ; stating that he had subscribed 1,000*l.* in a second general voyage now undertaken to the East Indies and that as he was not satisfied to take the oath formerly required of members of the said company he thereby promised and agreed to submit to and obey all orders to be made by the adventurers or the majority of them in this second general voyage, and as a security thereof he thereby deposited his stock.

A folio volume, newly bound, and lettered. "Letters and State Papers," 1648–1710.

February 21, 1647[-8]. Order made at a Committee of Lords and Commons at Derby House. With it are (1) a paper beginning :—" A cypher sent in a letter from the King to the Duke of York." Signed " Yorke."

(2.) A holograph letter from the Duke of York, with eight words in cipher. Signed "J. Darly."

(3.) A copy of the above deciphered.

(All the above are printed in *Lords' Journals*, vol. x. p. 77.)

[July 18 or 19, 1648.] Copy of a letter. On Friday the 14th of this instant July, the English and Scotch forces from Carlisle, Carden, Danston and thereabouts advanced in a body about 10,000 strong within two miles of Penrith, whereupon Major-General Lambert and his forces retreated at about 11 that night towards Appleby. The horse were in a body from then till Monday morning early, when having been so long on duty, and the weather foul and wet, they dispersed to quarters, leaving only Col. Harrison's regiment on guard on a moor beyond the town. That day at about one, the enemy forced them to retreat without much loss, only one lieutenant being slain and the colonel himself wounded, but not mortally. He is gone to Lancaster. The enemy then advanced to the town, but the water being raised by the great rain, they could only approach by the bridge, which was very well defended by our men, and after the enemy had been often repulsed, the dispute holding from about 3 to 7 p.m., they retreated, and our men attacked and followed them about a mile, until it was very dark. Many of their foot ran away and threw down their arms. 300 of the enemy are reported to be slain and 100 taken prisoners, while we did not lose above six or seven. That night towards morning, our men retreated towards Bowes and Barnard Castle, expecting more forces to join them, but did not hear that the enemy advanced after them the next day. (Cf. Rushworth, iv. 2, 1200.)

September 8, 1648. Draft of a Latin letter from the Houses of Parliament to the Estates of East Friesland, thanking them for preventing an officer from Lorraine levying troops there against England, and asking them to do the like in future.

September 14, 1648. Brancepeth, near Durham. Thomas Margetts to John Browne, Esq., Clerk of the Parliament. Has received his letter of August 15th only that day in consequence of his being out of the way with the party commanded by Major-General Lambert in pursuit of the Duke's horse that fled from their foot at Warrington. Had he received it sooner he would willingly have answered his desire. He presumes that now he has had a full relation of the battle, yet he believes not so fully and truly as it happened. He perceives more is attributed to some and less to others than they deserved. Is collecting the truth of the whole business, and hopes to send a copy by the next or second post at furthest. Has at present but little news only that Monro is gone into Scotland with all the Scots both horse and foot, the English under Sir Thomas Tildesley and Sir W^m Blackston are about Chillingham 10 miles on this side Berwick in Northumberland. The Lt. General [Cromwell] with all the horse and foot (except the Lancashire which stay in their own county and the 4 Regiments of Horse sent with Major-General Lambert) are (*sic*) about Alnwick and are marching to the borders, he having sent for these 4 Regiments (lying now about Durham) and Col. White's and Col. Hacker's (lying about Pontefract) to march up to him with all speed. 'Tis conceived we may march into Scotland, if there shall need. I presume you have heard that David Lesley with old Leven and Argyle are in the head of 8,000 horse and foot about Edinburgh and have made the Committee of Estates to fly, which is conceived to be the cause of Monro's speedy march into Scotland. It is true that Lesley, the Governor of Berwick, would not.

admit any of the Scottish or English cavaliers to come into that garrison in their passage, and reported that he affirmed that he always kept that place for the Parliament of England and will deliver it into their hands, the latter I cannot report for certain, but something there is in it. The English cavaliers both in Westmoreland, Cumberland, and Northumberland are now in so staggering a condition they know not what to do, swearing they are bewitched and will fight no more and do daily disband, depart from their colours, and shift for themselves." His absence from headquarters prevents his giving a better account. P.S. "I took the boldness as we marched from Uttoxeter through Derbyshire to visit Mrs. Gell, and found her and Mr. Gell with their little ones very well at Hopton Hall, but were preparing a little before the routing of the Scotts' army to remove their quarters. (This and all the other letters from the same writer are sealed with a seal bearing the device of a centaur and motto Nosse (*sic*) teipsum.)

LORD BRAYE'S MSS.

September 20, 1648. Belford. The same to the same. When I wrote to you last week I thought we should have overtaken the Lt.-General before this time with his party of horse, but he being far before us and marching as fast as we hath left us yet behind. Ludovic Lesley having returned answer to the Lt.Generals summons of Berwick very fair, viz., That being a servant to the Committee of Estates he cannot deliver it up without their order, but if they command, he is willing (that is the substance of it), the Lt.General drew up his army before it, lying himself within two mile, found a great deal of tameness, not any act of hostility past between them. Upon this answer, the Lt.General dispatched away Col. Bright and Major Strachan as Commissioners to the Committee of Estates, and it is much hoped they will carry both that and Carlisle. Mentions a report, which he believes, that Argyle being in a better condition than Lanrick and that party and they being near each other has offered him these terms: That he would forthwith lay down his arms and disband, sequester himself from all public employments till the next parliament, and surrender Berwick and Carlisle into the English hands, and he would receive him, but the Lt.General thinking it not amiss to strengthen the well affected with all speed hath resolved to march into Scotland, and accordingly Major-General Lambert yesterday morning passed Tweed with 4 regiments of horse and some dragoons and this morning the Lt.General with his own regiment of horse and all the foot is marching after him and to-morrow or next day I think we with this party of horse shall tread upon Scottish ground also. But the Lt. General before his entrance sent an express to the Committee of Estates to acquaint them with his intentions and to assure them that, as soon as he had strengthened the hands of the well affected party, and should have the garrisons surrendered, he would forthwith march out of that kingdom, and this he bid them be confident of for he spoke it out of the sincerity of his heart, and not out of hypocrisy or dissimulation, for he had so evidently seen the hand of God against Duke Hamilton for his invading England upon false pretences and hypocritical grounds, that if he did not really intend what he affirmed he durst not enter into their kingdom. It was rumoured that there had been some engagement in Scotland and that Argyle was worsted first, then that Lanerick was worsted by him, but I cannot hear of any such thing at all for certain, and do not believe it. Has not yet been able to finish his account of the battle.

September 21, 1648. A catalogue of the books and papers delivered to the Committee appointed to treat personally with the King.

LORD BRAYE'S
.MSS. September 26, 1648. Mordington. [Thomas Margetts] to John Browne, Esq., Clerk of the Parliament. On Thursday last, the Lieutenant-General [Cromwell] passed the Tweed, after the party he had sent over with Major-General Lambert, the present occasion being to face and block up the north as well as the south side of Berwick. After being at the rendezvous on that side, the town being faced on all sides by our army, he returned to his quarters at Mordington, the house of Lord Douglas, about two miles north of Berwick, and he received notice that the Marquess of Argyle would be with him on the following day.

On Friday morning, the Lieutenant-General [Cromwell], Major-General Lambert and other officers went out to meet the Marquess, and brought him to his quarters, accompanied by Lord Elcho, Col. Scott, and George Porterfield, as commissioners from the new Committees, with the Marquess, for procuring the delivery of Berwick and Carlisle, and for giving them into the hands of the English. Sir Ch. Erskine and Sir James Fraser came also as companions to them. That day the Marquess sent a trumpet into Berwick for a safe conduct for Lord Elcho and others to go in to the Governor and deliver their message from the Committee of Estates, which was not returned until the next night, and then the safe conduct was brought. They delivered letters of which copies are herein enclosed, but they returned with a negative answer.
· The next day, being Sunday (sic) the Marquess, the Lieutenant-General and others went again to the walls of Berwick and sent for the Governor to come forth. The Marquess (but not the Lieutenant-General) had private discourse with him. At last it was agreed that he should have liberty to send to Lanerick before giving any further resolution. Two gentlemen were despatched, to return by next Thursday night. No cessation was agreed on for the mean time, and we therefore drove away abundance of cattle from before the walls, which made them so angry that they have ever since been pelting at us with great and small pieces. As yet they have done us no harm. On the south side we have possession of the foot of the bridge and on the north we are very near. Neither party will be idle until the return of the messengers, whose good or ill report depends upon the agreement or non-agreement of the forces of Argyle and Lanerick. The latter are at Stirling Bridge, 26 miles north of Edinburgh, the former 12 miles on this side of Stirling. The substance of the agreement, if there be one, will be :—

1. That both the armies in the field, and the garrisons in Scotland, at Berwick and at Carlisle, shall be disbanded and "disgarrisoned."

2. That all differences of religion shall be referred to the General Assembly, and all civil differences to a Parliament to be speedily summoned.

3. That, to prevent a quarrel with England, none of Lanerick's party who were in the late Engagement against England shall be admitted to the Committee of Estates until the sitting of Parliament.

In Scotland the royal and Presbyterian parties are mixed, and it is uncertain which interest is the most powerful. The Independent party are "but as the gleaning of the harvest, and in their tender and budding state, but thriving and growing apace." The two former parties are both against the latter, and both against one another. When the sad divisions in England opened a gap, they strove which should first appear against it. The royalists were ready first, and invaded England with a mighty army. Since their defeat, the two parties have appeared in the field as friends lest the spreading evil of Independency should infect their Kirk. Argyle through his connection with the Kirk is likely to be powerful in the next Parliament. The Hamiltonian party must submit, else excommunication will be their doom.

If the two armies do not come to an agreement, we shall join Argyle and prosecute Lanerick and Monro, on account of the invasion of England. If they agree we shall have our garrisons and face about. A regiment of Argyle's has lately surprised and taken a regiment of Lanerick's, and a party of his men has also taken 1,000 arms which landed at Leith for Hamilton's army, coming from Dunkirk. It is the object of Scotland to live upon the divisions of England.

October 2, 1648. Berwick. Oliver Cromwell to ——. (Copy. Printed in Carlyle.)

October 3, 1648. Seaton, near Musselburgh. Thomas Margetts to John Browne, esq., Clerk of the Parliament. On Wednesday last Major-General Lambert advanced from his quarters at Mordington with 6 regiments of horse and two troops of dragoons, The next night his vanquarters reached within 5 or 6 mile of Edinburgh, which gave a hot alarm to the whole kingdom, and was the cause of the two armies making up their agreement so suddenly according to the articles inclosed. Berwick was delivered up to the Lieutenant General on Saturday last, and Lodovic Lesley marched forth with his forces and is now at Dunbar marching up to Edinburgh to be also disbanded." Cannot relate the particulars, having marched away with the Major General, except that he heard the English had no conditions given them. Colonel Overton's regiment was left to garrison Berwick, and all the horse and foot, except 5 regiments of horse left behind with the Major General, are marching to Carlisle and will be there next Friday. They think that place will be soon surrendered, as the Committee of Estates have sent the same orders about it as Berwick. These five regiments were also ordered to march to Carlisle, but the Committee of Estates sent a letter last night to the Major General, earnestly desiring his stay where he now is with his horse, because they have not yet heard whether Monro doth disband or not according to the articles agreed on. "Our army is their greatest strength, without which they could not have disbanded Lanerick, Crawford, Monro, &c. Nay Lanerick sent word to Lesley that had it not been for the English army he had scorned to have received conditions from him, but would have given him conditions. 'Tis happy for this kingdom that this army entered, for carrying so fair even beyond expectation, and thereby giving interest and respect they are like to be a means to procure its peace at least for a time. I wish the differences in England could be as easily reconciled as those in Scotland. On Saturday last, the Major General went to Edinburgh with divers of his officers to visit the place chiefly; much gaping there was upon him, some with smiling, some with sour faces. He went to visit my Lord Chancellor and the Earl of Leven (to whom he had before given notice of his approach) and had much discussion with them, and several lords and gentlemen of quality came to give him a visit at the Lord Chancellor's lodging while he stayed, which was about an hour, and then returned to my Lord Winton's at Seaton. Our time here will not be long, I hope (Scotland's accommodation (though we have as good quarters as any in the kingdom) comes far short of England), but I think we shall see all disbanded before we return. The Marquess of Argyle and the Lieutenant General (having settled Berwick) came this evening to this town, and the Marquess is gone this night to Edinburgh, and I believe the Lieutenant General himself thither tomorrow, partly out of desire to visit the town, but chiefly (I conceive) to gather a better understanding of the affairs and state of Scotland. There is much of outward compliment and salutation passing at all meetings between the great ones of both nations, striving each to exceed other, of which an ingenious spectator may make large comments. Cromwell hath the honor, but Lambert's discreet, humble, ingenious, sweet, and civil deportment gains him more hugs and ingenious respect and interest from the general parties. I could give you a large character of that man's great wisdom and valour, of which this kingdom reaps no little benefit.

October 10, 1648. Dalkeith. The same to the same. I have not failed to write to you by every post, directing my letters to Mr. Mabbet, according to your instructions. On Tuesday last, Lieutenant General Cromwell and Major General Lambert with certain officers went to Edinburgh, where they were very civilly entertained by the Marquess of Argyle. They remained there until Saturday night at the charge of the state. Most of the well-affected lords and lairds of the kingdom came to visit them at Lord Murray's house, which was specially provided for them. The well-affected rejoiced at our being there; the malignants gnashed their teeth, and some of them threatened to be the death of Cromwell and Lambert. Many of our soldiers and officers were very much abused and injured by some in the city who belonged to the late disbanded crew, whose inveterate malice made them desperate. Some of their horses also were stolen. In truth, all the while we were in Edinburgh, we were almost afraid to walk the streets or to lie in our beds, for fear of mischief. On Saturday after noon, before we left, the Marquess of Argyle took the Lieutenant General and all his officers to view the Castle, which is a very large and strong place, and had them in to a very nice banquet there prepared with all sorts of wine and sweetmeats. General Lesley was there to entertain the guests. It is noticed that David Lesley showed himself very little to the Lieutenant General, for he only paid him a visit of necessary civility on the morning after his entry, giving him a bare salute, and presently took his leave, and never saw him more. The Lieutenant General presented a paper to the Committee of Estates, the substance of which was that the chief places of the kingdom should be entrusted to persons well affected to the public good. To this he received a very full and satisfactory answer. The Committee of Estates for their own safety, asked that some of the horse should be left in Scotland. Major General Lambert is therefore left, with three regiments of horse. The rest of the army is marching to Carlisle, which, we hope, will be delivered in a very short time. The Committee of Estates has refused the King's desire as to three persons to treat with him on behalf of this kingdom, and have appointed Sir John Cheesley, and Mr. Robert Blair, ministers, to go to the Parliament of England. Our work here will not be difficult, but we live in great danger, "for an English soldier can scarce be alone a furlong from company, but he is sett upon and robbed and dismounted." Postscript. As we were coming out of the Castle at Edinburgh, they gave us nine or ten pieces of ordnance and a long volley of musket shot.

October 13, 1648. Edinburgh. Warrant to the lairds of Swinton Arnot (?) and Liberton to see such of the English forces as have had their horses plundered or been otherwise wronged recouped out of the estates of those who had been in the late engagement and had not submitted to the late agreement, and to take special care to keep a good correspondency betwixt this committee and them, and betwixt them and the country people where they are quartered. Signed—A. Henderson.

October 17, 1648. Seatoun. Thomas Margetts to John Browne, LORD BRAYE'S MSS. Esq. Several of our soldiers have lately been set upon in the highways and elsewhere, so that we dare not stir out without a good company "cockt and primed." Particulars about an attack on six men of Lambert's regiment. The Committee of Estates have taken these matters into consideration, which has given us some encouragement. We hope that our stay here will not be long. Within the next fourteen days they will have completed 600 horse in several troops and about 4,000 foot. It is believed that old Lesley will have the chief command. The next convention of Parliament will be in January. Most of the members are already elected, and those who are well affected towards the present Committee say that they are chosen well. The crushed party must therefore expect to be more trampled on.

November 1, 1648. Broxmouth. The same to the same. By your letter of this post I understand you have received mine which would have sufficiently satisfied me, had you been pleased not to have put yourself to the trouble of writing anything more, particularly in expressing so kind acceptance of that which is so unworthy of it. We are still in Scotland with our 3 regiments, attending the pleasure of the Committee of Estates, till they dismiss us, which we expect every day, but, I believe, will not be this ten days. They are very sensible of the benefit they have of our presence and countenance, being not yet in so good a posture as to act securely, their forces being not yet completed. We are very little burden to the well affected or those in the kingdom that were (not for, and) against the late Engagement, quartering altogether upon the contrary party, and have all this while been in the county of Lothian, till now Col. Twisleton's regiment is removed into the Merse, which is more Southward. The whole state of this kingdom is altered from what it lately was. The Committee of Estates consist only of those that were Anti-Engagers, and by that you may guess what they are doing, pulling down the other party, as fast as they can, and setting up themselves, according to the ordinary practice of all parties, when they are the most potent, to trample upon all others to advance their own interest, which I believe, were not we here, would soon crush out new commotions as they will in danger to appear when we are gone, for the differences between the Presbyterian and Royal interests are very wide and inconsistent, and cannot be at peace without the one holding his sword over the other and that's an ill tenure. By the many personal and reciprocal. civilities that have passed between the well affected Presbyterian party here and this army together with the great good done unto them by the army in freeing them from their late bondage and advancing their interest you may guess something at their correspondence. Their interest and practice are not the same, but ingenuity and honor, proceeding from a principle of gratitude will certainly lay a great tie, and now some misunderstandings are removed there is like to be the better harmony and correspondence, for ought I can perceive, and are in a nearer way of compliance than the two former. The last week the new parliament was indicted at Edinburgh Cross to convene the 4th of January according to the usual state of having the Cross hung with tapestry hangings. Being not very well at present I cannot enlarge to more particulars.

December 6, 1648. Petition of the East India Company to the House of Lords, signed—Wm. Cokayne, praying that the ship Ruth and the pinnace equipped by Alderman Andrews and others may not be permitted to proceed to the East Indies. (Cf. *Lords' Journals*, x. 617.)

It refers to the paper of January 8th, 1646–7 and to the paper of September 22nd, 1647 under the hand of Alderman Andrews.

January 24, 1648–[9]. Order of the High Court of Justice to Mr. Millington and Mr. Thomas Chaloner to repair to Mr. John Browne, Clerk of the House of Peers, for such papers as are in his custody which are conducible for the business and service of the court and to bring them, and requiring the said John Browne to send such papers accordingly.

January, 1648–[9]. Original receipt signed by Thomas Chaloner and Giles Millington for the papers delivered to them by John Browne, Esq., Clerk of Parliament, according to the foregoing order.

February 9, 1648[–9]. Life and character of Mr. John Packer, of Shillingford, [? father-in-law to Mr. John Browne], who died on that day. He was born at Twickenham on November 12, 1572, his father being clerk of the Privy Seal. He was educated at Westminster School, and then spent four years at Trinity College, Oxford, and then four years more at Trinity College, Cambridge. He afterwards travelled in France, and became secretary to Sir H. Nevill, the ambassador there, and on his departure served as agent till a new ambassador came. He was then agent in Denmark, and was made clerk of the Privy Seal in reversion and French Secretary. In 1612 he became secretary to the Earl of Somerset, and on his fall to Sir George Villiers, afterwards Duke of Buckingham, till his death in 1628. He often acted as secretary to King James, and was offered many times to be made Secretary of State, but always refused it. He was a diligent reader of the Scriptures, knowing by heart most of the New Testament, the Psalms, Proverbs, and Canticles. He frequented sermons not only on Sundays, but week days, and at his own expense sent able and orthodox ministers to preach in Lancashire, Staffordshire, Westmoreland, South Wales, and other remote parts of the kingdom, allowing some 50*l.*, some 40*l.*, and none less than 30*l.* a year, and to ministers elsewhere 10*l.* and 5*l.* In 1625 he built a chapel at Groombridge in Kent, which cost him above 500*l.*, and for the rest of his life allowed a preaching minister there 30*l.* a year, and endowed it by his will with 20*l.* a year for ever. In the same year he rebuilt Shillingford Church in Berkshire, costing at least 200*l.*, and in 1629 he bore most of the cost of rebuilding Chilton Foliat Church in Wiltshire. The writer then praises highly his behaviour to all that knew him, and his freedom from pride at his advancement, and his charity to the poor, of which several instances are given, mentioning the parishes to which he gave. He also mentions his gifts to the poor ministers banished the Palatinate and the Rochellois, and especially his gift of 100*l.* to the poor Protestants of Ireland, and his advance of 600*l.* for the recovery of that kingdom, half whereof he gave by his will for the bringing up of Irish children in the Protestant religion, and a second gift of 100*l.* the previous summer to 20 of those people "who were recommended to him to have lived in good fashion, and now were in want." His charitable gifts by will are then described. He was buried at St. Margaret's, Westminster.

March 15, 1649[–50].—"An assessment made by us whose names are underwritten by virtue of a warrant unto us directed for the raising and levying 28*l.* 11*s.* 10*d.* within this parish of Twickenham towards the maintenance of the troops for the Parliaments of England and Ireland

under the command of the Rt. Hon. Thomas Lord Fairfax, it being for LORD BRAYE'S
three months from the 25th of March to the 25th of June 1650," MSS.
containing the names of the persons assessed and the sum imposed on
each.

September 8, 1651.   Rowland Berkeley to his father-in-law, Sir
Thomas Cave.   I thank you for sending to enquire as to our condition
at this place, which has been of late very troublesome and hazardous.
The storm has fallen very heavily on the town of Worcester and four or
five miles around, to the ruin of very many families.   You cannot hear
too bad an account of the inhabitants of Worcester, all houses being
ransacked from top to bottom, the very persons of men and women not
excepted.   That the business succeeded so ill on the King of Scots side
is much attributed to the cowardice of the Scottish horse, who hardly
stood one charge, and to the unreadiness of that army in general.   The
officers not attending their duty could not be found to bring up their
men and to send relief where it was necessary.   The Parliamentary
army plied their business with reserve upon reserve until they had
routed all the Scottish forces on both sides of the river, and driven
them into the town, and then fell to storming without any reserve.
The fight began at Powick Bridge and in Weeke Fields ; the main of
it between Perry Wood and the town, and all those grounds between
that and the Diglesses (Douglas ?).   We hear that the Duke of Hamilton
is taken, being wounded in the body with a bullet, and also Sir James
Hamilton, who lies wounded at the Crown.   Your kinsman, Lord Grandi-
son, is a prisoner.   Being in great want he sent to my wife to inform
her of his condition, and she supplied him with 5l. and some provisions,
the town then yielding none.   The number of the slain is certainly great.
On Thursday morning the dead bodies lay in the way from Powick
Bridge to the town, and on the ground on either side of it, and in
almost every street of the town.   Many lie killed in the houses, in the
College and Church, on the green, and in the cloisters, and quite through
Sidbury, and for about a mile that way.   Where the King charged in
person the slaughter was very great, and the Parliamentary forces gave
back, but fresh reserves coming in did the work.   The King of Scots
fled northwards with about 4,000 horse and Highlanders with him.
The Parliament followed him with a greater number, and were about
three hours behind him.   I shall for the present forbear to trouble you
with the relation of the chances that have befallen me in this hurly-
burley.   As a man that meddled not on either side, I have had very
great deliverancies, in my person especially.   I have given the bearer
2s.   Heraldic seal affixed.

September 12, 1651.   Cotheridge.   The same to the same.   I hope
that you have before this received a letter from my wife and another
from me, by one College, who promised to be with you at Stanford by
10 o'clock yesterday.   In these letters you were informed of our late
troubles and present quiet.   I now thank you for your kind writing by
Major Smith's servant, and for your fatherly affection.   Your invitation
to myself, my wife, and my children, to come over to you is most comfortable, but I cannot be away from home, as you will perceive anon.   In
my last I only intimated to you some difficulties I passed through in the
late bustle ; I will now acquaint you more fully of them.   On the 3rd
of this month, the very day and time of the fight, I was taken from
hence by a Major with a party of horse, who had orders to bring me to
the King.   I had received several private messages from Worcester
while the King was there urging me to come to him, but resolving not

to meddle I had remained at home.   Before I came to the town the
fight was begun at Powick, and I, being dismissed from the Major and
his party to await the King's leisure, enquired the occasion of my being
sent for.   I was told that Major-General Massy was made Governor of
Worcester, and that there was a commission to certain gentlemen of the
county, whereof I was one, for the aiding and assisting of him, which
employment I not liking went presently to my horse, intending to get
home again with what speed I could, the battle being by this time hot
on both sides of the town.   By the time I came to the bridge the King's
forces were retreating from Weeke and the Parliament pursuing, and no
man was suffered to pass.   I presently made to the Foregate where I
was likewise stopped, and thence to St. Martin's Gate, and getting out
there endeavoured in vain to go into the Wick Road.   I then took
the footpath that goes to Perry Wood, and made up towards the battle
where there was hot service, and, being within musket shot, turned over
hedge and ditch on the left hand, and got into Wick Way at Barban
Bridge, not meeting a man to trouble me, and thence to Ombresley and
so to Holt fleet, as fast as I could.   Having well passed through the
army I rode through fields and closes for about a mile, and then
being to cross Worcester road I was taken by a party of Scots.   I
having neither sword nor pistol, they would not let me pass, and at
last began to quarrel as to whose prisoner I should be.   At last they
told me they would carry me to their party of about 120 horse that
were before.   When we came to the party they brought the news of the
defeat of their forces at Weeke, and finding them in disorder with it, I
lagged by degrees till I was in the reare, and, taking the opportunity of
a blind lane, clapped spurs over hedge and ditch, and was presently out
of sight.   About nine at night I came home, having been five hours
about it.   The next morning by sunrise came a party of the Parliament
horse and took me from hence, telling me that I must go to the General
and took my dun colt with them, but by the time I came to St. John's
I found that they had no order for what they did.   At last they were
all gone excepting him that led the colt, and for about half an hour we
rode about the fields amongst the dead bodies, and I persuaded him to
deliver the colt to my man again, and gave him all the silver I had in my
pocket, about 15s. or 16s.   Since then I have been informed that my
name is given in amongst many others for coming in to the King of
Scots, and that there are orders issued for inventorying the goods and
stopping the rents of all named in this list.   If there be any justice left
upon earth I hope they cannot touch me.   Heraldic seal affixed.

[January, 165¾.]   " To his highnesse the Lord Protector of the Commonwealth of England, Scotland, and Ireland, and our General, the
humble addresse of the officers and souldiers of the army whose names
are subscribed," declares, after a preamble, that we only shall not be
obedient unto you in the performance of your great trust, but in our
places most faithfully and diligently to the utmost hazard of our lives,
and whatsoever is near and dear to us be serviceable to you in the
station God hath placed you, against all oppositions, not doubting but
as God and man hath so highly intrusted you, so you will to the utmost
of your power and endeavour lay forth yourself for the glory of God
and good of his people, amongst whom, we have reason to think, there
are very many of the household of faith, over whom we shall therefore
take this boldness most humbly intreating your Highness more especially
to spread the wing of your protection, and to account of them as the
apple of your eye, which you continuing to do we are confident their
Father, which is in Heaven, will be unto you a buckler and a shield,

and an exceeding great reward, which is and shall be the prayers of your Highness' most humble and faithful servants. Then eleven "exceptions against subscription," being reasons against signing the above address, and "some queries and observations touching the army's late proceedings" follow. (Cf. Whitelocke's *Memorials*, 590.)

September 1, 1655. Madrid. A translation of the king of Spain's declaration laying an embargo on all English vessels and goods found in Spanish ports or territory in consequence of Penn's attack on San Domingo. This particular copy is addressed to the Corregidor of Biscay.

August 1, 1656. A long account by John Bradshaw, the regicide, of his dispute with Cromwell. It is headed:—"The substance of what passed at the Councell Table the 1st of August 1656, betweene the Lord Protector and the Lord Bradshawe."

May 30, 1660. Original Declaration made by Mr. John Browne to entitle him, to the-benefit of the General Pardon promised by the Declaration of-Breda. Witnessed by the Earl of Manchester, Speaker of the House of Peers, *pro tempore*. (Autograph.)

October 3, 1661. Warrant under the hand of William Whitehead, Messenger, ordering the persons therein named to appear before him at the Star at Southampton. On the back are names of persons summoned in the town and county of Gloucester.

Undated. Original petition of William Whitehead, Gentleman, to the King. Sets forth that for his loyalty in 1642 he was plundered in and near Winchester to the value of 500*l*. That in 1643 and 1644, being Commissary General to Lord Hopton, he furnished him with money and goods to the value of 500*l*. more, for which he never received any satisfaction or pay. In 1645 his estate was sequestered, and he lost by the Parliament party above 1,200*l*., and he was obliged to live abroad till the Restoration, since when he has been very instrumental in prosecuting some of those grand traitors lately executed at his own charge. He therefore prays that 3,000*l*. may be granted him out of the moneys arising from the seizure of prohibited goods by himself or his agents.

April 7, 8, 1662. Explanation proposed by the Bishop of Worcester of the clause about the Solemn League and Covenant in the Bill for Uniformity of Worship, but rejected by the House, viz., to add to the Clause (printed in *Lords' Journals*, xi. 422) "otherwise then in such things only whereunto I or any other person were legally and expressly obliged before the taking of the sayd Covenant." (Cf. *Lords' Journals*, xi. 423, 424.)

May 17, 1662. Original message from the King under the Sign Manual. (Printed in *Lords' Journals*, xi. 460.)

April 27, 1664. Certificate under the hand of the Earl of Manchester, of the appointment of William Whitehead as Messenger in Extraordinary to his Majesty. Signed, Manchester (autograph). Seal affixed.

August 23, 1665. Rules and Orders made by the Vice-Chancellor of the University of Oxford and the Justices of the Peace, for the good and safety of the University, City, and County of Oxford, during the plague.

LORD BRAYE'S
MSS.

1666. A table showing the rents at which the excise of each county was let to the farmers of it, for the year commencing Sept. 29, 1665 :—

| | | |
|---|---:|---|
| Berks - - - - | 2,800 | |
| Bucks - - - - | 2,400 | |
| Bedford - - - | 1,700 | |
| Bristol and County of | | |
| Gloucester - - | 8,000 | |
| Cambridgeshire and Isle | | |
| of Ely - - - | 4,380 | |
| Cheshire - - - | 2,800 | |
| Cornwall - - - | 2,100 | |
| Cumberland and West- | | |
| moreland - - - | 2,000 | |
| Derbyshire - - - | 2,400 | |
| Devonshire - - - | 9,500 | |
| Dorsetshire - - - | 2,700 | |
| Durham, Newcastle, | | |
| Northumberland, and | | |
| Berwick - - - | 4,700 | |
| Essex - - - - | 8,600 | |
| Hampshire and Isle of | | |
| Wight - - - | 3,200 | |
| Hertfordshire, with | | |
| South Mimms in | | |
| Middlesex - - | 4,600 | |
| Herefordshire - - | 1,700 | |

| | | |
|---|---:|---|
| Huntingdonshire - - | 1,400 | |
| Kent - - - - | 15,000 | |
| Lancashire - - - | 4,400 | |
| Leicester and Rutland - | 3,800 | |
| Lincolnshire - - | 7,200 | |
| Northamptonshire - | 3,200 | |
| Nottinghamshire - - | 3,100 | |
| Norfolk - - - | 13,800 | |
| Oxfordshire - - - | 4,200 | |
| Salop - - - - | 2,800 | |
| Somersetshire - - | 4,600 | |
| Staffordshire - - | 2,900 | |
| Suffolk - - - | 7,600 | |
| Sussex - - - | 3,800 | |
| Warwick - - - | 3,000 | |
| Wiltshire - - - | 3,300 | |
| North Wales - - | 2,000 | |
| South Wales - - | 3,500 | |
| Yorkshire - - - | 16,000 | |
| London, Middlesex, and | | |
| Surrey - - - | 140,000 | |
| Total - - | 312,180*l.* | |

October 7, 1665. New style. Madrid. The death of the King of Spain [Philip IV.] on September 7, at 4 in the morning, I know is no news to you, but his obsequies I believe may be, they being such as you would scarce expect. Sept. 8 his body was exposed to public view in the palace in the Chamber of Audience, a room very spacious, with a gilded roof, and hung with arras. There was nothing of black in the room, nor were the windows shut, though there were candles, but only such as stood on the 7 altars, which were set up to say some of the 300,000 masses that are to be said for the soul of him, the best altar was at his bed's foot, and three on each side the room. At the upper end there was a rail went athwart, within which under the ordinary canopy was placed a bedstead of silver. The valence seemed to be of fine red silk; curtains there were none. Over the bed was spread a counterpane of cloth of gold, whereon the body lay open in a coffin of silver gilt. His face and hands were painted very fresh, and his beard very neatly turned up. He had a white beaver hat on his head, his clothes were of light dove-coloured silk, laced with silver cord, his stockings of the same colour, and a pair of new shoes on his feet. Between his hands was put the globe. At the head of the bed was his coat of arms, the only one that was in the room. On the right side of the bed stood a man in mourning, but his face uncovered, with a plain gilded crown (for I heard nobody say it was gold) in his hand; on the left stood another with the sceptre which was set from one end to the other with diamonds, and on the top one about the bigness of a pigeon's egg at the least. There was no sign of mourning in the palace but in their habits, and so every person in the town mourns that is able, and but a few are not, for from the greatest grandees to their meanest servants nothing is worn but bayes. In this state the King lay till the next night, which was Saturday, and then about ten he was carried to the

Escurial in this pomp. First there went 4 several orders of friars on mules with torches in their hands, of each order twelve. Then followed some of the King's guard in mourning, with spears in their hands at the top whereof hung a little black pendant, then came the body laid on a plain bier, carried by two mules half covered with cloth of gold, The body was also covered with cloth of gold, and tied on to the bier with two white cords to keep it from tumbling, for they went at a round rate. At the corners of the bier were four glass lant-horns with large tapers burning in them, and about the corpse were carried very many torches. After the corpse followed a few noble-men on horseback, (as I was told, for they could not be known to be so, either by their habit or attendance), and then the rest of the guard. Many nobles went in their coaches, but in no order, nor as if they waited on the corpse. There was not one coach covered with black, nor one of the King's coaches went in State, nor a horse led. The two trumpeters of the guard had the King's arms on their trumpets, and these looked most like heralds of any that went by. And these in very truth are the funeral rites of the King of Spain.

The King in his will left the Crown to the Prince, who will be pro-claimed this week, and after him to the Infanta that is espoused to the Emperor, after her to the Emperor, and, upon his failing, to the Duke of Savoy. The King nor Queen of France are not mentioned, which his Ambassador here cannot forbear openly to manifest his resentment of. The Queen Mother is Regent, and though she hath six counsellors ap-pointed her, yet is she absolute. The King's last words to the Prince were these, "*Dios ti haga meior, y mas dichoso que yo.*" "God make thee better and more happy than I." No address or signature.

May 30, 1666. Philip Packer to his brother-in-law, John Browne. Could not get the navy list till the Thursday, too late for the carrier. Now sends it with one in print by the Banbury carrier. The report at Change yesterday was that Prince Rupert with Sir E. Spragg and Sir Thomas Allen and 30 ships are gone towards the fleet at Rochelle, but those who know how the wind hath stood to S.W. know it cannot be true for that cause. Others report that he has gone northward to take the Danish ships and so unite all together, but these are but rumours so far as I can learn. Addressed "To my very worthy good brother, John Browne, Esq., at his house at Eydon, Northamptonshire."

October 20, 1666. Hornby Castle. Lord D'Arcy and Meynill to Viscount Andover. (Printed in *Lords' Journals*, xii. 28.)

January 8, 1666[-7], Westminster. William Ryley, senior, to his son William Ryley, junior, at the Record Office in the Tower. Being unable from illness to go himself, he directs his son to bring the records desired by the Lords, being precedents of impeachments by the Com-mons of Peers, especially the Parliament Roll of 28 Hen. VI., the impeachment of the Duke of Suffolk. He is also to see if there is an impeachment against Lord Latymer in 50 or 51 Ed. III. Seal of arms. (Cf. *Lords' Journals*, xii. 70.)

June 20, 1667. Order made in the Queen [Mother's] Council Cham-ber, Denmark House, Strand. It being alleged that an arrear of rent was due for a messuage at Twickenham by John Browne, Esq. to Her Majesty, Mr. Blomley, Mr. Penny, Mr. Bound, and Mr. Hasell "having had a hand in the receipt of Her Majesty's rents within the said manor" are ordered to attend the board, so that the validity of the said allegation may be made manifest, and such course taken as may be for Her Majesty's service. Seal affixed.

LORD BRAYE'S
MSS.

July 4, 1667.  Parliament Office, Westminster.  John Walker to his kinsman, John Browne.  Was too late to acquaint Sir John Ayton " with your desire about venison."  Have looked over the Bills and shall wait on Mr. Attorney with the titles of them.  Cannot " say anything as to the likelihood of guessing what time the business of this Session may take up, but the comon opinion and talke of the towne is that we shall have hott worke as well as hot weather.  Yesterday the D. Yorke, D. Albemarle, and many others went hence toward Harwich where the Dutch have landed 3,000 men, but I find not any greate apprehension of feare here thereupon.  It was also yesterday very much talked of here that a general peace was on Fryday last concluded between English, French, Dutch, Dane, and Swede, but I am willing yet to suspend my beleefe thereof, though I was told last weeke at Whitehall that Mr. Secretary Morrice should say we should certainly have a peace before the Parliament meete.  The Earl of Bridgewater, (with whom I dined on Tuesday) said he thought we should sitt long, but, if it please God to send us peace, I rather beleeve the contrary.  His Lordship was then dispatching away letters to his Deputy Lieutenants and others to cause a meeting in Bucks for proposing the raising of money upon the credit of the eleven months' tax, on which Act betweene 60 and 70,000l. is already advanced."  He then mentions that he attended the Queen Mother's Council at Somerset House last Thursday, where Mr. Bloomley, Mr. Hasell, and Mr. Bound appeared, but no Penny.  It appears from his narrative of the proceedings that Penny, to whom Mr. Browne had paid his rents, had had no authority to receive them, so Mr. Browne had to pay them over again, and was left to his remedy against Penny, who could not be found.  He encloses a Gazette.

November 22, 1667.  Report of a conference with the House of Commons in the handwriting of Lord Ashley, afterwards Earl of Shaftesbury.  (Printed in *Lords' Journals*, xii., 144.)

December 2, 1667.  Report of three of the judges in the case of Heron *v.* Selvin.  (Printed in *Lords' Journals*, xii. 158; cf. *Lords' Journals* xii. 124.)  Attested by the signatures of Mr. Justice Wyndham, Baron Raynsford, and Mr. Justice Morton.

April 27, 1668.  " Presidents concerning the manner of proceeding against persons impeached by the House of Commons for misdemeanours."

June 7, 1668.  Lord Howard of Charlton and Andover to ————.  I send the copy of my speech very faithfully transcribed.

May 23, 1670.  Eydon.  Richard Ellis to his Master [John Browne].  Gives an account of what happened about the man and horse provided by Mr. Browne at the muster of the yeomanry.  Almost all the young men in the town were active about the maypole; it stands by the elm tree, carts and coaches may pass by.

May 27, 1670.  Dover.  Order in Council to William, Earl of Craven, Lord Lieutenant of Middlesex and the Borough of Southwark, directing him to make inquiry as to the alleged recent resorting of sectaries and disaffected persons especially such as were active in the late rebellion to the City of London and the neighbourhood, to search for them, and seize and detain them and their arms, till he sees cause to the contrary or till further order, and if necessary to employ the militia of the county and borough against all rebels and traitors.

September 22, 1670.  John Walker to his honoured cousin John Browne at Eydon.  Thanks him for directing him where to find the book he wanted, of which he had in the mean time "retrieved" the LORD BRAYE'S MSS. duplicate. On Saturday last the Commissioners [for an Union with Scotland] met at Somerset House (among whom was Lord Ashley), where Lord Arlington presented a written message from the King, expressing his sense of the Commissioners' readiness to comply with his desires in this work, and letting them know he had had many serious thoughts about it, and out of them had collected some heads which he thought fit to offer to them as matter of debate, out of which many particulars might arise, but left them free to propose what else their Lordships should think fit, and follow what method they please. The heads were—

1. The preserving to each kingdom their laws, civil and ecclesiastical, entire.
2. The bringing of both Parliaments into one.
3. The uniting both kingdoms into one monarchy under his Majesty, his heirs and successors inseparably.
4. The consideration of privileges, trade, and other advantages.
5. The securing the conditions of the union.

Upon which the Lords took time till to-day to consider of their methods and manner of proceeding hereupon. Mentions the death of his cousin Browne, and her burial at Marlow. On Saturday last when my Lord Keeper and Lord Arlington declared to the rest of the English Commissioners that his Majesty had appointed me to attend that service some of the Lords said merrily they had got the furniture of the House of Peers, to wit, 88 hangings and one of the clerks ; upon which it was replied, they hoped they should have no more of the clerks, for there was one who could not read, upon which I said I supposed you would take care their Lordships should be troubled with him no more. My Lord Keeper told Sir John Ayton and me on Friday last, that he hoped this treaty would be ended before Parliament meets, and that therefore they intended to sit every other day, but I hear since it is doubtful at the slow rate it begins. P.S.—The Commissioners have met and debated the 3rd head first, and have agreed to the substance of it, leaving out 'and successors,' and for the wording of it, a committee of three English and three Scotch Commissioners are named to prepare it as it is to be entered in their journal and ours, and also some preliminary rules agreed on for the better method of proceedings on both parts against Saturday morning, when is to be the next general meeting. Seal of arms.

January 12, 1672[-3]. Summons by H. Farmer and Edward Bromwich, the Commissioners appointed to take evidence in Brown v. Maunder, to the witnesses therein named to appear before them at the Red Lion at Moreton Pinkeney on the 22nd, to be examined on interrogatories. Seal affixed.

March 1, 1672[-3]. Report of the speech of the Lord Chancellor [Earl of Shaftesbury] acquainting the House, by his Majesty's command, with what passed between the King and the House of Commons with regard to his alleged exercise of the dispensing power in ecclesiastical matters. It concludes thus, " I cannot but observe to you that this reply [of the House of Commons] hath drawne in a new point besides the matter as it were by head and shoulders, viz., a coordination of the three estates, the King being made one of them. This is a matter of soe great moment that your Lordships will not wonder that the King is startled at it. I am commanded to open to you what foundation this coordination laid for the late war; it produced the ordinances which were the cause of it. Coordination makes the two Houses equal with

LORD BRAYE'S
MSS.

his Majesty in the legislature, whereas the sanction of lawes is in the King alone, without which any bill prepared is but as wast paper."

May 29, 1673. From aboard the Rupert. Wind S. and by E. J. H. to——, (Copy). We have for some time rid in sight of the Dutch fleet who kept their Banks, and although his Highness had resolved to engage them yet was prevented by foul weather until the 28th instant. He did me the honour to give me the command of 33 men-of-war, 13 fire-ships, and 20 other small ships drawn out of the several squadrons. I began the fight about 12 o'clock, and in one hour came the Prince with the whole fleet to our succour. We forced the Dutch fleet as far before us as we could go for the sands, the fight continued till night, and then (for fear of the sands) his Highness drew off the fleet. We ride now in sight of them, where they ride now as much under the protection of their Banks as they can. We presume their damage to be so considerable that they will seek the security of their Ports, but should they have other thoughts we are ready to receive them. We lost several captains, but of your acquaintance only Tho. Fowles, who seconding me (bravely) lost his life. The vessel is just going, which denies me the opportunity of enlarging. You may expect further by the next. All our ships are safe as he wrote. Captains lost, Finch, Fowles, Worden, Trevanion, Courtney. Land Officers, Col. Honble shot, Col. Hambleton lost his leg. The French fought well, but the captains of their fireships wanted dexterity. Van Trump was forced to change his ship three times.

August 16, 1673. Jermyn Street. Henry Heming to "my ever honoured good lord." (Copy.) I would not let slip this opportunity of giving your Lordship an account of the great affair which hath lately happened amongst us with engaging the Dutch fleet, which hath been longly (sic) expected this week, but nothing was heard at Court till Friday last, and then there came a letter from the Prince giving the King an account of our taking one of the Dutch East India ships, which is sent into Harwich, and upon the strict and several examinations of the persons therein he finds there are but five more in all of their whole fleet, who are (he is very confident) likewise taken, for they put into St. Hellen's Island [St. Helena] for fresh water, and that island we have now lately regained from the Dutch, (if so they are sure). It's said this ship we took is worth 100,000l. some say much more. She sailed quite through our fleet in the night, and wanting a little more night, sailing betwixt two French ships they discovered and fired, upon which she struck sail. The news this day is the engagement of the fleets which was this. Upon Sunday last the Dutch came out with their whole fleet and that within sight of ours. They bore northward and we after them. On Monday morning they had the wind of us and came up briskly to our fleet, upon which engagement Trump [Van Tromp] and Sprag [Sir E. Spragg] being in the rear they parted a great distance from the fleets and to work they went. Trump was forced to forsake his ship, and not long after Sprag was put to the same shift, but that would not serve the turn. Trump was forced thrice more to forsake his ship and Sprag twice, that is from the Prince (in which ship he was), having all his masts shot down to the decks, to the George, and from her to the Bristol, and she being likewise disabled, he got into her long boats, but by an unfortunate shot the boat was overset, and poor Sprag (as the King expressed it) was cast away. Some think he was shot in the boat, but dead he is to our great loss, and is much lamented here. Now Du Ruyter finding it very hot with the Prince tacked to Trump's squadron. The Prince tacked with him on one side and the French on the other, who had then the wind of the Dutch, so they fought all the way. The losses cannot yet bo known, only we have this certainty that we have lost no ship, and only Captain Neanes killed outright and Captain Heaward his left arm or shoulder shot off, and the Dutch have had in our sight three ships fired and two sunk, one by the Rear Admiral of the French, the other by Sir John Kempthorne. Towards night the Dutch got off as fast as possibly might be, (and if I forget not), homewards. The next morning nothing to be seen of them and the Prince cast anchor. It is otherwise reported that the Dutch went off northwards again and we after them, but I rather believe the first. It is likewise reported at Court that Lord Ossory had his deck cleared, and only himself and his page and Captain Herbert escaped. The Royal Sovereign had not 20 men killed nor wounded in her, the Dutch being very fearful of her.

LORD BRAYE'S MSS.

January 25, 1673[-4]. London. Copy of a paper from the French Ambassador, the Marquis de Ruvigny, remonstrating against the King's making a separate peace with the Dutch, inasmuch France had faithfully performed all the stipulations of the treaty of February 12, 1672.

1675. Petition of John Taylor, a prisoner in Bethlehem, to the King for his release. It begins with 14 lines of verse, the first letters of which form the words Charles Stuarte. (Cf. Lords' Journals, xii., 691, 701, xiii., 26.)

November, 1675. Copy of the narrative of M. de Luzancy of the manner in which a recantation of the Protestant religion was extorted from him by M. St. Germain and another Jesuit. Subjoined is a threatening letter sent to him on November 2nd. (Cf. Kennet's History iii., 307, Commons' Journals, ix., 369, 375.)

November, 1675. Copy of a bill brought in by the Duke of Buckingham for the ease and security of Protestant Dissenters (cf., Kennet, iii., 308). The chief provisions are that after January 24, 1675-6, two or more Justices of the Peace are empowered to license places of worship for Protestant Dissenters, and that any persons after that date on appearing before any justice and entering their names, and the sect or congregation to which they belong, and making a declaration shall have free liberty and exercise their religious worship in any place so licensed. Among the subsidiary provisions Dissenters are relieved from being Churchwardens, and no such meeting-houses are allowed within either of the Universities or their precincts.

April 3, 1677. The Reasons of the Lords for rejecting a proviso added by the Commons to the Bill for naturalizing the children of English subjects born in foreign countries during the late troubles. (Cf. Lords' Journals, xiii., 97, and Commons' Journals, ix. 416.)

February, [1677-8]. Reprimand of the Earl of Salisbury for maintaining that the long prorogation of Parliament had operated as a dissolution thereof, with the Earl's submission. (Cf. Kennet, iii. 309.) These documents were originally entered in the Lords' Journals, but were vacated by order of November 13, 1680, which is printed in Lords' Journals, xiii. 664.

[1678.] Case of the Earl of Cassilis. The Marquis of Athol and other lords had been empowered by the Privy Council by a Commission dated December 26,[1677] to raise the Highlanders within their bounds, and also all their vassals, and march to Stirling, and thence to wherever the Council should command, and to live at free quarters on the march, which the Earl submits was contrary to the fifth Act of his Majesty's first Parliament. The Earl of Strathmore and others having been warranted to convoke the militia of the shire of Angus and to march with them upon free quarters into the West Country, this accordingly was done, though the militia should be furnished with 40 days' provision out of the shire in which they are raised. The Earl of Cassilis in obedience to a summons attended the Committee of Council at Glasgow on January 26th, and by an order of the 29th, was, as bailiff principal of Carrick, ordered to get in the arms of all sorts in the Baylery, as muskets, pistols, swords, pikes, and halberds, Lochaber axes, dirks, and whingers—such as refused were to be quartered on—and an account of them to be given in at Ayr on February 7th, which was done accordingly. By an order of February 7th of the Lords of the Committee of Ayr the Earl was ordered to rase to the ground or burn all meeting-houses in the Bayley of Carrick, and to make an exact enquiry of the builders of them, and the actors or abettors thereof, and on whose ground they had been built. All this he did accordingly, though the Lords would not allow him any of the standing forces, nor the gentlemen, his friends, to go armed to assist him. He was then by a new warrant to bring back the timbers of the demolished meeting-houses to the places where they had stood, and to burn them there, which he accordingly did. The Lords of the Committee by letters of February 9th from Ayr, ordered the Earl to publish at the market-cross of Mayboll and at all the parish church doors in his baylery on the next Sabbath day, their proclamation requiring all heritors, liferenters, and others of the baylery to appear before them at Ayr on the 22nd, to subscribe such bonds as the committee should appoint, and it was published accordingly. Notwithstanding the Earl's ready obedience, on the 10th 1,500 men were sent upon free quarters into the jurisdiction of Carrick, most of whom were quartered on his estate, "whereby not onely free quarter but dry quarter, plunder, and other exactions, many insolencies and cruelties have beene committed too tedious and lamentable to report," of all which he gave an account by a letter to his Grace the Duke of Monmouth. On February 22nd the Earl in obedience to the proclamation appeared at Ayr, but refused to subscribe the bond tendered to him requiring that his whole family, tenants and cottagers, with their families should abstain from conventicles and should not recet (sic) supply or commune with forfeited persons, intercommuned ministers, or vagrant preachers, but should endeavour to apprehend them, as the bond was founded on no law, and was impossible for him to perform, and such practice was contrary to the laws and customs of all other nations. A libel was then given against him at the instance of his Majesty's Advocate, charging him to appear on the 23rd before the lords of the Committee under pain of rebellion for being present at conventicles, and other crimes of a very high nature, and to give his oath on the verity of the libel. He accordingly appeared and deposed negatively, only if there had been any conventicles on his ground, or if his tenants had been at them he knew no further thereof than by hearsay, swearing that he never saw such conventicles or any of his tenants at them. A proclamation was issued at the same time commanding all who would not subscribe the bond to sell all their horses which were worth more than 4l. before March 1st, under pain of forfeiting not only the horse but 100l. Scotch. Notwithstanding the Earl had cleared himself on oath, the lords appointed a messenger to charge him with letters of lawborrows to enact himself in the books of the Privy Council and that he, his wife, children, tenants, and servants should not go to the conventicles and other disorderly meetings &c. under penalty of double his yearly value rents, and in case of fail he was to be denounced rebel within six days. He asked a week's delay, which was refused, and he then went to Edinburgh to attend the Privy Council and offer them possible satisfaction according to law, but on his coming a proclamation was issued commanding all from the West Country to depart from Edinburgh within three days to their own houses, before which time he was actually denounced rebel at the market-cross of Ayr, and letters of caption issued to apprehend him. In this strait, not knowing how to find a remedy in Scotland, and being assured that many of these proceedings were illegal and not warranted by the statutes and customs of Scotland, he thought it his duty to repair to his sacred Majesty as the fountain of justice, to whose sentence he is content to submit his life and fortune; and therefore prays him to consider his case and examine how far these proceedings are warranted by the laws and customs of Scotland.

LORD BRAYE'S MSS.

May 3, 1678. Copy of a paper, in French, delivered by the King's Commissioners to the Ambassador and Envoyé (*sic*) of the States General, and a translation of the same.

May 4, 1678. Original answer in French of the Dutch Ambassadors to the last paper, and a translation of the same. These were communicated to the House of Lords on May 7th. (Cf. *Lords' Journals*, xiii., 214.)

April 21, 1685. St. James'. Copy of a letter from the Earl of Peterborough, Lord Lieutenant of Northamptonshire, to the Sheriff, forbidding him raise the militia at the time of election, so as to interfere with the freedom of election.

March 1, 1688[-9.] Draft of the address to the King desiring he will use means for the security of the Government. (Printed in *Lords' Journals*, xiv., 135). Where the address has "you have just ground to suspect divers persons of treasonable practices" in the draft " the Lord Arran and " was inserted before " divers."

March 8, 1688[-9.] Original address of the City of London to the House of Lords. (Printed in *Lords' Journals*, xiv., 146.)

April 20, 1689. Original message from the King with the Sign manual. (Printed in *Lords' Journals*, xiv. 183.)

May 2, 1689. George Bridges, a justice of the peace for the county of Southampton, to all constables and other officers thereof. Mary Collins, late of Dublin, has this day testified before him that she was lately in the company of 67 Irishmen and 6 Irishwomen who pretend themselves to be distressed Protestants forced out of Ireland, but that they are now dispersed into several companies. She declared upon her oath that their object in coming to England was to set towns and houses on fire, that they have set fire to several houses in a town near Sherborne, that they intended to set fire to the City of Winchester, and that on the 1st of this May they set the town of New Alresford on fire, so that the whole of it has been consumed. The names and descriptions of five of these men are appended. All the company are well armed, and their women carry their fire-balls. The hue and cry is to be raised after them. (Copy.)

May 14, 1689. Copy of an order to the keeper of Newgate to bring Sir Robert Wright before the House at 10 a.m. the following day, and of another ordering Sir Richard Holloway and Mr. Justice Powell to attend at the same time. (Cf. *Lords' Journals*, xiv. 211.)

LORD BRAYE'S
MSS.
—

May 25, 1689.  Draft of the reasons to be offered to the House of Commons at a conference on the additional Poll Bill.  (Printed in *Lords' Journals*, xiv., 221.  Some alterations in the original draft are in the handwriting of Bishop Burnet.)

June 1, 1689.  Certificate under the hand of John Allen, messenger, of his delivery of a letter from the Lord Halifax to the Earl of Yarmouth.

June 8, 1689.  Examination of John Allen concerning Edward Lord Griffin.  (Printed in *Lords' Journals*, xiv. 238.)

March 16, 1690[-1].  John Walker to John Browne, Esq., at Mrs. Mary Walker's at Colham Green, near Hillingdon.  Saw Dr. Mapletoffe yesterday, who had seen at the Secretary's Office the day before letters from the Bishop of London, stating that he with the Court Lords will be suddenly at home, and that the King is gone to the relief of Mons, which is besieged and stormed by the French, and it is thought by most will before this time be absolutely in the French hands, there being but 7,000 men in it, and the French 27,000 men and foot, and the King of France with all his court before it, with all his guards and best soldiers and officers.  If Mons be taken the French king will presently overrun Flanders and so hinder the confederates from doing anything to save even themselves.  Has taken the relation of the Queen's express out of the News-letter, the truth he knows not.

July 5, O.S. [1708.  Oudenarde].  Col. A. Oughton to Sir Thomas Cave.  We passed the Scheldt on the last of June, in the face of the enemy's army, which we immediately attacked.  We killed 3,000 of them upon the spot, took 8,000 prisoners and about 800 officers, besides nearly 120 colours and standards.  We yesterday passed their lines, and we are now actually encamped within them, between Lille and Ypres, the former of which places we are preparing to besiege as soon as our heavy cannon can be brought up.  In the meanwhile many people are employed in demolishing their lines, which are exceedingly strong.  The young Prince of Hanover, who is here this year as a volunteer, charged at the head of a squadron of dragoons.  He was slightly wounded in the belly, and his horse mortally in the neck.  Our battalion was very sharply engaged.  Two of my brother officers were killed, and two wounded.

March 3, 1710.  Sir Thomas Cave to Col. Oughton.  As you ask for information about the mob in Lincoln's Inn Fields, I can only give you such as I received from my friends in London.  The gutting of Burges's meeting-house is worthy of observation for the body of transgressors was a compound of dissenters headed by an Anabaptist.  The other most memorable actions of the mob were in Watling Street, from whence intelligence was brought to the Lieutenant Colonel of the Militia, who was at supper in the City with a friend of mine.  A detachment was then ordered to compose the tumult raised at the echoes of a score of old women, with the juvenile chorus of "God bless the Q[ueen] and S[acheverell]."  At the other end of the town the young ladies of the Exchange gave twelve pence a piece to dress up a figure of Dr. B. with a gown and a band, and burned it in a tub resembling a pulpit.  It is said that there were great rejoicings and illuminations after Dr. Sacheverell's trial.

The form of consecrating the New Chapel of University College, Oxford.

A number of Navy Lists of different dates between 1659 and 1688.

1659. "The summer fleet," giving the names of the ships, their LORD BRAYE's MSS. burden, number of crew, number of guns, and captains' names.

[1660]. A list of his Majesty's ships whose names have been changed since his Majesty's happy return to England," and a list of the Red, White, and Blue Squadrons.

1664. "The number and nature of guns proportioned in time of war by the officers of his Majesty's Ordinance." A list of the number carried by each ship, distinguished as Cannon, Demi-Cannon, Culverins, Demi-Culverins, Sakers, Demi-Calverin Cutts, 24 Pounders, 12 Pounders, 3 Pounders, Saker Cutts, Falcons, and Minions.

1665. [Before June]. A list of the English ships divided into Squadrons,—Red Squadron, the Duke of York,—White, Prince Rupert, —Blue, Earl of Sandwich.

[May 1665.] "List of the Dutch Fleet out of the Maes."

[Before September 1665.] A list of the Royal Navy, showing the names of each ship, her burden, her crew in war and peace respectively, the number of guns, the length of keel, the breadth, the depth in the hold, the draught of water, and the date of building, the dockyard where built, and the name of the builder.

[After September 1665.] "A list of his Majesty's ships in harbour and at sea."

[1666.] A list of the Red, White, and Blue Squadrons.

May 1, 1666. "A list of his Majesty's Fleet under the command of his Highness Prince Rupert and his Grace the Duke of Albemarle."

Lists of the French and Dutch fleets follow.

April 1, 1680. "The present disposal of all his Majesty's ships in sea-pay."

1688. "A list of his Majesty's fleet under the command of the Rt. Hon. the Earl of Dartmouth."

[1685?] An army list, probably of the army sent against the Duke of Monmouth, showing a total strength of 16,640 men.

Two plans of Culworth Church, one showing the existing arrangement and allotment of the pews, and the other the alterations proposed.

A folio volume, bound in white, containing—
(1.) A treatise on judicature in Parliament.
(2.) "Observations, rules, and orders collected out of divers journals of the House of Commons."

A folio volume, bound in white, containing extracts from the journals of both Houses of Parliament, fairly copied by John Browne (pp. 1–352).

A folio volume, bound in brown, containing extracts from the Rolls of Parliament and other documents, concerning the privileges of the Lords of Parliament (ff. 4–112).

A folio volume, bound in white, containing extracts from the Rolls of Parliament, and other documents concerning the privileges of the Lords of Parliament (ff. 1–192), and "A discourse of the priveledge and practice of the High Courte of Parliamente in Englande, collected out of the common lawes of the lande," by — Starkey (ff. 193–234).

A small 4to volume, newly bound in red, and lettered "Collections for a History of Grantham, F. Peck." It consists chiefly of extracts from the municipal records.

A similar volume, lettered "Collections for a History of Lincolnshire F. Peck."

A similar volume, lettered "Collections for a History of Leicester. F. Peck."

A similar volume, lettered "Topographical Collections. F. Peck."

A folio volume, bound in white, and marked "C. 19." It contains extracts from Inquisitiones post mortem and other public records from the reign of Henry III. to that of Richard III., relating to the county of Leicester.

A bundle of transcripts from the churchwardens' accounts of Southwold and Romford, A.D. 1495, and of an inventory of the goods of the church of Southwold, A.D. 1520, &c.

A packet of miscellaneous poems and ballads, mostly written in the early part of the 18th century. The following relate more or less to politics :—

"The golden age reversed." (A satire on the Whigs. A.D. 1700–1712.)

"The Merchant a la mode." (On the Duke D'Aumont. A.D. 1712–1713.)

"The parson of Walton-le-Dale." (A.D. 1714–1715.)

"Pasquin to the Queen's statue at St. Paul's, during the procession, January 20, 1714[–5]." (A scurrilous Jacobite effusion.)

"A ballad on the French King's marriage with Mme. Maintenon. 1708."

Ballad on Sir Thomas Abney's appearing at the funeral of Queen Anne in the garb of a member of the choir.

"Royal Mercy," by Edward Griffin. 1708.

"The British Ambassadress' Speech to the French King." (A.D. 1711–1713.)

Verses "upon the death of the Rev. Mr. Modd, Vice-Master of Trinity College, Cambridge. 1722."

"Semper eadem." (A parody on the 3rd ode of the 3rd Book of Horace, inscribed to William Bromley, Speaker of the House of Commons. A.D. 1710–1713.)

"A ballad on the Oxfordshire election."

"The May-pole in the Strand to the May-pole at Farnham." March, 1715–6.

"Oratio in comitiis prioribus Cantab. habita." (Endorsed "Terræ filius's speech at Cambridge." It contains allusions to William Whiston, Sir John Ellis, Dr. Henry James, of Queen's College, and others.)

A packet of transcripts in the handwriting of Francis Peck, whose authority for them, it appears by marginal notes, was a volume described by him as "MS. Mordaunt."

1658, May 16. Brussels.—The King to John Mordaunt. "I am willing to beleeve those who assure me, that you are very willing to do me service, and that you do thinke that the onely way to redeeme your countrey from the misery and slavery it groanes under, is, by the blessing of God, to restore that which belongs to me, the detayning whereof must continue that misery, and subject the people to a continual succession of afflictions. I hope all good men will be of this opinion with you. And if you shall imploy all your interest (which I know is considerable) to the advancing of mine, I doubt not but God will blesse you in it. And, I do give you my word, I shall acknowledge it with all the real kindness you can expect, and will alwayes be, Your affectionate friend Charles R."

1658. December 27. Brussels. — The King to John Mordaunt. "Yours of the 25th of the last month came not to me before the last night, and I make all the haste I can to let you know, that, if you have not heard from me or anybody about me, it hath only proceeded from our Care of you, and not to expose you to any hazarde. And yet care was taken by 247 (whom you trust) you should know how just and kinde I am to you, how tender I am of your safety and confident of your affection. And, if that letter to him miscarried (as I hope it hath not) it hath been no fault here.

258 tells me you have somewhat of great moment to impart to me, which I long very much to receive. And I assure you whatsoever it is, it shall only be to myself. In the mean time I am rather ready to receave advice from my friends who are upon the place, than [to] direct them what to doe. And therefore I am the more impatient to heare very particularly from you, and you may be most confident that you shall ever find me to be constantly Yours Charles R."

1658–9, March 11. Brussels.—The King to John Mordaunt and five others. "Charles, by the Grace of God, King of England, Scotland, France, and Ireland, Defender of the Faith, &c. to our right trusty and well-beloved John Mordaunt, 193, 161, 155, 152, 172, and to every of them, greeting.

We do, by these presents constitute and appoint your our Commissioners, giving you, or any one or more of you, power to treat with any our subjects of our Kingdom of England and Dominion of Wales that are, or have been, in Armes against us, or our father of blessed memory, or that have contributed to the present Rebellion in England ; (excepting only such as actually sate in judgment for the taking away the life of our said father, or pleaded as councell learned against his life, or attended as ministers in that odious pretended Court, or laid hands upon his person in the execution of that horrid murder) and to assure them in Our Name, that, if they shall forsake the present Rebellion, and joine heartily and effectually for the suppressing of the same, and for our restoration to the rights due to us by the laws of God and of that our Kingdome; that then we will not onely freely pardon their former opposing us and our said dear father, and all other their crimes and offences, in acting, adhering to, or complying with the said Rebellion, but that we will recompence and reward such of them, as shall, by any remarkable service merit of Us, either by reducing or rendering any towne, fort, or garison of the rebels into our Hands or into the Possession and Power of you or of any other trusted or imployed by Us or you for our service. And what you, or any one or more of you, shall, by virtue of this our Commission, in wrtting under your Hands or the Hands of any one or more of you, promise in Our name in this kinde, we shall ratifie, confirm, and performe.

Given at our Court at Bruxells this eleventh day of March 1658, in the eleventh year of our reigne."

1658–9, March 11.—The King to John Mordaunt and five others. (Printed in *Clarendon State Papers*, III. 437.)

1658–9, March 11.—The King to John Mordaunt and five others. "Since it is impossible for me to cause any service to be performed in that Order which I desire, and to grant such legal forms as were to be

LORD BRAYE'S
MSS. wished, I doe depend upon your affections that, knowing my intentious, you will with all freedom towards one another, consult together of Ways, which to your judgments may be necessary to advance and carry on my service.

And since, by the blessing of God, I doe intend to be myself with you as soon as the business is begun (or sooner if you shall advise it) and so to mend anything that is defective; I hope none of my friends will take it ill that they are not named by mee, since I only mention those few with whom I have had most correspondence, who, I know, wilbe redy to take the counsell, help, and assistance of all others who will joyn with them. And I well know many who (out of the apprehension that they have of their enemies, wilbe wary how they do engage before they see some probabilitie of success) will afterwards venture as freely as the rest; and to whose affection I shall think myself as much beholden. I would have 588, 606, 859, 458, and those who have always consulted together, and such whose advice they have usually taken, or as many of these as can opportunely meet together, look over and peruse the blank Commissions now sent by me, and then insert such names of themselves, or of others, (who to their knowledge, are willing and able to serve me in that condition) in that Commission which contains the main and great Trust, and who are to fill the blanks in the other Commissions for Countyes and Governments, presuming they will distribute themselves into several places in that manner as may both advance the work without any emulation or particular contention upon commands; since they may assure themselves and those that resort to them, and with whom they must have to do, that I shall think myself as much beholding to those who obey with cheerfulness as to any who command with success. Which I doe not say as necessary to those Persons to whom I commend the conduct of my business (whoe, I know, are superior to those thoughts) but in regard of the several humours they meet with in those who are full of zeal and affection to my service."

1658, March 11.—The Marquis of Ormonde to John Mordaunt. "When you have received all that this bearer brings you; it will evidently appear there remained little for me to say. I shall onely assure you, that your warmth and industry doe appear so clearly to my Master, that there remaines nothing for me to doe in your service towards him; and whatsoever markes you receive of his kindness are the effects of your merit and his justice. All I shall recommend to you is a care of yourself, and that you will beleeve the bearer when he shall tell you that I am your most affectionate Kinsman etc."

1658-9, March 12. Brussels. — The King to John Mordaunt. (Printed in *Clarendon State Papers*, III. 436.)

1658-9, March 12. Brussels.—The King to Mrs. Elizabeth Mordaunt. "I have information enough how much I am beholding to you, which considering all, shewes more courage in you than I could expect. I am persuaded I shall live to thank you when you shall neede be less afraid to receive it. In the meantime I send you the inclosed to borrow upon the person you think fittest to oblege, as an earnest of my kindness to you both, which shall be always constant to you upon the word of Your very affectionate frinde Charles R."

Blank Warrant enclosed, conferring the dignity of a Viscount.

1659, March.—John Mordaunt to the King. (Printed in *Clarendon State Papers*, III. 443.)

LORD BRAYE'S
MSS.

1659, April 10.—John Mordaunt to the King. " 1. Secure and safe councells find most adherents ; and it is much easier to create scruples and doubts than to satisfie them. In my opinion nothing at this time can prevent your establishment, but divisions amongst ourselves and difference in judgments. These misfortunes begin now to appear when union is most necessary. Yet I cannot but believe the Wary Gentlemen would as willingly have you restored as wee; but they are loth to venture much to contribute to it. If notions or discourses would reinthrone you, your Majestic might he sure of your kingdoms their way. But I referr it to your Majestie, whether in all your reading you have found any kingdom lost or recovered by silogismes. Scarce any thing under a demonstration will satisfie them : And they would leave all to tyme. I finde myself obliged in duty to represent to you the prejudices may happen by delay. And, to do them right, I will also lay down the advantages they seem to expect by it. By this ingenuous proceeding your Majestie will best judge which advice ought to be encouraged.

2. The first prejudice is, the Armyes Union ; towards which they have made this great progress. Two hundred Commissioned Officers they have thrown out, and filled their places with Sectaries, and such as they most confide in. Secondly, the Tower is in Colonel Fich his hands, a creature of Haselrig's. Thirdly, the Anabaptists are formed and armed every where. Which (if not certain, but surmised) it must be granted they may be, in few days; the Tower being in secure hands. Fourthly, several Captains of Horse we depended of (and some of these having it in their power to deliver considerable places to us) are in danger of loosing their charges, and wee the places; especially Lynn and Shrewsbury. Fifthly, it is an high discouragement to those who have been preparing and [are] prepared, to be consumed by the excessive expence of men and horses they must maintain ; and [add] to it, [be] still subject to discovery. And wee are infinitely happy it hath not yet befallen us. Sixthly, the reputation this Government gains abroad, by not being opposed. Seventhly, the diminution of the authority of those you honor to trust; when, by the delays [which] particular persons give to actions, others, who are commanded, see the power slighted, and begin to question whom they are to obey, those [who] have your warant and command for directing them, or those whose wariness and caution makes them to believe their care great and our orders rash ? Lastly and chiefly, your Majesties uncertain condition, having no assurance either of Lockart, Monck, Montague, or ——

3. The chief advantages they expect by delay are these. [First], The breach of the House. The hopes they found this upon is a speech of Sir H[enry] V[ane]s, which disrelished much yesterday. Secondly, gaine of time to put themselves in a posture for action ; which it appears yet they are not in. Thirdly, expectation of good effects from petitions which are sett on foot by the Grand Jurys. Fourthly, forraigne assistance. Fifthly and lastly, hopes of farther confusion yet.

4. To the first. If the Army be modul'd, as they wish it; they will not care to break the House. And, by the dissolving [of] the last Parliament (which had a face of legality) your Majestie finds you had little advantage. [And] this Parliament, being so odious and inconsiderable for number, tho', broke, wee shall have lesse; and the Government will fall, as they design it, into the hands of a few ; who will act more in a day to our prejudice than those mingled Councells of a Parliament and a Councell of State can possibly in a week (especially

as they are constituted) your Majestie having in both of them several, who think they can be only safe from you and under your Government. This knowledge makes mee desire the present Councells may continue and not be broke : since secrecy (which is the soul of all great undertakings) cannot be kept amongst men of such different opinions. And, when personal piques and animosities are so high, I make bold to presume I have reason on my side, when I assert, [that] confusion is likelier to happen these Councells standing, than if the Parliament were broke and Councell of State winnowed, and nothing but Sir H[enry] V[ane]s pure flour left to rule.

5. To the Second : 'Tis sad these gentlemen are not yet provided, having [had] for these four moneths, such allarms for action, both from their enemies and friends. Truly, by this it seems, they could not have contributed much for your Service had R[ichard] C[romwell] put it in blood ; which hee had certainly done, but that he was both coward and foole. Itt is great pitty wee must stand still till they overtake us ; by which negligence of theirs wee may be either disabled or discerned, before they will think they are ready enough.

6. To the third : I pray God the petitions may succeed ; but 'tis a great question, if the Grand Juries do present them ; and almost a certainty, the House will not receive them. Besides, this will take up much time.

7. Fourthly, for the forraigne assistance. 'Tis a sad cure for an ill disease, when more nobly wee may do it ourselves. And, I fear, by your Majestie's letter and Lord Chancellors no certain one.

8. The [fifth and] last truly may happen but 'tis but may : a contingent which I would not advise my Prince to venture his Crowns on, when he has a fair game.

9. These considerations I most dutifully and most humbly present your Majestie. And, with them, dare not venture to make it my desire, that, according to the joint sense of those worthy persons (whose names were to the last letter) you should, as yett, expose your person to this journey, till some way be found to unite opinions ; which I finde very differing, and truly with some willfulness rather than reason. But I shall not recriminate ; since I am a party concerned. Yet, I protest to God and your Majestie, I would most willingly have obeyed orders from any you had trusted, with a cheerful resignation, tho' against my sense. And I may say, [that] those [who] are received now into the Trust are every way superior in quality, fortune, number, and truly (in my poore Apprehension) not inferior in parts to those [who] refused the Trust now, yet will not willingly obey others. All yet stands very fair. But these divisions occasion sending this express, least when your Maiestie should be here, you may find them still unready for what they ought to undertake. I have instructed this person how to find a way to kiss your Majesties hands, tho' you should be removed. God of his infinite mercy preserve your Majestie."

1659, April 15.— ——to John Mordaunt. " 1. I received yours of the sixteenth of the last month, but on Tuesday last. And tho' 120 tells mee you have writt others to mee, of later dates, as yet I have not received any of them. 120 (to whom I give this) is so fully instructed of all things in these parts, that it is not necessary to me to say any thing else to you but that I was sorry not to have been 582. 147. when you and 95. 365. were there. Which is all I shall say, but that you shall always find mee.--The Same."

1659, April 21.—Mr. [Richard] Nicholls to John Mordaunt. " 1. The few occasions I have in Paris may easily be dispensed with when my Master sends mee word that his Journey is differ'd; upon which I LORD BRAYE'S<br>MSS. do yet attend.

2. I expect within four or five days some news of Mr. Montague, but as yet none is come. For the Court is upon their march to the pleasant battell which will be fought the tenth of May (*i.e.*, the King's marriage).

3. The expectations of the Palace Royal increase every week. I only doubt in poynt of time: and so suffer in opinion.

4. I have heard some ill offices have been done you to your best friend; but they made no impression. I suspect from what pen such stories flowe. For it is a trade some people drive because they write well.

5. I am confident all my friends have more justice in their nature and actions; neither will I robbe them of that meritt, to attribute any thing to my endeavors; which however shall be to serve you.

6. Present me very faithfully and kindly to those of our tribe and society, whether males or females. Direct yours to Mr. Boothe, as formerly."

1659, Easter Monday.—Sir John Greenvil to John Mordaunt. " My Lord, just now I received the inclosed from my friend, which will inform you fully concerning Lambert. Pray keep the Letter for mee 'till I shall waite on you in the afternoon.

2. I am going to Sir James, and will observe all your Commands, serve you upon all occasions to the utmost of my power; whereof and you may rest most confidently assured."

1659, May 3.—Sir Edward Hyde, Lord Chancellor, to John Mordaunt. " 1. Since my last to you of the eleventh of this moneth (which I hope came safely to your hands) yours to the King and my Lord Ormond of the twenty fourth of the last moneth arrived; and since your other of the 31, to the King and myself. I shall not enlarge upon many of the particulars, having said as much as I could in my former, with a prospect forward, even to those ill actions which have fallen out; which wee too well knew would always make a deep impression upon the spirits of many of our good friends.

2. Before I say any thing of the publique, I must desire you not to withdraw your kindness or good opinion from Sir James Hamilton, who hath frequently received so many instances of my kindness towards him, that I am confident he had no ill intentions in any of those expressions which some passion transported him to use, and of which no notice should have been taken by my consent.

3. His Majestie doth not well understand what is meant by his closing with the moderate Party upon tearmes which may be thought too rigid ; there not appearing the least application to him from any such Party. If there did, I doubt not but his Maiestie would give so gratious an answer, that they would receive satisfaction. And, in such a case (how gratious soever his Maiesty may be to any particular person who hath served him faithfully) I do not think any honest man will suffer himself to become the obstruction to such an agreement; but would choose rather, tho' against the King's will, to run to the Indies, and impose a perpetual banishment upon himself.

4. Now to your last letters, which express indeed a very great change as well in the success of [Richard] Cromwell, as in the dejection of our friends; who I know are usually cast down upon

such accidents.   And, the truth is, I should not be surprised, if Cromwell pursue his good fortune so far as quickly to get himself proclaymed and declared King.   And then he will himself put an end to the votes of those persons who serve him in the other House; and so they shall only vote during this Session.   It is not possible for the King to give orders, or indeed advice, from hence, what is to be done. But he is exceedingly troubled that, in such a conjuncture, there should want that mutual trust and confidence towards each other in those he hath referred his business to, that they should not take a view together of those advantages which might be made use of.   And if, upon such a consultation, it appeared to them that nothing were to be attempted, it would beget a calme and an acquiescence which would secure all.   And this was the fruit the King expected, and still hopes [for] from the commissions and instructions he sent by Mr. [Hartgill] Baron : nor have we received any such account of the contrary reasons you mention.

5. Give me leave, Sir, to tell you, if wee doe not use all freedom (as well concerning persons as things) we shall never apply proper remedies to any thing that is amisse.   And therefore I beseech you deale freely with us in the mention of those whom you finde most reserved and wary of engaging themselves, as well as those whom you finde forward and active.   And I will begin this freedome to you, by telling you all I know or think of persons there; since I cannot but conclude we should not deal well with you, if we do not give you all the light we have upon our observation and experience.

6. I do exceedingly wonder that any should think the instructions you have received needless, because themselves were impowred before. Which obliges me to tell you, for your own information, what you will reserve only to yourself.   It is very true that most of the persons named, and desired by you to bee together instructed with you, are those who have been formerly intrusted by the King, to the same general purposes ; but without such particular qualifications and directions as you have now received.   And truly I do not, in the lest degree, doubt their affection to his Maiesties service.   But I must tell you (as ours) their friends have always compiained of their want of freedom and communication with them, so, from the time of my Lord Ormonds return from thence, they have not sent the least advice or direction hither what they would have the King to doe.   But, on the contrary, have expressed a desire not to be called upon by our letters ; professing that they would watch all occasions to serve the King, and would then give him advertizement of all things necessary.   Only (as I formerly advertized you) the King did write to the Lord Bellasis concerning his nephew, and received a short answer from him, that matters were not yet ripe for that business.   And this, upon the matter, is all the correspondence we have had with any of them above this twelvemoneth.   And I doubt they have not had correspondence enough each with the other in the projection or design of what may be done ; if they have, it is more than we know.   However it is strange that they should believe the commissions and instructions lately sent to be impertinent, since they contain new matter to what they were possessed of before.   If I knew with which of them you have spoken, I could give you better information.

7. I advised Mr. [Hartgill] Baron, to bring you and Sir William Compton together first ; who could have brought the other best to you. And I wish that you speak with Sir Richard Willis, if you have not done it already.   I have writt to him by another way, which I hope

will come to his hands. Sir William Compton and Sir Richard Willis can best tell you what hope there is of the Republican Party. I confesse to you, I have seen little of sincerity from them. I believe my Lord Bellasis and Colonel John Russel are very shy, having been often in prison; tho' I make no doubt they will heartily engage when they think the business is ripe. I believe it is the joynt opinion of all of them (and I doubt, with too much reason) that, without a division of the Army, it is in vain for our friends to stirre; so farre they are from a confidence of the strength of our own Party. And I am sure the King endeavours, by all the wayes and means he can, to increase it, and thinks all men of his Party who are willing to be so. If these gentlemen knew all you can inform them of, and Sir William Waller and Lord Manchester, would conferre with any of them, I suppose it would raise their spirits. However, I hope it will be no hard matter to consult freely together, and thereupon to take a resolution as is fit.

8. I confesse I know not what to think of Colonel Brown, who seemes to have great obligations to the Court, contrary to what I conceived in your former letter. I long to hear that you have spoken with Massy or Titus, and that Sir William Waller hath done so too.

9. Wee heare that our friends are much troubled at the multitude of persons who come from these parts and pretend to be employed by the King. And we are not without a just sense of the mischief that might befall us upon any pretences of the discovery of plots. But we know not what remedy to apply to this inconvenience. For I do assure you (tho' it be no easie thing, in the condition we are, to restrain people who want bread, to seek it, when wee cannot help them to it, where they pretend they are sure to find it, yet) wee doe every day hinder those who would goe over. Nor hath the King knowne of the going over of any more than Massy and Titus, Mr. Baron (and one whom he desired to have with him), Mr. Hopton and [Nicholas] Armorer, every one of which I believe may be of use to that communication which our friends ought to have with each other.

10. I intended to have sent this to you by the last post; and then probably it would have been with you before this time. But having received none from our friends by the usual way, wee doubted there was some obstruction, and so resolved to keep this by us till another opportunity; to which I was the rather induced by an acknowledgment I had from Mr. [William] Rumball, that N[icholas] Armorer was arrived, and that you had received the dispatches I sent by him and am now to acknowledge (which I received by the last post from France) besides the duplicates of these above from Mr. Hart[gill] Baron.

11. Yours of the sixth to the King, and our English letters of this week persuade us, that your hopes there are not at all impaired. And wee are very well pleased that the Presbyterians and Republicans watch one another so warily. And no doubt the wiser men of either Party cannot be without apprehensions, that whilst they stand upon rigid terms, the other may gallop so fast towards the King's interest, that they may become less considerable. Whither they shall go together by the ears with each other ; or (by the dissolution of the Parliament) that Party shall prevail most which hath greatest interest in the Army; or whither the Army shall take the Government upon itself, without considering Richard Cromwell or the Parliament; in all these cases, nothing is more necessary, either to the King's service or your own securities, than a free communication ; which I hope the good changes

LORD BRAYE'S
MSS.

which have happened since your last, and the Diligence and Dexterity of Mr. W[illiam] Rumball (who I suppose bath signified the King's pleasure to them, if our letters to some of themselves have miscarried) hath in a good degree already accomplished.

12. Wee are so tender of exposing you (upon whose safety and liberty so much depends) that we never have, nor ever shall addresse any person to you (how honest soever in our Judgments) without your approbation. And therefore it is entirely left to your own choice when you will think fitt to speak with Massy. Yet I cannot but tell you, that I conceive there may be many convenieuces in your speaking freely with him; who, besides an integrity you may depend upon, is a briske man in any attempt, and is not satisfied with the general inclination of the Presbyterians, nor with the warines even of those who wish best ; insomuch as hee hath not been without some thoughts of returning hither out of pure indignation at the coldness of those from whom he found we expected most. He is much troubled at the temper of Brown, in whom he thought his own interest and Titus his to be unquestionable; and he hath absolutely refused to speak with either of them. Nor I do I find that Massey hath yet spoken with Sir William Waller. I am persuaded that if you and Massy speak together, you would give each other much useful information ; and he would tell you what hath passed between Mr. Alexander Popham and him; and you would understand how the business of Bristoll and Gloucester stands ; and would, thereupon, easily conclude, what attempts are to be made or depended upon in either of the cases I put before ; and to be sure of introducing a good strength of our own Party in any other [place] that pretends to wish us well. And you would do well to bring Mr. How and Massy acquainted ; which would be of much Availe.

13. I should be glad to hear from you, that, in either of the cases I have putt, or any other that is like to fall out, Sir Horatio Townshend would be able to make any notable appearance in Norfolk, which you know lies best for our landing. And it may be, upon late affront which every hour he is like to receive, he may be willing (how weary soever he hitherto hath been and is in [things of] this Nature [apt] to be) [to] see a good part in the business. And then, though we do not promise ourselves any notable [assistance] from the Catheliques in general towards the King's service, yet I hope none of our friends will refuse to joyn with those who will be forward, because they are Catholiques.

14. I find many are of opinion that the King should publish a Declaration (which wee think very unseasonable in this conjuncture) and might contribute towards their uniting. I am sure it is a very difficult work, and, without a joynt advice from our friends, in the matter as well as form, wee shall not adventure upon it. If you speak with Massy, he will shew you what I have writt to him upon that argument.

15. The last Diurnall mentions a Report made to the House of the state of their Debts and of the Publique Revenew both certain and casual, together with the Expences. I suppose it no difficult thing for you, by some friend in the House, to get an extract of that accompt ; which would be very well worth the seeing.

16. It is a great pity the House doth not prosecute the complaint against the High Court of Justice which would be a matter of great moment.

17. I must not forget to tell you, that (though I am very farr from con- fidence in Wildman, or that he hath not heretofore betrayed some of our friends) yet I am very secure he cannot corrupt Titus (upon whose integrity you may rely) and he will hardly overwit him. LORD BRAYE'S MSS.

18. There is a Party, among the Republicans, which is not satisfied with their leaders ; and, if they find that they are compounded with or (because of their greatest allies) frighted to appear any where but in Parliament, they are resolved to do somewhat briskly without them. And there are good fellows among them, who will use all their credit to spur them on.

19. It is very strange that all our friends (I mean, [those] who do not resolve to submit to any termes [which] shall be put upon them, [as] Oaths, Abjurations, or the like) do not think it necessary to consult together for their own preservation. I hear not from Mr. Rumball of the argument you mention. And I wish he would perswade those cold friends to send an expresse over to the King, to give him satisfaction of their temper.

20. If it should fall out, as some letters perswade us to expect it will, that the Army will comply neither with Cromwell nor the Parliament, but will set up for themselves, at least make both the one and the other properties, and oblige them to such lawes for the Government as they shall direct ; I hope there will be some found, of all Part[ie]s who will not only protest for the Priviledges of Parliament but betake themselves to arms for the defence thereof, in all parts of the King- dom. The quarrel would be so popular that they could never want hands, nor would the Army be engaged intirely to suppress them, nor their own lawes to punish them. I will adde no more but the very faithful service of, Sir, your most affectionate humble servant, Edward Hyde."

1659, May.—John Mordaunt to Sir Edward Hyde. (Printed in *Clarendon State Papers*, III. 459.)

1659, May 5, Dublin.— ——— to John Mordaunt. " 1. I have delayed my Intelligence, that I may give you a certain account what our friends resolves will be. They are well principled. What[soever] reports you possibly may heare, I can certainly inform you that it's necessity and only a stalking horse to gain the designe. Many obstacles have been thrown to thwart their intentions; but I hope carefulness and resolution may batter down all resistance.

2. Your friend and my relation is encouraged by the gentlemen of our County ; who are so well satisfied, that they have promised upon the least and shortest summons to aide him with all their power. I am not yet with them, nor will, untill they bring things unto maturity; but shall be ready to serve them with my life ande state as soone as they declare; which cannot be untill you and others shew themselves. They are in heart for a full and a free Parliament; though they declare for the Parliament [onely].

3. Sir, I am well certefied of your carefulness and reality in this cause; which makes mee write more boldly. I beseech you be carefull it be not known ; which may utterly ruine all the designe. This is all at present from your Countryman and Neighbour."
I have given the Character of the suspected Person."

1659, May 9.—Sir Edward Hyde, Lord Chancellor, to John Mor- daunt. " 1. Yours begun the eleventh and ended the fourteenth is come safe to us, as I hope my last to you is of the third of this month by the way of Calais. And therefore I shall not repeat any thing I said in that; and it may be I may likewise send you a duplicate of this the same way: and then, whether it be directed for Mr. Brown (as you appoint) or for Mr. Newman as Mr. [Hartgil] Baron directs, I suppose it will be all one, and, for ought I see, that way by Calais (when the custom of opening letters is broke loose again) will be not only the obscurest, but the shortest way wee can make use of; except some extraordinary opportunity falls in our way.

2. The King is exceedingly afflicted &c." (the remainder in *Clarendon State Papers*, III., 463).

1659, May 16.—Sir Edward Hyde, Lord Chancellor, to John Mordaunt. " 1. My last to you was of this day sennight, being indeed but a duplicate of what I sent the day before under a cover to Mr. William Rumball, which I doubt is not yet come to your hands, and I am the more sorry for it, because in it are all those letters from the King which you have written for (that is, for Mr. How, Sir William Waller, and Lord Manchester) and which I durst not send with the duplicate, though I believed it would come sooner to you.

2. I have since yours of the 21 [of April] which came not to me till yesterday, together with the last weeks letters of the 29th, the former having been stopped on your side the water, so that wee know in what distemper all things were then, and that is enough to make us imagine and hope they are much higher now. If they are not, the councell we can give from hence (upon the prospect wee have) would be as improper and unseasonable as if things were run to the highest extremities. All we can say must be upon generals, which you upon the place must judge how to reduce into particulars.

3. It hath been a great defect in the Parliament, that before its dissolution and when it saw what fate did attend them, they did not pass some such Votes and Declarations against Taxes and other arbitrary proceedings that may work upon the People.

4. If a right representation hath been made to us, the Army yet seems not to be of a piece, but to be governed by several Councells, and those of several interests; and it would be no hard matter to insinuate to those who are upon establishing the Republique, that they cannot lay a foundation that shall promise security without first taking all kind of vengeance upon the whole family of Richard Cromwell and [the] principal Ministers who contributed to his Tyranny. And, if this be soundly done, whither with formality or without, it would be a good beginning and excellent things would follow.

5. Though there seems to be a good disposition towards the reviving of the Long Parliament, yet there are so many objections against it, and there might presently be called into it so many new Members and such accounts for the dissolution and the circumstances of it, that I can hardly beleeve they will venture upon it; and, if they should, they will meet with difficulties enough.

6. The banishing of so many of our friends from London hath not made it less inconvenient that you did not meet before and consent upon what is to be done. And I doubt not but you will find great use of those Commissions for the putting of several Counties in a good posture, and will in due time dispose them accordingly.

7. You know very well that the persons trusted have authority to increase their number, by choosing other fit persons to join with them. So that, if for the present our other friends' wariness or absence keeps

them from joyning with you, it will be very well if you can procure Sir William Waller, Sir Horatio Townshent, Colonel Brown and other persons of quality to undertake the present worke with you.

8. The King is willing that you joyn Mr. [Job] Charlton to you, who is a person utterly unknown to us; though it seems of merit towards his Majestie and of interest to advance his service.

9. Wee can give from hence no other direction or advice for the election or admission of persons to joyne with you in the great work of moulding and designing than that you do the best you can to get persons of quality and interest, that others, upon any change, may be the better disposed to the conjunction, and to receive orders and directions from them. And you very well know, in the several Commissions for Counties and other services, there will be room enough for al! honest men to bear their parts according to their several qualities and faculties.

10. When I had written thus far, Mr. Baron came in ; who giving us other work to do, I shall refer you to him for particulars, rather than put them in writing.

11. I am sorry that Massy is not so easily satisfied upon conference with you as hee should be. It is very natural for men who are ready to expose themselves upon a particular action that hath danger in it, to desire to be assured that diversions shall be made by others, so that the whole power of the enemy may not fall upon him. And this, I presume, is all that he is inquisitive after. Wee know he is not without infirmities and weakness ; but his courage and integrity is unquestionable, and his reputation great, which will make the other more pardonable. He was sent over principally (besides that wee had reason to believe that he would find many friends 'on his own account) to assist in the business of Gloucester and Bristol; where our friends that looke after that affair sent us word, his presence would be very acceptable. And I have writ to him to betake himself to that; and that, if he can find encouragement to proceed therein, he need not doubt but that the Army will find somewhat els to do in other places. And in truth, methinks, any action that shall necessitate the Army to draw from London hath opened a fair door for all good fortune to enter to us. For (if Tichbourne and Ireton's interest can preserve the City for themselves, we have had an ill account given us) and then the neighbor Counties willbe at liberty.

12. I have [also] writt to Massy, that you will deliver all such Commissions as are necessary for that service. And truly if Mr. Popham and Mr. How joyn with him, and such persons of quality as are best known to you and them be inserted into those Commissions for those adjacent Counties who have power to choose the Commander in chief, I should hope that those places might be so good a foundation to begin upon, and such a retreat and security to our friends, that they would not need to fear any affront from the enemy, and that they might very reasonably assure themselves that other places would follow their example. And, though they might governe themselves and their councells by those Commissions from the King, they are not therefore obliged to use his name in any publique acts; but may only, in their declarations, own those specious grounds which have been so often mentioned between us. And, if you do at any time find Massy less prepared for that kind of reason which all understandings cannot comprehend, you will find Titus very capable of it, and as willing to doe those offices which the wise owe to the weak.

13. Mr. Baron will give you all those letters which you have desired from the King, in the delivery whereof you will cause that time and

LORD BRAYE's
MSS.
— method to be observed which you judge most reasonable. Only I must
desire you that that to R. Harlow may be put into the hands of Massy
or Titus who have most Friendship with him, and therefore may
reasonably expect the office."

1659, May 16.—Sir Edward Hyde, Lord Chancellor, to John Mordaunt. (Printed in *Clarendon State Papers*, III., 471.)

1659, May 23.—Sir Edward Hyde, Lord Chancellor, to John Mordaunt. " 1. A. N. (*i.e.*, Nicholas Armorer) is well come to us, and hath
brought yours to the King that was begun on the 28th and finished on
the 29th of the last [month ;] and your other on the 2nd of this moneth
to myself, which is all he brought. And therefore I do not well understand the Postcript in Mr. William Rumball's letter to Mr. Baron, in
which he desires that an answer be speedily sent to yours of the 25th.
To all your former, very full (and I hope, satisfactory) answers were
returned by Mr. Baron; who, after one day's stay, went from hence
on Saturday last, and I hope reached Calais by his time appointed;
though N. Armorer and he met not upon the way. And I doubt not
he is now safe with you, and shall not repeat what I then said, or he
was instructed in : which I hope hath given you satisfaction in many
particulars mentioned in these letters. And I shall once for all assure
you, that, upon receipt of any dispatch from you, I never delay returning an answer, but immediately go about it and send it away by the
first opportunity. And, if by cross winds or any accidents they sleep
too long by the way (as I doubt mine, by Mr. William Rumball's
messenger, hath done) it is not our fault. But hereafter I will very
rarely send by shipping, but preferr the way of Calais, if this, being a
speedier, do not prove secure.
2. The excellent Representation &c." (the remainder in *Clarendon
State Papers*, III., 475).

1659, May 27.—John Mordaunt to the Lord Chancellor. " 1.
Having since my last spoke with Titus, I find him so so clear in
opinion that the Engagement of Bristol and Gloucester stand fair yet,
that upon his encouragement (on whose prudence the King relies) we
think it our duty to represent to the King the advantages will accrue
to him, if he be in a posture to land 3000 men, which descent will
give a new life to his business, and the wariest then will fly in to
him without delay. This we have their promises for, and those
promises are all we can ever think ourselves secure in. This of the
3000 Foot we desire in case the war be begun in the West, and a diversion follow. But if, upon reinforcing these Towns or other discouragements, the Undertakers should draw back and refuse to hazard the
attempt, we think 3000 men too few to advise his Majestie to venture
his Person with.
2. Of your present condition we are in the dark ; but hope upon the
peace between the two Crowns, you can never want such a number of
Foot as we desire ; these to be ready in few days; since it hath been and
our care constantly and earnestly to beg of you, to put yourselves in the
best posture you could for present action.
3. The Offers of those French I gave you notice of, creates in us a
belief, that if the King of Spain, on the return of his rich Fleet,
supplies you with money, you can neither want men nor vessels to
transport them : the humor of both those Countries enclining them to
a war with us. If this be [        ] we have reason to hope you are
already prepared to second any attempt, if not to begin one ; for which

5000 men is here judged sufficient: the divisions here considered, LORD BRAYE's MSS. and the promises so universal.

4. We humbly leave to your considerations where you will land; and whether in one body or two; in Kent, or Norfolk, or more westward.

5. If it could be ordered so that, two *days* before you set sail, we might know your intentions, it would advantage you extreamly that, to so good a body of Foot, all the Horse we can engage might presently joyn. And more than two days notice might ruin all: secrecy being the soul of such resolves. All these particulars we, as becomes our duty, wholly resign our obedience to; and shall, in that, best manifest our inclinations to serve the King.

6. The particulars of the west Titus will give an account of, who is returned to those parts to perfect what he finds well begun. He humbly desires to be pardoned for not writing, being what you will find here is his sense as well as ours (*sic*).

7. I have lately had hopes to have transmitted to you a good sum of moneys, knowing how necessary it would have proved in this conjuncture, both as to the filling your own regiments, and as to the engaging other Forces; which we suppose money would easily do in so populous a Country. But the terms on which it was to be given were so conditional, that, to me, they seemed to take off much of the thanks they might have expected from so generous an offer. However I am not yet in despair but a sum may be raised very advantageous to you, if those People who are to give it may be permitted to lay it out their own way, and by their own instruments. Of this you shall have a fuller account, it being my care for the present to order it so that a friend of mine may be entrusted in it. Which if I succeed in, I shall think I have not done amiss. You may depend no time shall be lost in this affair; it being necessary that you post your fortune before the Fleet return from the Sound, or that Lawson get out of the River.

8. The base resignation of R[ichard] Cromwell will be made known to you by other hands, and of his brother's following his example. I am so straightened in time I can say no more, but that I am, &c.

I beseech you present my most humble duty to the King and my most humble service to Or: Ld. [Lord Ormond.]

I have now assurance of a good sum from a Lady whose purse may bear it. My Lord Bruce deserves a kind letter for it. This is to hasten your Levies; else I had not mentioned it till it was deposited: because accidents may change the resolution of Women."

1659, June 4. — Mr. Secretary Nicholas to John Mordaunt. " 1. Yours of the eleventh of the last moneth, brought by this worthy person Mr Alestre, would have made us very sad, had we not a little before received more comfortable news by the great diligence of honest Mr. Rumball.

2. I hope Mr. Baron hath satisfied your expectation in the dispatch he brought you.

3. Mr. Broderick is here esteemed a very discreet and faithful person; having given good proof of his loyalty and industry in his Majestie's service. He corresponds chiefly with the Lord Chancellor; is much confided in by Sir Richard Willis and others that have been privy to the trust reposed in that Knight, and others of that Knot.

· 4. The Lord Chancellor saith, he hath formerly written to you concerning the passing your patent. And, when his Lordship shall receive your answer to that letter, it will be proceeded in as you shall direct.

5. For that business whereof Mr. Baron hath discoursed with me concerning yourself, I have now spoken of it to both M[r.] M[ordaunt]s good friends here; who wish that we should consider of it, before any thing be moved in it to the King.

6. I assure you your dispatches are most welcome to the King. And your indefatigable industry and pains in all his Maiestie's concerns and interests, have that value and esteem set on them here by his Maiestie, and those with whom by your direction they are only communicated, as they well deserve. And I assure you the King, on all occasions, expresses his gratious sense of your singular merit.

7. Those that best know mee can tell you I am no man of compliment or courtship; but I shall faithfully serve you so far as it shall lie in my small power, as being with much truth and sincerity, Sir,
Your most humble Servant.

I write not to honest Mr. Baron; having not heard from him since I saw him."

1659, June 4.—Sir Edward Hyde, Lord Chancellor, to John Mordaunt. (Portions only of this letter are printed in *Clarendon State Papers*, III., 480, "Mr. Wright" being printed for "Mr. Rumball.")
"Sir, 1. I have yours of the 16 [past], and I hope Mr. Rumball hath received mine of the 27th which I sent through the same Hand by which his last came to me.

2. It is not possible for the King to give more particular directions in the great business, or to state his own condition more clearly, than he did by Mr. Baron.

3. Whatever advantage the Peace between the two Crowns may produce for the King in time, we cannot expect that fruit 'till that Peace be fully established. And that may take some time. The conveniences are enough, both at home and abroad; if our friends could make themselves appear considerable there; I mean so considerable as to possesse themselves of the places you mentioned: by which they would be secure from any affront from the enemy. Which would give us so great a reputation, that I presume they, who have been most cold towards us, would be most forward to give us help. Whereas, all being quiet and the King receiving no advantage by these mutations, people generally abroad believe the change to be no other than a Republique instead of R[ichard] Cromw[ell]. And even they, who wish it otherwise, do really fear that the King's party is not considerable. And the hast the Hollander makes so unreasonably to acknowledge these inconsiderable men for the Republique of England, Scotland and Ireland (which is the stile Newport prescribes to his masters for their address) will in a short time give them great reputation. And, if Spain should likewise enter into a publique and avowed Treaty (though it may be they may not afterwards agree) our friends there will have much more pretence for their wariness. Which is not said to hasten them to any rash attempt: which, you know, his Majestie hath always professed against. But he thinks still, if the business of Bristol and Gloucester be executed according to the design, it can never be held a rash attempt; and we should hope the fire would quickly go thro' the Kingdom. And the reputation of it would go near to make Spain, France, and Holland our friends. At least, I believe, they would connive at their subjects performing such offices towards us as would serve the turn. We are therefore full of longing to see what is determined in those particulars.

4. If those foundations fail, we shall be in great apprehension of the safety of particular persons, who have too much communicated their Purposes; and then many, who would have performed their parts well enough if there had been action, will betake themselves to the worst arts for their preservation. Yet even that is not so bad as offering at an Insurrection and being suppressed the next day; which can never be, if the other places be once possessed. And, if you had Lyn and Sandwich, the King would quickly be with you.

LORD BRAYE'S MSS.

5. His Majestie is very glad that Col. Brown makes good his professions, and gives him no other thing in charge for the present, but that he takes care of his person and preserves his liberty.

6. The King doth not write to my Lord Winchelsea (of whose affection he is very well satisfied) because he can give no other directions but what it seems is resolved between you : the pursuing whereof depends upon what is done in other places. Nor hath his Majestie been without those thoughts of Bulloigne and Calais which my Lord recommends to him. I am persuaded, if his Lordship be once up, and possessed of Sandwich we shall quickly throw over more men to his assistance than he proposes. And sure the army will in that case find it hath enough to do.

7. There are officers enough of all nations who would be very glad to transport men for England; and that course must be taken, if nothing else will do : though nobody thinks more unwillingly of it than I do.

8. I am heartily sorry for what you tell me of Col. John Russel: who, I hope, will be sorry himself and repair it.

9. We know not what to say to that spirit which hath possessed so many of them. If the designs on foot succeed, I doubt not but they will clearly declare themselves. And, if we are so much disappointed in what we have so much presumed upon, that it does not appear councelable to those upon whom we depend to proceed in those enterprises; we will not then despair, but hope the best from those arguments which our friends have given. And I am glad that they do not apprehend danger to their own person by delaying.

10. The King doth not conceive that Sir Horatio Townshent will be able to do him less service by being chosen [one] of the Councell ; or that that will hinder him from going into the country when the conjuncture requires it. And, till then, he will be able to give you the better advice at London. And therefore his Majestie referrs it to his own discretion, to doe what he shall, upon conference with his friends, find most conduceable to his Majestie's interest.

11. The King forbears to send you any letter for Colonel Norton ; because there is either one delivered to him, or remains in a gentleman's hands who knows him well, and will not omit the opportunity when he finds him capable of being prevailed with. And without doubt there hath been some apparent indisposition in him, that it hath been kept up so many moneths : For we do not suspect the fault to be in the person entrusted. However, if W[ill] Legg will let us know the person by whom he makes his approach; and that he believes there is reasonable hopes of prevailing: the King will send another letter. Which he is the more tender of doing now, because we have had an intimation within these fourteen days that we should speedily hear from the person entrusted.

12. Mr. Rumball's postscript is a very comfortable one. Which I wish he had a little enlarged; that we might have known in what manner my Lord of Hertford hath been treated with, and what he hath

undertaken to doe : that his Majestie might better have known what to write to him.

13. I told you in mine of the 30th [post,] that Mr. [Richard] Allestre was then come to town. And, if that letter came safe, there needs no other reply to any particular of that letter of yours of the eleventh. For (besides that both your postscript and the messenger left the affair desperate upon which the letter was written) I conclude it continues so still, by your not having mentioned a word of it in this last; in which I hoped to have found somewhat of Mr. Broderick upon the occasion of what I writt by Mr. Baron. And in whom if you are not satisfied, upon your farther enquiry and what I have informed you, I shall myself be the more wary.

14. If a little good fortune befal us we shall find both the great Lord and the great Lady very ready to acknowledge, that they have been very much mistaken in the character they have given our Master. And I am confident we shall all find that he will never deserve that reproach, of not being very punctual in keeping his word. And, if they that lay that imputation upon him would confess the truth, they would acknowledge that their quarrel is because he could not be prevailed with to make such promises as they wished; not that he hath broken any which he made.

15. I know not what to add nor what to advise, but that you make all the friends you can in the Parliament to pursue those councells which may provoke the army; and your friends in the army, to affront the Parliament; and the agitators, to do any act of outrage. And, without doubt, a very rude dissolution of this Parliament, with all circumstance of reproach upon the members, might produce many advantages to the King's service. And this you are desired to impart to Mr. Charlton and Mr. Beverley, who (this bearer saith) can forthwith bring it to pass, if the King thinks it convenient for his service. And his Majestie doth beleeve, that nothing can more advance his interest, both at home and abroad; and therefore I beseech you that it be pursued accordingly.

16. I wonder we hear nothing, or very little, in these great changes of Harrison; who, with his Fifth-Monarchy-Men, would be the fittest instruments to promote the confusion; and must be as little pleased with the form of government that is like to be established by this Parliament as we can be.

17. Upon farther thoughts, and the assurance Mr. W[illiam] Rumball gives of the Marquis of Hertford; the King thinks fit to take notice of his forwardness, and to send him his thanks. Which he hath done in the enclosed Letter marked M. which you will take care to get delivered by a trusty hand.

18. It is a thousand pities you have no way to be acquainted with my Lord Southampton; nor can I prescribe any. But you would find him one of the most excellent persons living. Of great affection to the King; of great honor; and of an understanding superior to most men. And, if the business of Portsmouth once succeeded, he would be the best countenance to the proceedings in those parts. We do not at all write to him; knowing it needs not. I think W[ill] Legg is acquainted with him. God send us a good and a speedy meeting; and mee opportunity to serve you."

1659, June 6.—John Mordaunt to Sir Edward Hyde, Lord Chancellor. " 1. Though no man living can be more against a rash attempt than I am, yet to loose such opportunities will distaste the whole world. Wee have such a veneration for a sacred person, that, though all seem still very fair to our apprehension, I dare not make it my desire his Majestie should come over, 'till by an express he hear wee are united, and then he [may] make it his own act. And the reason [is] the wary gentle-men differ wholly in opinion from us, and, I fear, may dispute orders, unless from the King himself. So that, 'till this be reconciled, I wish the King only ready and resolved to come.

2. Noe minute shall be lost to hasten all things. And, now so many considerable persons are in the great trust, affairs proceed properly.

3. This day my Lord          came to Abscourt, to have the advice of that worthy wise person; who will doubtless allow it freely.

4. The gentleman [who] will kiss your hands with this, is one extreamly honest; for which quality I have sent him; having never been abroad. Hee is my kinsman, and one [who] from the first war, engaged for the King: his name is Rowlandson. Pray, my Lord, dispatch him; and be pleased to think it is now a most secure time to pass the Patent, els I would not upon second thoughts desire it. I am, my Lord, certainly Your most humble and most oblieged servant.

(P.S.) Truly I must complain again of Mr. Br[oderick;] whom wine or desire of talk makes dangerous. For he continues to expose us in taverns before too many companies: so that we fear to be examined, especially Mr. R[umball] and your servant.

'Tis supposed for certain, notwithstanding all our endeavors, the army will not break with the Parliament 'till they have modell'd them-selves so as not to fear any prejudice by it. I was of opinion, the continuance of the Parliament would not hurt us (they being so divided) but, on better thoughts, I wish they were dissolved."

1659, June 6.—Sir Edward Hyde, Lord Chancellor, to John Mor-daunt. "1. I hope Mr. Cowper is by this time with you, and he hath then not only delivered you an answer to all you sent by him, but like-wise an acknowledgment from me to Mr. Rumball of the receipt of yours of the nineteenth [past] to the King. To which in truth, as I then told him, very little can be added to what hath been often said.

2. It may reasonably be hoped, that, when the Peace is with all the formalities established between the two Crowns, both Kings may be induced to joyn in such an enterprize for the re-establishment of our Master as may be worthy of them, or rather as they may think most agreable to their own interests. But, 'till the establishment be made, it is not imaginable that the King can procure forces or assistance from either of them to begin a design in England, and to take advantage of those revolutions which happen every day. The truth is, all the benefit this country yet enjoys, as from the Treaty of Peace, is, that they are not at the charge of drawing the army together, or of making any defence against an enterprize of the enemy, which they are very ill provided for; their poverty being as great as ever, nor one dollar yet returned from Spayne since the gallions came. Nor have they been able to supply the King in the least degree these many months. By reason whereof his necessities are so great they can hardly be imagined, and could not have been born, if the King had not received some small sums from some friends in England, which have been applied to buy him meat.

3. You will from hence easily conclude how impossible it is, from hence, upon a sudden, to procure either shipping or men to undertake the surprize of any place; especially while their ministers do beleeve, upon what Peter Talbot tells them, that the Republique is settled, and

that they shall have a Peace upon their own terms; and until they see somewhat appear that may persuade them to think the King hath a party in England, which they do, in no degree, beleeve; and the Cardinal himself (who enough detests a Republique) doth very much distrust [it].

4. But if, contrary to their expectation, there once appear a visible opposition to the present power, and places of importance possessed against it; wee shall have credit and reputation in all places, and the King will not only find a way in a short time to transport himself, but the numbers he hath formerly mentioned. And, if Sandwich were in the hands of his friends, you would I am confident have every day men sent over, as well from France, as from these countries. And wee only want a little credit from thence to make us considered every where. Therefore, though the King will never give any such orders as shall dispose his friends to rise against their own judgments, and to make himself the cause of their farther ruin; yet nothing can be so happy to him as to find, that their own understandings, as well as their inclinations, have disposed them to appear in arms. And, any considerable places being possessed, it will not be hard for them who rise in other countries (for then, I hope, the rising will be general) to retire thither; and the Parliament must, not only be forced to make a General (which, we perceive, they have no minds to do), but the army will be compelled to march from London: which is all you can desire. And, if it be so brought to pass (as very probably it will) that the army dissolve the Parliament, surely you have lost no time, but will then appear in any reasonable enterprize as seasonably and advantageously as can be wished.

5. The King is exceedingly pleased to hear that the Lord Willoughby and Sir Tho[mas] Peyton have joyned themselves to you. And, if the garrison of Lyn be so small, and the troop of horse prove faithful, his Majestie hopes my Lord Willoughby, by his interest, will be able to draw in men enough for that work; the town being generally well affected. And, though it be not possible for the King to send men hence to surprise it, it will not be difficult to send men thither as soon as it is declared. And, in the adjacent countries, we have many friends who will embrace the opportunities. And Boston may then likewise be easily possessed.

6. For the emulations upon particular command in the several countreys upon the first risings, I can say no more than I have done in my last to Mr. Rumball. And I hope Sir William Waller will persuade my Lord Winchelsea, not to affect a command that will not hold above ten or twelve days; and that is more honour to chuse the superior officer than to be one. And I believe he hath very much kindness for Sir John Boys, who may be as fit a person to be Major General of those forces as any man; and, if I am not deceived, is well beloved generally in the country.

7. It will not be possible, or at least convenient, for the King to send over any person of honor into Kent before the business be begun. And, shortly after (if you have Sandwich or any other proper place), his Majestie and the Duke of York will be quickly with you.

8. You will beleeve we are full of prayers for you, and that we may happily come together; which is faithfully hoped and believed by," &c.

1659, June 6.—The latter part of a letter to the King. (See Mordaunt's letter in *Clarendon State Papers*, III., 482.)

1659, June 7th.—John Mordaunt to [Secretary Nicholas]. " 1. I have now given so full an account to the Lord Chancellor, that I shall

give you only the trouble to press the signing my Patent. For the
other affair, I will not push it; because 'tis a reversion: and I have
a particular inclination to be near the King's person. For that I hope
I have, and shall serve him so considerably, that I shall not be refused
being of the Bed-chamber.

2. You are so extreamly obliging to me I can no ways endeavor
any return, but by offering myself to be disposed as you shall advise
me. And certainly I shall have so many obligations to you, that,
unless I prove a very ill man, you will have a perfect friend and obliged
servant of        M.

The Votes of this day are considerable. The seventh of May is set
[for] a period to this Sessions. [And] ordered, that all Commissions
be taken from the Parliament.

'Twill settle in [an] Oligarchy: and, what we do, must be done
quickly. And nothing can be done without the King, or the Duke of
York; whose interest here you ought not to be jealous of: since the
King's is clearly so far superior to it.

The Ch[ancellor] is believed to be the person [who] obstructs all
action; and no ways relished by the old Knot. You may shew the
postscript.

Pray ask the King if he treats with H[enry] C[romwell]: it will
concern us to know it.

This evening H[enry] C[romwell] is voted to come hither; and five
Commissioners to rule Ireland: Whereof two are already there, and
three go from hence."

1659, June 7. — John Mordaunt and others to the King.
"1. That your Nation should be so disposed to receive you, and
so concern'd for the injuries you have suffered, and yet that it should
not lye in the power of those [who] really honour and reverence you,
to make those good inclinations conducible to your Restoration, is so
sad [a thing] that I can scarce expresse it. The common discourse in
the very streets is, No Peace in England without the King. The
major part of this very House in private owne no lesse. Yet no man,
that is considerable for interest, will give beginning to a warre, [which]
cannot, in the opinion of the gravest men, last a month.

2. I would beg your permission, Sir, to lay the fault where truly it
is. And truly the obstruction proceeds from some flegmatick warinesse
in the Knot; many of them being too much at ease to hazard either
life or fortune. Yet were this humour only in them, the misfortune
were superable. But, to justifie this cold, inconcern'd, prudentiall
warinesse, they make it their businesse to gaine proselites; so that no
industry can hasten action, if, after our discourses, any of the contrary
opinion light upon the persons wee quicken with continuall solicitations,
and now, having suffer'd under rigour and tiranny, have not the use of
their reason so free, but that a graine of feare will operate more upon
them, then a far greater proportion of hope. I am very loath to name
those who are more industrious to prevent action, then ever they were
to appear solisitous in your behalf. But, if by a total delay they impede
your affaires so far, as that it appears likely to prejudice you farther,
I shall think my self tyed in conscience to let you know how far mallice
and envie possesse them.

3. By a worthy subiect I had secured to you 20,000l. which could
not be done but that some of these knew of it. To put [a] stop in this
likewise they objected, 'If the moneyes were sent, they were not satisfied
to what uses it would be layd out?' You may judge, Sir, how cooling
a speech this was; and how seasonable; and the difficulty not to be

removed unlesse I would, upon my Honour, see it layd out in the hire of vessels and buying armes and ammunition.

4. To this I was forced to condescend, beleeving it better to have the money on any termes, then not to have it at all. I mentioned something of this in my last; but now I think I ought to acquaint your Majestie, that, though the money be severall peoples yet my chiefly solicited this affaire and shee rules my lady Devonshire. These names I beg may be kept very secret. For the money is yet kept for your service, if it will serve to transport you with so considerable a number of men, as may give a stand to a part of the jury, and a shelter to your friends, who at first must be protected by a formed body.

5. I mentioned my Lord Bruce too, and desire the same for him, I doe for the Ladies. I feare H.C. [Chancellor Hyde] is not thought kind enough to them.

6. Indeed, Sir, these are a sort of men [who] will have their interest and security provided for, before they will act. But they, that will neither serve you themselves, nor suffer others to do it without reproach, are without excuse. Yet, upon conference with me, they seeme approvers of what is done; though by after hands, I know they discredit us as much as they can. Their way has so discourag'd my Lord Willoughby, that hee protests, if your Majestie can find no way to engage us in action, hee feares delay will ruine all. W. Legg is absolutely enraged at the loosing so faire an opportunity, and wishes you any where with 1000 men. 'Tis very unhappy if your fate must depend on the wills of your enemys, which is not to be denyed if wee follow the rule of these over-wise men, who say, without a breach here, nothing can in their opinion succeed. And 'tis to be feared since an established government was absolutely subverted without one drop of blood, that these may settle without coming to blowes. However, I am cleere in opinion, no occasion ought to be slipped when fairly presented; and, that wee have had a very faire one these six weeks, is the opinion of all the world. In short, Sir, these prudentiall gentlemen obstruct action, and, having been in your business formerly, their reputation is great; and what wee doe in the day, these destroy in the night.

7. Great use will now be made of the instructions, and, if wee cannot force it to a warre openly, wee will endeavour to undermine; which perhaps may succeed: But 'twill take time, and depend on contingents. Harrison and his party must be cajoled and all wayes used to hinder a settlement. In this your Majestie may assure yourself of industry and diligence; for your trust is in wise hands, and they will manage this part well.

8. I am now most concern'd as to your own condition, which I apprehend is tedious to you, and must give you sad houres, when a little arme of the sea obstructs all your hopes and our happinesse. I dare only say many are of opinion you ought to hazzard your selfe; but, whether it be reasonable in us to desire it, I will not venture it on my judgment. I had presum'd to have kiss'd your hands, if Captain Titus (on whose judgment and integrity I much rely) had not diswaded me from it; beleeving me more serviceable to your Majestie here.

9. The propositions you will receive from Ireland, I humbly beg may be gratiously received; and, that you will please to command us positively to obey what your Majestie commands: your instructions being undervalued here by those [who] deny to serve you in the instruments you please to think worthy [of] your trust. And these are, Sir, Your most dutifull and most obedient Subiects Willoughby of Parham, George

Booth, ... Newport, ... Mordaunt, W. Legg, William Waller, W. LORD BRAYE'S MSS.
Rumball, J. Charlton."

1659, June 13.—Sir Edward Hyde, Lord Chancellor, to John Mordaunt. "1. I have yours of the 27 [of May] and, methinks, while this good way of conveyance is open to us, wee have an excellent opportunity to communicate once a week all that is necessary. And I doe not finde [that] any of yours or Mr. Rumball's to us have miscarried. And, if ours to you have had the same good fortune you cannot complaine of being in the darke, with reference to the King's advice, which hath been, in severall letters, represented very clearly to you. And, though the state of our affairs there varie every day; yet nothing can varie ours [here] but either such good accidents in England as may give us reputation abroad, or the finall conclusion of the Peace between the two Crowns, by which they may be at ease to declare their full resolution towards us. And, 'till one of these things fall out, you may conclude us to be in the same condition we were a moneth since; and that the King can be no more ready to transport himself with two or three thousand men, then he was when Mr. Baron was here.

2. If the designe of Bristoll and Gloucester stands still faire, wee cannot imagine why it was not executed; nor doe we yet heare from Massy or Titus.

3. If such a sum of money could be raised as you mention, the persons who send it may, if they please, cause it to issue through such hands as they like; no body here desiring to touch a peny of it. And, there being no question, but, if money and shipping were ready, wee could have men enough; it is indeed great pity that, wee here and our friends there, have not been better prepar'd to appear in armes, upon these great mutations, which have lately happen'd. But, methinks, I doe not see any thing yet done, to make us despaire of the like opportunities; nor doe I conceive wee have at present one friend lesse, or one enemy more, then wee had two moneths agoe; (It is possible all men's hopes and feares are not the same they were; but those ebbes and floudes will happen under every wind) nor that the army and parliament will sooner agree upon a government, because they are out of apprehension of the Cromwells; nor that their tamenesse and dejection of spirit will finde the greater remorse. .

4. Now is the tyme for the parliament to raise monuments of their justice and severity, for the future terror of those whose ambition may dispose them to break their trusts. And I hope you want no instruments to kindle that fire. And I suppose a list of all the parliament men is in print which I would be very glad to see; as I would be to know, whither you continue the same good opinion of Sir Anthony Ashley Cowper? And whether hee received the King's letter?

5. I have seene a letter from Mr. Baron to the Secretary by which I perceive there remaines some jelousies and distances among our friends; which, I hope, proceeds rather from misunderstanding then from any waywardnesse; and that the interposition of discreet persons will qualify and extinguish all those distempers. Wee have yet heard from none of them; and you may be very confident, that the King will not gratifie any man's passions, by the disobliedging others that serve him faithfully. And I have too good an opinion of them to beleeve they can propose any extravagant thing."

1659, June 16.—John Mordaunt to Sir Edward Hyde (partly in cipher, printed in *Clarendon State Papers*, III., 489).

1659, June 20.—John Mordaunt to the King. "1. I have engaged my Lord Willoughby to endeavor to bring these gentlemen to our opinion; that all engagements may be ready at a time. And, if it succeed, wee shall be in a posture to receive you. However wee are diligent to do it, if possible, without them. Three weeks they think too little, but wee think it too much. I suppose Coll. Po. may give your Maiestie an account from thence.

2. Just now wee have hopes H[enry] C[romwell] may stand out."

1659, June 20.—Sir Edward Hyde to John Mordaunt. (Printed in *Clarendon State Papers*, III., 495, but without the following postscript]. "Is it not possible to get some good fellows, either of the army or the city, to petition the parliament, that [all] persons may be removed from either who have been instruments of tiranny? And that all those, who, by force and unheard of insolence dissolved the parliament in 1653, may be brought to condigne punishment?"

1659, June 20.—The King to John Mordaunt. (Printed in *Clarendon State Papers*, III., 498.)

1659, June    .—Sir Robert Howard to John Mordaunt. "1. I shall in London expect your returne!

2. Hitherto all my proceedings doe more then answer my expectations, especially the businesse in Staffordshire; which by my friend there, is grown to a considerable greatnesse.

3. At your return, I shall dispose of my self as the king's interest will best require mee. I only desire you, that a right use may be made of the distractions they are in here. Their own ruines, which is visible before them, may invite them, more then their consciences, to think of an accommodation; the managing of which is to put our selves in a capacity to enforce more then perhaps they entend; so that if they meane no deceit, wee are not lesse capable of judging; and their falsnesse will not have much power, if wee prepare in the worst expectation; and wee shall never have so free leave againe to arme our selves. But, without dispute, the King must at first appeare in person. Where that shall bee, I shall advise with you when you come, that wee may in the safest way hazzard him that is our all."

1659, July 2.—John Mordaunt to Mr. Hartgill Baron. "1. The obstructions the wary gentlemen have made, and the fears they infuse into them with whom they discourse, has wrought a great change in the minds of people since you went. And, though Sir John Bois and Will. Legg are clearly for present action, Mr. R[umball] is against it, and prevailes with many to own the same opinion. This strikes at the power the King has plac'd in us; which if not countenanc'd by the King, according to his instructions, a perfect confusion will follow. I doubt not but the King will make good his own act; and that since he offer'd Mr. Rumball and Sir Will[iam Compton] their shares in the trust, which they both refus'd, he will confirme the power to those great persons [that] now are in it; who act ingenuously, and who are, for quality and fortune, the most considerable in England.

2. My letter to the King (which I desire you may see) is not to discourage him at all, but to give him a true account of the present face of things, and the great division like to arise here by reason of Mr. Br[oderick;] who will have those of the Knott serve us as they did poor Penrudduc at Salisbury; engage us to [rise] and then never second us; but sit still, courting their [fortune].

3. All stands very fair at B[ristol,] and indeed every where. Only Lord Braye's MSS.
Mr. Br[oderick] has laid some of us so open, that we expect to be examined.

4. I am really yours, upon my honor; and depend upon the friendships you promis'd mee. I heare Major Hun . . plays false with you.

5. Send me word what fees are due for my patent, and to whom;
that I may send them. Ask H. C. [Chancellor Hyde].

6. Pray speak to the King to write a very kind letter to my Lord
Northampton; for hee very well deserves it."

1659, July 6.—John Mordaunt to the King. "1. I could never
have beleev'd so tame a spirit possest some that call themselves of
your party; but truly they are not of it, wholy given up to their
own ease and pleasure, and willing rather to live slaves, under the
worst of governments, than virtuously to assert your just title and
their own liberties. Every good man sure would be glad to expose his
life, that this good work might be done by your own subjects; and that
strangers might be excluded the glory and advantages of restoring you.
But since our wretched sloath, stupidnes, envy, and want of resolution
obstructs the begun work, let all the rable of our neighbours over-run
us, rather than your Majesty be kept out.

2. 'Tis to me so sensible an affliction to heare the engagements and
preparations all over England, and to see such an universal disposition
in all men to serve you, and yet that this cannot be made applicable, by
the crosness of some, the miserableness of others, the want of secrecy
in the rest; that truly, Sir, were I to be absolved from my duty to
your Majesty, I would never draw in the common ayre with such people.

3. Since we dispatch'd Mr. Baron to you, we met in councell, and
Titus was present, who was very well received by all; I undertaking
for your Majesty's confidence in him. Just before we met, Major
General Massey came in from the West, who assured us positively of
the certain surprisall of Br[istol] and Glo[cester,] and of a considerable
engagement in South Wales. By his account, I find, he has employed
his time well in those parts; reconciling to himself the dispersed interests of others. This falling in so, the offers from the North made it
appear to most present, that action was to be pressed, and a day sett.
But the keeping of the surprised places came in question, [and] 'twas
found we could not assure our selves of ammunition sufficient to defend
them; powder and match being continually wasting. And truly, Sir,
we have not foot armes sufficient for those numbers of men [which] will
appear in your quarrell. And for such armes wee allwayes depended to
have had them from your Majestie; not doubting, if they refused you
men, they would not, armes. But, wee giving them a true account of your
present condition, they discours'd of the readiest way to procure them.
And, though [the want of] money be the only obstacle in such affairs,
we found, by my Lord Willoughby's earnestnesse to serve you, a way
to raise a summe to be employ'd in Holland; and Captain Titus was then
thought fittest to see that perform'd. These are to be landed at or near
Lynne. Sir Thomas Peyton, after so good an example, undertooke for
Kent; but I fear the summe will not be so considerable.

4. This night we met Sir John Grinvile. And, if he and Colonel
Arundel will send immediately to Saint Malo's wee shall bee provided;
if all this can be done in convenient time, before the new Militia settle,
or we be secured. In case any of these faile, the supplies [which] were
sent your Majestie can never be better layd out. Which, if your
Majestie thinks reasonable, wee humbly desire may presently be done;

that no objection may remaine to those [who] seeme to be willing to serve you.

5. From Staffordshire Sir Charles Woocsley [Wolseley] assures of his interest, and his friend Sir John Whitcroft; and will leave himself wholly to your Majesties mercy. This engagement we hope will be considerable.

6. I sent Mr. B[aron] to Mr. Palmer, who returns your Majestie most humble thanks for your high favour to him. But says, he begs of your Majestie, that, in his old age, he may live quietly, and enjoy the satisfaction of seeing you restor'd as a private man and one no ways fit for the dutyes of that charge. He will get a pardon ready, which, when finished, I will see safely sent to your Majestie.

7. Wee extreamly want money for necessary .imployments, so that wee desire of your Majestie, that receipts, without name or summe, may be sent us; that, if any good, unexpected fortune befall us, we may raise a summe to contract for a town, or a port; privy seals procuring now no money at all.

8. A letter from the Fleet gives us some hopes Montague may prove honest. Which, if so, and the Treaty with Monck succeed, your Majesties game will be faire. The Duke of Yorke had hopes of some armes from France, and of some foot. T'would highly advance your Majesties reputation here, if but 500 men could be procured from France to land in Kent.

9. I am not forgetfull of the proposalls of Dunkerke; but, some money being sent them, they are quieter then when I was at Bruxells. I beseech God [to] bless my endeavours, which shall ever be imployed to make mee worthy [of] the name of, Sir, etc."

1659, July 7.—John Mordaunt to Mr. Hartgil Baron. (Printed in *Clarendon State Papers*, III., 518.)

1659, July 8.—The King to ———. (Printed in *Clarendon State Papers*, III., 519.)

1659, July 10.—John Mordaunt to the King. " 1. We are differing in opinion and so factious, that truly I think we best uphold your honor, when we set the most value on the trust you have pleased to think us worthy of. And, now there are so many considerable persons entred into it, that your Majesties affairs cannot well mis-carry, if private piques and emulations divide us not; I have many good witnesses with what willingness I courted Mr. R[ussel] and Sir W[illiam] C[ompton] to it. But, Sir, they refused too long to accept it when so fairly offered. And, though they seemed to approve of what we did upon the account we gave them, yet in private I am assured at that very time they lessen'd and disparaged both the persons and pro-ceedings.

2. I have just cause most humbly to thank God, that not any. of all these transactions passed through our hands, has yet been discovered, or any particular person so much as examined about them. Which is more then these gentlemen can say, when they remember Salisbury, and Cromwell's telling them all the businesses they transacted, and all the persons in it. But recrimination is not fit for a person, who ought to submitt quietly to whatever God ordaynes for him. But I could not say lesse than I doe, to justifie those who have acted with mee, against the aspertions [which] lye upon us. Apprehending prejudice might accrew to your Majesties affaires by these misunderstandings, I went my self to Mr. R[ussel] and Sir W[illiam] C[ompton] to assure them, if any

scruple was entertayn'd of mee, by either of them, that I would most gladly write to your Majestie, for your permission to quit my share of the trust. They both told mee [that] no discouragement from the report of the world, or idle people, ought to make me quit an action I had so happily begun, and continued; and that at any time I should have their advice and assistance. But, Sir, all we finde from them is, that they are scepticall, and will have demonstration of everything, or allow no progress in it.

3. The reputation of these gentlemen is great, and the youth of the town are led wholy by them. So that wee may discourse what wee please [yet] in an houre these gentlemen shall sway them against what wee agree of as necessary to your service. And the people of quality, finding they will own no trust nor power from you, are uncertaine who to follow, either those, out of esteem and kindnesse to them ; or us, out of the authority your trust places in us. In this miserable confusion wee now are; these opposing your coming; the country's enraged at delayes, when their hearts are up, and the army so inconsiderable for number or discipline.

4. This being the true state of our present condition, I think it my duty to represent it as it is ; that, by our confusion and division, we expose not your royal person to hazzards [which] our unity amongst our selves might prevent: it being visible, if wee now draw not severall wayes, wee have it in our power to establish you.

5. These gentlemen are of opinion, [that] under 7000 men, you ought not to land. Others, that your appearance only will do it with the present preparations. These gentlemen beleeve the army cannot settle. Others beleeve it may ; being already they have put out 200 officers, and introduced anabaptists and such in their roomes. In fine, Sir, these gentlemen would, as willingly as wee, have you here ; but they are loath to venture for it, and expect from delays what we pretend to gain by action. Theirs is the safest way, if it succeed; ours, the noblest. Now, whether you will please to run a risque by comming over and commanding them speedily to forme, or expect what tyme will doe, is most humbly refer'd to your Majesties great wisdome. I only feare, [that] the hearts of most, [which] are alredy [so well] prepar'd, may fall so low, [as] no encouragement hereafter will raise them.

6. But, Sir, on the other side, the reverence we owe your sacred person is so great, we know not what to say, this division being amongst us. If your Majestie resolves to come, or the Duke of York, or both, many of these considerable persons must be writt to, that they may have no pretence to excuse them. And surely a common Fate ought to be runne, when you appeare ; none deserving the name of a gentleman that will refuse to lay down his life on this account.

7. I am so perplext at the delay and objections they make, that (though last night it was the full sence of those whose names I sent, and who were consulted yesterday, that your Majestie should be invited to come) I cannot but of my self send this expresse to your Majestie, to acquaint you of all particulars.

8. The engagements stand every where very faire ; of which wee can be no better assured, then by those [who] manage and looke into them : and they give us their faith and word for it. God of heaven protect your person, and inspire you for the best; which I cannot question but he will, since He hath [already] so miraculously preserved you. I shall ever be ready to lay down life and all, to appprove my self, Sir, your Majesties most loyall and most faithfull servant."

1659, July 11.—John Mordaunt to the King. (Printed in *Claren-don State Papers*, III., 524.)

1659, July 12.—[Sir Edward Hyde, Lord Chancellor] to John Mordaunt]. " 1. Yesterday I received, in a letter from R. W. [William Rumball] one from him for you, in which was another also in cipher, superscribed with R. W. his hand for your self ; which opening, I found this later to be written by another hand, in the cipher you left with me, but it is not subscribed with any name.  So although I have decipherd it, I know not certainly from whom it came ; but confesse I now guesse at it.
2. I shewed R. W. his letter to the K[ing] of E[ngland,] and acquainted his maiestie with so much of the other letters as I conceived necessary for his maiestie to know.
3. Mr. R. W. can tell you the reason why there are no bills of exchange yett come to mee.  When any shall be sent me, I pray let me have a particular direction how I shall dispose of the money that shall be remitted to me.
4. Your patent hath already passed the signet, and shall be forthwith set in hand to be ingrossed.  And I hope to let you know by the next it is pass'd the great seale.  I long passionately to hear of your safe arrival, which is heartily prayed for by &c."

1659, July 12.—John Mordaunt to the King. " 1. Being assured Captain Titus will give a large account to your Majestie of the whole, I shall only with great satisfaction present to your Majestie the hopes of our reconciling all mistakes, opinions, and clashes amongst us, as I am sure nothing was wanting in me to have done it sooner.  But now all looks fair, I would have, if possible, all remembrances of past negligences forgot, and that every one apply himself to propose considerably to serve you.  Yet your Majestie will receive reasons, which are now drawing up, to obstruct your remove and divert action.  'Tis our duty to refer all to your wisdome ; els I might find something to say in this poynt.  But, though these wary gentlemen would deferre the time, they resolve to act, in case either your Majestie or the Duke come.  I beseech God to direct your Majestie in it, and to blesse your resolution with successe.  My most ready obedience and humble duty to all your Majesties commands will make me appear, Sir, your Majesties most loyall and faithful subject and servant."

1659, July 13.—Sir George Booth to John Mordaunt. " 1. This gentleman, the bearer hereof (one that lookes to my affaires in my own private fortune) I have had experience of his fidelity and honesty, he has something considerable to acquaint you with from me.  Pray give him credit, and fear not to say to him what you have to say to mee.  I am still the same you expect while my power continues, as befitts, Sir, your most faithful servant——the person you did chide for not leaving my agent in London."

"(P.S.) The same reproofe I had from the lady in St. Martins Lane."

1659, July 15.—Sir George Booth to John Mordaunt. " 1. The businesse you pleased to intrust me with that concernes the Lady [i.e. the King] in this country, I have been very faithful in.  My unkle and my brother (who with his own hands presents you this) have been very serviceable to you in it.  You will therefore please to take notice of it to my brother (the bearer hereof) to whom you may as safely impart any thing as to my self.

2. Sir, You will also please to encourage both my unkle and my brother, by owning their care and endeavors : it will not be lost,

3. I know it will not be unpleasing to you to know how my little family here does. I have therefore desired my brother to wait on you, from what you may receive a perfect account of whatsoever you shall please to ask him. And by him I hope to heare your sweet lady, your self, and all yours are well."

1659, July 16.—John Mordaunt to the King. " 1. I must dispatch this expresse to you with a sad heart ; since I looke on all delayes as ruinous to your present businesse. But the reverence those you trust have for your person directs us humbly to represent to your Majestie the slow and incertaine preparations of some here on whom you depend. Some miscarriage too has happened ; which disturbs Mr. Popham. And Har[ry] Cromwell's base compliance, checks Sir George Boothe, who apprehends enemys from Ireland.

2. These particulars, without more, are of force to prevaile with Capt. Titus and me, to give your majestie this advertisement before you leave Bruxells. And, least by accident at sea or land this person miscarry, either I or a fit person shall wait on you at Calais, to give your majestie a free and faithful account of the whole (the day your majestie first pleased to appoint) that you may not run an unnecessary risque at sea.

3. And if, in the mean time, these gentlemen will clearlye and frankly runn your fortune and come to some determinate resolution of a day, either the person I send to Callais, or my selfe, will come to Bruxells with all imaginable diligence, and wait on you back. There being nothing I desire more than to see a warre begunne being of opinion it can last no longer then to make your majestie appear as brave and wise as any prince, [who] ever ruled this unstedy people.

4. This hasty and ingenious account I hope your majestie will pardon, and accept it as the duty of Sir, your majesties most loyal and most faithful servant and subject Mordaunt.

I am glad I find the supplies transmitted and Mr. W. Mordaunt gone."

1659, December 30.—The King to John Mordaunt. " 1. I writt to you two or three days since, which, it may be, may not come sooner to your hands than this. But having since seen a letter of yours to one whose name is not in the cypher, and who (tho' he be a very honest man) is not fit for all kinds of trust, I make all the hast I can (which I take to be one necessary part of kindness to you) to undeceive you in some particulars, which I perceive have given you trouble, and might well do so, as long as you give credit to the information.

2. But I do, in the first place, assure you, and not only for myself, but those about me that have been trusted by you (and who are as just to you as they ought to be, and as any can be whom you can trust) that we have only forborne saying anything to yourself, which you might well expect to heare, out of tenderness to you ; which 665 expressed at large, with all my sense of your carriage to 247 if his letters have not miscarried. And, I do assure you, I have never heard any such discourse or censure as you mention, but, on the contrary, all men have exceedingly commended what you did, not without trouble that another very good man did not do the same. Therefore I must conjure you not only not to believe any reports of that kinde, but to look upon the reporters as persons who do not wish well to me or you, whatsoever they pretend. And I pray hearken not to any body who shall discourse

with you upon my affaires, except you are sure they are trusted by me; which, upon my word, many are not, who pretend to much, and who would be thought to understand my business better than myself.

3. I was once moved in a particular concerning you, upon the desire of him who shewed me your letter; which I concluded was not by your desire, and so answered accordingly: tho', for the thing that was asked, I intend it you with all my heart.

4. I shall he glad to receive advice from you in all particulars. And, what you do not write to myself, write to 665 or to 513, who are very faithful to you. I will add no more that that, if I am not very kind to you, I deserve no more such friends. Pray remember me very kindly to your wife. Charles R."

## THE STUART PAPERS.

## VOL. I.

f. 1. 1701. Copies of the wills and codicils of James II. and Queen Mary.

f. 7. Abstracts in Italian of the same.

f. 11. April 5, 1717. Ohlau [in Silesia]. Acknowledgment by Pelucchi in Italian of a blank paper signed and sealed by James [Louis], Prince of Poland and the Grand Duchy of Lithuania.

f. 12. Same date. Acknowledgment in Italian by Giono Pelucchi of a similar blank power from Constantine, brother of the preceding Prince.

At the foot is the acknowledgment of the receipt of a bill from the deceased Queen [Dowager of Poland] for 25,000 scudi.

f. 13. The blank powers above referred to. In addition are three blank papers signed, but not sealed, by Prince Constantine, and two others formerly in an envelope, endorsed—"Blancs signés par le Prince Constantin."

f. 27. Narrative in French entitled :—"Recit distinct et fidele de l'evasion de S. A. R. Madame la Princesse Sobieski, et de quelques petits evenemens arrivés dans la voiage qu'elle fit de Inspruck à Bologne. Escrit par H. Gaydon, Major du Regiment d'Infanterie Irlandoise de Dillon. A Bologne le 9ᵉ May, 1719."

f. 55. A different narrative of the same events entitled :—"Relation exacte de l'arrêt, de l'evasion, et du mariage de la Princesse Clémentine Sobiesky, Reine d'Argleterre." It gives a copy of a letter from Secretary Stanhope to General St. Saphorin, dated at London, November 4, 1718.

f. 75. Paper of accounts in French, relating to the property left by the late Queen Dowager of Poland, widow of King John Sobieski.

f. 79. Letter in French from the Comte de Shaffgotsch to M. le Chevalier Passarini, recounting a conversation with his Highness [Prince James Sobieski]. The latter had announced his intention of taking his daughters with him to Poland, in the event of the death of his wife. The Count then disclosed the orders he had received from his Majesty [the Emperor]. Endorsed in Italian—"Breslauia (Breslau) the 28th of July 1722. Received the 29th by courier."

f. 81. Extract from the *London Gazette* in August 1722, giving an account of the death on August 10th, at Ohlau, in Silesia, of the Princess Hedwig Elizabeth wife of Prince James Sobieski, and mother of the wife of James III. (the old Pretender).

f. 83.   September 5, 1722.   Rome.   Autograph letter in Italian of     LORD BRAYE'S
Pope Innocent XIII. to the wife of the old Pretender, then at the Baths     MSS.
of Lucca.   Rejoices at hearing good reports of her health and of that of
the Prince of Wales.

f. 85.   July 5, 1723.   A sermon in German by George Mocki,
almoner and secretary of Prince James Louis Sobieski, delivered at
the Church of the Château of Ohlau, being a panegyric on Her Most
Serene Highness the Princess Maria Casimira Josepha Anna Theresia
Carolina, the eldest daughter of the said prince, who had died on the
previous 18th of May, and dedicated to her sister Maria Clementina,
the wife of James III.   At the end are six quatrains of Latin elegiacs,
one on each name of the Princess.

f. 113.   October 1723.   Breslau.   Legal opinion in German,
addressed to His Royal Highness Prince [James Sobieski], advising
him how he should proceed in order to make a valid will.   Signed—
Johannes Schwartz.

f. 117.   February 20, 1726.   Copy of a letter in French from the
old Pretender to his wife.   During the three months that she has spent
in the convent of Ste Cecile, she has had leisure to reflect on the consequences of her retreat, which is not only contrary to their mutual
satisfaction, but injurious to their interests and the interests of their
children.   He has ever been anxious to please her in all matters that do
not concern his honour and their common interests.   Her continued
retreat is opposed to the tenderness and affection which, he is sure, she
has for him, and to the ordinary rules of prudence.   She must have
been persuaded to it by the intrigues of some discontented, factious,
persons.   She has never pressed for anything except the dismissal of
the Earl of Inverness, and she has never explained her reason for dis-
trusting him.   The situation of Europe was and is very critical.   The
Earl had all his correspondence, and he had nobody capable of taking
his place.   Being sure of his capacity, fidelity and discretion, he could
not dismiss him without ruinous consequences.   He must have some-
body to serve him, and if she had anything to urge against the Earl,
she ought to have urged it before going into the convent.   As to his
own son, he desired to give him a governor personally known to himself
and capable of watching over him.   He fixed on Lord Dunbar the more
readily because he was acceptable to her.   Lord Dunbar did not seek
the office, and he only took it in obedience.   He has since heard that
she does not approve of the appointment.   She ought at least to have
expressed her opinion on the question of appointing a person so
esteemed by the King and so beloved by his subjects as the Duke of
Ormond.   Lord Dunbar has mentioned this as a very advantageous
step in the present state of affairs.   Lord Inverness is vexed at being
considered the cause of their separation, and he is only restrained from
resigning his duties by the King's express orders.   He cannot imagine
what other grievance she can have, and he urges her to follow the
dictates of her own heart.

f. 119.   June 27, 1726.   Rome.   Copy of another letter from the
same to the same.   After reproaching her for her conduct, he assures
her that he will receive her with open arms, if she will return to her
duty.

f. 120.   September 17, 1726.   Rome.   Copy of another letter from
the same to the same.   (A translation of it is printed in Ellis's
*Original Letters* 1st series, vol. iii., pp. 397, 398.   The two letters
which are there mentioned as having been written by the Pretender to

his wife, are dated Nov^r 9 and Nov^r 11, 1725. See *The Memorial of the Chevalier de St. George.*)

f. 121.   February 6, 1727.   Legal document in Polish, addressed to the Secretary of Prince James Sobieski, apparently relating to the property of his deceased brother, Prince Constantine.   Heraldic seal affixed.

f. 123.   October 22, 1728.   Lublin.   Copy of an agreement in Latin between Prince James Sobieski and Princess Maria Josepha, the widow of his brother Constantine.   By the mediation of Elizabeth Sicniawska, Castellan of Cracow, Grand Duchess of the Kingdom of Poland, the Princess agreed to relinquish in favour of Prince James all her rights to the property of Zolkiew, which had belonged to her husband, in consideration of 729,000 Polish florins, of which 229,000 were to be paid within a week after Martinmas next, and the balance secured on mortgage of two estates of the Prince as therein mentioned.   Signed and sealed by the said Elizabeth Sicniawska, and by the commissaries of the two parties.

f. 129.   August 31, 1731.   Zolkiew.   Document in Italian.   The writer had, on the recommendation of the Queen Maria Clementina, been appointed by her father manager of his three manufactories of glass, iron, and tallow, by a diploma of August 12th, 1731, on condition that he should pay him a fixed sum of 6,400 Polish florins per annum.   By this document, in which he expresses a hope that the Duke of York will inherit his grandfather's great possessions, which are sufficient to maintain a king, he pledges himself to render a regular yearly account.   Signed—De Ronchber (?), and sealed with heraldic seal.

f. 131.   List in French of the legatees of the Queen Dowager of Poland, whose pensions for life, to begin on July 1st, 1722, had been settled by an instrument dated December 9th, 1721.   It was drawn up after the death of Prince James Sobieski in 1737, and states which of the legatees were then alive and which were dead.

f. 133.   February 1737.   Deed of gift in Latin, by Prince James Louis, described as "Regius Regni Poloniæ et Magni Ducatus Lithuaniæ Princeps, Bonorum et Fortalitiorum Zolkievien, Zloczovien, Tarnopolien, Pomerganensium Dominus et Heres," to his grandsons, Princes Charles Edward and Henry, of the jewels he had pledged at Rome for 100,000 Roman crowns, including the Polish crown jewels which had been pledged to the house of Sobieski, and which he had in 1732 bequeathed to their mother.   By the same deed he gives them all sums due to him from the Republic of Poland, and especially the 400,000 Rhenish florins advanced on the security of the Duchy of Ohlau.   A life interest and a power of revocation are reserved to the donor.   Dated "at our residence of Zolkieviez in Russia" (the palatinate of that name in Poland), February 12th, 1737, and registered at the Court at Leopolis (Lemberg) on the 15th.   A notarial copy made at Rome from and compared with the original in the possession of James III. on Nov. 20th, 1739.

f. 135.   Another copy of the same document.

f. 139.   January 24, 1739.   Palace of the SS. Apostoli at Rome. Deed of gift in Latin by Prince Charles Edward and Prince Henry of the 400,000 Rhenish florins secured upon the Duchy of Ohlau to the Apostolic See.   Witnessed by the prothonotaries Bolognetti and Acciajuoli, and by Thomas Sheridan, Hugh Dicconson, and Peter Martius.   A true copy, certified by Gregorio Castellani, Secretary and Chancellor of the Apostolic Chamber.

f. 141. Same date. Copy of a deed in Latin, whereby the afore-said Gregorio Castellani declares that, in his presence, the most illustrious and reverend Cardinal Sacripanti, Treasurer of the Pope and the Apostolic Chamber, with the Pope's approval, had appointed Paulucci, the Nuncio at the Emperor's Court, his Procurator to receive the 400,000 florins mentioned in the last document, and the revenues of the Duchy of Ohlau, till payment of the debt. Dated at the palace of Monte Citorio, Rome.

f. 143. September 17, 1741. Paper in French, which, after mentioning the deed of gift of Feb. 12th, 1737, by Prince James Sobieski, his death in the following December, and the deed of gift by the Princes to the Holy See of the 400,000 florins secured on Ohlau, states that their reason for it was that they could not proceed to recover their rights at Vienna in their own names. When the Nuncio was on the point of taking possession, the changes in Silesia (the Prussian invasion) suspended everything. Endorsed in Italian:—" Short note on the affairs of Ohlau of Sept. 17th, 1741."

f. 145. 1741. Paper in French, stating the gift of the 400,000 florins secured on Ohlau to the Princes, the assignment of their interests to the Pope, and the adverse claim by the Duchess of Bouillon, daughter of Prince James Sobieski. The Chancery of Bohemia had decided in favour of the Nuncio, but 80,000 florins of rents were in arrear, which would increase while the appeal of the Duchess was pending. The Princes, or rather their father, propose that when the final decision is given in their favour these arrears shall be capitalized and added to the principal. Endorsed in Italian:—" Memoir on the affair of Ohlau, to be presented to his Royal Highness the Grand Duke of Tuscany, Duke of Lorraine, &c., and afterwards the Emperor Francis I., in 1741."

f. 149. December 22, 1742. Rome. Agreement in Italian between Prince Charles Edward and Henry Duke of York, approved by their father James, as to the division of the jewels and other property of their late mother, and also of the jewels comprised in the deed of gift by Prince James Sobieski of Feb. 12th, 1737, pledged at the Monte della Pieta at Rome for 100,000 scudi, and redeemed by them out of the proceeds of sale of their rights to his property in Poland.

1. The proceeds of the jewels comprised in the deed of gift which had already been sold to be equally divided between the Prince and Duke.

2. The Duke permits the Prince to have the use and custody of the crown jewels of the Republic of Poland pledged to the Sobieskis, namely, a great ruby, two large diamonds with their gold settings, and a small ruby ring, until they are redeemed or the right of redemption is barred, but in the former case the redemption money, and in the latter the jewels shall be equally divided between the brothers.

3. The remaining jewels, both those of their mother and their grandfather, to be divided between them, according to the schedule annexed.

4. Of the remaining effects of their mother, the Duke reserves a gold watch and chain, a silver toilet service, and a walnut wardrobe, and gives the rest to his brother.

Signed—" Carlo P.," " Enrico," " Giacomo R." The schedule is also signed—" Carlo P.," " Enrico." Heraldic seals of James III. and his two sons affixed.

LORD BRAYE'S  f. 153. Memoir in French in support of the claims of the Prince
  ——  de Turenne and his sister, the Duchesse de Montbazon, to a moiety of
the 400,000 florins and the jewels. Reasons—i. That the Princes
Charles Edward and Henry, having exercised their rights as heirs of
their grandfather, were bound to bring the 400,000 florins and the
jewels into hotchpot. ii. That the donation was null, not having been
" insinuated," *i.e.* properly registered. iii. (applicable only to the
400,000 florins) that 300,000 of them were subject to the stipulations
of the marriage contract of Prince James Sobieski. It appears incidentally that the Princes had sold all their rights in Poland and
Lithuania, as heirs of their grandfather, to Prince Radziwill in September
1740, confirmed by an Act at Rome dated January 20th, 1741, for
800,000 Polish florins, of which 630,000 had been paid down to Father
Lascaris, the Princes' agent. Undated, but later than January 1741.

f. 167. Paper in French endorsed—" Summary of the Affair of
Olau," consisting of three distinct parts. The first, written shortly
after the end of 1741, deals solely with the claims of the House of
Bouillon to share in the 400,000 florins secured on Ohlau. It appears
that on Frederic the Great's invasion of Silesia the château and its
contents were taken possession of by Gen. Kleist. The second is
entitled—" Reasons in support of the contention of the Royal Family
of England against that of the Dukes of Bouillon." The third, written
after the death of James III. and therefore after Jan. 1766, refers to the
Polish crown jewels which had been pledged to the House of Sobieski
and were comprised in the deed of gift of Feb. 12th, 1737 from Prince
James Sobieski to his grandsons.

f. 175. Paper containing another copy of the second and third
parts of the last, in reversed order. At the end of part three, there are
some additions written in the same hand as the copies of the " Short
Note " and " the Memoir on the affair of Ohlau " of 1741.

f. 183. April 26, 1754. Monte Citorio, Rome. Copy of deed in
Latin in exactly the same form as the second deed of Jan. 24, 1739, by
which Crivelli, the Nuncio at the Imperial Court, is appointed procurator
for the same purposes as those for which the Nuncio Paulucci had been
appointed.

f. 185. Copy of opinion in Latin in favour of the rights of the
Stuart Princes to the jewels and the 400,000 florins included in the deed
of gift of Feb. 12, 1737. Undated. Endorsed in Italian :—" Reply of
the Advocate Acqua to the case from France on the donation from
Prince James of Poland to the Royal Princes of England."

f. 209. Translation in Italian of a writing, or memorial, presented
in the name of the Prince de Turenne to His Royal Highness the
Cardinal Duke of York by the Abbé Cojer (Coyer). According to it
(1.) The gift of the 12th Feb. 1737, confirmed by a second deed of the 16th
July following, was a gift *inter vivos* and not a *donatio mortis causa*,
and the donees, being *heredes* of the donor, were bound to bring into
hotchpot what they received under these deeds. (2.) The gifts were
themselves void, not having immediately been communicated to the
donees.

f. 215. Opinion in Latin in favour of the claims of the Stuarts as
against the Bouillon family. Signed—Guaret. Undated. Endorsed in
Italian:—" Responsio Juris to the writing, or memorial, in French (of
which the last document is a translation) presented by the Abbé Cojer
(Coyer) to His Royal Highness the Cardinal Duke of York, in the name
of the Prince de Turenne his cousin, with regard to the gift of jewels

made by their grandfather, James Sobieski, to the Cardinal and his royal LORD BRAYE'S<br>MSS. brother Charles Edward."

f. 237. Opinion in Italian in favour of the Stuart claims against the Bouillon family. Unsigned and undated, perhaps that mentioned in the memoir of 1772 (?) as by Monsignor Petrucci.

f. 245. March 28, 1763. Vienna. Letter in Italian from the Abbé Giuseppe Bernardo Serravalle to a Cardinal [not the Cardinal of York]. The writer had been consulted on the rights of the Stuart Princes to the 400,000 florins comprised in the deed of Feb. 12, 1737, and the best means of proceeding to recover them. For the reasons he gives he considers that the Princes had best proceed directly themselves, and not through the Apostolic Chamber. The bearer was Stefano Bianchino, chocolate seller, of Milan.

Annexed are four minutes. The first is a report to James III. by his minister dated 1763, mentioning that the said Serravalle had been charged with the business in 1752, and advising the King to request the Pope to direct the Nuncio at Vienna to exert his influence. The next two are apparently a draft appointment of Serravalle as procurator at Vienna and a draft petition by the minister to the Pope asking him to order the Nuncio at Vienna to assist Serravalle, and the fourth a note by James approving of a letter of commendation being obtained.

f. 249. Copy of the will of "James III. King of Great Britain, &c." dated at Rome, November 21, 1760, and of a codicil thereto dated May 26, 1762.

f. 257. Abstract of the same in Italian.

f. 261. Extracts in French of the parts of the same relating to the rentes payable at the Hôtel de Ville at Paris, and various documents showing that the Cardinal Duke had ratified the provisions in question and renounced his rights to them in favour of his brother.

f. 267. June 2, 1766. Act of renunciation by the Cardinal Duke of his rights to the said rentes. Certified by the Chancellor of the French Consulate at Rome. Seal of the Consulate affixed.

f. 269. Three different drafts of a Latin Epitaph on James III.

f. 272. A series of papers in French, being extracts from the registers of the French rentes payable at the Hôtel de Ville de Paris and relating to the rentes belonging to the Stuart family.

The first, dated February 9, 1708, is a copy of the contract relating to the investment by the Queen Dowager of Poland of 240,000 livres in the loan authorised by the edict of December 1707, the principal of which was 5,000,000 livres. Each subscriber was to receive a perpetual annuity of 5 per cent. and in addition a life annuity of 5 per cent. She thus received a perpetual rente of 12,000 livres, and a life annuity of like amount, the life nominated being that of her son Prince Alexander. A memorandum follows stating that in 1720 the perpetual rente was reduced to 2½ per cent. on the capital, or 6,000 livres. On the death of the Queen Dowager, the capital was divided between her sons Prince Constantine and Prince James Sobieski, the former receiving 168,000 livres and the latter 72,000 livres, corresponding to rentes of 4,200 and 1,800 livres respectively. In September 1732, 200 livres of the first rente were sold, reducing it to 4,000.

The second consists of copies of entries in the register to the following effect :—

No. 1. That the said Prince Constantine became entitled on his mother's death to 12,000, subsequently reduced to 6,000 livres of rente, and that James III. is now entitled thereto by virtue of a transfer to his wife Maria Clementina from her father, who had become entitled thereto on his brother's death.

No. 2. That Prince Constantine was further entitled to the rente of 4,200 livres above mentioned.

That Prince James was entitled on his mother's death to 6,000 livres of rente.

That he was also entitled to the said 1,800 livres of rente.

And finally, that James III. was entitled in all to 8,325 livres of rente, namely to 4,000 out of the 4,200, 4,275 out of the 6,000, and 50 out of the 1,800 by virtue of a transfer made to him and his deceased wife.

These extracts are all dated at Paris, March 29, 1765.

No. 3. That Marie Josephe, Princess of Poland, Countess of Wesel, widow of Prince Constantine, was entitled to 2,250 livres of rente, and that James III. was now entitled thereto by virtue of a transfer made to his wife by her father.

This extract is dated Paris, February 1, 1765.

The total rentes therefore to which James III. was entitled under these instruments were 16,575 livres.

The third paper is a document which, after reciting an edict of December 1764 consolidating all outstanding French loans into a 5 per cent. stock, certifies that Charles Edward being entitled to 4,000 livres of rente (being the 4,000 mentioned in the last paper), is entitled to the capital sum of 80,000 livres. Dated Paris, March 31st, 1767.

The fourth paper is in the same form as the first, and relates to the investment by M. de Tencin, then Archbishop of Embrun [afterwards Cardinal] of 150,000 livres producing 3,750 livres of rente in the 2½ per cent. loan of 2,500,000 livres issued by the royal Edict of June 1720.

The fifth contains declarations by M. de Tencin, dated December 31st, 1725, and March 8, 1726, to the effect that the investments of six sums of 150,000 livres each (of which that mentioned in the last paper was one) were made out of the moneys of James III., and that he had merely given the use of his name, and had no interest in the respective rentes.

The sixth paper is in the same form as the third, and certifies that Charles Edward being entitled to the 3,750 livres mentioned in the fourth paper is entitled to the capital sum of 150,000 livres. Dated September 20th, 1766.

VOL. II.

f. 1. March 15, 1771. Mesnil. Letter in English from Lord Caryll to Charles Edward. Narrates a conversation with the Duc de Noailles. " I have just received a letter from my agent in England, who assures me that things are now so farr advanced that he only expected my answer to put an end to this long depending affair." Regrets that new regulations of the French Posts will interfere with his procuring the public papers (from England).

f. 3. A number of scraps endorsed in Caryll's hand :—" Some memoranda or notes of no consequence found among the papers brought from Paris by the King." Among them are three pieces of paper with memoranda in Charles Edward's hand, one being a sketch of a note to the Duc de Fitz-James, and another as follows: " Monday morning at 10½. The two houses by se or land. The D. signing present L. d. de F. [le duc de Fitz-James], and only Doun to be consulted before making any attempt far off. My sayin to Gros and his brother in trede (*sic*) the affair enjoining the secret, as also the soverain of the place ; a renewall of Carignian's proposition. The economy, as one dose not even know if Gros'[? the King of France] will guive funds, which would derange me very much ; Ryan's writing immediately on or off. Iff on, wait for all things and what is desiered to be done, in as little time as possible and come with it himself, to guive it in Mr. Gordon's name for a necessary security, and remain near or at Paris for the answer." There are also two notes in his hand both dated Monday September 9, [1771] to Mr. Gordon, the Principal of the Scotch College at Paris, and the Marquise d'Azi, Rue Neuve Lunembourg (Luxembourg) la seconde porte cochére du Coté du Boulevard, quartier Place Vendôme. There is also the card of the keeper of the hotel where Charles Edward stayed, "Didelot, Maitre et Marchand Tailleur, Hôtel de Brunswick, Rue des Prouvaires, la 2$^{de}$ porte cochére à gauche, par la Rue St. Honoré."

f. 8. Note in French (by the Marquis de Fitz-James), dated Thursday morning (Aug. 29, 1771) to the effect that his father could not come that day to Paris, but would probably do so on Sunday morning, while the writer went to Versailles to receive the answers expected.

fol. 9. Monday morning, September 2, 1771. Note in French from the Duc de Fitz-James to Mr. Stonor (Charles Edward) to the effect that he had arrived the previous evening from Versailles and would have the honour to wait with his son upon him at 10 that morning. Hopes he will excuse his being in country dress. Addressed "A Monsieur Monsieur Stonor, a l'hotel de Brunswick, Rue des Prouvaires."

f. 11. September 15, 1771. Paris. Copy of power to M. Ryan, Colonel of foot in the French service, Major in Berwick's regiment, to negotiate with the Prince of Salm-Kyrburg a marriage between his daughter Marie Louise Ferdinande, born Nov. 18, 1753, and Charles Edward. Signed :—"C.R."

f. 12. Same date and place. Copy of power to Ryan, in case his negotiations with the Prince of Salm prove unsuccessful, to effect a marriage between Charles Edward and any other Princess or Countess of the Empire, and for that purpose to go to Brussels, Cologne, Mannheim, or elsewhere. The Princess Marie Isabelle de Mansfeld, born August 29, 1750, is suggested as likely to be eligible. Signed as the last.

f. 13. Same date and place. Copy of a third power to Ryan to negotiate a marriage between Charles Edward and any Princess or Countess of the Empire whose rank, birth, age, and appearance would be suitable. Signed as the last.

f. 14. Two copies in French of the instructions to Ryan for negotiating a marriage with the Princess of Salm, one in the same hand as the last three powers, and the other in Caryll's hand. The last endorsed in his hand :—"Copy of Instructions left with Ryan concerning the marriage with the Princesse de Salm. N.B. They served after as his instructions for the treaty with the Princesse de Stolberg." They are in the form of questions and answers as to the position, residence, jointure, pin-money, household, and place of marriage of the future Queen.

f. 18. October 9, 1771. Mons.—Copy of a certificate in French of the death of the Prince de Stollberg [father of the Princess] at the battle of Lissa [Leuthen] on December 5, 1757, under the hand of officers who were present, with further certificates of the identity of the certifying officers. The copy was made March 26, 1772.

f. 20. Paper in French in the hand of the Marquis de Fitz-James. The King, intending to marry, can no longer remain in his present state ;

he ought to be treated as the late King his father; the incognito which he has voluntarily assumed can no longer continue; it is therefore necessary that his Highness the Cardinal Duke should communicate it to his Holiness as well as the fact that he has communicated to his Most Christian Majesty his intended marriage. At the same time his Holiness might be informed of the satisfactory manner in which his Most Christian Majesty has received the King's confidence, and of the pleasure he has manifested in seeing everything turn out according to his desires. It remains to add that the person charged with the negociation of the King's marriage has had permission to say, if necessary, that his Most Christian Majesty has been informed of it, and at the same time to make it known that he is favourably inclined to supply the subsidies which have become absolutely necessary. Cardinal Marefoschi has been informed of all this, and the greatest secrecy is earnestly recommended. Endorsed in Caryll's hand:—"1772, Instructions in the hand of the Marquis. Jan. Intended for the Duke."

f. 22. Another copy in the same hand, with the addition in Charles Edward's hand:—"Donè au Duc a Frascati le 21º Octo. 1771 . . .," the words after "Duc" being erased.

f. 23. Narrative in French by the Marquis de Fitz-James of the steps taken by Charles Edward before his marriage. He wrote to the Duc de Fitz-James for a passport to enable him to go to Paris. The Duke accordingly applied to the Duc d'Aiguillon for one in the name of Douglas. D'Aiguillon having consulted the King replied that none was necessary. Charles Edward, having been informed of this by the Duc de Fitz-James, started for Paris from Siena on August 18th (1771), under the name of Stonor. On his arrival, he charged the Duc de Fitz-James to inform the King of his arrival, to present his compliments to him, and to inform him through the Duc d'Aiguillon that the object of his journey was to forward a marriage he had in view, and to ask the King for his assistance in that matter, and in particular for permission to employ a colonel in his service, and to remind him that the subsidies granted to his late father, which had not been continued to himself, had become absolutely necessary now that he was thinking of marrying.

The Duc de Fitz-James performed his mission, and received the following reply:—"The marriage of the King would be agreeable to him. The necessary furloughs and passports would be immediately given to the colonel or to any other persons the King might require, and that they would endeavour by the intervention of the Duc de Fitz-James to settle the subsidies which the state of the finances had hitherto prevented them from arranging."

The Duc d'Aiguillon charged the Duc de Fitz-James to assure the King of his zeal and devotion and that he would have delivered in person his master's reply, were it not for the secrecy the affair required, the King himself having declared that he wished to see no one, and to preserve the strictest incognito.

The King, satisfied with the reply of the King of France, with the interest he took in his affairs, and with the zeal of the Duc d'Aiguillon, immediately despatched the colonel charged with the negotiation of the marriage, having furnished him with all the necessary powers, and with answers to the questions which would be probably put to him.

There is every reason to hope for success if the King finds as much good-will and affection at the Court of Rome.

As the marriage is being arranged in concert with the Court of France, the colonel is authorised to apprise those whom it may concern thereof, but under pledges of the greatest secrecy, his Most Christian LORD BRAYE'S<br>MSS. Majesty not wishing to appear publicly to be informed of it.

The King having declared that it was indispensable to apprise the Cardinal Duke, his Holiness, and Cardinal Marefoschi, of his agreement with France, he was permitted to do so, but with the utmost secrecy, and only verbally, without leaving anything in writing.

The subsidies now in course of being granted in France, prove how satisfied his Most Christian Majesty would be to see similar subsidies granted by the Courts of Rome and Madrid on the ratification of the marriage.

The King seeing his affairs about to be settled, and desiring to return to Rome to finish them there, has thought that the zeal and attachment of the Marquis de Fitz-James might be useful to him, and therefore his Most Christian Majesty has given the Marquis leave to accompany him, and has expressed his satisfaction at his doing so.

Annexed is a copy of the instructions to Ryan.

Endorsed in Caryll's hand :—" 1771.—Notes of the steps taken by the King previous to his marriage and the answer of the Court of France when inform'd of it and apply'd to for their assistance."

f. 27.   Key to cipher in the hand of the Marquis de Fitz-James.

| | |
|---|---|
| " Rome = canton. | Ryan = edmondt. |
| civitaveccia = peekin. | d. fitzjames = mansfieldt. |
| livourne = tunkin. | m. fitz-james = stuart. |
| genes = tunis. | Salm = burton. |
| turin = gibraltar. | daughter = speedy. |
| antibes = alger. | pape = st paul. |
| toulon = tripoli. | R. de france = le grand. |
| marseille = chipre. | R. d'espagne = durand. |
| paris = nanci. | Card. duc = dickson. |
| bruxelles = toul. | Card. Marefoichi = le monge. |
| viterbe = luneville. | stonor = le blanc. |
| | Card. Bernis = le noir. |
| C h a r l e s b d f g    i. | d'aiguillon = le fils. |
| K m n o p q t v x y z   &c. | d. pedro = le capitaine. |
| | Gordon = st andré. |
| | Moore = james. |
| | Ld. Caryll = smith. |
| | C. R. = douglas." |

A part of the cipher containing the name of "Charles " and the remaining letters of the alphabet in their due order, was to be used by substituting letters in the lower line for those immediately above them, and *vice versâ*.   Thus C was to be used for K, M for H, A for N, and so on.   Compare the Jacobite cipher given in the 10th *Report of the Historical MSS. Commission.*   App. iv., p. 331.)

f. 28.   November 6, 1771.   Rome.   Paper on which is written in French, in the hand of the Marquis de Fitz-James with a few interlineations in that of Charles Edward, a draft letter to Edmondt [Ryan], and instructions to Stuart [the Marquis de Fitz-James.]

The letter acknowledges Ryan's of October 16, directs him to go to the Duc d'Aiguillon and point out it is indispensable he should make some positive statement about the subsidies, as the success of the negotiation depends on this, and the least delay may be most prejudicial.   The Marquis de Fitz-James, who is returning to France, will assist him.

The instructions refer to the question of the subsidies.   The person (Mad<sup>lle</sup> de Salm) cannot pass through the States of the King of

Sardinia.  Her only route must be from Marseilles or Toulon direct to Civita Vecchia.

f. 29.  Paper in French containing on one side the questions of M. Burton (the Prince of Salm, the proper names being according to the cipher) and on the other the replies of Colonel Ryan.  At the bottom in Charles Edward's hand is written—" aprouvé et donnant en même tems Cart Blanche a Mr. Edmond (Ryan).  Rome ce 11ᵐ Decemʳ 1771."

f. 31.  Draft in Italian of an instrument to be executed by Charles Edward appointing N. his proxy to contract a marriage with N.  Endorsed in Caryll's hand.  "Sketch of powers proposed to be sent to Ryan but not sent.  Jan. (1772)."

f. 32.  Draft in French in Caryll's hand with some words added in that of Charles Edward of an appointment of a proxy to contract a marriage with the Princess of Stolberg.

f. 33.  Copies in French in Caryll's hand of the several powers and letters sent from Rome by a courier on January 22, 1772.

1. Power to Ryan to conclude the marriage contract.

2. Note by the Cardinal Duke declaring his approval.

3. Form of the last as proposed by the King.

4. Power to Ryan with regard to the dowry and pin-money, and secret article relating thereto.  Dowry to be 40,000 and pin-money 12,000 livres per annum.

5. Short letter from Charles Edward to the Duc de Fitz-James.

6. Letter from the same to the Marquis de Fitz-James.  " I have already informed you that I have chosen the eldest of the sisters, her age is the most suitable for me, and what you have told me about the health of the younger confirms me in my resolution."

7. Letter from the same to Ryan, with full instructions about the contract and general arrangements, particularly as to the route of the Princess, which was to be from Brussels through the Tirol by Trent to Bologna and thence by Ancona and Macerata to Viterbo where Charles was to meet her, and the marriage to be solemnized.  If possible no stay to be made at Mantua.  Letter enclosed for Mr. Conway there in case of necessity and also one for M. Angeletti at Bologna.  Ryan to accompany the Princess.

8. Itinerary from Bologna to Macerata.

9. Letter from Caryll to the Marquis de Fitz-James about the courier's expenses.

10. Letter from Charles Edward to Mr. Conway.

11. Letter from the same to M. Angeletti.

f. 39.  Another copy of the above powers and letters, in a different hand.

f. 45.  January 28, 1772.  Original certificate in English under the hand of Mr. Stonor by virtue of the faculties granted by Cardinal Colonna, Vicar to the Pope.  He has received the oath of " his Majesty King Charles III." that he was at liberty to contract marriage.  At the same time the said Cardinal granted his Majesty a dispensation from publication of banns.  Signed :—Christopher Stonor.  Seal affixed.

f. 47.  Letter in Italian on the question whether a dispensation from the publication of banns was necessary.  Advises Charles Edward to entrust the secret to Mˢʳ Lascaris, who being a member of the Vicariate Tribunal, could obtain the dispensation secretly.  Endorsed in Caryll's hand :—" 1772, note from Cardˡ M[arefoschi] about the dispensation of banns."

f. 49.  Letter in Italian from Marefoschi to Caryll.  Advises Charles Edward to show confidence in the Minister of State, and in no case to disgust the Sovereign of the country (the Pope), "whose sentiments cannot be doubted, though circumstances do not permit him to do as he pleases. Your conduct full of prudence and moderation could not fail to be praised by Princes, and would mortify to the utmost the enemies of the Royal House, who seek nothing but a rupture to remove the best props that your house could have, and to triumph as they did under the late Government." He also adds a warning against disgusting his Royal Highness (? the Cardinal of York), and explains that he is writing unofficially. Endorsed in Caryll's hand "1772, C. M.'s opinion in a note to me C."

f. 51. Draft, or rather rough notes, in French in the handwriting of Charles Edward, with several alterations and mistakes in spelling, beginning "Memoire pour le C. M." (Cardinal Marefoschi.)

"A Blank dispensation is demanded giving power to celebrate a marriage by proxy without being obliged to have the banns published, to wit the form of such a proxy, and it is proposed to consult Mr. Stonor.—How I ought to keep my counsel (me contenir) in the presence of Mr. Dixon (the Cardinal of York.)—Sketch of a letter of notification to his Holiness.—His Eminence the Cardinal Pallavicini, Secretary of State, is requested to present himself to the Pope as soon as he shall be able to lay for me before his feet [an erasure] and to inform him of the marriage I have agreed upon with the Princess, &c. I flatter myself that his Holiness will find it good that the Queen should come to Rome to reside with me.

Rome, The &c., &c.                                                        C. R.

I believe it is not necessary to have a dispensation for a marriage by proxy, but one is demanded of me.—Memorandum for Ld Caryll. (In English.) To C. M. (Card. Marefoschi) To tell him that I had forgot mentioning how he had been received by the C. Secretary of State as also he wood bee the properes person to deliver my Billet to the said Secretary of State and think Ld Caryll the moste proper person on all accounts."

On the back of the same sheet, in French, in Charles Edward's handwriting, " I shall point out to my proxy that no dispensation of Banns is necessary for the proxy, but that when I shall join the Princess in the Papal States, I shall bring with me everything that will be necessary to conclude (the marriage) effectively. M. Lascaris is a very proper person to be employed if they find it necessary at the time." Endorsed in Caryll's hand :—" 1772, Instructions to Ld Caryll."

f. 52. Memorandum in English in Caryll's hand :—"To tell the Cardinal that the King has no objection to employ M.'Lascaris at the proper time if it prove necessary. That the King had forgot to mention how well I was received by the Secretary of State and to add that he has since been to see me, also that he mentioned the King by name *of his Majesty*. To show the Billet and desire his thoughts of it, that the K. intends to sign it at full length and seal it with his Arms, but to put no address to it, if the Card. judges it proper, and in the same size and form as he sees it, that he judges proper for me to deliver it into the Secretary's own hands without waiting any answer, and only staying till he shall have opened it. Desire the Cardinal's opinion as to everything concerning these matters." Endorsed in Caryll's hand :—" 1772, Instructions to Lord Caryll."

f. 53. Paper in French, in Caryll's hand, requesting the opinion of Cardinal Marefoschi on a plan that had occurred to Charles Edward after sending the note of that morning, namely, instead of making his

LORD BRAYE'S proposal to the Cardinal Secretary of State as he had at first resolved, to
MSS.     notify his resolution in the forms annexed without asking or waiting for
any answer, so as to spare the Pope the embarrassment of making one,
and he would regard the Pope's silence as consent. Annexed are the
forms in which Caryll is to communicate with the Cardinal Secretary of
State and the Cardinal Duke. Only that the marriage was to be with a
Princess of Stolberg was to be mentioned, and the utmost secrecy was
requested till her arrival in the Papal States.

Below is Cardinal's Marefoschi's reply in Italian, to the effect that if
silence in the present case was equivalent to a tacit consent the proposed
plan would do, but something more was necessary which he will explain
better verbally. Endorsed :—" 1772. Instructions for Lord Caryll with
Card. M's opinion."

f. 55. Paper in French in the hand of Charles Edward, endorsed in
Caryll's hand :—" 1772. Notes sent by the King to Cardinal Marefoschi
by my hand, C. Sometime in (erased) Jan^y." (Numerous mispellings,
e.g. palé for palais, cera for sera, and occasional words illegible.)

" Since the election of this Pope I have voluntarily assumed an
incognito in the perfect confidence which I felt that his Holiness would
desire nothing better than to replace things in the position they ought to
be, and his proceedings hitherto have shown clearly that I was not
deceived. He has little by little hinted that it does not displease him
that his subjects pay me the honour due to my birth, and the Cardinals,
particularly Calini, Canale, Corsini, Borghese, and Orsini, who have given
me the title of Majesty. As for our friend Marefoschi, minister of the
King of the Two Sicilies, the feudatory of the Pope, he has come and does
come continually to our palace. Thus for an interval of laying aside the
not being recognised, an expression which is used (?) and which I
cannot admit, nor doubt that I shall be received like the late King my
father as soon as I wish to lay aside the incognito in order to be in a
position to be treated in the same manner as all the predecessors of the
present Pope have done. It will be necessary for this purpose that Cardinal Marefoschi should be kind enough to accept the commission which
I shall give him, namely, to present himself on my behalf to the Secretary
of State, to ask for an immediate audience of the Pope as representing
my person, to notify to him that the Queen has safely arrived in his
States. I hope that his Holiness will excuse me for substituting another
at this moment, but this proceeds from my eagerness to meet her, in order
that I may be the sooner in a position to present her myself to his
Holiness, being quite certain that his Holiness will receive her in the
same manner and with the same kindness that the late Queen was always
received by his predecessors, being particularly convinced of his good
feelings towards us. It may be seen in all this that I do not speak in
doubt and that I only speak of the Queen ; it is for the Pope to do the
rest, and Cardinal Marefoschi can hint to the Pope at a proper opportunity to send a guard to our palace of the SS. Apostoli at the arrival
of the Queen, and have it there as in times past. At the same time I
should wish it to be composed of the Company of Avignon, and on my
arrival I shall thank the officers while naming (with the permission of
his Holiness) one of my gentlemen to command the troop consisting of
50 men as in the late King's time. It would be desirable that his Holiness should give orders for some furniture for the Queen's suite ; the large
rooms are already prepared. Formerly the Chamber used to provide all
the furniture of the palace both at Rome and in the country. I should
wish also for the courier Ossolinski to go before the Queen. His
Eminence sees clearly the reasons there are for his going himself to the

Pope on the arrival of the courier with news of the arrival (of the Queen), and not Lord Caryll, on acount of the need there is of hinting all these matters which ought not to be understood to come from me and would be consequently too marked in his mouth. Who knows that the Pope has not also given me [the title] of Majesty on the two occasions I have already seen him and by all this the thing proceeds of itself, the Cardinals will come to see the Queen and me. We shall be on a sofa, as was the custom formerly, and everything will go on the same way and I shall be *cavaliere servente* to the Queen. As to complaisance, I pay no regard to my brother or to anyone else when the maintenance of the dignity due to me is concerned, and a low economy ought to be still less regarded on this occasion. The Queen is entitled to the same ceremonies as the King, and the Prince of Wales also, when there shall be one. The guard is offered to the Prince even in the greatest incognito, and I had when Prince of Wales at Gaeta, on my return from Naples, a guard of 50 men, an officer, and a flag. It will be proper to say to the Pope that one of the first conditions of the marriage was that the Queen should be treated like the late Queen, and that I should place myself on the same footing as the late King. The treatment at Leghorn, and the Dauphin at Paris were everything that could have been done, if I had been upon the throne. The late King also was frequently incognito, although with all his honours, so I do not know if what is intended is to annihilate me and make himself ridiculous." (This document must have been written shortly before the dated message of February 17.)

f. 57. Paper in English in Caryll's hand endorsed :—" Queries to Cardinal Marefoschi, February 17, 1772, and answers."

The first is that if the Cardinal declines to go to the Pope or the Cardinal Secretary of State with the first notice of the Queen's arrival, he is to be persuaded to go after Caryll has spoken. The fourth mentions the courier Ossolinski, while the sixth question and answer are—" If the King does not find them [guards in attendance] on his arrival he should not resent it, but may with great propriety apply for them some day after his return with the Queen, making use of an argument I (Caryll) proposed that there will now be more to be apprehended from the attempts of England when there is a prospect of succession." The seventh relates to the furniture for the Queen's suite.

f. 59. Draft note in French addressed "To his Majesty," stating that in the marriage negotiations his instructions have been literally followed, and only deviated from when absolutely necessary, or when the advocate of the Princess Mother had insisted on it. The instructions had only dealt with three points, the dowry, the allowance, and the jewels. Another difficulty was whether matters unprovided for by the marriage contract should be regulated by the law of Flanders, of France, or of Italy. The writer recommends it should be stated in the contract that such matters should be decided according to English law. A note approved by the Princess Mother is enclosed, relating to the manner in which the contract should be executed—whether before notaries, or privately. The last course is recommended among other reasons " because, if so, the English minister, if by any occurrence he had suspicions of the marriage, could not acquaint himself with the contract, as he could do if it were executed before notaries." Undated and unsigned.

f. 63. March 22. 1772. Paris. In the same hand as the last. Original certificate in French, certifying that the Princess of Stolberg is free and competent to contract a marriage. Signed by the Duc de Fitz-James, the

Marquis de Fitz-James, the Duc de Berwick, and the Marquis de la
Jamaïque, whose seals are affixed.

f. 65. March 22, 1772. Paris. Settlement in French, in the same
hand as the last, on the marriage between Charles Edward and the
Princess of Stolberg, executed on the above date by Ryan and De
Betagh as the procurators of the Prince and the Princess and her
mother respectively. At the foot are copies of the powers to the procurators from the respective principals. Below, in Caryll's hand, is a
form of ratification by Charles Edward, sealed, but undated and unsigned. (See memorandum, f. 102.)

f. 67. Paper in French in Caryll's hand, being a true copy of the
paper written in " his Majesty's hand, March 29, 1772." "The C. de B.
[Cardinal de Bernis] should be informed that the Pope was informed
through the Cardinal Duke as soon as I arrived from France that it was
impossible for me to contract a marriage without one of the first articles
relating to our being on the same footing as the late King and Queen at
Rome, and I have succeeded by promising it. On all the articles being
concluded, I communicated them to the Pope by the Cardinal Secretary
of State, and informed him at the same time that his Holiness had
already been acquainted with it some months before. The message was
given by the Cardinal Secretary, and the answer was that his Holiness
felt extreme pleasure at it, an evident sign of his approval. On the
other hand the marriage has been contracted in concert with, and with
the approval of, the King of France, by my agents, who will give an
exact account of everything to the Duc d'Aiguillon, to be communicated
to the King of France, so that he cannot be ignorant that one of the
first articles was that I should place myself on the same footing as the
late King, my father, and the Cardinal de Bernis has had orders to say
to the Pope, if an occasion should present itself, that his Most Christian
Majesty would agree to all that the Pope might do in my favour. I
must observe that I should be wronging the Pope and myself were I
to doubt for a moment that he would treat me and the Queen in the
same manner and with the same attention as all his predecessors have
acted towards the late King and Queen. Am I not equally excluded
from the throne of my ancestors only for being a Catholic? Therefore I
have only to acquaint his Holiness by Lord Caryll as soon as the
Queen shall have arrived in the States, and on her arrival at Rome to
send him again to the Cardinal Secretary of State, in order to impress on
him our eagerness to render him our homage by placing ourselves at
his feet after the example of the late King and Queen."

f. 68. Memorandum in English in Caryll's hand for the Cardinal.
The necessity of the marriage being put in the public papers in due
form.

The Princess Palestrini to be consulted by Thomasi after the King's
departure, and her opinion acted on about the reception of the lady.

Thomasi and Carlini to receive the Cardinal's orders about their
different spheres, furniture, &c.

Tell of the Duke's refusing the affair of the courier, and ask the
Cardinal's opinion how to act.

Lopez to be on guard with his Avignonese.

Desire him to apply for permissions for Lent as last year. This is a
good pretext to name the King, which he hopes the Cardinal will profit
of, if occasion offers. Q. if leave for forbidden books which the K. will
keep under lock and key.

To send Fitzgerald on Wednesday about noon to me, that in case of
news by the post he may be informed, and desire he may bring the

answer about the permission and the forbidden books if he has received it. Endorsed:—" 1772. Memoranda of instructions. March. To Lord Caryll."

f. 70. April 13, 1772. Instructions in French to Caryll, in Caryll's hand, desiring him to apprise the Secretary of State that the Princess of Stolberg has arrived, and that the King is just starting to bring her to Rome and present her to his Holiness. "The Pope must be informed that the King can no longer call himself Baron de Renfrew, one of the first articles of the marriage contract having been that he should place himself on the same footing as the late King, and that he does not doubt that his Holiness will show the same kindness to himself and the Queen as all his predecessors showed to the late King and Queen." Signed "C.R."

f. 72. Memoranda in French, in Caryll's hand, relating to the titles which should be given to the King and the Princess in the marriage register—his recognition as king by the Papal Court—the guards to be furnished to him—whether the Cardinal Duke should be told of the King's having changed his resolution as to where he should meet the new Queen—whether an extract of the register of the King's baptism will be required—the absolute necessity of the Pope's doing what he will do without delay, to show the world that the previous state of things was due to the mutual consent of the King and his Holiness—the King hopes that his marriage will be published in the first *Gazette de Rome* with his titles. Endorsed:—" 1772. Instructions from the King in April to L. C."

f. 74. Fragment endorsed by Caryll:—" 1772. Titles to be put in the Contract of marriage." In Charles Edward's hand "Carolus III. D.G. Mag. Bri. Fran. et Hiber. Rex Fideique Defensor. At present there is added before the 'Fideique' 'and of the Dependent Dominions.'" The last words are in Italian.

f. 75. April 18, 1772. Certificate in Latin of the marriage between "His Majesty Charles III., by the Grace of God King of Great Britain, France and Ireland, Defender of the Faith, and her Most Serene Highness Louisa Maximiliana Carolina Emanuella daughter of the deceased Gustavus Adolphus of Stolberg, Prince of the Holy Roman Empire, Count of Königstein, Roccafort, Vernigerode, and Hohenstein," celebrated on Good Friday, April 17, 1772, at 19 o'clock (about 2 p.m.) in the private chapel of the Palace of the de Compagnoni Marefoschi family at Macerata by the Bishop of Macerata and Tolentino.

At the foot is an Italian translation of the instrument appointing Colonel Ryan as representative of the Princess Dowager of Stolberg at the marriage, dated at Paris, March 27, 1772, and also a document in Latin from the priest of the parish of the Santi Apostoli at Rome empowering any priest appointed by the Bishop of Macerata to celebrate the marriage in his stead, dated at Rome, April 13, 1772. Seal of the Bishop of Macerata and Tolentino affixed.

f. 81. April 17, 1772. Macerata. French copy in Caryll's hand of the writing whereby the King secures to the Queen the payment of her jointure of 40,000 livres and her pin-money, the last being 15,000 livres per annum and not 10,000 as in the contract of March 26, Charles having made the increase on sight of the Princess. The original was delivered to the Queen by his Majesty himself after the marriage.

f. 83. Another copy of the same in a different hand.

f. 84. Paper containing copies in Caryll's hand of several letters all dated at Macerata, April 17, 1772.

(1) In English, from Charles Edward to his brother, announcing his marriage.

(2) In French, from the same to Cardinal Marefoschi, addressed to M. le Grand, announcing his marriage and saying the Queen will be much mortified if she does not find the guards at the gate of the palace on her arrival.

(3) Instructions sent by the King's order to Count Tommasi, directing him to call on the Cardinal Secretary of State and request him to inform the Pope of the marriage, and that he was repairing with the utmost speed to Rome with the Queen, to be ready to present her to him the moment he should find it good.

(4.) Instructions from the same to the same, directing him to deliver the enclosed to Cardinal Marefoschi and to his brother respectively.

(5.) Letter in French to the same from Caryll, announcing by Charles Edward's order his marriage with the Princess of Stolberg. "The Queen, who is perfectly well after her long journey, has all the good qualities her most devoted subjects could wish her." The King orders Caryll to ask Tommasi to call upon Card. Marefoschi, as he also directs in the enclosed letter, which he is to show the Cardinal, and also to repeat to Tommasi what the King has told him verbally, that there is now no longer any Baron de Renfrew.

A postscript gives "the names of the King and Queen" as they were inscribed in the register, and requests Tommasi to tell Caryll's wife that he is well, and hopes soon to see her, and that she must be ready by Tuesday evening to be presented to their Majesties. It concludes "The King has just given me the letter you will find addressed to M. le Grand, which is for Card. Marefoschi, to whom you will deliver it yourself. You should acquaint the Secretary of State with the contents of the letter, and show it, if he asks for it."

f. 86. Rough drafts of the last five letters and instructions.

f. 91. April 19, 1772. Macerata. Copies in Caryll's hand of his letters to the Duc de Fitz-James, in French, and Mr. Gordon, in English, both dated at Macerata, April 19, 1772, announcing the marriage, "which had been celebrated at this place the very day of her arrival, as such was the earnest desire of the Queen's friends, and the Bishop of the place yielded with pleasure to all that was required by the King." One of the three certificates of the marriage is enclosed to Gordon to be placed among his archives, and he is requested to have proper notices of the marriage inserted in the *Gazettes* of Utrecht and Amsterdam.

f. 93. Rough drafts of the last two letters.

f. 95. Paper containing copies in French of letters from Prince Charles Edward to the King of France (1), the King of Spain (2), the Duc d'Aiguillon (3), the Marquis Grimaldi (4), the Marquis de St. Leonard (son of the eldest brother of the Duc de Fitz-James and younger brother of the Duc de Berwick) (5), and the Duc de Fitz-James (6), announcing his intended marriage with the Princess of Stolberg. (1) contains the following passage : "Your Majesty must feel at the same time that the loss of my kingdoms makes it impossible for me to sustain the rank to which my birth entitles me, without having subsidies sufficient to keep it up." (2) concludes thus :—"Your Majesty must at the same time feel the necessity of the subsidies indispensable to keep up the dignity of a king who has lost his kingdom for the sake of religion." (3) was sent with (1) to request the Duke to

present it to the King of France.  It asks that the King of France
will use his influence with the King of Spain and the Court of
Rome. (4) was similarly sent with (2) to request the Marquis to
deliver it to the King of Spain. (5) was also sent with (2) and (4),
copies of which were enclosed.  The Marquis is requested to acquaint
Charles Edward with the manner in which the King of Spain received
his letter.  With (6) were enclosed copies of the others which the Duke
was asked to show to the Duc d'Aiguillon, but not to leave them with
him.

Endorsed :—" 1772.  Copies of letters sent to French and Spanish
Courts on occasion of the King's marriage.  N.B. These were according to the drafts left by the Marquis de Fitz-James when he went away
from Rome."

f. 98.  Paper beginning thus in French, in the hand of Charles
Edward :—" Lord Caryll should call upon the Cardinal Secretary of State
to request him to place me at the feet of his Holiness and notify to him
the Queen's arrival here with me.  Awaiting his orders.  C. R.  Rome
this 22ᵈ of April 1772."

Then in Caryll's hand, in English :—" The above was shewn by me
according to the King's order to the Cardinal Secretary of State who
returning one to the following purpose (sic) :—

(In French.) I have acquainted his Holiness with the arrival of
the Baron de Renfrew and his wife, and he has commanded me to
assure them that he will be very glad to receive them, but as he is now
very busy, he wishes to defer it till he is less engaged than at present.'

(In English) This is the purport but not the wording of the
message which I cannot positively remember.  The King on reading
the above mentioned paper declared he could not receive it, and ordered
me to take it to the Cardinal Marefoschi who might retain it or dispose
of it as he judged proper.  Caryll."

f. 100.  Paper, in French, in Charles Edward's hand.  "I was so
shocked at the beginning of Canon Fitzgerald's communication that I
did not perhaps give him time to say all that he had to say.  The priest
was waiting for me at my residence (à l'Hôtel) and I believed I would
find him again after the Mass.  I should have been myself this morning
with le C. M. [Card. Marefoschi], but in order to make less scandal I
sent Lord Caryll to inform his Eminence and to assure him that, notwithstanding the bad treatment of this Court, I should not abandon the
friendship esteem and veneration which I shall always preserve for his
Eminence, convinced that he could never have had any part in the evil ;
I could not have believed that the Pope would have wished to make an
event tragical, for which every good Catholic ought to have given his
services to make it splendid and agreeable.  Did they wish to perpetuate
the family of Hanover and to cut off the Legitimate Catholic race ?
Finally, did they wish to compel me to leave this country ?  How could
they imagine that the Catholic Courts would not be scandalised and
chilled by such proceedings?  It is for the Pope to go before them,
showing them a good and not a bad example.  The sheep usually follow
their shepherd, and it is his duty not to disgust them by showing a path
of brambles and thorns."

Endorsed in Caryll's hand :—" 1772, Message sent from the K. to C.
Marefoschi concerning his opinion of the acknowledgment being to be
refused."

f. 102.  1772 (?).  Memorandum in French by Caryll.  When the
marriage contract had been read to the King in the form in which it

LORD BRAYE'S MSS.

had been executed by Ryan and Betagh, the King ordered him to add his ratification at the foot and seal it, in order that he might sign it himself, but though he had often requested the King and Queen to do so, they had always deferred it. A copy of the form of ratification is subjoined. (See fol. 65.)

f. 104. Extracts, in Caryll's hand, from a memoir in French concerning the rights of the Stuart princes as to the jewels and 100,000 florins comprised in the deed of gift of February 1737. It mentions the occupation of the Chateau of Ohlau by a Prussian general in the first Silesian war, and the burning of it and its contents, gives an account of the litigation between the Stuarts and the representatives of the House of Bouillon, and states that Austria contended that the King of Prussia was now responsible for the debt. It concludes by stating that the princes had appointed the Prince de Rohan, the French ambassador at Vienna, their agent with full powers, on Nov. 19, 1771, but that no information had been received from him, though Lord Caryll had written to him in August 1772.

Undated, but it appears in part 4 of the list of documents (Vol. III. fol. 268) as No. 9 and is there dated 1774.

f. 114. June 20, ·1773. The Quirinal, Rome. Two drafts in Italian in different hands of a letter from the Cardinal Secretary of State to Monsignor de Lascaris, Patriarch of Jerusalem. If Madame Clementina Walkingshaw refuses to leave Rome, he must convince her of the uselessness of her resistance, and of the worse position she will consequently be in.

f. 116. June 24, 1773. The Quirinal, Rome. Two similar drafts of a letter in Italian from the same to the same about the same business. It mentions the greater opportunities for molestation the ladies would have in Rome, and refers to the wish of Miss Walkingshaw's daughter for removal from the convent at Meaux to one in Paris, and to the indifference of His Royal Highness and Eminence (the Cardinal Duke) as to the place of retirement of the unfortunate young lady, provided she remain always in a nunnery.

f. 118. Original letter in French, with envelope from Charlotte Stuart (natural daughter of Charles Edward) to M. de Lascaris. Acknowledges receipt of his letter. Thanks him "for all the trouble you have taken to soften a little my unhappy lot. I hope that his Eminence will not refuse my demand for changing my convent from Meaux to one in Paris." The intended route is from Genoa to Antibes, from Antibes to Aix, from Aix by Avignon to Lyons. She sends on the part of her mother "mille hommage." Signed :—" Charlotte Stuart." No place or date, but written in the summer of 1773. Seal on envelope.

f. 121. Note and envelope to the same in the same hand, but headed Madame La Comtesse d'Albestroff (Clementina Walkingshaw) requesting him to send her letters under cover to La Marquise d'Alberi at her residence in the Faubourg St. Germain. Same seal as last. A note on the envelope states erroneously that it is in the handwriting of the Princess of Stolberg.

f. 123. Paper with two draft testimonials in Latin in favour of two clergymen named Armineus (?) Francia and Dominicus Buttaoni (?). The first is dated in August 1774.

f. 124. Undated, but between July 13, 1761, the date of his appointment to Tusculum, and September 26, 1803, that of his translation to Ostia and Velletri. Draft testimonial by the Cardinal Duke in favour of the monks of the order of St. Basil at the monastery of S. Maria at Crypta (Grotta) Ferrata.

f. 126. A list in French of the documents handed over to Wm. Cowley, Prior of the English Benedictines in Paris, on April 26, 1777, by George Jean, Comte de Waters, banker, at Paris, in virtue of the letter of Charles Edward of April 4. They mostly relate to the French Rentes belonging to the Stuarts.

f. 130. March 23, 25, 1783. Florence. Copy of the will and codicil of Charles Edward in Italian. The will appoints Charlotte Stuart, Duchess of Albany, then in the Convent of S. Marie at Paris, his heir, and leaves to John Stuart his major-domo and to his wife and sons a legacy of 100 Florentine scudi per mensem during their lives, and the right to inhabit an apartment in his Palace at Florence. The brothers Count Camillo and Canon Tommaso della Gherardesca are appointed executors. The codicil bequeaths annuities to his different servants. Sealed with the Royal Arms of England, France, Scotland, and Ireland.

f. 136. March 30, 1783. Florence. Copy of the Act of Legitimation, in Italian, of Charlotte Stuart by her father Charles Edward. Certified by M. Sémonin, chef du Dépôt des Affaires Etrangères, whose signature is verified by M. de Vergennes.

f. 140. September 18, 1783. Albano. Draft or copy of a letter from the Cardinal Duke of York to the King of Spain, in reply to one announcing that his daughter-in-law, the Princess of the Asturias, has been delivered of twins.

f. 142. April 3, 1784. Florence. Copy of the letter in French from Charles Edward, permitting his wife to live separate and apart from him at Rome, or wherever else she may think fit.

Certified to be a true copy of the original sent to the King of Sweden at Rome to be delivered to the Countess of Albany.

f. 144. September 21, 1784. Extract in French from the *Gazette de Leyde*, of that date, giving an account of the Duchess of Albany and the affairs of Charles Edward. It mentions that he complained to the King of Sweden that his brother, the Cardinal Duke, kept possession of the family diamonds, that the King on going to Rome requested him to restore them, but that the interposition of the Pope had been required to make him do so.

f. 145. Extract from the register of the Church of S. Maria ad fontes at Liége of the entry of the baptism of Charlotte Stuart on October 29, 1753, therein described as the daughter "nobilis domini Guillelmi Johnson et nobilis Dominæ Pit."

Dated October 20, 1784. A certificate below from the Prince Bishop of Liége, Duke of Bouillon, &c., that the extract was in the hand of the priest of the parish. The seals of the Church of S. Maria ad Fontes, and of the Prince Bishop of Liége are affixed.

f. 147. November 16, 1784. Florence. Copy of a letter in French from Charles Edward to the Pope. Thanks him for his letter to the Duchess of Albany, entreats his protection for her, and asks that he should grant her the reversion of his pension after his death. States that his father used to give her a pension of 12,000 francs, had paid all the expenses of her education, and placed her and her mother in a convent, and had charged the Cardinal Duke to continue the pension. Complains that after his father's death the Cardinal Duke had reduced the pension to 1,000 scudi, and now that she had come to live with him had discontinued it altogether.

f. 149. November 16, 1784. Versailles. Original letter with envelope in French from M. de Vergennes to "Myladi Stwart d'Albany," informing her that the King of France has granted her father "M. le Comte d'Albany" an annual pension of 60,000 livres, with a reversion in her favour on his death as to 10,000 livres thereof. The pension being charged on the Royal treasury, some confidential person should be appointed to receive it and give receipts for it at Paris. Seal on envelope.

f. 151. Suggestions, in French, for a medal in honour of the Duchess of Albany.

On one side her portrait with the legend—

"Charlotte, Duchesse d'Albanie, fille de Charles III., Roi de la Grande Bretagne, de France et d'Irlande, defenseur de la Foi," or in Latin, "Carolina, Albaniæ Ducissa, filia Caroli III. Magnæ Britanniæ, Franciæ, et Hiberniæ Regis, Fidei defensoris." For the reverse four different designs are given :—

i. Figure of Hope pointing to a crown placed on a map of England. Legend :—"*Spem juvat amplecti, quæ non juvat irrita semper.*"

ii. — The Princess herself, with her left arm resting on a scutcheon bearing the Stuart arms, to which she points with her right hand, and with her eyes fixed upon a throne. Legend—"*Spem etsi infinitam persequar.*"

iii. — Hope, holding a flower in her right hand, and leaning with the other on a scutcheon with the Stuart arms. Legend—"*Spes tamen es una.*"

iv. — A tempest-tost ship, nearing the English coast, whose flag bears the Stuart arms. Legend—"*Pendet Salus Spe exiguâ et extremâ.*"

f. 153. February 18, 1785. Two certificates in Latin of the deposit at the Archive Office and Chancellery at Florence on the previous day of copies of two documents in French, the first attesting the deposit by Col. Ryan and M. de Betagh of the sealed copy of the contract of March 26, 1772, which was not to be opened without the authorization of one of the parties, and the second being a declaration made at Rome July 12, 1772, by Ryan, that he had acted only as the agent and made the deposit only on behalf of Charles Edward, and declaring that the latter is entitled to authorize the opening of the sealed packet.

f. 157. March 4, 1785. Copy of the marriage contract of Charles Edward and the Princess of Stolberg, of March 26, 1772, extracted and delivered to Colonel Ryan by M. Picquais the notary.

f. 163. March 11, 1785. Florence. Declaration in Italian by Charles Edward that Charlotte Stuart, created by him Duchess of Albany and legitimated with the approval of the Most Christian King, now living in his palace at Florence, was the same as the child of himself and Clementina Walkingshaw, born at Liége and baptized there under the name of Charlotte Johnson, she being his only daughter. He further declares that he never had any other children, and in particular none by the Princess of Stolberg. Signed :—"Charles R."

f. 165. Same date. Original declaration in Italian by the same of the nullity of the obligations imposed on him by his marriage contract in favour of the Countess of Albany, not only by virtue of her renunciation, but also for whatever cause, although he had not named it for the sake of decency, and that this declaration should enure in favour of the person who should be his heiress. Same handwriting and signature as the last.

f. 167. A French translation of the last.

f. 169. March 21, 1785. Dunkirk. Letter in French from Caryll to the Duchess of Albany. Thanks her for his restoration to favour with her father. He has been endeavouring to establish the right of Charles Edward to the arrears of the ointure of his grandmother Mary of

Modena. He suggests that the good offices of the Court of France should be solicited, especially as France has a right by treaty to demand payment of the arrears, which had been recognised both by William III. and Anne, and that they should direct their Ambassador to England to make representations to that effect. On receiving his full powers from Charles Edward, he would have at once proceeded to Paris, but had not the sum necessary for the journey. He therefore requests a small remittance. "There are in the present (British) cabinet persons suspected of being attached at heart to their legitimate Prince, and further I know for certain, that the Elector himself [George III.] has more than once declared that if the King [Charles Edward] were ever in distress it would be a real pleasure to him to assist him." Mentions the probable success of the Earl of Newburgh's petition for the restoration of his family estates, as a proof of the favourable disposition of the Government. Gives his reasons for desiring the cross of St. Andrew, notwithstanding his life of retirement at Dunkirk. Refutes the arguments against its being granted. Mentions incidentally that the Marquis of Seaforth was his uncle.

f. 173. June 22, 1785. Florence. Original document in Italian whereby Charles Edward revokes and declares null the letter of April 17, 1772, whereby he had charged the jointure and pin-money of the Princess of Stolberg upon the first subsidies he might receive and had increased the latter to 15,000 francs. Sealed and signed :—"Charles Comte d'Albanie." At foot is a certificate under seal from the Comte de Durfort, French Minister Plenipotentiary at Florence, that the notary who has signed the act is such as he is therein described.

f. 175. Copy of a memorial in Italian from the Cardinal Duke to the Pope. Refers to some circumstances attending the legitimation of the Duchess of Albany as being offensive towards him. He has however been won over by the young lady's disposition. Through her intervention, his brother had written a letter of reconciliation to him. Mentions Charles Edward's letter to the French Foreign Minister complaining of the conduct of his wife, referring to "lo scandalo col Conte Alfieri," and to her journey to Baden to rejoin him there, and requesting that the French Court should stop the pension granted to her. The letter had been drawn in the names of Charles Edward and the Cardinal Duke, and had been signed by both. One of the principal causes of disunion between the brothers had been the supposition of Charles Edward that his wife was protected by the Cardinal Duke. Gives a summary of a letter of his sister-in-law to him, who represents herself as in despair at not hearing from him, assures him of her attachment to him, &c., excusing her conduct in various points with regard to which it had never been impeached, but saying not one word about Alfieri. Hears that she is afraid her jointure may according to French law turn out to be invalid, no particular property of Charles Edward having been specifically charged with it. Fears also she may lose her French pension in case of war. She will too late repent of her conduct, which has brought upon her universal disapprobation.

Unsigned and undated, but probably written in 1785.

f. 181. January 23, 1786. Rome. Copy of the registration in Latin of the deed of donation in Italian dated January 18, 1786, by Charles Edward and the Cardinal Duke of certain jewels to the Duchess of Albany.

f. 185. Opinion in French and Italian on the question whether the covenants relating to the payment of the Princess of Stolberg's

LORD BRAYE'S
MSS.

jointure and pin-money were satisfied by the pension of 60,000 francs granted by the King of France. The writer is of opinion that they were, but, that, if possible, a declaration should be obtained from the King that he had granted the pension in consideration of her marriage with Charles Edward, and to relieve him of the obligations he had undertaken. Unsigned and undated.

f. 191. Draft memorial in French to be addressed by Charles Edward to the King of France, requesting him to make such a declaration as is suggested in the foregoing opinion. Unsigned and undated.

f. 193. Undated. Florence. Draft in Italian of a full power from Charles Edward to the advocate Vulpian to settle every question relating to the jointure of the Princess of Stolberg, under certain conditions. The fourth is that the agreement shall contain an absolute release and discharge of all claims and demands whatsoever apart from the stipulations therein so that " we Charles Edward and the said Princess of Stolberg may be considered for all civil purposes, as if we were totally strangers to each other, and that it shall be declared in the same instrument that we have not, and never have had any issue by the said Princess of Stolberg." The object of entering into the agreement is stated to be " to assure for the future fully and finally the tranquillity of ourselves and those connected with us, with which object we have adopted this system of conciliation, which for many reasons we have hitherto been induced to reject."

f. 195. September 27, 1786. Rome. Original power in French executed by Charles Edward before the Chancellor of the French Consulate at Rome to M. Busoni, empowering him, in presence of or acting with the advice of Mons. J. B. Vulpian, to execute along with the Countess of Albany or her representative the agreement whereof a draft is subjoined. Signed:—" Charles Comte d'Albanie " Seal of French Consulate at Rome affixed ; executed in duplicate. The draft agreement after reciting the securing of the jointure of 40,000, and the pin-money of 12,000 livres upon the marriage contract upon the first subsidies received by Charles Edward, the letter of April 17, 1772, the letter of separation of April 3, 1784, the grant by Louis XVI. of a pension of 60,000 francs to the Countess of Albany and of the same sum to Charles Edward, and the claim of the Countess to the jointure of 40,000 secured by the contract in addition to the pension of 60,000 francs, whereas her husband contended that the contract had been satisfied by the grant of the pension, witnesses that the Countess agrees to accept a reduced jointure of 20,000 livres charged on all the property of her husband, and redeemable at any time after a year from his decease at her option for 200,000 livres. Signed as the power.

f. 199. A draft of the said power and agreement.

f. 205. March 10, 1788. Versailles. Letter in French, with envelope, from the Comte de Montmorin to the Duchess of Albany, condoling with her on her father's death and informing her that the king of France would increase her reversionary pension of 10,000 to 20,000 livres. Envelope sealed with seal of French Foreign Office.

f. 208. April 5, 1788. List in French of the letters and papers belonging to the House of Stuart deposited at the English Benedictine Monastery in Paris. Signed by Wm. Cowley.

f. 209. July 22, 1788. List of silver plate, to the value of 3,407 scudi, received from the Duchess of Albany by Tommaso Zapporti, silversmith.

f. 211. September 30, 1788. Copy of a document, partly in Latin and partly in Italian, executed by the Cardinal of York, by which, after reciting that after his father's death he had allowed his brother Charles Edward the sole enjoyment of three rentes of 6,000, 500, and 2,250 livres respectively payable at the Hotel de Ville de Paris, he granted to his niece Charlotte Stuart, Duchess of Albany, to enjoy the same rentes in the same way as his brother had enjoyed them. Extracted by Francesco Gritti of Tusculum, notary public, from the archives of the Roman curia.

f. 213. Calculation, in French, of the income and expenditure of the Duchess of Albany after her father's death. A list is given of the pensions payable under Charles Edward's will, of the household of the duchess, and of the pensions she had to pay. Among them is one of 3,000 scudi to "une personne à Paris" (her mother) one of 100 to Lord Nairne and one of 400 to the Countess of Norton; It appears that she had to pay 4,000 scudi a year to the Countess of Albany, and received 11,000 from her uncle the Cardinal.

f. 215. Accounts, all except the last, in Spanish, relating to the Spanish pensions of the Cardinal of York, consisting of five parts.

The first is a summary of all the receipts from February 15th, 1765, to December 31st, 1788, amounting in all to 15,333,775·3 reals vellon. In addition 222,500 R⁵ Vⁿ the proceeds of previous years had been remitted to Rome in 1789 by bills of exchange and 13,584 in Tobacco and Chocolate by order of the Cardinal.

The second is a detailed account of the revenue derived from each source. It appears by it that the Cardinal had pensions charged on the bishoprics of Jaen, Cordova, Malaga, Segovia and the prebends of Chinchilla, Moron, Heurta de Olmos, Jaca, Hermedes, Puerto de Sánta Maria, Seville, Utrera and Mexico.

The third gives the sum received yearly from each bishopric and the fourth that from each prebend.

The fifth and last is a note in Italian of the payments made by the Cardinal for the administration of his Spanish revenues.

A memorandum in Italian in the Cardinal's hand (?) estimates the yield of the pensions and prebends together for 1787 at 19,840 scudi.

f. 236. Copy of the will and codicil, in Italian, of the Duchess of Albany, made at Bologna, November 14, 1789. Seal of the Archbishop of Bologna affixed.

f. 244 and 247. February 15, 1790. July 18, 1791. Paris. Two original letters in French from Clementine Walkin[g]shaw (Countess D'Albestroff) to the Cardinal of York, written after the death of her daughter the Duchess of Albany. Both are addressed :—"A sa Majesté le Roy D'Angleterre, a Rome." Original envelopes with seals.

f. 250. Account in Italian showing how the sum of 223, 536.63, the proceeds of the sale to the Duke of San Clemente of Charles Edward's palace at Florence had been disposed of. After January 30th, 1790.

f. 252. March 1, 1790. Paris. Letter in French from MM. Busoni and Co. to M. Waters, stating that Mᵣ Barker, the Prior of the English Benedictines in Paris, had placed in their hands two diamonds weighing 22 and 18 carats for the Cardinal Duke.

f. 254. March 12, 1791. Marennes. Letter in French from M. Lortie Dumaine, enclosed in the following. After apologising for his delay from illness in sending the accounts, he states that all salt dues whether belonging to the King or to Seigneurs had been suppressed by the decree of May 16th, 1790. Since April 1st salt has been free. M. de Richelieu and many other seigneurs are in the same position as the King of England's representative, and demand from the National Assembly repayment of the sums they had paid for their rights, but

as the King of England's pension was a present from Louis XVI. he
doubts if his Royal Highness will be allowed an indemnity.

f. 255. May 16, 1791. Paris. Letter in Italian from MM.
Busoni and Company to Louis Giammarile at Rome. After acknowledging his letter of the 27th ult. with an order from the Cardinal of
York to hold 60,000 livres at the disposition of the Marquis Jerome
Belloni, they enclose the foregoing letter. Have received the remit-
tances mentioned and have credited them to the accounts of the Duchess
of Albany and the Cardinal Duke as directed.

Enclosed are accounts signed Lortie Dumaine of the sums received
by him in 1788, 1789, and the first three months of 1790 on account of
the salt dues of the Duchess of Albany amounting in all to 19,961.10.11
livres, from which were deducted vingtièmes and expenses amounting to
2,462.11.6 livres.

f. 259. July 18, 1791. Paris. Letter from MM. Busoni & Co.
to Louis Giammarile, mentioning their payment of 50,000 livres to the
Countess d'Albestroff.

f. 262. July 26, 1791. Paris. Receipt in Italian for the 50,000
livres paid to her by MM. Busoni and Co. on account of the Cardinal
Duke. Signed :—" Clementine Walkin[g]shaw, Comtesse d'Albestroff."
An act of attestation by a notary is added.

f. 267. August 4, 1791. Rome. Draft note in Italian mentioning the arrival of the Countess' receipt, and referring to Busoni's letter
about the diamonds. Unsigned.

f. 268. August 8, 1791. Letter in Italian from Louis Giammarile.
Has received letters from Busoni giving the state of the capital of his
Royal Highness producing a net annual revenue of 45,430 livres.
Refers also to letter of July 18.

f. 270. Copy of memorial in Italian addressed by the Cardinal
Duke to the Pope praying for a declaration that the inventory of the
effects of the Duchess of Albany drawn up by her executor should be
held to be lawful notwithstanding any technical objections to it.
The reply endorsed on it is dated July 14, 1791.

f. 272. Appointment by the Cardinal Duke of York as heir of the
Duchess of Albany, of the Abbé Giuseppe Luigi Flaviani as his pro-
curator for the purpose of concluding the sale to Signor Michele
Maselli of the jewels therein described, the property of the late Duchess,
for the sum of 7,600 scudi to be paid by instalments. Signed—" Enrico
Cardinale." (Undated, but written in 1792.)

f. 274. April 4, 1792. Rome. The act of sale, in Italian, in pursuance of the last powers.

f. 276. Account in Italian showing the payments made by Maselli
and the interest on the unpaid balance carried down to December
1793.

## VOL. III.

f. 1. February 1, 1794. Alost. Letter in French from D. B.
Lescailler, Grand Prior of Anchin, to the Cardinal Duke. Relates
to the sufferings of himself and his monks in consequence of the
French Revolution. Deprecates the distraints which he has heard
the Cardinal Duke intends to levy by means of the Comte de Walsh
Serrant on the property of the Abbey in the Netherlands, to enforce
payment of his share, a measure which has already been taken as to the
property of the abbey of St. Amand. Has sent two of his monks to the
Nuncio at Brussels to request his mediation.

f. 5. February 2, 1794. Brussels. Note in French from M. de LORD BRAYE'S MSS. Limon to the Nuncio at Brussels, stating that he had forwarded to the Comte de Walsh the letter of the Cardinal Duke. Had been appointed to act for the Comte during his absence in London, and in particular to consent to the removal of the sequestration, provided that the monks would give at least a general account.

f. 7. Monday, Febuary 3, [1794]. Letter in French, in the hand of the Duchess of Fitz-James, to the Cardinal of York. Acknowledges a letter of January 21st. M. de Serran (Walsh) had on his departure left his powers and instructions with M. de Limon. Assures him of her devotion. If he has not heard from her for four months, her letters must have been lost. Postscript. Has seen the Nuncio since she wrote.

f. 9. February 4, 1794. Brussels. Letter in French from M. de Limon to the Cardinal Duke enclosing a copy of that of the Comte de Walsh, dated January 31st. Remarks that the monks seem to be intriguing with the Nuncio.

f. 13. January 31, [1794]. London. The copy referred to in the last in French from the Comte de Walsh-Serrant to M. de Limon. He defends the active steps he had taken to put an end to the monks' delays, and bring matters to a conclusion. As general news, he mentions that the bishop of Autun [Talleyrand] has been positively ordered to leave the country, and a report that M. Mack [afterwards capitulator of Ulm] has just arrived to settle the plan of the campaign.

f. 17. February 4, 1794. Brussels. Letter in Italian from the Nuncio at Brussels (Cæsar, Archbishop of Nisibis *in partibus*) to the Cardinal Duke, on the affairs of the Abbeys of St. Amand and Anchin. Mentions that the Duchess of Fitz-James was then at Brussels. Seal of arms.

f. 22. Same date. A second letter from the same to the same, enclosing a letter from the Duchess [of Fitz-James], which she had asked him to forward, and also one from M. de Limon. He likewise encloses the copy of the letters of January 31, with his marginal observations.

f. 24. Letter in French to the Nuncio from M. de Limon, being that enclosed in the last, enclosing a copy of that of January 31st, and requesting him to forward to the Cardinal Duke his letters of the same date. There are some observations in Italian by the Nuncio, addressed to the Cardinal Duke in the margin of the letter and inclosure.

f. 26. Letter in French from the Duchess of Fitz-James to the Cardinal Duke. Has just returned from Paris. Has not succeeded about her affairs. Her husband exceedingly ill. (Undated, but probably written from Brussels early in 1794.)

f. 28. February 18, 1794. Rome. Letter in Italian sending a draft reply to the letter of M. Lescailler of the 1st instant for the Cardinal Duke's approval. Makes various suggestions for his reply to the Nuncio's letters of the 4th instant. Unsigned.

f. 29. The draft answer in French referred to in the last. Announces that the sequestration on the property of the abbey will be removed. It is necessary for him to have an agent at Brussels.

f. 31. Feb. 21, 1794. Letter in Italian from the Nuncio to the Cardinal Duke, on the affairs of St. Amand and Anchin. His reasons for delay. Disapproves of M. de Limon. Encloses a copy of the accounts of St. Amand, and a complaint of the monks of Anchin relating to waste committed in their woods. The inclosures mentioned in the last, are :—

f. 35. (1.) February 17, 1794. Alost. Letter in French from
Louis Brunion, monk of Anchin, to Monseigneur [the Nuncio at Brussels]
complaining of the waste committed in the woods of Carinois, and
asking him to remonstrate with the Government at Brussels.

f. 37. (2.) A fragment of an unsigned and undated memorial on the
same subject as the last. Endorsed in Italian—"Original memorial of
the monks of Anchin."

f. 30. (3.) February 20, 1794. Detailed account of the rents and
profits, and also of the charges and outgoings, of the property of the
Abbey of St. Amand, in the Netherlands, and in the part of France
conquered by the allies, from which it appears that the net revenue was
50, 191 livres, but that much of it was derived from uncertain sources,
and was difficult to collect. Signed :—Philippe Devienne.

f. 47. February 27, 1794. London. Letter in French from the
Comte de Walsh to the Cardinal Duke. The Count fears that some one
has been prejudicing him against him. The Nuncio from the month of
August last had in his letters to Rome appeared to be engaged in the affairs
of the Abbey of St. Amand, but the Count found, on his arrival at Brussels
on the 8th of October, that he had done nothing. The Count immediately
went to the abbey, and his letter from Tournay had informed the Cardinal
of the monks' insubordinate tone and of their plan for gaining time. The
Nuncio on the Count's return paralysed his proceedings, and did not write
to the monks till December. Complains of his conduct in general, and
defends himself. Will return to Brussels in a fortnight. Seal of
arms.

f. 50. March 2, 1794. St. Amand. Letter in French from the
Secretary of the Chapter of St. Amand, on behalf of the superior and
monks, to the Nuncio at Brussels. After mentioning his request that
they should make an offer to the Cardinal Duke, they offer for that
year 20,000 livres, and ask for his good offices on their behalf.

f. 52. March 4, 1794. Note in French from M. de Limon to the
Nuncio, forwarding the letter of February 27th from the Comte de
Walsh to the Cardinal of York, and mentioning that the writer would
be at his then address on the 15th of this month.

f. 54. March 18, 1794. Brussels. Letter in French from the
Comte de Walsh to the Cardinal Duke. Mentions the arrival of the
Emperor at Brussels on the 9th, and the steps he had since taken and
his reasons for them. Has not time to copy the memorial he had drawn
up to Count Traut[t]smansdorff, but will send it by the next post. Seal
of arms.

f. 57. Copy of the long memorial in French referred to in the last,
addressed to Count Trauttmansdorff, Privy Councillor and Minister of
State of his Majesty the Emperor and King, Chancellor of the Netherlands, by the Comte de Walsh-Serrant, as procurator of the Cardinal
Duke for everything concerning the abbeys of St. Amand and Anchin.
It sets forth the special circumstances distinguishing the claims of the
Cardinal Duke for relief against the sequestration of the property
situated in Flanders of the French abbeys from those of all other
sufferers from the same sequestration. His exceptional position
prevents any favour shown him being used as a precedent by others.

f. 59. December 19, 1795. Penna. Letter in English from M. . .
Countess Norton to the Cardinal Duke, thanking him for his benevolence to her.

f. 61. October 29, 1799. Grosvenor Street. Extract from a letter from
Sir John Cox Hippisley, Bart., to Andrew Stuart, Esq., M.P. He encloses

a letter from Cardinal Borgia, setting forth the present poverty of the Cardinal of York. In such a case the relief is not to be decorously sought in the liberality of private individuals, although many who have witnessed the acts of princely benevolence of the Cardinal would doubtless press forward to alleviate his sufferings. Cardinal Borgia is allowed to be a prelate of great probity, intelligence, and urbanity, and his palace was the resort of all lovers of science and virtu. The late Pope, anticipating the calamities that soon after befel him, appointed Cardinal Borgia President of the Congregation to whom the whole authority of the See was delegated. His Eminence probably recollects that the writer, during his last residence in Rome, was in correspondence with His Majesty's Ministers on subjects of considerable importance to both states, and knows that his proper resort is to the highest authority in the nation.

Appended is a memorandum that the original of this letter, with that of Mr. Stuart to Mr. Secretary Dundas, and additional observations by Sir John Cox Hippisley were transmitted to the King by Mr. Pitt. "Sir J. C. H. had the pleasure to receive letters from the Duke of Portland, Lord Chatham, Lord Spencer, and Mr. Secretary Windham (all Ministers of State), strongly expressing their satisfaction in acquiescing in any measure that could offer relief to the illustrious and venerable Cardinal of York. It was sufficient that the knowledge of his sufferings should reach the Throne, to assure both sympathy and relief. Mr. Pitt, Mr. Secretary Dundas, and the Lord Chancellor, also expressed to Sir John Hippisley the extreme pleasure they felt in recommending the measure to the royal consideration."

f. 64. October 30, 1799. Lower Grosvenor Street. Extract of a letter from Andrew Stuart, Esq., M.P., to Mr. Secretary Dundas. He encloses a letter from Cardinal Borgia to Sir John Hippisley, dated the 14th of September, from Padua, where Cardinal York then was with the other Cardinals for the election of a Pope. He also encloses a letter from Sir John Hippesley. While at Rome, he was informed of the very heavy losses the Cardinal sustained from the French Revolution, amounting to no less than 48,000 crowns annually. At a later period, the largest parts of his valuable jewels were sacrificed amid the contributions levied by the French.

f. 67. January 20, 1800. London. Letter from Thomas Coutts to the Cardinal Duke of York. The Cardinal will remember to have seen at Frascati in 1790, a Mr. Coutts and his wife and three daughters. The eldest daughter is now married to the Earl of Guildford, and the second to Sir Francis Burdett, whose family has been much attached to the House of Stuart as late as 1745 and since. "The third is unmarried and living with her mother and me, and remembers the distinguished honour she received at Frascati, when you put on her finger with your own royal hand the ring which King Charles wore at his coronation. On my return to England, giving an account of what I had seen abroad to his Majesty King George the Third, I did not ommit (sic) a particular detail of the honours I had received at Frascati, and of the uncommon politeness as well as the elegant and princely manner in which they were conferred. Neither did I fail to notice the very handsome and most liberal terms in which your sentiments of his character were expressed. I had also the honour of showing at that time to his Majesty the silver medal given to me with so much condescension at Frascati. He questioned me on the likeness, said he was much pleased to have seen it, imply'd that few he supposed would have mentioned the subject to him, but that they were much mistaken

who imagined he did not very sincerely regard the family of Stuart,
who were worthy of all good men's attention, were it only for their misfortune.  He was so good [as] to receive and accept from me with his
own hand the medal I had the honour to receive from yours."  " I have
long been acknowledged his banker, and I have also transacted the
business of all his royal sons, and have from them all received the
most flattering marks of approbation. . . . . . My remaining and only
ambition is to be the hand by which the benevolence of Britain from
the best of men shall be conveyed to the last of that illustrious line,
the rightful former sovereigns of Scotland, England, and Ireland."  It
lies with you to make the choice.  Two words from you to my relation Lord Minto, to Mr. Pitt, or to Lord Grenville, my friends, to Mr.
Dundas, or to the Lord Chancellor, my schoolfellow, would settle the
matter.

f. 69.  A duplicate of the last letter.

f. 72.  Two pieces of paper with the name and address of Mr.
Coutts.  Two are in the Cardinal Duke's hand.

f. 74.  February 9, 1800.  Vienna.  Letter in French from Lord
Minto to the Cardinal of York.  He has received orders from the
King of Great Britain to remit to his Eminence the sum of 2,000*l.*
(Printed, but not quite accurately, in Jesse's *Memorials of the Pre-
tenders*, vol. ii., p. 159.)

f. 79.  Letter of same date from the same to the same in French.
Recommends Mr. Oakley, who has undertaken to be the bearer of
the last, and assures the Cardinal that if he has any observations to
make on the details, he can safely do so through him.

A note is enclosed advising the Cardinal how he should draw the
money placed to his credit at Coutts'.

f. 82.  Draft, or copy, in English, of the Cardinal's answer expressing his gratitude.  (Printed in Ewald's *Life and Times of Prince
Charles Stuart*, vol. ii., p. 340.)

f. 84.  March 15, 1800.  Vienna.  Letter from Lord Minto to Mr.
Oakley, expressing his satisfaction at the manner in which he has performed his mission.

f. 87.  Draft, or copy, of a letter in English from the Cardinal Duke
to Sir J. C. Hippisley, expressing his gratitude.  (In the hand of
Father Connolly, of San Clemente, Rome.  Undated, but probably
written about this time.  Perhaps that referred to as of February 26th
in the next.)

f. 89.  March 31, 1800.  Letter from Sir J. C. Hippisley to the
Cardinal Duke.  (Printed in Jesse's *Memorials of the Pretenders*,
vol. ii., p. 162.)

f. 91.  April 15, 1800.  Grosvenor Street.  Copy of a letter in
Italian (or a translation of one) from Sir J. C. Hippisley to the
Cardinal Duke, enclosing a note to Sig. Patrick Moir, English banker
at Rome.  Refers to the mode of drawing the allowance, and also to a
temporary advance of 500*l.* made by the writer's bankers.

f. 93.  The note enclosed in the last of the same date advises Mr.
Moir, that 2,000*l.* will be credited at Coutts' to the Cardinal in the
middle of the following July, and requests Mr. Moir to assist him, in
case he wishes to draw part of it previously.

f. 95.  April 23, 1800.  Draft, or copy, of note in Italian to Mr.
Coutts, acknowledging his letter in duplicate of January 20.

f. 97.  Same date.  Draft, or copy, of letter in Italian to Mr.
Andrew Stuart from the Cardinal Duke, thanking him for his services.

f. 99. July 6, 1800. Draft, or copy, in the hand of Father Connolly, LORD BRAYE'S MSS. of a letter from the Cardinal of York to Sir J. C. Hippisley. Has returned to Rome on June 25th. He is actually in greater distress than he was in some months ago, for on going southwards he has been informed of the devastation of his residences at Rome and Frascati. He would like to be able to draw upon a banker, half-yearly.

f. 101. August 20, 1800. Grosvenor Street. Letter from Sir J. C. Hippisley to the Cardinal of York. He suggests that the Cardinal should in his next letter mention the loss of the Italian "Luogi di Monti" etc., not so much for the satisfaction of his Majesty, as for that of the minister of finance. He hopes that the Cardinal will support the reform which Pius VI. considered so reasonable, that of national superiors [of the English, Irish, and Scotch Colleges at Rome]. If it is not confirmed, the English Ministers will be greatly dissatisfied. The Pope, in a letter to him of the 10th of May last, expressed his wish to show the same favourable sentiments towards England as distinguished his predecessor. Ministers have requested him to draw up a memoir on the subject of the Catholics of Ireland, arrangements for whom will soon be brought forward.

f. 103. August 2, 1800. London. Letter from Andrew Stuart to the Cardinal Duke, apologising for his delay, caused by bad health in replying to the Cardinal's letter of April 23rd, and referring to his *Genealogical History of the Stuarts.* (Enclosed in the last.)

f. 105. October 17, 1800. Frascati. Draft, or copy, in the hand of Father Connolly, of a letter in English from the Cardinal Duke to Sir J. C. Hippisley. Conscience, inclination, honour and obligation alike require him to use all possible endeavours, where there is a question of his nation and country as in the affair of the national colleges.

f. 107. October 21, 1800. Frascati. Draft, or copy, in the same hand of a letter from the same to the same, mentioning that he had enclosed in the last a copy of his letter of July 6th, which had not reached Sir J. C. Hippisley, and enclosing another copy thereof, and also one of the last letter.

f. 109. December 5, 1800. Grosvenor Street. Letter from Sir J. C. Hippisley to the Cardinal Duke, acknowledging the last two letters, and also that of July 6th. Advises him to draw at once on Messrs. Coutts for 2,000l., with a letter of advice stating it is for the half yearly payment, which he understood was settled to be drawn at their house. Seal of arms.

f. 111. January 8, 1801. Rome. Copy of a receipt from Cardinal York for 2,000l., the allowance for the first half of 1801.

f. 112. February 10, 1801. London. Letter from Sir J. C. Hippisley to the Cardinal Duke. Announces "the extraordinary change in our administration, Lord Grenville, Lord Spencer, Lord Camden, Mr. Pitt, Mr. Dundas and Mr. Windham having resigned their places as cabinet ministers, differing in opinion with the King on the subject of the Roman Catholic measures proposed by them to be adopted in favour of the subjects of that Communion. The King considers the *extent* of those measures as militating against his Coronation Oath, but has avowed every sentiment of conviction of the merits of those who seek further extension of their privileges. The Duke of Portland now at the head of the Administration has ever been a fast friend of the Catholics." Hopes that Rome will not consider this as any *hostile* act against her. Difficult position of the Duke of Portland on account of the Dissenters, and of his position as Chancellor of the University of Oxford. Requests the Cardinal to communicate these facts to the

Cardinal Secretary of State, such events being always liable to mis-interpretation. Will arrange the Cardinal's business with the Duke of Portland to his entire satisfaction. Announces his intended marriage to a friend of his late wife, "having paid the tribute of 18 months' mourning." Requests the Cardinal to convey his thanks to the Pope for his favourable intention with regard to the national colleges. It will be an excellent argument in support of Mr. Pitt's opinion.

*Postscript.*—He has just heard that the Duke of Portland prefers to remain Secretary of State, but he will settle the Cardinal's business equally well with Mr. Addington if he takes the Treasury.

f. 115. An Italian translation of part of the last letter (in Father Connolly's hand).

f. 117. March 30, 1801. Downing Street. Copy of a letter from Lord Hawkesbury, Secretary of State for the Foreign Department, to Sir J. C. Hippisley, announcing that care will be taken that future payments of the allowance to the Cardinal of York shall be regularly made.

f. 119. An Italian translation of the last letter.

f. 121. April 7, 1801. Grosvenor Street. Letter from Sir J. C. Hippisley to the Cardinal Duke, enclosing the above copy of the letter of Lord Hawkesbury, to whom he had transmitted the correspondence relating to the allowance, and assuring the Cardinal that he will always take care of "that delicate and important business" in any future change of ministers.

f. 123. May 11, 1801. Copy, in Father Conolly's hand, of the reply of the Cardinal to the last letter, thanking Sir John for his services, and referring to the affair of the national colleges.

f. 125. June 1, 1801. Grosvenor Street. Sir J. C. Hippisley to the Cardinal Duke, enclosing another copy of Lord Hawkesbury's letter. Mentions the death of Mr. Andrew Stuart.

f. 127. Copy of a letter [from the Cardinal Duke to Lord Minto] probably written in the spring of 1801. Refers to the letter received from him at Venice about this time last year. His situation is worse if possible than it was a twelvemonth ago.

f. 130. November 2, 1802. Florence. Autograph letter in French from the Countess of Albany, acknowledging the receipt from the Cardinal Duke of 1,000 scudi, in full discharge of all arrears up to September 30th, 1802, and, in consideration of his written promise to pay her in future 1,000 scudi quarterly, releasing all other claims and demands.

f. 132. January 3, 1803. Frascati. Copy, in Father Connolly's hand, of a letter in English from the Cardinal Duke to Messrs. Coutts, stating that he has committed the entire management of his domestic economy to Monseigneur Angelo Cesarini, Bishop of Milevi, whom he has authorized to draw on him for the allowance.

f. 134. January 6, 1803. Frascati. Draft letter in Italian from the Bishop of Milevi to Messrs. Coutts, announcing that he has been authorised to draw the pension, and referring to the arrangements for remitting it.

f. 136. Same date. Draft in Italian of the appointment of the Bishop by the Cardinal Duke, and an Italian translation of the letter of the 3rd.

f. 140. January 30, [1803]. Lyons. Letter from Cardinal Fesch (maternal uncle of Napoleon Buonaparte) to the Cardinal Duke, thanking him for his letter of congratulation on his elevation to the Cardinalate, and also for his having employed his interest in his favour.

f. 142. February 4, 1803. The Strand, London. Letter from LORD BRAYE'S MSS. Mr. Coutts to the Cardinal Duke, stating that he has received the Christmas half-year of the allowance, and that he has used every means in his power to obtain an addition to the allowance, but hitherto without success.

f. 144. February 11, 1803. London. Letter in French from Messrs. Coutts to the Bishop of Milevi, acknowledging his letter and enclosures of January 6th, and stating that they have accordingly opened an account in his name to which they have credited the 2,000*l.* received for the half-year ended on January 5th. They decline to charge any commission for their services.

f. 147. March 2, May 8, June 18, 1803. Drafts in Italian of three letters from the Bishop of Milevi to Messrs. Coutts, advising them that he has drawn on them in favour of Mr. Alexander Sloane.

f. 150. July 5, 1803. Draft receipt in Italian by the Bishop of Milevi to Messrs. Coutts for the allowance of the first six months of 1803.

f. 151. August 2, September 15, November 5, 1803. December 24, 1804 [3]. Two drafts in Italian, and two drafts or copies in French, of business letters from the Bishop of Milevi to Messrs. Coutts.

f. 156. Copy of receipt enclosed in the last for the first six months of 1804.

f. 157. January 13, February 10, June 12, April 17, June 16, 1804. Three business letters from Messrs. Coutts to the Bishop of Milevi, with copies of two replies of the Bishop.

f. 166. July 5, 1804. Copy of receipt enclosed in the last letter for the last six months of 1804.

f. 167. September 14, 1804. Rome. Copy of a letter from the Bishop of Milevi to Messrs. Coutts, announcing Mr. Sloane's failure, and that he will consequently in future draw upon them in favour of M. Joseph Aquari.

f. 168. December 15, 1804. Rome. Copy of a letter from the same to Mr. Coutts, enclosing the Cardinal Duke's receipt for the allowance for the first six months of 1805, and mentioning certain drafts. He entreats him to use his good offices with the Court to procure an increase of the allowance, without which the Cardinal will find himself much embarrassed, and refers to the loss of his subsidies from France since 1790.

f. 170. 1804. Two drafts in Latin of an inscription to be placed on a nunnery of which Henrietta Cesarini was abbess, commemorating the bounty of the Cardinal Duke in discharging its debts.

f. 173. 1804. Draft in Latin of an inscription commemorating the munificence of the Cardinal Duke in removing a seminary which was unhealthy in summer from malaria, and re-erecting it on a more healthy site.

f. 175. Draft decree in Italian by the Cardinal Duke, directed to be published by every parson in his dioceses of Ostia and Velletri relating to the education of the clergy at the seminary at Velletri. Undated, but later than September 26, 1803, the date of his translation to Ostia and Velletri.

f. 176. February 1, 1805. London. Letter from Messrs. Coutts to the Bishop of Milevi. Concludes with assuring him that they will make representations with regard to the last part of his letter in the proper quarter, but holding out no hopes of success in consequence of the bad circumstances of the times.

f. 178. March 9, 1805. Copy of a business letter from the Bishop to Messrs. Coutts.

f. 180.  June 8, 1805.  Copy of a letter from the same to the same. After referring to some business, he again hopes they will be able to procure some increase in the allowance.  Assures them that the Cardinal's firmness in refusing to apply for assistance elsewhere is surprising at the age of 80.

f. 184.  July 19, 1805.  Reply to the last letter.

f. 186.  September 11, 1805.  Paris.  Original letter in French from Edward, Duke of Fitz-James, to his Majesty the Cardinal of York, announcing the death of his father.

f. 188.  October 3, 1805.  Frascati.  Copy of the answer thereto.

f. 189.  September 21, December 1, 1805, March 1, March 4, 1806. Drafts of three business letters from the Bishop of Milevi to Messrs. Coutts, and the reply of Messrs. Coutts to the first two.

f. 196.  April 8, 1806.  S. Clemente, Rome.  Letter in Italian from Father Conolly to the Bishop of Milevi.  He had the honour three years before to present at Frascati young Lord Althorp to his Highness, who had received him most graciously, and promised to send him one of his medals.  Lord Althorp not having received it before his departure requested Father Conolly to forward it to him in England.  On the recent change of Ministry on Mr. Pitt's death, Lord Althorp has been appointed a Lord of the Treasury, and his father, Lord Spencer, Home Secretary.  He is convinced that they will be much gratified, if in the letter of congratulation which he is writing to Lord Althorp, he can inform him that he has received the medal for him.  He therefore requests that it may be sent.

f. 198.  June 4, August 27, October 24, August 1, 1806.  Three business letters from the Bishop of Milevi to Messrs. Coutts, and answer of Messrs. Coutts to the letters of March 1 and 4.

f. 206.  Copies of the receipts for the allowance payable July 5, 1806, and January 5, 1806.

f. 208.  October 15, 1806.  Frascati.  Draft letter in Italian from the Bishop of Milevi to Prince Augustus [Duke of Sussex].  Has lately heard of him through Mr. Fagan who has been at Frascati.  The Cardinal Duke has directed him to write and present his compliments to him.  The Cardinal Duke is as well as his age of 82 permits.  His circumstances would be much reduced but for the generosity of the Royal Family, which he attributes in great measure to the Duke's influence.  The writer will ever preserve a grateful recollection of the attention shown him by the Duke during his stay in those parts.

f. 209.  February 28, July 11, May 8, 1807.  Drafts of two business letters from the Bishop of Milevi to Messrs. Coutts, with their reply to the first.

f. 214.  March 28, 1807.  Lisbon.  Letter in Italian from Monsignor Caleppi, the Nuncio at Lisbon, to the Bishop of Milevi.  Thanks him for charging him with the commission of forwarding the letter of February 28 to Messrs. Coutts.

f. 216.  Account in Italian of the post mortem examination of the remains of the Cardinal Duke of York made at Rocca del Tuscolo, on the evening of July 14th, 1807, by Giuseppe Gegeo.

f. 218.  July 18, 1807.  Rome.  Copy of a letter in French from the Bishop of Milevi to Messrs. Coutts announcing the death of the Cardinal on July 13th at two hours of the night [between 9 and 10 p.m.].

f. 219.  July 21, [1807].  Letter in French from the Countess of Albany to the Bishop of Milevi.  Condoles with him on the separation after a friendship of 40 years.  Approves that the Cardinal Duke appointed him his executor.  Cannot express how sensible she is of the

Cardinal Duke's remembrance of her; is confident that her jointure will be paid regularly. Signed:—"Louise de Stolberg, C. d'Albany."

f. 221. August 25, 1807. Duplicate of a letter in French dated August 21, 1807, from Messrs. Coutts to the Bishop of Milevi, expressing their regret at the death of the Cardinal Duke, and stating there was now standing to the credit of the Bishop of Milevi 1,999*l.* 3*s.* 0*d.* At the end is added a letter acknowledging the Bishop's of October 24, 1806, which has just arrived.

f. 223. August 30, 1807. Rome. Draft of a letter in Italian from the Bishop of Milevi to the Prince of Wales. Refers to his intimacy for more than 38 years with the deceased Cardinal Duke, as placing him in a position to testify to the sentiments of gratitude felt by the Cardinal towards the English Royal Family for their assistance, and his desire to show them some mark of it. Among the property left by the Cardinal the only objects he has found which can deserve the acceptance of the Prince are the Cross of St. Andrew set with diamonds, which had been worn by King Charles I., and a ring set with a ruby engraved with a cross, which he had often heard from the Cardinal was placed on the finger of the Kings of Scotland at their Coronation. These he desires to offer the Prince, and requests him to indicate some safe means for transmitting them.

f. 225. Another draft of the same, differing in some respects, in which the cross is said to have been worn by James I. and James II.

f. 227. French translations of the drafts.

f. 231. Same date. Copy of a letter from the Bishop to Messrs. Coutts, requesting them to forward the enclosed letter to the Prince of Wales, and mentioning that the Cardinal Duke wished to leave them as a legacy (blank) which he will send them on the first opportunity.

f. 233. Same date. Draft letter in Italian from the Bishop to Monsignor Caleppi, the Nuncio at Lisbon, enclosing the packet for Messrs. Coutts, which he requests him to forward on the first opportunity. Mentions that the Cardinal Duke has left him a small legacy.

f. 234. October 10, 1807. Lisbon. Reply of the Nuncio to the last letter. Has forwarded the packet and has also written as requested to Prince Augustus [the Duke of Sussex], asking him to use his influence to procure the continuance for at least a year of the pensions enjoyed by the Cardinal Duke.

f. 236. Friday, November 13, [1807]. Letter in French from the Countess of Albany to the Bishop of Milevi. Acknowledges the receipt of the presents left her by the Cardinal of York and of the picture he had chosen for her, which she considers is better than any work of the same painter at Florence. Thanks the Bishop for having her cipher placed on the watch left her by the Cardinal. She would have been satisfied had she been left only a pin as a remembrance. Was sure that the Bishop would not have delayed sending her her legacy without excellent reasons. Signed and addressed as the letter of July 21st, but directed "a Frascati."

f. 238. November 14, 1807. Ston Easton, Somerset. Letter in French from Sir J. C. Hippisley to the Bishop of Milevi, expressing his regret at the news of the death of the Cardinal Duke. Encloses a copy of a letter from the Prince of Wales in reply to that of August 30. The Prince directs him to express "the profound respect which he will always preserve for the memory of the late Cardinal Duke, and the great pleasure the presents will give him, which the friendship of his Royal Highness had destined for him." The Prince has charged him with the care of their transmission to England. He therefore requests the Bishop to place them in the hands of his brother-in-law, M. Cicciaporci, through M. Orsi, banker at Florence, who will find a safe opportunity to forward them to England. The King has ordered him to acquaint the Countess of Albany of his intention to allow her a pension of 1,600*l.* a year for her life. Has received a second letter from the Secretary of the Prince of Wales, charging him to express the above stated sentiments of the Prince.

The enclosure is from Colonel J. McMahon, M.P., Private Secretary of the Prince, to Sir J. C. Hippisley, and is dated at Carlton House, November 10th, forwarding the letters of the Bishop of Milevi and requesting him to take such steps as may be proper and necessary for the Prince to observe on the occasion, as H.R.H. invests him with full powers to act for him in this business and to receive whatever the late Cardinal York may have desired to be given to H.R.H.

f. 240.    An Italian translation of the last letter and enclosure.

f. 242.    Draft or copy in Italian of the answer to the last. Had he known where Sir J. C. Hippisley was, he would have communicated to him the death of the Cardinal Duke, and forwarded through him his letters to the Prince of Wales, but being informed he had been appointed Governor of some part of India he has sent them through Messrs. Coutts. Is gratified that the Prince has charged Sir John with the transmission of the gifts to England. Will send them to Florence as desired on the first safe opportunity. At present it would be dangerous, as all the roads are closed and Tuscany is entirely in the hands of the French. Is glad to hear that the King has granted the pension to the Countess of Albany, but points out that she already has 4,000 scudi a year, which absorbs almost all the proceeds of the assets of the Cardinal Duke, so that his own dependents cannot have their pay during her life. (Unsigned and undated, but written early in 1808.)

.    f. 244.    November 29, 1807.    Frascati.    Letter from the Bishop of of Milevi to the Minister D. Antonio Vargas.    Assures him he will search as requested for any papers that may be interesting to the Duchess of Berwick, but reminds him that owing to the quantity of documents it will require time to go through them all.

f. 246.    November 30, 1807.    Rome.    Draft letter from the Bishop of Milevi to Monsignor Caleppi, in answer to his letter of October 10. Thanks him for writing " al neto personaggio " [the Duke of Sussex]. The only cause for his importunity is his wish to provide for the Cardinal Duke's poor household.

f. 248.    January 2, 1808.    Rome.    Draft letter in Italian from the Bishop of Milevi to the Countess of Albany.    Has received through Cardinal Consalvi the letter of Sir J. C. Hippisley, and congratulates her on the pension granted her by the King, and hopes she may live many years to enjoy it.    Hopes she will again visit these parts.    His villa will be always at her disposal.

f. 249.    January 26, [1808].    The answer to the last.    " I thank you with all my heart for your interest in me.    I was sure that you would have been gratified at the favour the King of England has granted me.    I find that you have done well in having sent to the Prince of Wales the Order of St. Andrew.    In your whole behaviour since the death of my brother-in-law, you have shown yourself worthy of his confidence, and that he could have not have made a better choice." Hopes at her next journey to Rome to visit him at his hermitage at Frascati. Signed, addressed, and directed as the letter of November 13. Seal of arms.

f. 251. July 6, 1808. Rome. Draft copy of a letter in a mixture of French and Italian from the Bishop of Milevi to Messrs. Coutts, stating that he has not yet drawn the 1,000*l.* remaining to his credit from the difficulty of finding buyers of letters of exchange on London. Mentions that he has a legacy for Mr. Coutts and one for Sir John Hippisley, which he is waiting for an opportunity to send.

f. 253. Another draft of the same letter written the previous April.

f. 255. September 22, 1808. Reply of Messrs. Coutts. After the business part of the letter, they enquire what the legacy is.

f. 257. September 1, 1808. Draft of another reply of the Bishop of Milevi to Sir J. C. Hippisley's letter of November 14th, written because he doubted whether the first had reached him. Refers to the legacies left to Sir John by the Cardinal Duke, viz., a Plutarch in two volumes folio, a MS. with miniatures, and a gold medal, and the veil of Mary Stuart. Had forgotten in his grief that the best way of sending them was through M. Cicciaporci. Refers to the pension granted to the Countess of Albany, and suggests it would be worthy of the generosity of the King of England, to make some provision for the household, amounting to 56 persons, of the Cardinal Duke, as his assets are swallowed up by the charges on them, and they have nothing to depend on except what may have been due at his death from his Spanish benefices. His importunity is due only to his desire that some assistance may be given to the poor household, and to his wish to erect a monument in St. Peter's, where the Cardinal Duke and his father and brother are buried. Asks Sir John to press his request on the Prince of Wales, whenever he may have a favourable opportunity. Forwarded by the agent of the Nuncio at Lisbon.

(The Plutarch, which is a fine copy of the first Latin edition printed by Ulric Han, probably in 1470, (a copy of the same edition is in Lord Spencer's library, see *Bibliotheca Spenceriana*, ii. 376), the veil, and the medal are now in the possession of J. Fortescue Horner, Esq., of Mells Park, Frome, a maternal descendant of Sir John Hippisley.)

f. 261. December 19, 1808. Rome. Draft of another reply in the same terms as the last, to be forwarded through MM. Busoni & Co. to Messrs. Coutts.

f. 263. January 28, 1809. Rome. Draft letter in French from the Bishop of Milevi to Messrs. Coutts, acknowledging their letter of September 22, 1808, and advising them that he has drawn bills upon them for the balance at his credit. The legacy is a gold enamelled snuff-box, on the lid of which is a portrait of the Cardinal Duke, with a border of Oriental pearls, an etui à voyage, two small porcelain vases set with gold, and a gold medal of James II. Has informed Sir John Hippisley of the particulars of his legacy.

f. 265. March 1, 1809. Rome. Draft letter in Italian from the Bishop of Milevi to Sir J. C. Hippisley. Renews his application on behalf of the Cardinal Duke's household, and intreats that at least a temporary allowance of 1,000*l.* may be granted them during the life of the Countess of Albany.

LORD BRAYE'S MSS.  f. 267.   Extract from will and codicil of Tiburzio Tuzi of Musellaro bequeathing a dowry of 30 scudi (reduced to 20 by the codicil), to be given yearly on the day of his death to a poor girl of Musellaro, to be nominated by the Marquis Valerio di Sanctacroce and his descendants.  Italian.  Undated.

f. 268.   List, in Italian, of the documents, some originals and some copies, relative to the interests in Poland of the Royal house of Stuart.

The latest dated document is assigned to 1774, but, as a copy of the will of the Cardinal Duke of York is mentioned, the list was apparently compiled after his death.

---

## THE MANUSCRIPTS OF B. R. T. BALFOUR, ESQ., OF TOWNLEY HALL, DROGHEDA.

MR. BALFOUR'S MSS.  DURING a recent visit to Ireland I came across the following documents at Townley Hall, near Drogheda :—

A small 4° volume of 173 pages of paper, bound in red morocco, containing private devotions, meditations, and other notes, in the hand of King James the Second.  It was bought at Rome in 1842, together with some Jacobite relics, from the Marchese Sigismondo Malatesta, nephew and heir of Bishop Cesarini, who formerly had all the personal effects of Cardinal York.  Some extracts from this volume have been already printed in the " *Life of James the Second*," edited by J. S. Clarke, but I have made a few others which seem to possess some historical interest.  In these I have retained the original spelling.

f. 1.  " T'was the divine Providence that drove me early out of my native county, and obliged me for self preservation to save myself from the hands of my enemys, and seek for shelter in foraine partes, and t'was the same providence ordred it so that I past most of the twelve years I was abroad in Catholike kingdomes, by which means I came to know what their religion was, which is all liklyhood I never had been so happy as to have done, had not that dismal revolution happned, for had I remained in quiat at home, in all appearence, it would have been impossible for me (considering the care was taken to breed me up with a prejudice to Catholike Religion) ever to have known the true maxims of it, and conceqnently continud in the errors I had been bred up in, which nothing but tyme and the grace of God could have effected in me, espesially considering how little aplication yonge men of the age I was then of have to any thing that is good or of that kind, being for the most part led away by the heat of their temper and ill example ; notwithstanding all which the devine providence ordred it so that I began to be sensible *by experiance* that I had had wrong notions given me of the Ca[tholike] Rei[igion], and that they were not guilty of several things they were falsely taxed with, so that by degrees I was convinced that the Prot[estants] had wrongfully seperated themselves and were fallen of[f] from the true Church. . . . My cheef designe of writing this paper is to give some advice to new converts, and to such whose harts are touched, and have inclinations to find out the truth, and when they have found it, to behave themselves as becomes true converts, which is to live up to the height of Christianity, or at least to do thier parts to endeavor it, and tho I acknowlidg to my owne shame I did not do it so sone as I was throwly convinced of the truth of the Religion I now

proffesse, I am desirous others should not follow my ill example, but do their parts to take warning from me. . . .
New converts are bound to be more regular and even to deprive themselves from some things which are not ill in themselves, for mortification. Even hunting and other manlyke exercises should be used with moderation and with as little expence as may be, and the quality of the person requires. One must be carefull not to lose masse any day for those recreation[s], nor indeed use any of them on days of obligation, they being more particularly sett apart by the Church to be kept holy.
. . . . T'is a duble scandal to see the theaters and other dangerous divertions so frequented on those days, when we have all the rest of the weeke to ourselves to please ourselves in innocent recreations. . . . Such of you as have yonge persons under your charge should not lett them reade Romances, more espesialy the womenkind ; at best 'tis but losse of tyme, and is apt to put foolish and rediculus thoughts into their heads, espesially the female. History is usefull and as diverting.'
f. 24. " King Charles the 2 papers, which I gave and desired you to read, sufficiantly explaine to you that there can be but one Cath[olike] and Apos[tolical] Ch[urch], and which it is. The late Dutchesse [of York] in hers, letts you see that those who made and carryed on the Pro[testant] Ref[ormation] in Ed[ward] 6 tyme had no resemblance to those who in the first Coun[cil] at Jerusalem used the phrase mentioned in the Acts of the Apos[tles] of ' it seemed good to the Holy Ghost and to us.' " August 1694.
f. 71. Resolutions to hear mass daily, to receive the Blessed Sacrament once in fifteen days or oftener, to observe days of fasting and abstinence, to be carefull in making friendships, to avoid idleness, to avoid balls, operas, and plays, as far as possible, to give all one can spare in charity, etc.
f. 79. Resolutions. " To rise at seven or half an houer after, not to be above eight houers in bed. So sone as one is up and so far drest as not to catch cold, to say ons first morning prayers. So sone as quit drest to retire into an oratory or closett alone there to say ons other morning prayrs, make some meditations, or read some good book for half an houer. Immediately after which to heare ons first masse, and then to dispatch what businesse one has, then to walke to take the aire, and then to go and heare ons last masse, if one has any spaire tyme before that to spend it well in reading or writing so as never to be idle. After diner to converse with the company one is in for some tyme, then if one can to retyre to rest ons self for some tyme and read a little in some good book, and about three to say the prayrs out of the manual for the evening, after which to follow ones affairs, make visits or take the aire, and to assist at the Rosairey in the chappel.
" On Sondays, Holy days, and Thursdays in the afternone to assist at comply[ne] and the benediction at the Parish or some other Church, if not hindred by some just impediment, and on Frydays at the Chapel, and to order so ons necessary affairs as not to faile if possible assisting at those prayers ; the same as to those every third Wensday of the month, for establishing Catholike Religion in the three Kingdoms, and to fast that day.
" To make the speritual Retreat of one day in the month out of P[ere] Croissettes books printed at Lyons, 1694.
" Not to go to plays or operas except it be with the M[ost] C[hristian] King, and even to avoyd that as much as one can without affectation.
" To observe days of fasting and abstinence as are done by Catholikes in England, with leave of ones Confessor.

"To receve twice a weeke as Wensdays or Sonday, or such other days as shall be most proper."

f. 85. "Reasons for desiring to dy. Nov. 1696."

f. 111. " 1697. Altho I am a great admirer of La Trappe and of the holy and exemplary life the monks led there, and am over joyd when I hear of any that leave the world and retire thether, and have found great reason to praise the devine goodnesse for having put it into my hart to see that place, since I have visibly found great advantage by it; yett I cannot be so partial to it as to thinke one may not worke out ones salvation in the world without retiring thether or to some strict order, seing that persons of all qualitys, of all callings, have been great Saints, and may be so still."

f. 125. A prayer for the distressed part of the persecuted church in the three kingdoms, for the Queen and all the King's children, for the King of France, his family, and his church. "Preserve the Duke and Dutchesse of Savoye, and all their children thou has already given them, and grant that the D[utches]s in deu tyme may bring him more sons. Touch L[ord] S[underland's] hart that he may know and embrace thy Cat[holike] Reli[gion] . . . Have mercy on the P[rince] of Or[ange], toutch his hart that he may speedily repent his past life, which doing, he may become a true convert, and so attaine everlasting life."

f. 129. "Have mercy on the Emp[eror], all Cath[olike] K[ing]s, P[rince]s, and Pot[entates], that they all may live in all things up to what they professe as becomes true and zealous Christians, and to consider well and wicely their obligations as such, and not to lett themselves be imposed on by revenge or false or bribed councellors."

f. 135. A letter of advice to the Duke of Berwick.

f. 143. Another letter to the same concerning the approaching death of the Duchess.

f. 152. A letter in French, concerning the death of the Duke of Modena. Dated at St. Germain, October 4, 1694.

A thin 8° volume bound in red morocco and richly tooled, bearing on one cover the arms of Pope Clement and on the other a shield of four quarters, 1 Scotland; 2, England; 3, France ; 4, Ireland, surmounted by a crown, with the motto " *Hony soit qui mal y pence.*" It contains four leaves of vellum richly illuminated. The first has the royal arms as before impaled with those of Poland. The second and third, written on both sides, have a certificate by Sebastian Pompilius Bonaventura, patrician of Urbino, bishop of Montefiascone, that on the 1st of September 1719, about 24 o'clock, according to Italian time, he, pontifically attired and assisted by two dignitaries of his cathedral church, in the hall of his episcopal residence, by virtue of the papal authority conveyed in a letter of Cardinal Paulucci dated at Rome on the 31st of August, 1719, conjoined in marriage James III., king of Great Britain, France, and Ireland, F.D., and H.R.H. Maria Clementina Subieschi, third daughter of James, king of Poland, their previous consent having been expressed in French, in the presence of Sir John Hay and James Murray of the kingdom of Scotland, and Charles Wogan and John O'Brien of the kingdom of Ireland, who subscribed in the presence of Sebastian Antonini, Protonotary Apostolic, and John Brown, of the order of the Preachers, confessor in ordinary of both their Majesties. On the third page is the signature of the bishop, and that of the Old Pretender—" *Nos Jacobus tertius Magnæ Brittaniæ Rex, &c., affirmamus ut supra, et propria manu subscripsimus, J. R.*" On the fourth page are the signatures of Maria Clementina "*Magne* Mr. BALFOUR's *Brittannic Regina*," and the six witnesses, and the attestation of a MSS. notary.

June 18, 1561, Dillenburg Castle. Commission from William, Prince of Orange, to Sir Henry de Balfour, a Scottish gentleman of prudence and experience in warfare, to arm and equip a ship, and to levy soldiers for the same, to go to the coasts of Spain and Portugal, in order to attack the Prince's enemies and do damage to their persons and goods. He is expressly forbidden to do damage to any subjects of the Queen of England, the Kings of Denmark and Sweden, or any other potentates well disposed to the Christian religion or to the Prince. Signed " Wille de Nassau." Heraldic seal affixed. (French.) Endorsed: —"Commission of the Prince. Letter of marke."

June 15, 1574. Rotterdam. Commission from William, Prince of Orange, to Sir Henry Balfour, to be colonel and superintendent of all the companies of Scotch foot-guards, in his service. Signed " Guille de Nassau." Seal attached but defaced. (French.)

November 5, 1575. Order by the nobles and delegates (*delecti*) of the cities of Holland, for the issue of a yearly pension of 800 florins of 20 stivers apiece to Henry Balfour for so long as he shall live and show himself friendly to the people of Holland, in consideration of his services against the Spaniards. Seal affixed. (Latin.)

December 22, 1576. Brussels. Commission from the King [Philip II. of Spain], to Henry de Beaufort (*sic*) to be colonel of sixteen ensigns of Scotch foot-soldiers, at a yearly salary of 500 *livres*, with suitable salaries specified for the inferior officers. Signed:—*Par le Roy.* D'Ouerboepe. (French.) Parchment. Seal broken. (See *Calendar of State Papers, Foreign Series,* 1575–1577.)

May 22, 16 Jac. I. Westminster. Warrant from James I. to the Deputy, the Chancellor, the Deputy Governor, and other officers of the realm of Ireland, to issue letters patent, confirming to Sir James Balfour, knt., one of the Privy Council there, all the castles, manors, &c., formerly granted to Lord Balfour of Burley, in the county of Fermanagh, and other possessions in the province of Ulster. Signed " James R." Heraldic seal affixed. Paper.

December 30, 1619. Original will of James, Lord Balfour, Baron of Glennawlye, one of His Majesty's Privy Council in Ireland.

November 1, " 1638." (The real date must be between 1622 and 1630.) Whitehall. Order by the Lords of the Council of Scotland for the issue of a yearly pension of 500*l.* to Sir William Balfour, gentleman of his Majesty's Privy Chamber, for the term of his life, in consideration of his recall from the service of the estates of the Low Countries for the King's special service in France, and for a yearly pension of 250*l.* to William Balfour, his son, for the term of his life after the death of Sir William. Signed by George [Hay], Chancellor ; John, Earl of Mar, Treasurer ; Lord Naper, Deputy Treasurer, the Earl of Haddington, the Earl of Linlithgow, and four others. Countersigned :—" Charles R."

June 1, 1642. Commissions from Robert, Earl of Leicester, to Sir William Balfour, knt., to be captain of a troop of carabines that are to attend the Scotch army in Ireland, and to be Commissary-General of the troops attending the Scotch army in Ireland. Heraldic seals.

August 31, 1644, 8 p.m. Plymouth. William Balfour to Lieut.-General Midleton. " Sir I am come hither by order from his Excellency to joyne with you, and I have brought all our cavalry with me to Salt

Ashe, from whence I shall transport them tomorrow over the ferry to Devonshyre syde and refresh my horse hereabouts two or three dayes, and I shall expect to hear from you and of your strength. In expectacon whereof I rest your very affectionate servant." (Written on a small piece of yellow silk, probably part of the lining of a coat.)

February 5, 1688. St. James's. Commission from William Henry, Prince of Orange, to William Balfour, Esq., to be captain-of a troop in the regiment of dragoons commanded by Col. James Hamilton of Carneyshure. Signed :—" d'Orange." Heraldic seal affixed.

October 10, 1689. Cambridge. Isaac Newton to Mr. N[icholas] Falio de Duillier. " I intend to be in London the next week, and should be very glad to be in the same lodgings with you. I will bring my books and your letters with me. Mr. Boyle has divers times offered to communicate and correspond with me in these matters, but I ever declined it because of his ——— — and conversing with all sorts of people, and being in my opinion too open and too desirous of fame." Heraldic seal.

November 21, 1692. Trinity College, Cambridge. The same to the same. " I have the book, and last night received your letter, with which how much I was affected I cannot express. Pray procure the advice and assistance of physitians before it be too late, and if you want any money I will supply you. I rely upon the character you give of your elder brother, and if I find that my acquaintance may be to his advantage I intend he shall have it, and I hope that you may still live to bring it about, but for fear of the worst pray let me know how I may send a letter and, if need be, a parcel to him, and pray let me know his character more fully, and particularly whether his genius lyes in any measure for sciences or only for buisiness of the world."

January 24, 1692-3. Cambridge. The same to the same. Enquires about his health, and invites him to Cambridge. Heraldic seal.

February 14, 1692-3. Cambridge. The same to the same. " When I invited you hither, I was contriving how you might subsist here a year or two, but since the death of your mother, and the concerns you have left by her in Switzerland call you thither, I must be content to want your good company, at least for some time. Yet Mr. Deirquens gives me hopes that you may be fixed in the Mathematick Professorship at Amsterdam, and I should be very glad to have you so near England. You left here 12 doses of the first imperial powder for the first region, which I am to return to you or the value of them in money. . . . I have also two chymical books of yours, which I beleive will be of no use to you. . . . I am glad you have taken the prophesies into consideration, and I beleive there is much in what you say about them, but I fear you indulge too much to fancy in some things." Heraldic seal.

March 7, 1692-3. Cambridge. The same to the same. Sends 12l. for twelve doses of his powder for the first region and two books, and also 5l. for three rulers. (On the same page is an acquittance from N. Falio de Duillier for 14l. for the value of certain goods left by him with Isaac Newton, esq.)

January 29, 1693-4. Oates. J. Locke to Mr. Falio, near Soho Square. " Having never had the honour to write to my Lady Russell in all my life, I thought it not very gracefull to begin now that her Ladyship can noe longer read. This however I was resolved should not hinder me from shewing my desire and readynesse to serve you as far as I am

able." I have therefore joined Lord Ashley's powerful interest with MR. BALFOUR'S MSS.
my own.

June 29 [1694]. Salisbury. Gi[lbert], Bishop of Salisbury to Mr. Falio at Southampton House. "I return you my most humble thanks for the particular account that you are pleased to give me of the good successe of the operation on my Lady Russell's eye. I rejoice in it with all my heart, and doe sincerly blesse God that the use of light is again restored to one that deserves it so well. Pray return my most humble thanks to my Lady for thinking on me in so critical a time. I am very sensible of the honour of so noble a frendship ; give my most humble service to my Lord Tavistoke. I am sorry that he loses his time so much. You must make the most you can of the few minutes he gives you, and throw away as few of them as may be in chiding, That is now too late and will but alienate him the more both from you and from that which you may instill in him." Heraldic seal.

March 3, 1742-3. London. John Pringle to Blayney Townley. "The gin bill has passed both houses, notwithstanding an opposition even from the whole bench of bishops ; the late obstruction being removed, we expect nothing less than an inundation to follow, and therefore the Riot Act ought to be first repealed to prevent the inconveniencies must necessarily follow thereon. The thinking people speak against it with great warmth and I fear reason also ; the Earl of Chester[field] calls it the Drinking Fund, and the onely one that had not already a tax annexed. The King is preparing for Flanders, but few persons believe there will be any action this summer."

July 14, 1750. London. The same to the same. "The Prince intending this summer to call a Parliament in Cornwall has put the Court in some commotion, least, under the colour of the tin, gold may be introduced for the convenience of the electors. This week he honours Lord Bathurst with a visit, but [I] much doubt of his makeing any further progress (whatever the publick papers insinuate to the contrary) than that of Bath. The general sett of mankind (who onely judge from appearances) are much surprized att present on an execution for debt on Dr. Mead's goods and chattels, but they who are more conversant with the world are astonished it was kept off so long, from a consideration of his extravagance and such a variety of wayes of squandering his fortune."

November 14, 1754. London. The same to the same. "Great are the disputes at present between the rival theatres, vieing with each other in different characters, which afford unusual entertainment to all frequenters of the stage. His Majesty on Saturday payed his first visit to Covent Garden in preference to the Opera and Drury Lane, when Lady Townley by Pegg Woff[ington] gave him great pleasure, with the addition of unusual huzzas in a part of the Miller of Mansfield. The birthday was solemnized with great splendour. . . . . Last night the special jury on the Richmond Parke gave their verdict for P. Emilia after a debate of 3 quarters of an hour, which is by no means agreeable to the town. It is expected there will be a new election for Oxfordshire, which will much aggravate the expense, which has been already almost incredible. . . . . I fear the Ministry has not the American expedition so warmly att heart as the town generally believes, by the present embarkation of troops."

February 5, 1755. Bath. Hamilton Gorges to the same. "There was an odd speech made in the House of Commons by Mr. [Henry]

MR. BALFOUR'S
MSS.
Fox, to repeal the Act making the 30th of January a church holyday. The whole House seemed amazed at the motion, and he was obliged to make a motion to withdraw his former one. It was an ambition to please his Sovereign, but he fixed on the wrong method. Quin says there's nere a king in Europe but has a creek in his neck on that day."

H. C. MAXWELL LYTE.

# INDEX.

## A.

Abbott, George, letter of; 95.
Aberdour; 77.
Abergavenny:
    Marquis of, report on his manuscripts; 1–72.
    Lord (1783); 61.
    Lady, her death; 71.
Abernetthe, Sir William de; 78.
Abney, Sir Thomas, ballad on; 188.
Abscourt; 205.
Acciajuoli, prothonotary; 218.
Achelees; 94.
Acqua, Italian advocate; 220.
Adam, Mr.; 66.
Adams, Samuel:
    letter to; 19.
    ambassador from America; 21.
Addington:
    Dr.; 21.
    Mr., at the Treasury; 246.
Addiscombe Place, letters dated at; 27–42 passim, 53, 60, 64, 65, 68–70.
Admiralty Office; 3.
Affleck; 45.
    Sir Edmund, letters of; 67.
Aiguillon:
    Duke D'; 4, 224, 230.
    —— letter to; 232.
Ailesbury, Earl of (1781), letter of; 45.
Aix-les-Bains; 234.
Akehurst, John, instructions to; 85.
Akenhed, Sir William de; 78.
Albano, letter dated at; 235.
Albany:
    Count of, pension to; 235. *See* Stuart, Charles Edward.
    Countess of, wife of Prince Charles Edward; 235, 236, 237.
    —— her allowance and presents from the Cardinal of York; 246, 249.
    —— letters of; 246, 248, 249.
    —— pension to; 239.
    —— pension granted by George III. to; 250, 251. *See* Stolberg, Princess of.

Albany—*cont.*
    Duke of (1402), his son; 77.
    Duchess of, natural daughter and heiress of Prince Charles Edward, papers concerning; 235.
    —— her legitimation; 236, 237.
    —— gift of jewels to; 237.
    —— proposed medal in her honour; 236.
    —— declaration concerning; *ib.*
    —— letters to; 236, 238.
    —— her inheritance from her father; 238, 239.
    —— her will and death; 239.
Albemarle, Duke of:
    (1666), fleet under; 187.
    (1667), at Harwich; 180.
Alberi, Marquise d'; 234.
Albestroff, Comtesse d', Clementina Walkingshaw; 234. *See* Walkingshaw, Clementina.
Alehouses, suppression of; 111.
Alfieri, Count, and the Countess of Albany; 237.
Alford:
    Sir F., speech of; 126, 127.
    John, grant by; 74.
Allen:
    John, certificate of; 186.
    —— examination of; *ib.*
    Sir Thomas, with Prince Rupert's fleet; 179.
Allestre, Mr. or Richard; 204.
Allispath:
    Gerard de; 99.
    church of; *ib.*
Almsworthy manor; 75.
Alost, letters dated at; 240, 242.
Alresford, New, alleged burning of; 185.
Althorp, Lord, and the Cardinal Duke of York (1806); 248.
Alton; 150.
Altona; 12.
Alured:
    Captain, his troop; 90.
    —— suspicions against; *ib.*
    John, letter of; 146.
Alva, Duke of; 126.
America:
    Gen. Burgoyne's plan regarding (1775); 8.
    Wedderburn on affairs in; 9.
    and France; 15, 17, 20.
    and Spain; 16.
    Commissioners of, at Paris; 19, 20.
    the treaty with; 56, 57.

R 2

S

LONDON: Printed by EYRE and SPOTTISWOODE,
Printers to the Queen's most Excellent Majesty.
For Her Majesty's Stationery Office.

www.ingramcontent.com/pod-product-compliance
Lightning Source LLC
Chambersburg PA
CBHW031407270326
41929CB00010BA/1365